THE TRUE NAME

Talks on the Japuji-Saheb of Guru Nanak Dev

- First in the Morning
- Gita Darshan (Vol-I)
- Gita Darshan (Vol-II)
- Tao: The Pathless Path
- Inner War and Peace
- Die O' Yogi Die
- Behind A Thousand Names
- Meditation: The Only Way
- Freedom from the Past
- Ah This!
- The Way of the Sufi
- The Silence of the Heart
- The True Name
- The Secret
- Truth Simply Is
- In Search of Celebration
- From Sex to Superconsciousness
- Never Born, Never Died
- Walk without feet, Fly without wings...
- Won't you Join the Dance?
- Priests & Politicians – The Mafia of the Soul
- My Diamond Days with Osho
- Tantra – The Supreme Understanding
- The Goose is Out
- Sex, Money and Power
- The Rebel
- A New Vision of Women's Liberation
- I Teach Religiousness Not Religion
- Words From A Man of No Words

Also in Hardcover
- The True Name (HC)

OSHO

THE TRUE NAME

Talks on the Japuji-Saheb of Guru Nanak Dev

THE TRUE NAME

Copyright © 1974, 2006 Osho International Foundation. All Rights reserved.

First paperback edition, 2007
First paperback reprint, 2007
Second paperback reprint, 2007
Third paperback reprint, 2009
Fourth paperback reprint, 2010
Fifth paperback reprint, 2011
Sixth paperback reprint, 2013
Seventh paperback reprint, 2014
Eight paperback reprint, 2015
Ninth paperback reprint, 2017 (2)
Tenth paperback reprint, 2018

ISBN 978-81-7621-207-6

Published by **FULL CIRCLE** PUBLISHING
J-40, Jorbagh Lane, New Delhi-110003
Tel: +011-24620063, 24621011 • Fax: 24645795
E-mail: contact@fullcirclebooks.in *website:* www.fullcirclebooks.in

All rights reserved. No part of this book may be reproduced or transmitted in any form or by any means, electronic or mechanical, including photocopying, recording, or by any information storage and retrieval system, without prior written permission from OSHO International Foundation.

OSHO is a registered trademark of OSHO International Foundation, used under license.
For more information: www.osho.com

Originally published in Hindi under the title: **Ek Omkar Satnam**

Designing & Layout: *SCANSET*
J-40, Jorbagh Lane, New Delhi-110003

Printed at Gopsons Papers Ltd. , Noida

PRINTED IN INDIA
07/17/09/0.6/SCANSET/TP/YP/YP/OP350/NP375

Contents

Chapter 1	The Singer	9
Chapter 2	The Weight of a Flower	37
Chapter 3	Solving the Riddle	61
Chapter 4	Some Other Ganges	87
Chapter 5	The Art of Listening	113
Chapter 6	Only Contemplating Can Know	135
Chapter 7	The Journey Ends	160
Chapter 8	Countless Ways	183
Chapter 9	Dyed in His Hue	204
Chapter 10	The Lure of the Infinite	229
Chapter 11	Fear Is a Beggar	252
Chapter 12	Steeped in the Wine of Love	283
Chapter 13	Birds Don't Go to College	306
Chapter 14	Posture Is a Template	326
Chapter 15	One Becomes Three	350
Chapter 16	Your Boat Is Useless on Land	375
Chapter 17	The Mines of Meditation	402
Chapter 18	There Is No End to It	430
Chapter 19	He Exults in His Creation	460
Chapter 20	Patience Is the Goldsmith	487

Introduction

Every few thousand years an individual appears who irrevocably changes the world around them in ways that are never immediately apparent, except to the most perceptive.

Osho is one such individual: his spoken words will resonate for centuries to come.

All those words have been recorded and transcribed into books like this one, written words that can carry a transforming message to the reader.

For Osho, all change is individual. There is no "society" to change — it can only happen to each one of us, one at a time.

So, no matter what the subject matter of the book, the thread that runs through all Osho's words is like a love song that we can suddenly, mysteriously, hear at just the right moment. And strangely, no matter what the words seem to be referring to, they are really only referring to us.

And this is no ordinary love song, more an invitation to open our hearts to hear something beyond the words, beyond the heart...a silence beyond all understanding. Where we all belong.

CHAPTER 1

The Singer

He is one. He is Omkar, the supreme truth.
He is the creator, beyond fear, beyond rancor.
His is the timeless form.
Never born, self-creating.
He is attained by the guru's grace.
He was truth before the ages and as time ran its course.
Nanak says: Now is he truth eternal, and forever will he be.
We cannot comprehend him though we think a million times;
Nor quiet the mind by silence, however long we sit;
Nor a mountain of bread appease the hunger of the soul;
Nor one hundred thousand feats of mind achieve unity with him.
How can truth be attained and the veil of falsehood torn?
Nanak says: By submission to the divine order which is
   preordained.

It was a dark moonless night; the clouds were heavy with rain because it was the monsoon season. Suddenly thunder sounded and lightning flashed as a few rain drops started to fall. The village was asleep. Only Nanak was awake and the echo of his song filled the air.

Nanak's mother was worried because the night was more than half over and the lamp in his room was still burning. She could hear his voice as he sang. She could restrain herself no longer and knocked at his door, "Go to sleep now, my son. Soon it will be dawn." Nanak became silent. From the darkness sounded the call of the sparrowhawk. "Piyu, piyu, piyu!" it called.

"Listen, mother!" Nanak called out. "The sparrowhawk is calling to his beloved; how can I be silent, because I am competing with him? I will call my beloved as long as he calls his — even longer, because his beloved is nearby, perhaps in the next tree! My beloved is so far away. I will have to sing for lives upon lives before my voice reaches him." Nanak resumed his song.

Nanak attained God by singing to him; Nanak's quest is very unusual — his path was decorated with songs. The first thing to be realized is that Nanak practiced no austerities or meditation or yoga; he only sang, and singing, he arrived. He sang with all his heart and soul, so much so that his singing became meditation; his singing became his purification and his yoga.

Whenever a person performs any act with all his heart and soul, that act becomes the path. Endless meditation, if half-hearted, will take you nowhere; whereas just singing a simple song with all your being merged in it, or dance a dance with the same total absorption and you will reach God. The question is not what you do, but how much of yourself you involved in the act.

Nanak's path to supreme realization, to godliness, is scattered with song and flowers. Whatever he has said was said in verse. His path was full of melody and soft, filled with the flavor of ambrosia.

Kabir says: "My enchanted mind was so intoxicated that it drained the filled cup without caring to measure the quantity." So it was with Nanak: he drank without caring how much he drank; then he sang, and sang, and sang. And his songs are not those of an ordinary singer. They have sprung from within one who had known. There is the ring of truth, the reflection of God within them.

Now another thing about the *Japuji*. The moonless night described at the beginning was an incident from Nanak's life when he was about sixteen or seventeen years of age. When the Japuji was conceived, Nanak was thirty years, six months and fifteen days old. The first incident refers to the days when he was still a seeker in quest of the beloved. The call to the beloved, the refrain, "Piyu, Piyu, Piyu..." was still the sparrowhawk calling; he had not yet met the beloved.

The Japuji was his first proclamation after the union with the beloved. The sparrowhawk had found his beloved; the call of "Piyu,

Piyu" was now over. The Japuji are the very first words uttered by Nanak after self-realization; therefore they hold a very special place in the sayings of Nanak. They are the latest news brought back from the kingdom of heaven.

The incident preceding the birth of the Japuji needs to be understood also. Nanak sat on the bank of the river in total darkness with his friend and follower, Mardana. Suddenly, without saying a word, he removed his clothes and walked into the river. Mardana called after him, "Where are you going? The night is so dark and cold!" Nanak went further and further; he plunged into the depths of the river. Mardana waited, thinking he would be out soon, but Nanak did not return.

Mardana waited for five minutes; when ten minutes had passed he became anxious. Where could he be? There was no sign of him. Mardana began to run along the shore calling to him, "Where are you? Answer me! Where are you?" He felt he heard a voice saying, "Be patient, be patient!" but there was no sign of Nanak.

Mardana ran back to the village and woke up everyone. It was the middle of the night, but a crowd collected at the riverside because everyone in the village loved Nanak. They all had some sense, a glimpse, of what Nanak was going to be. They had felt the fragrance of his presence, just as the bud gives off its fragrance before the flower has opened. All the village wept. They ran back and forth the whole length of the river bank but to no avail.

Three days passed. By now it was certain that Nanak had drowned. The people imagined that his body must have been carried away by the swift current and perhaps eaten by wild animals. The village was drowned in sorrow. Though everyone thought him dead, on the third night Nanak appeared from the river. The first words he spoke became the Japuji.

So goes the story — and a story means that which is true and yet not true. It is true because it gives the essential truth; it is false in the sense that it is only symbolic. And it is evident that the more profound the subject matter, the greater the need for symbols.

When Nanak disappeared in the river, the story goes that he stood before the gate of God. He experienced God. There before his eyes stood the beloved he pined for, for whom he sang night and day. He who had become the thirst of his every heartbeat stood revealed before Nanak! All his desires were fulfilled. Then God spoke to him, "Now go back and give unto others what I have given unto you." The Japuji is Nanak's first offering after he returned from God.

Now, this is a story; what it symbolizes must be understood. First, unless you lose yourself completely, until you die, you cannot hope to meet God. Whether you lose yourself in a river or on a mountain top is of little consequence; but you must die. Your annihilation becomes his being. As long as you are, he cannot be. You are the obstacle, the wall that separates you. This is the symbolic meaning of drowning in the river.

You too will have to lose yourself; you too will have to drown. Death is only completed after three days, because the ego does not give up easily. The three days in Nanak's story represent the time required for his ego to dissolve completely. Since the people could only see the ego and not the soul, they thought Nanak was dead.

Whenever a person becomes a *sannyasin* and sets out on the quest for God, the family members understand and give him up for dead. Now he is no longer the same person; the old links are broken, the past is no more, and the new has dawned. Between the old and the new is a vast gap; hence this symbol of three days before Nanak's reappearance.

The one who is lost invariably returns, but he returns as new. He who treads the path most certainly returns. While he was on the path he was thirsty, but when he returns he is a benefactor; he has left a beggar, he returns a king. Whoever follows the path carries his begging bowl; when he comes back he possesses infinite treasures.

The Japuji is the first gift from Nanak to the world.

To appear before God, to attain the beloved, are purely symbolic terms and not to be taken literally. There is no God sitting somewhere on high before whom you appear. But to speak of it, how else can it be expressed? When the ego is eradicated, when *you* disappear, whatever is before your eyes, is God himself. God is not a person — God is an energy beyond form.

To stand before this formless energy means to see him wherever you look, whatever you see. When the eyes open, everything is he. It only requires that you should cease to be and that your eyes be opened. Ego is like the mote in your eye; the minute it is removed, God stands revealed before you. And no sooner does God manifest, than you also become God, because there is nothing besides him.

Nanak returned, but the Nanak who returned was also God himself. Then each word uttered became so invaluable as to be beyond price, each word equal to the words of the Vedas.

Now let us try to understand the Japuji:

> Ek Omkar Satnam
> He is one. He is Omkar, the supreme truth.
> He is the creator, beyond fear, beyond rancor.
> His is the timeless form.
> Never born, self-creating.
> He is attained by the guru's grace.

He is one: *Ek Omkar Satnam.*

In order to be visible to us, things must have many levels, many forms. That's why whenever we see, we see multiplicity. At the seashore we see only the waves, we never see the ocean. The fact is, however, only the ocean *is*, the waves are only superficial.

But we can see only the superficial because we have only external eyes. To see within requires internal eyes. As the eyes, so the sight. You cannot see deeper than your eyes. With your external eyes you see the waves and think you have seen the ocean. To know the ocean, you must leave the surface and dive below. So in the story Nanak did not remain on the surface, but dived deep into the river. Only then can you know.

Waves alone are not the ocean, and the ocean is much more than a mere collection of waves. The basic fact is that the wave that is now, after a moment no longer will be; nor did it exist a moment ago.

There was a Sufi fakir by the name of Junnaid. His son, whom he loved dearly, was killed suddenly in an accident. Junnaid went and buried him. His wife was astonished at his behavior. She expected him to go mad with grief at the death of the son he loved so dearly. And here was Junnaid acting as if nothing had happened, as if the son had not died! When everyone had left, his wife asked him, "Aren't you sad at all? I was so worried you would break down, you loved him so much."

Junnaid replied, "For a moment I was shocked but then I remembered that before, when this son was not born, I already was and I was quite happy. Now when the son is not, what is the reason for sorrow? I became as I was before. In between, the son came and went. When I was not unhappy before his birth, why should I be unhappy now to be without a son? What is the difference? In between was only a dream that is no longer."

What was formed and then destroyed, is now no more than a dream. Everything that comes and goes is a dream. Each wave is but a dream; the ocean is the reality. The waves are many, the ocean only one, but we see it as so many waves. Until we see the unity, the oneness of the ocean, we shall continue wandering.

There is one reality, truth is only one: Ek Omkar Satnam. And says Nanak, the name of this one, is *Omkar*. All other names are given by man: Ram, Krishna, Allah. These are all symbols, and all created by man. There is only one name that is not given by man and that is Omkar, and Omkar means the sound of *Om*.

Why Omkar? — because when words are lost and the mind becomes void, when the individual is immersed in the ocean, even then the strain of Omkar remains audible within him. It is not a man-made tune but the melody of existence. Omkar is the very being of existence; therefore Om has no meaning. Om is not a word but a resonance that is unique, having no source, no creation by anyone. It is the resonance of the being of existence. It is like a waterfall: you sit beside a waterfall and you hear its song but the sound is created by the water hitting against the rocks. Sit by a river and listen to its sound; it is caused by the river striking against the banks.

We need to go deeper to understand things. Science tries to break down the whole of existence. What it first discovered was energy in the form of electricity, and then charged particles like the electron of which all of existence is made. Electricity is only a form of energy. If we ask a scientist what sound is made of, he will say that it is nothing but waves of electricity, waves of energy. So energy is at the root of everything. The sages say the same thing; they are in agreement with the scientists except for a slight difference of language. Sages have come to know that all existence is created out of sound, and sound is only an expression of energy. Existence, sound, energy — all are one.

The approach of science is to analyze and break things down, to reach the conclusion. The sage's approach is absolutely different: through synthesis they have discovered the indivisibility of the self.

The wind rises creating a murmur in the branches of the tree, a collision of air against the leaves. When the musician plays a chord on an instrument, the sound is produced by a blow. All sound is produced by an impact, and an impact requires *two* — the strings of the instrument and the fingers of the musician. Two are necessary to form any sound.

But God's name is beyond all separateness. His name is the resonance that remains when all dualities have faded and cease to exist. Within this indivisible whole you come across this resonance. When a person reaches the state of *samadhi*, Omkar resounds within him. He hears it resounding inside him and all around him; all creation seems to be vibrating with it.

He is struck with wonder when it first happens knowing that he is not creating the sound. He is doing nothing and yet this resonance is coming — from where? Then he realizes that this sound is not created by any impact, any friction; it is the *anahat nad*, the frictionless sound, the unstruck sound.

Nanak says: "Omkar alone is God's name." Nanak refers to name a great deal. Whenever Nanak speaks of his name — "His name is the path," or "He who remembers his name attains" — he is referring to Omkar, because Omkar is the only name that is not given to him by man, but is his very own. None of the names given by man can carry you very far. If they do go some distance towards him, it is only because of some slight shadow of Omkar within them.

For instance the word *Ram*. When Ram is repeated over and over it begins to transport you a little, since the sound *m* in Ram is also the consonant in Om. Now if you keep repeating it for a long time, you will suddenly discover that the sound of Ram subtly changes into the resonance of Om, because as the repetition begins to quieten the mind, Omkar intrudes and penetrates Ram; Ram gradually fades and Om steps in. It is the experience of all the wise men that no matter with what name they started their journey, at the end it is always Om. As soon as you start to become quiet, Om steps in. Om is always there waiting; it only requires your becoming tranquil.

Says Nanak: "Ek Omkar Satnam."

The word *sat* needs to be understood. In Sanskrit there are two words: *sat* means beingness, existence, and *satya* means truth, validity. There is a great difference between the two, though both contain the same original root. Let us see the difference between them.

Satya is the quest of the philosopher. He seeks truth. What is the truth? It lies in the rules whereby two plus two always equals four, and never five or three. So satya is a mathematical formula, a manmade calculation, but it is not sat. It is logical truth but not existential reality.

You dream in the night. Dreams exist. They are sat, reality, but not satya, truth. Dreams *are* — or else how would you see them? Their being is there but you cannot say they are true, because in the morning you find they have evaporated into nothingness. So there are happenings in life which are true but not existential. Then there are other occurrences that are existent but are not logically true. All mathematics is true but not existential; it is satya but not sat. Dreams are; they are existential, but they are not true.

God is both. He is sat as well as satya, existence as well as truth. Being both, he can neither be fully attained through science, which probes truth, nor through the arts, which explores existence. Both are incomplete in their search, because they are directed only towards one half of him.

The quest of religion is entirely different from all other quests. It combines both sat and satya: it is in quest of that which is more authentic and true than any mathematical formula. It is in quest of that which is more existential, more empirical, than any poetic imagery.

What religion seeks is both. Looking from any one angle, you will fail; from both directions, then only shall you attain.

So when Nanak says: "Ek Omkar Satnam," both sat and satya are contained in his expression. The name of that supreme existence is as true as a mathematical formula and as real as any work of art; it is as beautiful as a dream and as correct as a scientific formula; it contains the emotions of the heart, and the knowledge and experience of the mind.

Where the mind and the heart meet, religion begins. If the mind overpowers the heart, science is born. If the heart overpowers the head, the realm of art is entered: poetry, music, song, painting, sculpture. But if head and heart are united, you enter into Omkar.

A religious person stands above the greatest scientist; he looks down on the greatest artist, because his search contains the essentials of both. Science and art are dualities; religion is the synthesis.

Nanak says: *"Ek Omkar Satnam. He is one. He is Omkar, the supreme truth. He is the creator..."*

To take them literally limits your understanding of Nanak's words. It will be a mistake.

One difficulty of the sage lies in the need to use words in general usage. He has to talk to you and so he must speak your language, but what he means to say is beyond words. Your language cannot contain it; it is very limited, whereas truth is very vast. It is just as if someone were trying to compress all the sky into his house, or to gather all the light within his palm. Yet he has to use your language.

It is because of words, because of language, that there are so many sects. For instance, Buddha was born two thousand years before Nanak and used the language of his time. Krishna was born yet another two thousand years before Buddha. His was quite a different kind of language because he belonged to a different country, a different climate, a different culture, and so it was with Mahavira and Jesus. The difference is one of language alone, and languages differ because of people; otherwise there is no real point of difference between the enlightened ones. Nanak made use of the language prevailing during his lifetime.

Nanak says: "He is the creator." But at once the thought arises: "If he is the creator, and we are the created, that establishes a difference between the two," but Nanak has denied duality in the very beginning, saying that "God is one." It is language that is responsible for all the obstacles, and these will increase as we proceed further into Nanak's words.

The first words uttered by Nanak after samadhi were: "Ek Omkar Satnam."

Now the fact is that the entire Sikh religion is contained in those three words. Everything else is merely an effort to teach you, to help you understand. Nanak's message was complete in these three words. Because it was not possible for ordinary people to understand the message directly, an effort had to be made to expand on it. Explanations are given out of your inability to understand; otherwise Nanak had said all he wanted to convey: "Ek Omkar Satnam." The mantra was complete. But for you it has no meaning yet. These three words alone cannot solve the mystery for you; then language must be used.

God is the creator. But realize that he does not stand apart from his creation. He is absorbed and one with all that he has created. This is why Nanak never separated the sannyasin from the householder. If the creator was separate from his creation, then you would drop all worldly activities in order to seek him, abandoning the shop, the office, the marketplace. Nanak did not give up his worldly duties till the very end. As soon as he returned from his travels he would go to work in the fields. All his life he ploughed the fields. He named the village in which he settled, Kartarpur, which means the village of the creator.

God is the creator, but do not think he is separated from his creation. When man sculpts an idol and the idol is completed, the sculptor and the sculpture are no longer one; they are separate. And the sculpture will remain long after the sculptor is dead. If the image fractures, the sculptor is not also broken, because the two are separate. But there is no such distance between God and his creation.

What kind of relationship exists between God and his creation? It is like a dancer with his dance. When man dances can you separate him from his dance? Can he return home leaving the dance behind? If the dancer dies, the dance dies with him. When the dance stops, he is no longer the dancer. They are united. This is why since ancient times, Hindus have looked upon God as the dancer, "Nataraj." In this symbol the dancer and the dance are one.

The poet is no longer related to his poem, once it is finished. The sculptor is separated from his sculpture as soon as it is completed. A mother gives birth to a child, and they are separate; the father is always distinct from the child. But God is not distinct from his creation; he is contained in it. It would be more accurate to say: the creator is the creation, or the creator is nothing but creativity.

Discarding all idea of separateness Nanak says there is no need to renounce or run away from the world. Wherever you are, he is. Nanak has given birth to a unique religion in which householder and sannyasin are one. He alone is entitled to call himself a Sikh who, being a householder is yet a sannyasin; who, being a sannyasin is still a householder.

You cannot become a Sikh merely by growing your hair or wearing a turban. It is difficult to be a Sikh. It is easy to be a householder or to be a sannyasin, but to be a Sikh you have to be both. You have to remain in the house — but as if you are not there, as if you are in the Himalayas. Keep running the shop, but maintain the remembrance of his name ever throbbing within; you can count your cash but take his name along with it.

Before attaining samadhi, Nanak had many small glimpses of God — what we call *satori*. The first occurred when Nanak was working in a grain shop where his job was to weigh wheat and other grains for the customers. One day as he measured, "One, two, three..." he reached the number thirteen. Now the number thirteen is *tera* in the Punjabi language. "Tera" also means "yours." When Nanak reached thirteen, tera, he lost all consciousness of the outside world because he was reminded of his beloved lord.

He would fill a measure and repeat "tera, thine, thou." Again and again he filled it... "tera" — as if all numbers ended at tera. Tera became his mantra. The destination was reached; everything ended at tera for Nanak. People thought him mad and tried to stop him, but Nanak was in a different world altogether: "Tera! Tera! Tera!" He could not move past tera. There was nothing beyond it.

There are really only two halting places; one is I and the other is you. You start with I and finish at you.

Nanak is not against the mundane world. In fact he is in love with it, because to him the world and its creator are one. Love the world and through the world, love God; see him through his own creation.

When Nanak came of age, his parents told him to get married. Nanak did not refuse, though people feared he would because his ways were so different from others since his childhood. His father was very much troubled on his account. He could never understand Nanak — all these devotional songs and always in the company of holy men.

Once he sent him on a business trip to the adjoining village with twenty rupees to buy some goods for resale at a profit. Since the way of business is to buy cheaply and sell at a higher price, his father told him to buy something which would be profitable. Nanak made a few purchases. On the way back he came across a band of holy men who had not eaten for five days. Nanak pleaded with them to come to his village instead of sitting there expecting food to come to them.

"But that is the vow we have taken," they replied. "God will provide when he pleases. We are happy to abide by his will. Hunger is no problem to us."

Now Nanak thought to himself, "What can be more profitable and worthwhile than feeding these great holy men? I should distribute among them my food I have bought. Didn't my father say to do something profitable and worthwhile?"

So he gave away to the sadhus whatever he had brought from the village, though his companion, Bala, tried to stop him, and said, "Are you mad that you do that?"

Nanak insisted: "I am doing something worthwhile, as my father wished," and returned home very pleased with himself.

His ways were strange and his father was very angry. "What a fool you are. Is this how you make a profit? You will ruin me!"

Nanak answered, "What could be more profitable than this?"

But nobody else could see the profit either, much less Kale Mehta, Nanak's father. He could not see any good in this act. He was certain the boy had gone astray in the company of these holy men and lost his senses. He hoped marriage would make him more reasonable. People generally think that since the sannyasin renounces women and runs away, the way to keep a man in the world is to tie him to a woman. This trick did not work on him because Nanak was not against anything.

When his father told him to get married Nanak readily agreed. He married and had children, but this did not change his ways at all. There was no way to spoil this man, because he saw no difference between God and the world. How can such a person be defiled? If a man leaves wealth behind to become a sannyasin, you can tempt him just by giving him riches. If another has left a wife behind, give him a woman and in no time he falls. But how can you spoil a man who has left nothing? There is no way to bring about his downfall. Nanak cannot be corrupted.

My view of the sannyasin is similar to Nanak's, because he is a formidable sannyasin who cannot be corrupted. He who sits right in your world and yet is not of it can in no way be tempted.

This God Nanak refers to as the creator, the fearless, because fear is when the other is. An expression of Jean Paul Sartre has become famous: "The other is hell." It describes your experience. How often do you want to escape from the other, as if he is the source of all your trouble? When the other is closer to you, the turbulence is less than when the other is more remote, stranger. But the other is always troublesome.

What is fear? Fear always involves the other: if someone can take something away from you it destroys your security. Then there is death and there is illness — both are the other. Hell is being surrounded by the other; hell *is* the other.

But how can you escape the other? Should you run away to the Himalayas you will still not be alone. Sit under a tree; a crow's dropping falls on your head, and you are filled with anger towards the crow. There are the rains and the sun — irritations everywhere. How will you escape the other who is present everywhere? The only way to escape the other is to seek the one; then no other remains. Then all fear fades away. There is no death, no illness; there are no inconveniences, because there is no other. Finally you are alone. Fear persists as long as the other remains the other for you.

Ek Omkar Satnam. Once this mantra has penetrated your being, where is fear? God has no fear. Whom should he fear? He is the only one, there is no one besides him.

> *He is the creator, beyond fear, beyond rancor.*
> *His is the timeless form.*
> *Never born...*

Understand that time means change. If nothing changes you will not be aware of time. You cannot tell the time if the hands of the clock do not move. Things are changing constantly: the sun comes out and it is morning; then it is afternoon, then evening. First there is the infant, then the youth, then the old man. A healthy man becomes ill, an ill person becomes healthy; a rich man becomes a pauper, a pauper becomes a king. There is constant change. The river is forever flowing. Change is time.

Time means the distance between two changes.

Just imagine getting up one morning and no events occurring till evening. There are no changes: the sun stands still, the hands of the clock do not move, the leaves do not wither, you do not grow older – everything is at a standstill. Then how will you know the time? There will be no time.

You are aware of time because you are surrounded by change. For God there is no time because he is eternal, perpetual, immortal. He is forever. For him nothing is changing; everything is static. Change is the experience of sightless eyes that do not see things in their full perspective. If we could see things from the furthest vantage point all change drops away, and then time stops; it ceases to exist. For God all things are as they are; nothing changes, everything is static.

> *His is the timeless form.*
> *Never born, self-creating.*

He is not born of someone. God has no father, no mother. All who are begotten by the process of procreation enter the world of change. You have to find within your own self the unborn one. This body is born, it will die. It is born by the conjunction of two bodies; it will disintegrate some day. When the bodies that gave birth to it have perished, how can something remain which is a component of the two?

But within this, there is also that which was never born but has nevertheless come with the embryo. It was there even before the formation of the fetus, and without it the body will one day return to no more than clay. The timeless has penetrated within this body; the body is no more than a piece of clothing to the timeless. That which is beyond time dwells within the time-bound. Only when you attain the timeless being within your own self will you be able to understand Nanak's words. You have to seek within yourself that which never changes, that which is changeless.

If you practice just sitting with your eyes closed, you will be unable to make out within yourself what age you are. You would feel yourself the same inside at the age of fifty as you felt at the age of five — as if time has not passed for the world within you. Close your eyes and you will discover that nothing has changed inside.

What is changeless within is not born through the womb. You have come through your parents, but they are only the path for your coming; they do not bestow life on you. You have passed through them because the requirements of your body were nourished by them, but what has entered into your body has come from beyond. The day you attain the unborn within you, you will know that God has no origin, no source, because God is the entirety; he is the aggregate of all things. God means the totality. How can the totality be born to a particular someone? There is nothing beyond totality for there to be a mother and father, so he is *never born, self-creating.*

The meaning of self-creating is that he exists by himself and has no support except his own; he is self-begotten and has no origin. The day you glimpse, however briefly, this fact within yourself, you will be rid of all anxieties and worries. Why do you worry? Your worry always arises out of your dependence on things, because any support can be snatched away from you at any moment. Today you have wealth? It may be gone tomorrow. What will you do then if you consider you are rich because of your wealth, not because of yourself?

A sannyasin is rich by his own right; he is rich because of himself so you cannot rob him of his riches. What will you steal from Buddha or from Nanak? You cannot make them poorer by taking anything from them; you cannot add to their wealth nor subtract from it. Whatever Nanak is derives from being one with the supreme support. You have nothing to lean on.

The supreme being is not a separate entity. God is without support. The day you too are prepared to be without support, your union with God will take place.

This definition of God is not the philosopher's interpretation, but is valid for the seeker so that he may know the characteristics of God. If you want to attain God, you will have to make these characteristics your religious practice. You have to try to be God in a small way. As you gradually begin to become like him, you will find a rhythm establishing itself and a resonance struck between you and God.

Never born, self-creating.
He is attained by the guru's grace.

Why does Nanak say *by the guru's grace*? Is not man's own labor enough? It is necessary to understand this very subtle point, because Nanak stresses the guru a great deal. Later Nanak says that without the guru God cannot be attained. What is the reason for this? If God is omnipresent why can't I meet him directly? What is the need to bring in the guru?

Krishnamurti says there is no need of a guru at all. This idea appeals to the intellect and to reasoning. What need to introduce the guru since I am born of God, as is the guru? Mind does not approve of the guru; so a congregation of egoists revolve around Krishnamurti. What he says is perfectly correct, that there is no need of a guru — provided you are capable of annihilating your ego yourself.

But it is as difficult to drop the ego yourself as it is to lift oneself up by your bootstraps. It is just like a dog trying to catch his tail. The quicker he turns, the further his trail swishes away. If, however, a person is competent enough, then Krishnamurti is absolutely right that no guru is necessary.

But here lie all the complications. No sooner have you somehow conquered your ego then you will say, "*I* have dropped my ego," and there you introduce a new form of ego even more dangerous than the old. The guru is needed so that this new ego is not born. Even as you say, "By the grace of the guru," you can convey by your behavior: "See how humble I am! No one can be more humble!" And now these new paths are etched out by the ego. Till yesterday you were proud of your wealth; today you are proud of its renunciation and your humility. The rope is burned but the twists remain. How is this arrogance to be destroyed? — hence Nanak's emphasis on the guru.

There is no difficulty in attaining God directly, because he is present right in front of you. Wherever you go, there he is. But the one difficulty is that *you* stand within yourself, and how will you remove this interfering you? Hence, "the guru's grace." The seeker may labor but the attainment will always be by the guru's grace. This concept of the guru's grace will not allow your ego to form. It will destroy the old ego and prevent the new from forming; otherwise, you rid yourself of one ailment and contract another.

A very funny situation has arisen. A crowd of egoists have collected around Krishnamurti, people who do not wish to bow before anyone. They are completely at ease since they don't have to touch anyone's feet; they bow to no one. They firmly believe that the guru is not required, they will arrive by themselves. And this itself is the difficulty.

If there were a person like Nanak or Ramakrishna around Krishnamurti then his message would have been effective, but the crowd around him consists of those very people who are unable to drop their egos — the ones in most urgent need of a guru. This is the ultimate irony: all those around Krishnamurti need a guru. Those who surrounded Nanak were people who could have done without a guru.

Now, you might say this is all a riddle, but it is a fact that those around Nanak would have arrived even without a guru, because they were people ready and eager to accept the guru's gift; they were ready to renounce their own selves. The attainment comes without the guru, but the idea of the guru is effective in destroying the ego so that you are not filled with arrogance for whatever you accomplish. Otherwise you will boast, "I can stand on my head for three hours, and I meditate every morning!"

The wife of a Sikh gentleman once complained to me: "Things are getting out of control. My husband comes to see you, so please advise him."

"What is the matter?" I asked.

"He gets up at two in the morning and begins to recite the *Japuji*. It is impossible for the rest of the family to sleep. If I complain he tells us that we should all get up and chant too! What should we do?"

I called the husband to me. "When do you recite the *Japuji*?" I asked him.

"Early every morning, about two," he replied proudly.

"That is proving to be quite a nuisance to others," I said.

"That is their fault," he said. "They are lazy and indolent! — they should all get up at that time. Besides, I'm doing them a service by reciting aloud so that the holy words can fall not only on the family's ears but the neighbor's as well."

"Take it easier with your practices," I advised him. "You can get up at four in the future." You have to bring down such a person by degrees, or else it is impossible to bring him down at all.

"Never!" he replied. "I never expected to hear such words from you. Do you want to rob me of my religion?" He couldn't believe his ears.

Now this was his arrogance — that no one could recite the *Japuji* like him. This alone is his obstacle. You may repeat the *Japuji* all life long, but the real need is to destroy your arrogance.

Therefore Nanak says time and again, "Nothing can be attained by whatever you do, unless you eradicate your own self." This concept of the guru is a priceless alchemical device to annihilate the ego, because whatever you do, you just say, "It is all the grace of the guru." I am doing is the difficulty. If you can eradicate your I without any help, you do not need a guru. But it is one in a million who can do this; he is the exception for whom we need not make any rules or regulations.

It happens sometimes that some person drops his ego without the help of a guru, but it requires a very deep and profound understanding which you do not have. The understanding should be so deep that you can order your ego to stand before your eyes — and by your mere looking, the ego *must* drop. Your eyes must be like the eyes of Shiva, through whose very glance the god of love turned to ashes. You should have such awareness. A Buddha, a Krishnamurti, surveys the ego with such intensity that it melts into nothingness. No other feeling then arises in its place; and they are not even aware of having done something, it just happens.

But you are not they. Whatever you do, a voice within constantly repeats: "I have done this, I have done that...." If you sing hymns, you are conscious that *you* are singing the hymns. If you meditate, the feeling within is: "*I* am meditating." With your prayer or your worship your ego is replenished and recreated every moment.

Let us leave these one-in-a-million exceptions aside, because they are bound to attain. For the millions of others there is only one way: whatever they do, whatever practice or ritual or repetition, the feeling should be that whatever results is due to the guru's grace.

He was truth before the ages began and as time ran its course.
Nanak says: Now is he truth eternal, and forever will he be.

There is a very old saying in India that during the *Sat Yuga*, the age of truth, the guru was not needed much, but in *Kali Yuga*, the age of darkness, which began about five years ago, the guru will be a necessity. What is the reason? The Sat Yuga was the period when people were very alert, full of awareness. In the Kali Yuga people are insensitive, slumbering, almost unconscious.

Therefore the religions of Buddha or Mahavira born in the Sat Yuga, are not of as much use in today's world as the religion of Nanak. Nanak's religion is the newest, though it too is now five hundred years

The Singer 27

old. We need another new religion, because those who heard Mahavira and Buddha were relatively more alert than us; they were also wiser, simpler and more artless. And even further back, the people who listened to Krishna were even more aware and alert.

As we move backward we find more innocence...just as when a person recounts his life backwards, he arrives at the period of his childhood. In infancy he is simple and innocent; in youth he begins to become complicated. It is difficult to conquer an old man filled with wisdom. He knows nothing and yet he feels he knows everything. He has been thrown about by life. Through his suffering he feels he is very experienced; he has gathered trash and he thinks he has collected diamonds.

The child is simple, innocent; he is the symbol of Sat Yuga. The old man is highly complicated, and his insensitivity increases day by day as death is drawing near — he is the symbol of Kali Yuga. The child's consciousness is very fresh because the fountain of life is very close to him. He is like a wave just arisen from God. The old man is dirty, weighted down by dust, and about to fall back into God. The child is a fresh bud; the old man is a withered flower whose life breath is just about spent.

Kali Yuga means that period where the end is near. Life is now old. In Kali Yuga you cannot, under any circumstances, do without the guru because you will be constantly filled with ego. When each little thing that you do fills you with ego, how will you not be filled with arrogance when you do your spiritual practice? If you build a small house and pride yourself on it, fill your treasure chest and your conceit will know no bounds; and when you start on the quest for the supreme treasure your self-importance and vanity will be unfathomable.

Notice the contemptuous look of the man who goes to the temple or to the mosque towards those who do not. His eyes tell you: "You sinners will rot and burn in hellfire! Look at me! I pray every day and I am saved." He recites, "Ram, Ram," and thinks the gates of heaven are open for him and all others will go to hell.

The greater your insensitivity, the more somnolent you are, the greater your need for a guru. Understand that. If you are fast asleep, how can you awaken yourself? Someone else will have to shake you. Even then the chances are that you will roll over and fall back asleep again.

He was truth before the ages began and as time ran its course. Nanak says: Now is he truth eternal, and forever will he be.

This is the definition of *satya*, truth, and *asatya*, untruth. Asatya is that which never was, which now is, but again will fade into nothingness. It means that which is nonexistent at both ends and exists only in the middle. Take dreams for example: during the night as you slept, dreams existed; in the morning when you awake the dream is lost and then you say that dreams are untrue.

Once in the past your body did not exist, and one day again it will cease to be. Thus body is a falsity. Anger comes; a moment before it was not there, and after a while it shall again not be there. Anger is like a dream because it is not truth. Only that is true which is forever. If you can only grasp this thought and allow it to penetrate you deeply, your life will undergo a transformation. Don't be taken by things that are not. Seek only what is unchanging and unmoving.

Who it is within you who never changes, look only for him. All changes occur around him like the shaft of the wheel: it never moves but the wheel revolves around it and because of it. If you remove the shaft the wheel falls. All changes that take place occur around the eternal; the hub of the soul is static, while the wheel of the body revolves around it. No sooner does the hub disintegrate than the wheel falls apart.

Nanak says that God alone is the truth, that one alone, because he was beyond all beginning of things. He still is; he always will be; he is forever. All else is a dream. Let these words penetrate deep within you.

When anger comes or hatred or greed, repeat these words to yourself. Let it remind you of what is real, what is true. Remember, what wasn't before but which now is, can only be a dream and will fade away. There is no need to become too involved in it, but maintain the attitude of the witness. Gradually, all that was useless will fall away from you on its own because your connection with it has broken;

and that which is useful, meaningful, will begin to take root within you. The eternal has begun to arise, the world has begun to fade away.

> *We cannot comprehend him though we think a million times;*
> *Now quiet the mind by silence, however long we sit;*
> *Now a mountain of bread appease the hunger of the soul;*
> *Nor one hundred thousand feats of mind achieve unity with him.*
> *How can truth be attained and the veil of falsehood torn?*
> *Nanak says: By submission to the divine order which is preordained.*

This is a very valuable sutra. It is the quintessence of Nanak's teachings. With all our thinking we cannot think of God. We think a million times, yet we cannot think about him. Nobody has ever arrived at him by thought; in fact we have lost him through excessive thinking. The more we think, the more we lose ourselves in thought.

God is not a concept, not a thought. He is not the settlement of an argument, not an outcome of the mind. God is truth. Thinking isn't relevant — you have to *see*. By thinking you will only wander. You have to open your eyes, but if they are filled with thoughts and concepts, they will remain sightless. Only eyes without thoughts enable you to see.

It requires what Zen masters call no-mind, which Kabir names the *Unmani* state, the state of no-mind. Buddha refers to it as the dissolution of the mind and Patanjali named it *nirvikalpa samadhi*, the samadhi without thoughts. They are all describing the same state in which all doubts and debates end. This is what Nanak is referring to.

We cannot think of God even with infinite thoughts, although we think a million times. By keeping quiet we cannot attain this silence, although we can remain in continuous meditation. Why is it that with all our thoughts we are not able to conceive of him? Why is it that we cannot attain silence by effort?

You will find that the harder you try, the more impossible it is to become silent. Certain things cannot be attained by effort. Sleep cannot be brought about by effort; the harder you try, the more difficult it becomes. The essence of sleep is the absence of all effort, then only does sleep come. Effort keeps you awake, but stretch out on the bed completely relaxed with all activities suspended and sleep comes. Similarly, how can you make yourself silent? You may force yourself to remain seated in a buddhalike posture while the mind keeps boiling within.

Nanak was a guest of a Mohammedan nawab. For Nanak there were no Hindus and no Mohammedans; the sage observes no sectarian boundaries. The nawab said to Nanak, "If you really mean what you say — that there is no Hindu, no Mohammedan — then come along with us to the mosque. Since today is Friday, let us pray together."

Nanak readily agreed, but he insisted, "I shall offer prayers only if you also pray." The nawab replied, "What a strange condition to set! That is exactly why I am going."

The news spread like wildfire through the village. Everyone gathered at the mosque. The Hindus were greatly upset, and the members of Nanak's family were particularly abusive; everyone thought Nanak was becoming a Mohammedan. In such a way do people burden others with their own fears.

Nanak reached the mosque and the prayers were begun. The nawab was very annoyed with Nanak because, whenever he turned around to look, he found Nanak still erect, neither bowing now offering prayers, but just standing like a statue. The nawab raced through his prayers as quickly as possible, because how can a person pray when he is angry? Finally he turned to Nanak and said, "You are a fraud. You are neither saint nor seeker! You promised to pray but you never did."

Nanak said, "I did promise, but have you forgotten the conditions? I said I would pray provided you also prayed. But you didn't, so how could I pray?"

"What are you saying? Are you in your right senses? There are so many witnesses here; everyone saw me offering prayers!"

"I can't believe these other witnesses because I was looking within you all the time. You were buying horses in Kabul."

The nawab was taken aback because that was exactly what he was doing. His favorite horse had died just that morning and he was still strongly affected by the loss of such a fine animal. His mind was preoccupied with how to reach Kabul as early as possible to buy another thoroughbred. To him a horse was a symbol of status and honor.

"And the priest who led the prayers," continued Nanak, "was busy gathering the harvest in his fields." The priest admitted that he was worried about his harvest that was ready to be reaped. "Now please tell me, did you offer your prayers so that I could offer mine?"

You force yourself to pray, you force yourself to worship, to meditate — it is all meaningless. By bending the body into certain postures you cannot force the mind to follow suit. The cacophony of the mind continues, and in fact it becomes louder and more intense. When the body was engaged in some activity the energy was divided. Now when the body sits absolutely inactive, all the energy flows to the mind and the thoughts spin at even greater speed!

This is why when people sit to meditate, the mind becomes more and more active...a real avalanche of thoughts cascading one upon the other! You sit to worship, but the marketplace still grips your thoughts. You go to the temple and ring the bells, but the mind races in other directions. Normally the mind is not so restless. You go to see a film and the mind is quiet and you feel at peace, but no sooner do you enter the temple or mosque or church it becomes its most restive. What is the reason? The theater is linked to your desires. In the movies all the things that you are filled with are brought out, all the rubbish, all the trash. It strikes a chord within you. In the temple what you hear touches nothing within, and hence the confusion.

Nanak is saying that by enforcing silence you will gain nothing, because you cannot attain *that* silence. Even if you remain in constant meditation, nothing is going to happen. The hunger cannot be appeased even by a mountain of bread, because this is not a hunger that can be appeased by bread. The hunger for meditation, the hunger for God, is not an ordinary hunger. Nothing of the world can appease it. This thirst is unique. It can only be quenched if God himself descends on the seeker.

How can we become authentic, true? How can the veil of falsehood be destroyed? The answer, says Nanak, is to follow when God orders, according to his wish alone. Everything should be left in his hands; everything should be left to his will, to his design, and that alone will help.

> *How can truth be attained and the veil of falsehood torn? Nanak says: By submission to the divine order which is pre-ordained.*

Nothing will happen by your doing. Whatever you do, it will be your doing. Even when you tell a truth, because it arises out of your false personality, it will be a falsehood. From where can you utter truth when you are absolutely false?

Nanak was a guest of Lalu, a poor carpenter. The rich landlord of the village was performing a religious sacrifice to which he had invited the whole village. He sent a special invitation to Nanak. When Nanak did not appear the landlord himself came to bring him along.

He said, "How can you refuse to come to my mansion and partake in such a feast? Everything is of the best and purest ingredients, and it is specially prepared by *brahmins* who have first bathed and performed their rituals. Can you refuse this food cooked with the water of the Ganges and prefer the meager meal of this lowly carpenter who is not even a brahmin?"

Nanak said, "If you insist, I will go with you," but he asked Lalu to follow him and bring his food.

It is said — and this is a symbolic story — that Nanak took Lalu's dry bread and squeezed. A stream of milk poured forth. With the other hand he squeezed the landlord's bread and a stream of blood came out.

Nanak said to the landlord, "You cannot hide your impurity. Whether you have your food cooked by brahmins, whether you clean each grain with the Ganges water, it makes no difference. Your whole life is one long tale of exploitation, deceit, theft and lies. Blood is hidden in every bite of your bread."

Whether blood actually came out of the bread or not is inconsequential, but the story deals with truth. Only if you are true in your very being, can you be truth. Otherwise who can remedy it?

Nanak says nothing will happen by your doing. You are dishonest, so dishonesty will creep into your truth also. Your truths will somehow be made to serve your dishonesty, and in such a way that it harms others. You will look for such truths that will pierce another person's heart. Before you harmed the world with your lies, now you harm the world with your truths. Whatever you do will be wrong if you are wrong.

What is the cure? Nanak says the only remedy is to leave everything to God: his will be done. Await his pleasure. Live the way he wants you to. Be whatever he wants you to. Go wherever he takes you. Let his command be your one and only spiritual practice. Brush aside hopes and desires, and fill yourself with wonder and gratitude. If he has brought you sorrow there must be a reason behind it, some meaning, some mystery. Do not complain but be filled with gratitude: "Come joy, come sorrow, keep me as your will!" If he has kept you poor, welcome poverty; if he has made you rich, be grateful. In happiness or in sorrow let one tune play incessantly within you. "I am happy the way you keep me. Your command is my life."

Suddenly you will find yourself tranquil. What did not happen through a thousand meditations begins merely by leaving all to his will; and it is bound to happen, because now there is no cause to worry.

What do you mean by "worry"? Worry arises whenever things are not happening as you wished them. Your son lies dying; that should not happen, is your worry. You have gone bankrupt; this should not be is the anxiety. You are trying to impose your will on existence. Things should not have happened as they have happened, and things should not be happening as they are happening: this is your anxiety, and then you suffer because of it.

With all these troubles plaguing you, you sit down to meditate. What can you do but go on reaping your harvest or buying a horse in Kabul! Your anxieties infiltrate and take over your meditation. Then how can you possibly become tranquil? There is only one formula for this: *Accept whatever is.* If you grasp it, you have understood the entire quest of the East from Lao-Tzu to Nanak.

The ancient name for this is fate or destiny. The words have been spoiled as all words are through long usage, because the wrong kind of people use them and hence attribute wrong meanings. Now to insult someone as irresponsible or old-fashioned you accuse him of believing in fate. Nanak says: *By submission to the divine order which is preordained.* Everything should be left in his hands; everything should be left to his will, to his design, and that alone will help.

Think, take a chance, experiment a little; live as he wishes you to. Haven't you tried hard enough? Are you any better off than you were? You are perhaps more deformed, but certainly no *better* than what he made you. You have not even preserved, the innocence and simplicity that were yours in infancy. You have filled to capacity the book of your life with your scribbling. It stands spoiled, defiled, and what have you gained besides suffering, pain, tension and remorse?

Try to listen to Nanak's words and act on them for a few days. "Leave all unto him," Nanak says – no prayers, no mantra, no penance, no meditation, no resolutions. There is only one spiritual practice — his wish. As soon as the thought is nourished deeply within you that all happens at his command, an intense peace, a gentle shower inside washes away all tension, all anxiety.

The West is filled with anxiety and tension. It is much more prevalent than in the East in spite of the East's backwardness, its poor and its diseased; there is not enough to eat or to cover the body, nor even a roof over everyone's head. The West has everything, and yet it is filled with such tension and anxiety that large numbers of people are on the verge of breaking down or require tranquilizers.

What is the reason? It is clear. The West has tried to force its own will on existence. The West has tried to have its own way. Western man has faith only in himself: We shall do everything for ourselves. There is no God! And he *has* done a great deal, but the man in him is almost lost as he is turning schizophrenic. He has performed wonders outside, but within himself everything has become sick and diseased.

If this verse penetrates you, nothing remains to be done. Just let things happen by themselves. Do not swim, float. Do no fight with the river because it is not your enemy but your friend. Float! By fighting, you create enmity; when you swim against the current, the river opposes you. It is not the river but you who introduces the struggle. The river flows along its course; it is not even aware of you. Of your own will you begin swimming against the tide. You are asserting your will by going in the opposite direction, and that means you are nourishing and strengthening your ego.

His wish...and you become one with the current. Now wherever the river takes you is your destination. Wherever it takes you is the shore. If it drowns you, that is your destination. Then where is the anxiety, then where is the pain? You have cut off the very roots of suffering. What Nanak says is invaluable — that all be left to God's will and command. Only by following the path he has etched out for you can everything happen.

Nanak has closed all doors on the ego: first, by emphasizing the guru's grace – that whatever you attain through your effort is attained only by the guru's grace — and then, that whatever happens, wherever the current of life takes you, is by his command. Then nothing remains to be done. Then it will not be long before you realize that:

> *We cannot comprehend him though we think a million times;*
> *Nor quiet the mind by silence, however long we sit;*
> *Nor a mountain of bread appease the hunger of the soul;*
> *Nor one hundred thousand feats of mind achieve unity with*
>   *him.*
> *How can truth be attained and the veil of falsehood torn?*
> *Nanak says: By submission to the divine order, which is*
>   *preordained.*

CHAPTER 2

The Weight of a Flower

By divine order all form was created,
But his order cannot be described.
Divine order has created all life,
And by it all greatness bestowed;
By divine order are some high and some low,
And pain and pleasure granted;
By his order do some attain salvation,
Or endlessly wander through cycles of death and birth.
All are subject to his order; none is beyond his reach.
Nanak says: He who understands his order becomes freed from his self.
Those who know power will sing of his might.
Knowing charity, some sing of his bounty as the sign.
Some sing of his virtues and his greatness.
Some sing of his knowledge, when scholarship is their bent.
Some sing that he creates the body and turns it back to dust.
Some sing that the life he takes will again be reborn.
Some sing that he is far, far away.
Some sing that he sees all and is everywhere.
There is no end to his attributes,
Though a million describe him in a million ways.
The giver gives eternally, though the receiver tires of receiving;
Since the beginning of time have they subsisted on his endless bounty.
He is the ordainer and by his order does the universe turn.
Says Nanak: He is without a care, endlessly blissful.

There are two ways of living. One is the way of conflict, the other is the way of surrender. In conflict you feel that your will is different from the will of the whole. In surrender you feel that you are a part of the whole, with no question of your will being different or apart. If you are aloof and apart, conflict is natural and inevitable. If you are one with the whole, surrender is natural. Conflict brings tension, restlessness, worry, and anxiety. Surrender brings emptiness, peace, joy and finally the supreme knowledge.

The ego thrives on conflict and is destroyed in surrender. The worldly man is always in conflict; the religious man has given up all struggles and surrendered himself. Religion has nothing to do with your going to a church or a mosque or a Sikh temple. If your tendency is to fight, if you are struggling even with God, if you are trying to enforce your own will — albeit through prayer or worship — you are irreligious.

When you have no desire of your own, then his wish is your wish; if you have no separate goal of your own, wherever he takes you is your destination. When you are ready to move as he pleases, when you have no expectations of your own, when you make no decisions, then you cease swimming and begin to float.

Have you watched a hawk soaring high in the sky? When it has flown to a sufficient height, it stretches its wings wide and floats in the air. When your mind reaches that stage it is in a state of surrender. You need no longer flap your wings, you merely float, weightless in his atmosphere. For all weight is caused by conflict; it is born through resistance. The more you fight the lower you fall. The more you abandon the fight, the lighter you become; and the lighter you are, the higher you soar. If you leave all conflict completely, you reach God's heights, which signifies being free of all burden, weightless. Ego is like a stone tied round your neck; the more you fight, the heavier it becomes.

Once Nanak happened to camp by the side of a well outside a village inhabited by Sufi fakirs. Early the next morning when the head of the Sufis came to know of Nanak's arrival, he sent Nanak a cup of milk filled to the brim. It was so full that not a drop could be added. Nanak broke a flower from a nearby shrub, put it in the cup and sent it back to the Sufi guru. The flower floated on the milk, because what weight has a flower? Nanak's disciple, Mardana, was puzzled and asked Nanak what all this meant.

Nanak explained: "The Sufi's message said there was no room, that the village is so full of sages that it can accommodate no more. My reply let him know that I shall ask for no extra space, because I am as light as the flower and shall float at the top!"

He who is unburdened is a sage. He who has weight is still ignorant and his weight can harm others until he is completely free of all burdens. Nonviolence occurs on its own. Love flowers on its own. No one can bring about love or implant compassion; if you become free of all burdens, it all happens on its own. As a shadow follows a man, so hatred, anger, malice and violence follow the man weighted down with anxiety. Love, compassion, pity, prayer follow in the wake of a weightless person. So the primary issue is to annihilate the ego within.

There is only one way to annihilate the ego. The Vedas have referred to it as *Rit;* Lao Tzu calls it *Tao;* Buddha has called it *Dhamma;* Mahavira's word is *Dharma;* Nanak refers to it as *Hukum* – divine order. He who conducts himself according to his command without making a single movement on his own, with no desires or feelings of his own, or need to introduce his own self, is alone the religious man.

And he who puts himself under his command attains all; there is nothing left to be attained. To obey his command is the gateway to his heart. To believe in oneself is to turn your back on God; obey his will, and you face him again. You may lead your life with your back to the sun and you will never be able to shake off the darkness; no sooner do you turn your face towards the sun than the darkness of innumerable lives vanishes. The only way to stand before God is to leave your own will. To float is enough. There is no need to swim and carry a load unnecessarily. All defeats and all victories are diseases of your own ego.

Your condition is like that of the fly who sat on the hub of a huge chariot's wheel which raised an immense cloud of dust as it moved. The fly looked around and saw nothing but dust. It said to itself, "I am raising so much dust that I must be very big myself!" Whether you are successful or suffer defeat, it is all because of this dust. You are nothing more than the fly on the chariot wheel, so don't bring in your puny self by thinking it is you who is raising the dust. The dust is of his chariot, as is the journey.

You must have heard the story of the lizard. Once his friends invited him for a walk in the jungle. "I am sorry, I can't go," he answered, "because if I were to leave, who will support the ceiling of the king's palace? If the ceiling falls, the responsibility will be mine." The poor thing thinks so much depends on it! And if it is possible for a lizard to think so....

Then there was the old lady who owned a rooster that crowed every morning as the sun came out. The old woman became haughty and arrogant. She told the villagers to be careful of their manners towards her because if she went away to another place with her rooster, the sun would rise no more for them.

Now it was a fact that every day when the cock crowed the sun came out, but the villagers laughed and made fun of her. They told her she was out of her senses. Finally in anger the old woman left and went to another village. There also the cock crowed and the sun came out. She thought, "Now they will beat their breasts and cry. The rooster is no longer there to make the sun rise!"

Your arguments and the old woman's logic are very similar. It has never happened that the cock has crowed and the sun did not come out, yet you have it all backwards. But who can explain this to the old woman and make you understand too? When the old woman saw the sun come out in the new village she was certain that if it had risen there, it could be nowhere else.

Your intelligence and capacity to think is also so limited. God is not because of you; you are because of him. Your breath flows from him; not because of you. It is not you who prays; it is he who prays through you.

If this feeling penetrates your understanding, Nanak's priceless words will become clear. Each word is a jewel.

> *By divine order all form was created,*
> *But his order cannot be described.*
> *Divine order has created all life,*
> *And by it all greatness bestowed.*

Nanak uses the word *hukum,* which means the divine order or the cosmic law which governs all of existence. All life is born out of the divine order, and it is hukum that gives you greatness.

When you are successful, do not consider yourself the victor. Then you will not consider defeat as your defeat. It is he who is victorious, it is he who is defeated. All is his play. In fact the Hindus look upon the whole world as play. This signifies that it is he who wins and he who loses. He wins with one hand and loses with the other; however, the apparent winners and the losers, who are no more than a means, an implement, mistakenly consider themselves doers.

Krishna says to Arjuna in the Gita, "Don't bring yourself into things. It is he who does, and he who gets things done. It is he who has brought this battle about. He will kill those he wants to kill, he will save those he wants to save. Do not imagine that you are the killer or the savior." What Krishna has expressed in the whole Gita, Nanak has said in this sutra: It is he who has created the great and the small.

Let us ponder over this: if it is he who has created all things great and small, then no one is big, no one is small, because all are his creations. You make a small idol, you make a big idol, but you are the sculptor of both. When there is but one maker, what issue can there be which is big or small? Our trouble throughout life is that we think in terms of great and small. No matter how hard we try, we cannot become great enough to satisfy our ego.

As soon as you begin to see the hand of the formless within yourself, you immediately become great. The maker is one. He who makes the lowliest flower also creates the majestic pine tree that seems to touch the skies! If the hand behind both is one and the same, who is great and who is small? The victory is his, the defeat is his. We are just pawns in the chess game.

You must have heard many a devotee saying: "All that is good in me is Yours; all that is bad is mine." On the surface the devotee attributes all his virtues to God while holding himself responsible for all his shortcomings. This apparent humility is not genuine. Because if all the goodness is his, how can all the badness be yours? Genuine egolessness would give way completely at the feet of the Lord, keeping *nothing* for itself — not even the bad. It is the ego in the garb of humility that holds back this little support for itself. However much you may insist, how can success be his and failure yours; goodness be his and evil yours? This talk is hollow; it holds no substance. Either both are his or both are yours.

There is a difference between true humility and false humility. False humility says: "I am only dust at your feet." When a person says that to you, look into his eyes and you will see that he expects you to say: "Oh, no! How can you say that? It is I who am dust at your feet." If however you accept his statement and say, "Yes, you are quite right. That is exactly what I think," then you have earned an enemy for life. He will never forgive you.

All praise is his, all blame his. We have no part in it. We are but the bamboo flute; let him play on it as he will. It is still arrogance that says: "If there is any fault it is mine," because then the ego is still preserved. The I is such a disease: guard even a speck of it and the whole is saved. Either you let go of it completely or it remains completely, hidden safely within you.

Nanak says: all forms have arisen out of the divine order. It cannot be expressed in words. All that is most significant in life cannot be put into words. Divine order is the most significant. There is nothing beyond it. Words are adequate only for the purpose they ordinarily serve, to carry on our day-to-day life. But there is no way of expressing the extraordinary in words. There are many reasons for this.

Knowledge of the supernatural occurs only in silence. And what is experienced in silence, how can that be expressed in speech? Silence and speech are antithetical. When he is experienced within there are no words, only complete silence. How can you find in words what you have known in emptiness? The medium has changed. Emptiness is a different medium altogether — the formless — whereas words have shape and form. How can you give form to what is formless? This has been a problem for all who have known. How can it be expressed? Imagine hearing a beautiful song and trying to explain it to a deaf person.

There is an old Sufi story: A deaf shepherd was grazing his sheep near a mountain. It was afternoon, long past the usual hour his wife brought his lunch and he was very hungry. As she had never been late before he began to worry whether she was taken ill or had met with an accident. The shepherd looked around and saw a woodcutter perched high on a tree. He reached up to him and said, "Brother, would you keep an eye on my lambs? I would like to run home and get my food."

Now, as it happened, the woodcutter also was deaf. He said, "On your way! I have no time to waste in idle gossip." The shepherd understood from his gestures that he had agreed to his request. He ran home as fast as he could and returned with his food. He counted his sheep and all was in order. He thought it would be nice to offer a gift to the woodcutter as a gesture of his gratitude and good will. Having a lame sheep which he would have to kill some day, he took it with him to where the woodcutter was.

Now when the woodcutter saw the shepherd with the lame lamb, he cried out in anger, "What? Do you mean to say I made her lame?"

The more the shepherd offered the lamb to him, the louder shouted the woodcutter. Now it happened that a horseback rider who had lost his way came upon the two. He meant to ask them the way but immediately the two of them caught hold of him. As luck would have it, the rider, who also was stone-deaf, had just stolen the horse and was riding away with it. When these two caught hold of him he thought they must be the owners of the horse. Meanwhile the shepherd asked him earnestly to explain to the woodcutter that he was presenting the lamb as a gift to him.

The woodcutter said, "Please tell this man I did not so much as look at his sheep, much less make this one lame!"

The horseman said, "You may take back the horse. I admit my guilt, please forgive me."

While all this confusion was going on a Sufi fakir happened to pass by. All three rushed at him, caught hold of his clothing and begged him to clear things up for them. The fakir had taken a lifelong vow of silence, and although he understood each of their problems, what was he to do? He looked deep and long into the eyes of the rider, who began to get restless. He thought this man was hypnotizing him. He became so frightened that he jumped on the horse and rode away.

Now the fakir turned and looked piercingly at the shepherd who also felt he was losing consciousness. He quickly gathered his sheep and went on his way. When the fakir turned to the third man, he was equally frightened.

The fakir's eyes were very powerful. Those who observe prolonged silence develop a unique luster in their eyes. All the energy accumulates and the eyes become the channel for expression. When the fakir looked at him deeply, he quickly tied his bundle of sticks and went off. The Sufi laughed and continued on his way. He had solved their problem without saying a word.

This is the difficulty that holy men experience, and there are not only three who are deaf; there are three billion deaf in this world! And each one makes his point but nobody listens; nobody hears anybody else. There is no dialogue in life, only debates and disputes. What is the saint to do then? He has developed the art of silence so there is no way to speak. Besides, however much he speaks, as in the case of the Sufi fakir, deaf men are never able to follow. He would only have added to the confusion. So he merely looked deep into their eyes.

The saint has always tried to solve your problems by looking deep into your eyes. He tries to pour into your eyes what is contained within himself. Therefore Nanak talks a great deal of the company of saints. He says, "Associate with holy men if you want to know what they have known. Keep the company of saints, because mere hearing and talking will not take you far." You will be told one thing, you will interpret it in another way people are deaf. You will be shown something and you will see something else people are blind. You will draw your own conclusions, give different meanings to the saint's words.

Nanak says the divine order cannot be expressed, yet hints can be given. These hints are not mere words, because the divine order cannot be contained in the words. These words are like milestones telling you that you are on the right path, that the destination lies ahead. Many cling to the milestones and go no further.

You can also do this. If you get up each morning and merely repeat the Japuji you will know the Japuji by heart and no more. You will be clinging to the milestone! Instead, travel the way the Japuji directs you to go. Understand it; don't cling to it. Travel you must, because religion is a journey, but to hold on to Japuji or the Koran or the Bible or the Gita is clinging to the milestones. Understand them, go forward and the mystery will unravel itself!

> *By divine order all form was created,*
> *But his order cannot be described.*
> *Divine order has created all life,*
> *And by it all greatness bestowed.*
> *By divine order are some high and some low,*
> *And pain and pleasure granted.*

Think a little: when you are unhappy, you hold the other responsible for your sufferings. If you must do this, hold the divine order responsible. When the husband is unhappy he blames his wife, when the wife is unhappy she lays the blame on her husband. The father holds the son responsible, the son rebukes the father. If you must hold someone responsible, let it be the divine order. You cannot settle for less.

It is most ironic that when you are in trouble you blame another, but when you are happy you take the credit entirely for yourself. What logic is this? — happiness is on your own account, but your unhappiness you put on another's account! This is why you can neither overcome your sufferings nor unravel the secret of happiness, because you are wrong on both counts: neither is the other responsible for your sufferings nor are you responsible for your happiness. God alone is responsible for both. And if joy and sorrow come to you from the same hand, why make a difference between the two?

There was a Mohammedan king. He was very fond of a particular slave, and the slave worshipped his master. One day as they were going through a forest the king saw one lone fruit hanging from a tree. The king picked it and as was his habit, he gave some of it to the slave. When the slave tasted it he said, "Master, give me a little more."

The slave asked for more and more till there was hardly any left for the king. Yet he kept insisting and even tried to snatch what remained from the king's hands. The king quickly put the remaining bit in his mouth but spat it out immediately.

"Have you gone mad?" he shouted at the slave. "This fruit is poisonous and you stand there smiling at me! Why didn't you tell me?"

The slave fell at his master's feet as he said, "The hands that gave me the sweetest of fruits — should I complain against those hands if they gave me but one bitter fruit?"

Notice that he ignored the fruits, but only took account of the hands.

The day this wisdom dawns on you, that it is through his hands alone that sorrow comes to you, then would you still look upon it as pain? You only know suffering *as* suffering because you do not see his hand behind it. The day you realize that both joy and sorrow are given by him, they lose their impact. Then happiness will no longer raise you up nor sorrow produce pain. When joy and sorrow become equal to you, bliss appears to take their place. When the duality of joy and sorrow ceases, the indivisible descends and you are filled with bliss!

Do not hold anyone around you to blame — neither husband nor wife, neither son nor daughter, neither friend nor foe. Let God be the owner of all responsibility. When joy comes or success, don't fill your ego. He is master of all success, the owner of any rewards, of all sweet fruits! If you leave everything to him, joy and sorrow disappear and only bliss will remain.

> *By divine order are some high and some low,*
> *And pain and pleasure granted.*
> *By his order do some attain salvation,*
> *Or endlessly wander through cycles of rebirths.*
> *All are subject to his order; none is beyond his reach.*
> *Nanak says: He who understands his order becomes freed from his self.*

Once you understand the essential, that all is his, what remains of the I? There is no one left to say I. Understand that you desire to get rid of the ego when it causes you pain; yet the trouble is, it is the same ego through which you can experience happiness. That ego gives you pain is well known: when a person abuses you, your ego feels hurt and you want to be free of it.

People come and ask me how they can be freed from sorrow. They also say they know that it is the ego that is the cause of all suffering. Then they ask how to get rid of the ego. I tell them: *"How is not the question. If you really felt that the ego was the cause of all your ills, you would have abandoned it long ago. There is no need then to ask!"*

But it is not so simple; you want to rid yourself of the ego half of the time; you want a fifty-fifty arrangement. The same you that is hurt by accusation and wants to get rid of the ego is delighted when praise comes and the ego feels nourished. Make a mistake and you suffer, perform well and you are delighted; when people abuse you it hurts, when they sing your praises you are all smiles. Both alternatives take place on the plane of the ego.

The trouble is that if you let go of the ego your joys will end along with your sorrows. You want to preserve your happiness and be rid of unhappiness. This has never happened, nor can it ever happen. If they stay, they remain together; if they go, they depart together. They are the two sides of the same coin. You want to throw away one side and keep the other. Since that is impossible, you alternate: one minute you throw the coin aside and the next you pick it up again. You can't keep — or abandon — one side without the other.

Understand the plight of the ego: if you leave both sorrow and joy to God, who is the authentic source of all life, your ego has no place to stand. Then how will you say, "I am"? I is nothing but a collection of all your actions. It is not an object, and has no independent existence. If you let go of the doership and say, "You are the doer, I am only an instrument," then where is the ego? Then whatever he directs, you do; whatever he does not direct, you do not do. If he makes you a sinner, you are a sinner; if he makes you a saint, you are a saint.

Try to understand the uniqueness of Nanak's statement. He says that only through divine order does a person attain knowledge, and it is through divine order alone that a man wanders through countless cycles of life and death. What Nanak means to convey is that if you are a sinner do not brand yourself a sinner. Rather, say "His will."

You might think there is the danger of a person gaily committing crimes blaming his will. The crux of the matter is that once a person *knows* it is all his will, whatever he does is a worthy deed. As long as you do not know, there is a continuous conflict between you and him, which by definition, gives rise to sin. Sin is the result of the struggle between you and God. This conflict brings about the state of inflicting suffering on oneself as well as on others. The day you leave everything to him ,all sins flee.

Nanak says that too is happening through him. If you are a sinner, it is he; if you are a saint, it is he. Don't think it is you who has done the good deed nor that it is you who has committed the sin. The very concept "I have done" is an error, a mistake.

There is only one ignorance; it lies in the belief that "I have done..." There is only one knowledge; it consists in recognizing the ultimate creator. The creator does everything; I am only the means, the instrument. There is no one and nothing outside of the divine order. Everything resides within it.

> Those who know power will sing of his might.
> Knowing charity, some sing of his bounty as the sign.
> Some sing of his virtues and his greatness,
> Some sing of his knowledge, when scholarship is their bent.
> Some sing that he creates the body and turns it back to dust.
> Some sing that the life he takes will again be reborn.
> Some sing that he is far, far away.
> Some sing that he sees all and is everywhere.
> There is no end to his attributes,
> Though a million describe him in a million ways.
> The giver gives eternally, though the receiver tires of receiving;
> Since the beginning of time have they subsisted on his endless bounty.
> He is the ordainer and by his order does the universe turn.
> Says Nanak: He is without a care, endlessly blissful.

His definitions are countless, and still incomplete. How can man who is himself incomplete define the complete? Whatever he says will be incomplete. How can the part bear witness to the whole? Whatever the part utters will relate only to itself. Can the atom know the absolute? Whatever it understands cannot transcend itself.

So those who can sing, sing of his attributes, and yet the unknown remains unknown. The Upanishads sang his praises till they were tired, as did the Gita, the Koran, the Bible. His is indescribable, undefinable — he is made that way. It has been impossible to define him completely. All scriptures are incomplete and they are bound to be, because they are limited man's effort to manifest the infinite.

The sun comes out, and the artist paints a picture of it. However well he paints, the picture will give off no light. You cannot keep the painting in a dark room and expect the room to be lit by it. If a poet witnesses the sunrise and writes a beautiful song about it, no matter how earnest and profound the feelings he conveys, his song cannot light the darkened room.

All songs sung in praise of God, all pictures representing His attributes, are incomplete. No song can tell of him completely, because we cannot bring his being down into them. Words are hollow and must remain hollow. If you are thirsty, the word *water* will not quench your thirst. If you are hungry, the word *fire* is not going to cook your food. And if the desire of God has arisen within you, the word *god* is not enough. It is enough only for those with no desire.

Understand well: if you are not thirsty, the word *water* or H_2O is enough to name it. But if you *are* thirsty, the difficulty begins. Then neither the word *water* nor the symbol H_2O works. You may gather together all the words for water — there may be three thousand languages in the world — and tie them round your neck, they will not yield a single drop of water. If you are not thirsty, you may play with the words.

Philosophy is a game for people who are not thirsty. Religion is the journey of those who are thirsty. Therefore philosophy plays with words; not so religion. Religion takes cognizance of the hints the words give and follows them. When the quest is for the lake, what can the word *lake* do? When the search is for life, the word *life* alone sounds hollow.

The Weight of a Flower

Let us understand a little about a profound question facing the philosopher. A tourist comes to India and he is given a map of India. What is the relationship between India and the map? If the map is the same as India then it must be as vast. If it is exactly like India, it would be useless, because you couldn't carry it in your car, much less put it in your pocket. If it is not like India, how can it still be useful?

The map is a symbol. It is not like India and yet by means of its lines, it conveys useful information *about* India. You may roam the whole of India without ever seeing a map of India. Wherever you go you will find India; the map is nowhere to be seen. But if you have the map with you and understand it and use it, the journey will be made easier. By either keeping the map in your pocket, or by looking at the map and never leaving your room, you will not learn a great deal. Both together make for the fullest understanding of the experience.

Religious people the world over hold the maps to their chests as if the maps were the actuality, the totality. Scriptures, holy books, images, temples – all contain hidden pointers that keep the maps from being just a burden. The Hindu is carrying his load of maps, the Mohammedan his, the Christian his. The maps have become so numerous that the journey is now almost impossible, so weighted down are you by maps. The maps should be short, abridged, and they are not to be worshipped in themselves, but to be utilized on the journey.

Nanak drew his essentials from both the Hindu and the Mohammedan religions. He cannot be called Hindu nor Mohammedan; he is both or neither. It was very difficult for people to understand Nanak. There was a saying: "Baba Nanak is the king of the fakirs. He is the guru of the Hindus and the saint of the Mohammedans."

He is both. Of his two special disciples, Mardana and Bala, one was Hindu and the other a Mohammedan. Yet Nanak has no place in the Hindu temple or in the Mohammedan mosque. Both doubt his position and do not know where to place him. Nanak is the confluence of the two rivers, of Hinduism and Islam. He harvested the essence from both. Therefore the Sikh is neither Hindu nor

Mohammedan; they must be both or none since their religion arises out of their junction.

Now it is difficult to understand this confluence; when there is a river on the map it is clear-cut, but here two rivers have become one. Some words relate to Islam while others reflect Hinduism, and together they became hazy, but gradually the fog clears when you enter into the experience. If you keep Nanak's words on your chest as you do other scriptures, it becomes like any other holy book — and we do find the Sikh worshipping his words as if they were the guru. Is it not astonishing how we repeat our mistakes?

Nanak went to Mecca. The priests there told him to be careful not to point his feet toward Kaaba while he slept. As the story goes, Nanak's reply was that they should turn his feet where God was not, and, it is said, the holy stone of Mecca turned wherever they turned his feet. The symbolism means only this: wherever you turn your feet, there God is. Where will you put your feet if he is omnipresent?

I was invited to the Golden Temple at Amritsar. When I went they stopped me at the entrance saying I must cover my head before entering the place of God. I reminded them of the incident with Nanak at Kaaba and asked them, "Does it mean that right here where I stand with my head uncovered, there is no God, no temple?" We keep on repeating our mistakes. I further asked, "Then please show me a place where I can be without a head-covering. And don't you remove your turbans while bathing, and while sleeping? Then isn't that also an affront to the Lord?"

Man's foolishness is the same everywhere. Whatever Buddha says, his followers paint with their own brush to suit them. And so also with Nanak. The same web is woven once a master has pronounced his words, because man's foolishness has not changed, nor has his deafness improved. He hears, but he draws his own individual conclusions which he then follows accordingly, never putting into practice what he actually hears.

Nanak says: no matter how many songs are sung about the lord, nobody has covered it completely. Different people sing different songs because there are many paths to reach him. However antithetical their songs may seem there is no contradiction anywhere because they all contain the same message. The Vedas say exactly what the Koran says, but the method by which Mohammed reached is different from Patanjali's approach. Buddha also says the same thing but his method is entirely different.

Infinite are the gates to his abode. Whichever way you go leads to his gate. Once arrived you can begin to define the gate through which you entered, and describe the path you have trodden. Another person will likewise describe his own door and his road. Besides, it is not only the path that differs, but your understanding, your perception, your emotional attitude all play a significant part.

When a poet enters a garden, he sings in ecstasy; an artist would paint a picture; if a flower-merchant comes along, he will think in terms of sale and profit; a scientist will analyze the flowers or soil to find out their chemical composition and why they grow; a drunk will be oblivious to the beauty around him, he will not even know that he went through a garden. Whatever you see passes through the windows of your own eyes which impose their own color on everything.

Says Nanak: Some sing the praise of his power — he is all powerful, omnipotent. Some sing of his benefaction and munificence — he is the supreme giver. Some sing of the glory of his attributes, his beauty — he is the most beautiful. Some call him truth, some call him Shiva, some call him the beautiful."

Rabindranath has written: "I found him in beauty." This says nothing of God; rather, it tells of Rabindranath. Gandhi says: "For me, he is truth — truth is God." This speaks of Gandhi rather than of God. Rabindranath is a poet; for a poet God resides in beauty, supreme beauty. Gandhi was no poet, he is practical, and it is natural that such a mind sees God as truth. From the point of a lover — he is the beloved.

How we see him reflects our insight. He is everything simultaneously and also — none of these. In this context Mahavira's reflection is wonderful. He says, "Unless and until your sense of vision drops, you cannot know him." For whatever you will know, you will know through your own seeing; it will be your view of knowing. Mahavira calls his method no-view. Seeing only occurs when all vision drops.

But then you will lapse into silence, because how will you speak without a viewpoint? When you are freed of your vision, you will become like him; because you will be so extensive, so comprehensive, you will be one with the open skies. How will you speak? You will no longer be separate unto yourself, but one with the absolute. A viewpoint means that you stand apart from what you see; to have a viewpoint means that you are separate from him.

Therefore Nanak says that all the viewpoints are correct but none is complete; when the partial is proclaimed as complete and perfect, the illusions begin. Any sect or organization claims one particular incomplete vision as perfect. One sect stands against another, whereas all sects are different aspects of religion, and no one sect is a religion. If we were to amalgamate all possible sects that have been, that are and that will be, then religion would be born. No sect on its own can be called religion.

The word for sect in Hindi, *sampradaya*, also means the path, that which takes you to the goal; whereas religion, *dharma*, means the destination. The destination is one, the paths, many.

> *Those who know power will sing of his might.*
> *Knowing charity, some sing of his bounty as the sign.*
> *Some sing of his virtues and his greatness.*
> *Some sing of his knowledge, when scholarship is their bent.*
> *Some sing that he creates the body and turns it back to dust.*
> *Some sing that the life he takes will again be reborn.*
> *Some sing that he is far, far away.*
> *Some sing that he sees all and is everywhere.*
> *There is no end to his attributes,*
> *Though a million describe him in a million ways.*
> *The giver gives eternally, though the receiver tires of receiving.*

In spite of saying it millions of times, there is much more left unsung. The benefactor gives and gives and gives, while the receiver drops with exhaustion.

These are very significant words. It is he who gives life. It is he who breathes your breath. It is he who pulsates in every heartbeat. He keeps on giving...giving. There is no end to his giving, and he asks for nothing in return.

As a result you mistakenly feel life to be a cheap commodity and other things appear expensive. You are always ready to abandon life and aliveness but not wealth; because wealth is acquired with great difficulty and life is given you without any effort on your part — it comes free! Whatever he has given you, he has given freely and you have given nothing in return.

When this begins to occur to you, you begin to question your own worthiness for all that you have received: "Would it have mattered one bit if I were not?" The life potential, the flowering of consciousness that has bloomed within you — if it had not, to whom would you have complained? And what is your worth that makes you eligible for life? How have you earned it?

For every small thing in life you need proof of worthiness. To be a clerk in an office or a schoolteacher, you have to be qualified for the post; you have to earn your place in life. How have you earned your life itself? It is a gift freely given and not because of some special qualification of yours. The day you begin to realize this, prayer will arise within you. You will say, "What shall I do to express my gratitude? How shall I repay Thee?"

Prayer is not begging but an expression of gratitude for what is already received. Prayer of another kind, when you go to the temple to ask for something, is false prayer.

Nanak also goes to the temple, but only to express his thanks and gratitude: "I cannot believe all that You have given me! I see no reason why you should cover me with so many gifts, because I am not worthy. If you do not give I have no complaints, but you are such that you give and give...and give."

And us? It would be difficult to find more thankless people than us. We offer no thanks, show no gratitude. His gifts are unending and our ungratefulness knows no bounds! We cannot so much as thank him; we find it so difficult our throats seem to choke.

You are ready to say thank you if you drop your handkerchief and someone picks it up for you, but you have no word of thanks for the one who has given you life. If you ever go to pray, it is always a complaint. You tell him of all the wrong he is doing, "My son is ill, my wife does not treat me well, my business is failing." And you exaggerate your complaints so! You manage to convey: "You aren't there. And if you are, why don't you satisfy all my desires!"

Atheism means that your complaints have reached such a pitch that you can no longer believe there is a God. Your complaints kill God.

And what is the meaning of theism? You are so filled with gratitude and thanksgiving that you see him all around you. Everywhere you see his hand, everywhere his reflection; everywhere you feel his presence. Theism is the peak of thanksgiving; atheism, the nadir of complaints.

> *The giver gives eternally, though the receiver tires of receiving;*
> *Since the beginning of time have they subsisted on his endless bounty.*

Enjoy him as much as you will, you cannot exhaust him. To empty an ocean with a teaspoon is more possible, because whereas the scope of the spoon is limited, so also is the ocean limited. But you can never drain God because he is boundless. For eons upon eons you have been enjoying his bounty but never has a word of thankfulness risen from your heart to proclaim how grateful you are that all he has given is boundless. Whenever you have spoken, it has always been to express your dissatisfaction, emphasizing your worthiness and minimizing what you received.

A high official came to visit me from Delhi. The higher the post the greater is the number of complaints. He felt he was treated very unjustly and should have become a minister, preferably prime minister. He said, "Show me how to bear up under this injustice I have suffered."

Every person lives with this pain that he has not been awarded what he deserved. He who was worthy of becoming a vice-chancellor, lands up an ordinary schoolmaster; another feels he should be the master, but becomes a *peon*. And it goes on and on. Even the prime minister aims at becoming an international figure, having attained the highest position in his own country. You cannot satisfy an Alexander the Great — and everyone is an Alexander in his own right — big or small.

Desires always go ahead of you, as you think yourself worthy of more and more. These are the characteristics of an irreligious person. A religious person believes: Whatever I am given is beyond my worth.

Think it over for yourself. Whatever life has given you — is it more or less than what you deserve? It is always more — much more. For we have done nothing to earn this vast existence that we have attained unasked and undeserved, and yet there is no sign of gratefulness within us!

Nanak says we cannot exhaust him even by partaking of him for infinite ages. The divine order shows the way through his command.

Here is a very deep clue, a critical part of Nanak's thoughts: He governs the world through his commands and is forever ordering you. Had you the slightest ability to listen, you could understand his command and flow accordingly. But you never listen!

You go to steal. He tells you inside, "Don't, don't!" twice, a thousand times. But you do as you please. The voice gradually becomes weaker and weaker until you become deaf towards it. Then you don't hear him at all though he keeps calling.

There is not a single sinner who has lost his internal voice, the voice of the divine order. You cannot find the most evil person whom he has stopped calling. He never tires of you; he is never disappointed; he never considers you beyond redemption. However deep your illness, he has a cure. God has infinite hope, infinite potential. He is never disappointed in you.

There was a Sufi fakir by the name of Bayazid. His neighbor was a total rogue, a cheat, a criminal. He had committed every sin under the sun and the whole village was terrified of him. One day Bayazid prayed to God: "Oh Lord, I have never asked anything from you. But this man is now going beyond all limits. Please remove him from our midst."

At once the inner voice spoke to Bayazid: "I am not as yet tired of him, then why are you? And if I still have faith in him, why don't you?"

You cannot make him tired of you, no matter how much you

sin for unnumbered lives. You cannot outlive him. He keeps on calling. He never gives up on you.

And if you become silent for a moment and listen, you will surely hear his voice within you. Whatever you do, the internal voice ordains how you should do it.

He is the ordainer and by his order does the universe turn.

This is why Nanak calls him the ordainer — for it is his order that comes. The consciousness that is within your heart is the instrument that brings his voice to you. He speaks through your consciousness. Before doing anything, close your eyes and listen to him. If you obey his command, bliss will shower on your existence. To go against it is to create your own hell, by your own hands. Turn your back to the voice, and you are taking a dangerous step. Before deciding on anything, before taking any step, close your eyes and ask him. This is the thread in all meditation, that first we shall ask — seek the voice, then proceed. We should not take a single step without his permission. We should close our eyes and hear his voice, and follow his voice, not ours.

Once you acquire this key, it will open infinite doors for you. The key is within you; each child is born with it. We develop the child's intellect but do nothing to develop its consciousness. It remains undeveloped, incomplete. We heap so many layers of thoughts over the voice, it gets hidden so deep that we no longer can hear it, though it calls all the same.

That art of hearing the inner voice is called meditation. It is imperative to know his command. We must know what he wishes, what is his will.

He is the ordainer and by his order does the universe turn.
Says Nanak: He is without a care, endlessly blissful.

He keeps on giving but expects nothing in return — not even an answer. He keeps calling out to you whether you hear or not. He does not care, he does not worry that you do not listen. He never feels he should stop since you have turned a deaf ear to him, much less would he cast you aside as a lost cause.

You cannot make God anxious. And for this very reason, a man who has begun to see the reflection of God within himself has no anxiety. He will be simultaneously concerned and unconcerned. He will care for you and at the same time he will be carefree. You cannot make him anxious or worried.

Here I am! God knows how many people I am concerned about and yet I am carefree. You come to me with your woes and though I am concerned you do not cause me worry or anxiety. I do not become sad with your sorrow or I would not be able to help you. Though I need to sympathize with your troubles and find ways and means to lighten your distress, I cannot be so concerned that your worry grips me too.

And I should not be displeased with you if you come the next day without acting on my advice — which will surely happen. I don't feel: "I took so much trouble and you disregarded my advice." I still care, and through it all I remain carefree.

God is concerned about the whole world. He is forever ready to raise you up but he is not in a hurry. And if you wish to wander a little longer in fleeting pleasures, you are welcome to do so, by all means, but then he is carefree.

His concern is boundless and unaffected by you. He is always full of bliss — or you can imagine what state he would have been in by now! He would surely have gone mad with all the people there like you, and what trouble they are creating all around. God is one — and you are so many. You would have pushed him into madness long ago; but existence is carefree, which is why it is saved from going berserk.

Carefree does not mean indifferent. Note the subtlety. His endeavors for you remain unchanged — his desire to raise you, to change you, to transform you. But his desire is nonaggressive. He will wait. Every morning the sun and his beams knock at your door and your door is closed. The sun will not force his way in. He will wait. It never happens that he will be angry and turn back. Whenever the door opens, he will come in.

God is concerned about you; existence cares about you. This is bound to be true for existence creates you, has developed you; it has great expectations of you. Existence is endeavoring to become conscious within you, to attain buddhahood from within you. God is endeavoring to bring forth flowers within you. But if you delay, he will not be troubled, he will not be anxious; he remains unaffected if you do not listen to him, or refuse to heed him. If you can understand both these things together, then you will understand why existence is filled with bliss. God is bliss.

Nanak says: he gives commands, and shows the way, and yet he has not a care! He keeps evolving in supreme bliss. His flower keeps blooming — always and always.

For us there are only two possibilities: either we care and that gives rise to worry, or we are unconcerned and there is no anxiety. This is why tradition has separated the sannyasin from the everyday world. If you stay at home you are bound to be involved with the family, then how could you be unconcerned and carefree? If your wife is ill you will worry; if your child has some disorder you will worry about his treatment and be filled with pain if he does not improve. But if wife and children are not before our eyes, we shall forget them — out of sight, out of mind! So we run away to the mountains and turn our backs to the world, so that by and by we shall forget.

We see only two alternatives: if we stay in the world we cannot remain unconcerned, and if we are concerned we are bound to worry, then there is no way of being blissful. The other choice is to run away and become carefree and unconcerned, so without worry the prospects of bliss increase.

But this is not the way of God. Therefore Nanak remained a householder as well as a sannyasin. He was concerned and also unconcerned. And this is the art, the spiritual course — to be concerned and yet free from anxiety. Outwardly you do everything required of you but nothing attaches to you inside. You educate your son, and take great care of his upbringing; but if he turns out useless, or does not study, or fails in life, you are not worried.

Until you combine the two, and be a sannyasin within the household, you cannot reach God, because that is God's way. He is *in* the world and yet not *of* it. His way should be yours, on a lesser scale, in order to reach him.

The Weight of a Flower

If the child is ill, take care of him with all the medical care he requires but what is the need to be worried? What value is there in disturbing or destroying your internal carefreeness?

Outwardly be in the world, inwardly be in God. Let the outer physical boundary be in contact with the world but let the center remain untouched. This is the essence.

And this is what troubled people about Nanak — that he was a householder but he wore the robes of a sannyasin. People could not categorize him. The Hindus would ask: "Are you a householder or are you a sannyasin? You talk like a sannyasin, your way and manners are those of a sannyasin and yet...this wife and child? If you plow the fields and look after your family, what sort of a sannyasin can you be?"

The Mohammedans questioned him in the same manner. They would say, "You dress like a fakir then why haven't you left your house and family?" At many places many gurus told him to leave everything and become their disciple. But Nanak did not budge from his path. He was constantly practicing the art of remaining outside of everything while remaining within everything, and that alone is the way of God; and that alone should be the way of the seeker.

People ask me: "What are you doing giving sannyasins' robes to householders!" But that is the way of God; he is in the world and yet not in it. And this should be your path too.

He is the ordainer and by his order does the universe turn.
Says Nanak: He is without a care, endlessly blissful.

He is cheerful, filled with bliss, blooming like a flower and yet he has not a care! He is concerned about you — but he does not worry.

Put this experiment into practice in your life: work, mind your shop, but let there be a distance between your work and your being. Let your work be a play, a *leela,* and do not be the doer, that is all. Be an actor, let the art of acting become your life's thread; because that is the way of God and that should be your way, your practice.

CHAPTER 3

Solving the Riddle

The Lord is truth. Truth is his name.
His praises are sung in endless ways.
Even while praising they ask for more and more,
And the Lord keeps on giving.
Then what offering can we make to gain a glimpse of his court?
And what language shall we speak to endear us to him?
Nanak says: Remember the true name and meditate on its
  glory in the ambrosial hour.
Through your actions you receive this body,
And by his grace the door to salvation opens.
Nanak says: Know then his truth, because he alone is everything.
He cannot be installed in any temple, nor fashioned by any skill.
The faultless one exists unto himself.
Those who serve him attain the glory.
Nanak says: Sing his praises, lord of all attributes.
Sing and hear only of him; engrave him in your heart.
So banish sorrow and suffering, and make bliss your abode.
The guru's word is the sound of sounds, and the Vedas too.
The Lord abides in his words.
The guru is Shiva, the destroyer; the guru is Vishnu, the sustainer;
The guru is Brahma, the creator; he is the trio of goddesses —
  Parvati, Laxmi and Saraswati.
However well I know him, he cannot be described.
He cannot be expressed by words.
The guru is the secret that solves the riddle.
He is the benefactor of all. Let me never forget him.

Sahib, the Lord, is the name given by Nanak to God. We can write about God in two ways. The way of the philosophers is to talk about God, but their words are dry and without love. Their words are intellectual and lack emotion completely.

The other is the way of the devotee. His words are juicy; he looks upon God not as a doctrine, but as a relationship. Unless there is a relationship the heart is not influenced. We can call God truth but what the word *Lord* conveys can never be conveyed by truth. How can we establish a relationship with truth? What would be the bridge that would connect truth to our heart?

The Lord is a loving relationship. The Lord immediately becomes the beloved and now we can be related; the way is open. The devotee longs for something that he can touch, something he can dance around, sing around. The devotee wants a place to lay his head. Lord is such a beautiful, lovable name. It means: the master, the owner. Thus the relationship can be of many kinds.

The Sufis look upon God as the beloved, so the seeker becomes a lover. The Hindus, the Jews and the Christians have spoken of God as the father, so the seeker becomes a child. Nanak saw God as the lord and master so the seeker becomes a servant.

It needs to be understood that for each relationship the path is different. With the beloved we stand as equals: neither is higher, nor lower. The relationship between a father and son is a relationship of circumstances: because we are born in a particular household, so the relationship. Since, given the opportunity we ourselves would like to be the master and make God the servant, the role of servant best serves to obliterate the ego. The ego does not disappear either in the father-son relationship or the lover-beloved relationship; it can only drop away in the master-servant relationship.

And this is the most difficult relationship, because it is the state which is exactly the opposite of ego. Ego believes: I am the master, all existence is my slave. The devotee says: All existence is my master, I am the slave. And this is the authentic yoga headstand — not literally standing on one's head: you must let the ego touch the ground, because the ego is the actual head. Therefore it is the servant — the devotee — who practices the real headstand. He turns upside down. As you have observed the world through the eyes of a master, it is different from the world you see when you develop the servant attitude.

When a beggar begs from you, is there a chord struck within you which builds a relationship between you? No, just the opposite is the case. As soon as he asks, you shrink within; then even if you give, it is done unwillingly. You make a mental note not to pass that place again. When someone asks something of you, you pull back and want to withhold; when a person does not ask, you feel more like giving.

Try to understand yourself a little and the way towards God will become clear. When someone asks, you do not want to give, because his asking seems like an act of aggression. All demands are aggressive. But when nobody makes demands on you, you become lighter and you give more easily.

Buddha had told his monks that when they went to the village to obtain alms, they were not to beg. They could only go and stand at a door; if there was no response they should move on.

This is the difference between a begging monk and a beggar. We have honored certain begging monks as we have never honored our kings; whereas beggars remain last in our minds. We barely hold them worthy of insult and try to avoid them. The monks asked, "How will people give if we do not ask?" Buddha replied, "Things are easily obtained in this world merely by not asking." As soon as you ask, you constrict the other and create difficulty for yourself. When you do not ask you make others eager to give.

You will find this story hidden in all life's relationships. Your wife asks for something, and giving becomes difficult. If you do get it for her, it is halfheartedly, only to ward off a quarrel. It arises not out of a bond of love, but as a way to maintain peace in the household. If the wife never makes demands you feel like giving her something. Giving is possible when not asked.

You are separated from God by your demands. All your prayers consist of: Give me! Give me! You want God to serve you. You wish to use him as a servant. You say, "My foot pains. Take away the pain...My financial condition is bad, improve it." You say, "The wife is ill, make her well," or "I have lost my job, give me another." You always stand a beggar at his door. Your very asking shows you consider yourself the master whom God is to serve. Are your needs so important that you press even God into your service?

If God is the master and you are the slave then what is left of the demands? The most amazing thing was that you kept asking, and he kept on giving. It is not that you are refused when you ask — you keep on getting; but the more you get this way, as you keep on asking for more and more, the further away from him you become.

A demand can never be a prayer. A desire can never be a prayer. A longing can never be worship. The essence of prayer is to offer thanksgiving and not ask for handouts. He has already given enough — more than necessary, more than we deserve. The cup is full to the brim and already overflowing.

The genuine devotee offers thanks, his prayer is full of gratitude, saying: "You have given me so much, I am not fit to receive it all." And at the other extreme, there you stand: "See the injustice, I deserve more: *I* want *more!*"

Nanak says people keep on asking, and he keeps on giving. Yet there is no end to their asking. He keeps giving, and the beggars keep asking. If you are constantly asking, when will you pray? When will your worship begin? If you fulfill one desire ten others take its place. For how many births have you thus been asking? And you are still not full!

You can never be satisfied, because it is not the mind's nature to be full; its essential quality is to be unsatisfied. Only when one is rid of the mind, does satisfaction appear. You will never find a man who can say that his mind is satisfied. If you ever happen to hear someone say that, look deep into him because he is sure not to have a mind.

What is the mind but a collection of all your demands: "Give, give and give more...." There is no greater beggar than the mind, caring not how much we receive. Even Alexander the Great was a beggar, no better than any beggar soliciting by the side of the road. It is necessary to understand the nature of the mind.

How can the mind pray, for prayer is a state of no-mind? The whole viewpoint is changed as soon as you put the mind aside. It means you have come for thanksgiving and not begging. Reintroduce the mind and you feel you don't have enough, you need more. Mind keeps its eyes on the absence of things. Abolish the mind and you begin to see existence.

It is like this: take a man who sees only thorns to a rosebush. He begins counting the thorns and does not even look at the flower. Try your utmost, he will not notice the flower. Where there are so many thorns, what worth is a simple flower? And be very careful. Don't touch the flower. It might be thorns in disguise!

Who can refute his argument? If his heart has been pricked by a thousand thorns, he is naturally afraid of them, and he is bound not to trust in flowers either. He will take them to be an illusion, a trick to deceive him, a dream. Who could see the flower amongst such a plethora of thorns?

Now if you take into account only the flowers — lost among them, and filled with their touch, and their scent — another state is born in you. Then you think: "Where there are such lovely flowers how can there be thorns! And the few there are, are only there to protect the flowers and help them to bloom. And it is God's will that they should exist too. Perhaps the flowers could not be without horns; they are the protectors to save the flowers from all harm."

And as your attention to the flower increases, you will realize that the same sap flows in the thorns as in the flowers. Therefore how could there be conflict between the two? The mind tends to concentrate on the thorns; it turns its attention to what is not, to where the fault is, the complaint, the failing. It has an eye for dissatisfaction, nonfulfillment. What is left but to make demands? So a man filled with the mind goes to a temple to ask; he is a beggar.

If you set the mind aside a little, you begin to see more and more flowers; you attain to the power and the joy of life. So much have you received from the very beginning what source is there for complaint? And if he who has given so much has kept something back, there must be a reason for it. Perhaps you are not yet prepared to receive it, or lack the worthiness.

Anything that comes before its time brings suffering rather than joy. Everything has its own time to ripen. When you have ripened

God will give. Infinite are his ways of giving; thousands are his hands, spread in all directions — raining bounty on one and all!

The Hindu concept of God is a thousand-armed being. This concept is full of love. They say: "He gives with a thousand hands, not just two! You will not be able to hold his gifts because you have only two. He gives with a thousand hands — but at the right time, so wait for the moment without complaint — and his grace begins to rain in torrents."

Nanak says even when they sing the Lord's praise they do not fail to ask, and the Lord keeps on giving. But these blind people see not, and still clamor for more. While his grace pours down on them, they wail endlessly that they are thirsty, as if they have fallen in love with their suffering!

Then what offering can we make to gain a glimpse of his court?

This is very significant. Nanak says God has given so much, there is nothing left to be asked for. When complaints fall away and you are filled with gratitude, you wonder what you should take as a love-offering to his feet.

What shall we offer at his court? What shall we place before his feet when we express our thanksgiving? How shall we worship, how shall we adore him? You take flowers, pluck them from bushes — his bushes. They were better off on the plant, still living. You plucked them and killed them. You kill his flowers and offer them at his feet — and you are not ashamed? What can you give him — everything is his!

When you spend your money to build a church or mosque, what are you doing? You are returning to him his own things, and yet you are filled with pride. You say, "I built the temple. I fed so many poor. I distributed so many clothes." You give so little, yet you become arrogant.

What does this show but that you have not understood? Returning a little bit of the infinite gifts you receive from above is not a matter of pride. Yet you go to offer the gift and you are not even ashamed!

"What will you put before him?" Nanak asks. How shall we

approach — with what — so that we can see his courts, and can come near him? What shall we put before him — rice dipped in saffron, flowers from the market, wealth, treasures — what?

No! No gift will serve the purpose. To understand that everything is his, is enough. The gift is accepted! As long as you feel something belongs to you, you think of offering something. As long as you consider yourself the master you may give if you like, but you err. Anything you may offer — your whole kingdom — is nothing. For everything is his, even you are his! Whatever you have earned, whatever you have gathered is all his play.

Nanak says: "What shall we do to stand in your court, to stand in your presence? To look into each other's eyes? When you come to understand that everything is already his, there is no need to take anything. The flowers on the tree are already an offering to him; everything stands offered at his lotus feet — even the sun and the moon and the stars. What will your miserable lamps do before the orb of the sun? Open your eyes and see that all of existence stands offered at his feet. This exactly is the meaning of the word *master*. He is the master of all, everything stands as an offering to him."

So Nanak says: "What are we to give?" This is Nanak's question: "What language shall we speak, hearing which, he may love us? What shall we say to him? What words shall we use? How should we entertain him? How shall we please him? What shall we do so that his love pours on us?"

Nanak does not seem to give any answer. He raises the question and leaves it unanswered. And that is the art, because he says that whatever we say, it is he who speaks through us. What is so exceptional in offering his own words to him? Only in ignorance can it be done. Wisdom recognizes that: "Nothing is left to offer him because I too am an offering at his feet." No words can become a prayer, because all words are his. It is he who speaks; it is he who throbs within the heart; it is he who is the breath of breaths. Then what is the wise one to do?

Nanak says: Remember *satnam*, the true name, and its glories in the ambrosial hour. There is nothing else to be done. What is the wise one, the sensible person to do?

Remember the true name and meditate on its glory in the ambrosial hour.

The Hindus call it *sandhya* which literally means evening; it is used to designate the hour of prayer at twilight and at dawn. Nanak calls it *amrit vela* which means nectar or ambrosia time. It is an even more appropriate name. The Hindus have been working on this path for thousands of years. In search of the reality of existence and exploring consciousness, they have found paths in almost all directions; almost nothing is left undiscovered. They have gradually determined that in the twenty-four hours of the day there are two short periods of *sandhya*.

In the night when you retire to bed, there is a short period when you are neither asleep nor awake. At this particular moment your consciousness, so to speak, changes gears. In changing the gears of the car, you have to move through the neutral gear before going to the second gear. So for a moment, the car is in no gear.

Sleep and wakefulness are two very different states. When awake you may be filled with misery; in sleep you become an emperor! You do not even wonder that the one who is a beggar in the day can be a king at night. You are in an altogether different gear. You are on a plane of consciousness that is entirely different from your ordinary daytime consciousness; and these two levels have nothing to do with each other. Otherwise you would have remembered for an instant, that you are a beggar and why have you become a king? But when you dream you are entirely identified with the dream. You experience the waking hours of the day as a different existence altogether from the world of sleep. You enter an entirely different world.

In the day you are a saint, at night you are a sinner — and do you even wonder at it? Have you ever doubted your dreams while dreaming? Once you do the dream will break apart, for doubting is part of wakefulness; it is a part of waking consciousness. In dreams you are not conscious of the fact that you are dreaming.

There are many orders of seekers where the spiritual exercise is taught that when they prepare to sleep at night, they should keep one thought in mind: "This is a dream...this is a dream." It takes three years for this remembrance to become strong enough for the seeker to recognize the dream as a dream — at which point it breaks. From then on, there are no dreams for him, because now the gears are not separate. The two planes of consciousness merge into one: now he is awake even when sleeping. This is what Krishna means when he says the yogi is awake when others sleep. The wall between the compartments has fallen and now it is one big room.

Both in the night when you are about to fall asleep and in the morning just as sleep departs and you are about to awake — these are the two moments when consciousness, in its process of changing gears, drops for a moment into neutral, when you are drifting between sleeping and waking consciousness. This is the time that Hindus call sandhya and Nanak calls amrit vela. *Sandhya kal* is a scientific term. *Kal* means hour, and *sandhya* refers to middle, neither here nor there — neither belonging to this world nor to that. At the moment of sandhya kal you are nearest to God; therefore the Hindus have made use of this time for prayer. Amrit vela, nectar time, is sweeter — the moment you are nearest to ambrosia.

It all happens in this temporal body: with one mechanism of the body you sleep, with another you awake. All dreams pertain to the body. All waking and sleeping happens to the body. Behind this body is hidden a *you*, who never sleeps, never awakens. How can he who never sleeps, awaken? There is a you who never dreams, because that requires sleep, and that never sleeps. Behind the various states of this body hides the ambrosia, the nectar that is never born, never dies. If you succeed in locating the sandhya kal, you will come to know of the bodiless within the body; you will know the master hidden behind the slave. You are both. If you look at the body alone, you are the slave; if you look at the master within, you become the master.

So, says Nanak, there is only one thing worth doing and that is to meditate on the glory of satnam, the true name, in amrit vela. You will gain nothing by going to temples making various demands. Nothing will result from worship and sacrifices, by offering leaves and flowers, because what sense is there in offering him what is already his? There is only one thing worth doing — pray in the ambrosial hour.

Sandhya kal lasts but a moment, but your mind is never in the present, therefore you always miss it. Every day it comes — once in every twelve hours you are nearest to God, but you miss him, because your eyes are not alert enough to the present, to catch this subtle moment.

As you sit here now, are you here or have you gone to your office and started your daily work? Are you involved in what I say or are your thoughts engaged in *thinking about* what I say? If so, you will miss the present.

If you want to catch the ambrosial moment, you must become conscious of the present at every moment! When you eat, let only eating be — no other thought should fill your mind. When you bathe — bathe only; no other thought should be in the mind. When you are in your office, let your thoughts be only of the work, not thinking of home. When you go home, forget about the office. Be completely, wholly, within each moment and not here, there and everywhere. This way the subtle sight will develop gradually and you will be able to see the present moment.

It is only after this, that you can meditate in the nectar hour, because that is a very subtle moment. It passes by in a flash. You may be thinking of something else and the moment has come and gone!

Before falling to sleep, lie in bed completely relaxed. Still the mind in every way, don't let any thoughts drag you here and there, or else you will miss the moment. Let the mind become like the cloudless sky: not a trace of a cloud, that's how empty the mind should be. Keep watching, be alert; because when the mind becomes empty there is the danger of your falling asleep. Keep watch within. If you succeed in remaining awake, soon you will hear a sound — the changing of gear — but it is a very, very subtle sound. If thoughts are rambling within, you will never hear it. Then you will be able to witness the day turn into night, waking turn into slumber, and also sleep turning into awakening. You stand apart, witnessing the various processes.

The one who is witnessing, the seer, is the nectar. Then you will easily observe waking consciousness fading out and sleep coming in; and in the morning you will see slumber depart and consciousness dawning. When you become capable of seeing both sleep and awaking, you will stand apart from both. You become the seer. This is the nectar moment. Nanak says: at this moment — the amrit vela — let your experience be of his glories.

And this feeling should be: he is truth, his name is truth. Do not say the words, keep only the feeling within. If you begin reciting the Japuji you will miss it; no words, no thoughts — only feelings. If in that moment you begin reciting his attributes: "You are great, you are boundless, you are such..." you will miss it. The moment is so very subtle.

Remember the experience of falling in love. Did you need to express your feelings over and over? Do you need to sing the beauty of your beloved every time you meet? Words make everything hollow and superficial. The truth is, as soon as you begin to express it, the glory of love is gone! You cannot express love in words.

When you sit with your beloved in silence a feeling of the glory of love resounds within the heart. You are thrilled, you are in bliss, you are happy and cheerful without any reason. You feel filled to the brim for no reason. All emptiness is gone; you are replete with love. The lover feels the stream of love overflowing, like a river so full that it pours over its banks! You will always find lovers silent, while husband and wife are always talking. They are afraid to be silent. In silence there would be no connection between them, because their relationship is one of conversation and words. If the husband is quiet the wife is worried; if the wife is quiet the husband feels something has gone wrong. Only when they quarrel are they quiet. The silence you now use for quarrels should be used for the highest love.

When two people are intensely in love they are so overwhelmed with feeling that there is no room for words. In this state they may hold hands or embrace, but speech is completely lost. Lovers become dumb; talking seems trivial, it seems an obstruction. For speech would destroy the profound silence; speech would snap the strings of the heart; speech would disturb the surface of the ocean and waves would begin to form. Therefore lovers become silent.

In that moment of nectar you are not to allow a single thought, or form any words. You have to preserve the mood, the feeling of his supreme glory, of loving gratitude for all he has given. You are full — overfull; you want nothing. Let thankfulness, gratitude flow from you.

What language shall we speak to endear him to us?

There is nothing to say, what can we say to him? All words are useless. Meditate on satnam. Be filled with the true name and you will feel you have established a rhythm with the amrit vela. Be alert and you will be shocked! You will feel you have become a flame of light without beginning or end, which always is, true and eternal. It is in this flame that the doors of existence open and the hidden truth is revealed.

Nanak says: Through your actions this body is achieved. In that intense moment you will know that the body is a result of actions, of karma; and it is his benevolent, all-compassionate eyes that open the door of salvation. The body is the fruit of your actions.

A few things need to be clarified here. First: only certain things can be attained by actions, only what is petty and trivial. The vast absolute cannot be attained through actions. Kabir has said, "All happens by nondoing." You have to be in the state of nondoing in order to attain the absolute.

Whatever I do cannot be greater than myself. How could it be otherwise? The action can never be greater than its doer. The sculpture is never greater than the sculptor, the poem never transcends the poet. It is just not possible. Whatever comes out of you is invariably less than you, or at the most, it can be equal to you — but never greater. How will you attain God? Your actions will achieve nothing; the more you try through action the more you will wander.

In a vain attempt to hide this wandering you have carved images in temples. There is no way to fashion God, because God fashions us. You make idols, you make temples — these bear the imprint of your hands and therefore are insignificant. How can the absolute that is so vast come out of *your* hands? But it is also possible that your creation may bear the stamp of God — when you leave yourself completely to him; then it is he who acts, and you are only the implement.

A wealthy Indian industrialist has constructed many temples bearing his name. No trace of God will ever be found there. What has it to do with God? You will not find him in the temple, nor in the church, nor in the mosque, nor even in the *gurudwara*, because these bear the stamp of Hindu, Christian, Mohammedan and Sikh.

There can be no name to God's temple. He is without name; therefore his temple also has to be nameless. Whatever you make, however beautiful, however loaded with precious stones, it will bear the stamp of man. Your temple may be bigger than other temples, it cannot be bigger than you. And he can only manifest in your temple when you become completely nonmanifest; there should not be a trace of you anywhere.

Until now we have been unable to construct a temple where there is no stamp of man. All temples belong to someone or other. The builder of the temple is very much in the atmosphere of the temple. No temple is truly his. The truth in fact is, there is no need to build a temple to him because the whole of existence is his temple. It is he twittering in the birds; it is he blooming within the flowers; it is he wafting in the breeze; it is he gurgling in the rivers and brooks. The whole wide sky is his expanse and you are a wave that has arisen in him. His temple is so vast, how can you contain him in your small places of worship?

Man can do a great deal through his performance. The West is an example of this. They have attained a great deal through actions. They have succeeded in building good houses, good roads. They have made scientific discoveries, made the hydrogen bomb. They have made great preparation for death and destruction. But they are completely bereft of God.

The more they attained in the physical field, the more they lost all those things that are born of the nondoer state. The very first thing they lost was God. Nietzsche said a hundred years ago: "God is dead," and for the West, God was really dead. When they are filled with actions and deeds, all connection with him is broken — then he is as good as dead for them. And since God was almost lost to them, all prayers became hollow and superficial. Meditation was completely lost. There was no point in meditating. For if everything is to be attained by action, what is left to *in*action? And meditation is inaction.

Therefore the occidental mind takes the Easterner to be lethargic and indolent. Nanak's father thought the same of Nanak, that he was lazy, indolent. What was he doing just sitting all day? The father had a business mind and this son posed a problem for him by doing no work and showing no inclination to follow any trade. Whenever he went to work he was thrown out. He did not study, because he would invariably get into an argument with the teacher. For he would tell him, "The last word is already spoken. What more is there to know? And have you attained him in spite of all your learning?" When the teacher had to reply in the negative, Nanak said, "Then I shall seek a way to know him myself," and the teacher regretfully took him home, acknowledging his inability to teach him.

Kabir says: "All the world has learned books upon books, and never has even one become a learned man. He who learns the four letters of *l-o-v-e*, becomes a wise man."

Nanak set out to learn these four letters of love in order to attain knowledge. Why should he endure the business of all this knowledge which has such a different goal altogether?

Mulla Nasruddin was a school teacher. Every day for many years he rode his donkey to school. At last the attitude of learning caught hold of the ass too, and one day he turned to the rider on his back and asked, "Mulla, why do you go to school every day?"

The Mulla was quite taken aback. Was he hearing right? Did the donkey really speak? He had heard many donkeys speak, but never a four-legged one! However, if those others can talk why not this one? The Mulla thought, "It must be that all this going to school has had an effect on him and he has just begun to speak. It was my own fault bringing him to school every day."

"Why do you want to know?" asked the Mulla.

"I am curious, that's all. Why do you come to school every day?" said the donkey.

"I come to teach the children."

"Why?"

"So the children can learn."

"What happens by learning?"

"A person gains intelligence and wisdom."

"What use is intelligence?" persisted the ass.

"What use you say? It is because of my intelligence that I am riding you!" said the Mulla.

"Teach me also, Mulla. Give me intelligence!" said the donkey.

"Oh, no," said the Mulla, "I am not that foolish. Then you will be riding me!"

All that we learn in this world serves as a means of getting the better of one another. It is a plan for your conflicts in life. You will be able to fight better and win out if you have more degrees. The universities are a reflection of your aggression; armed with its weapons you can compete and exploit others more efficiently. You can harass them more systematically, and commit crimes lawfully. With the right rules and methods you can do effectively all that you otherwise could not do, and which you should not do. Education teaches dishonesty and deceit. As a result you may win out over others, but you will never be wise. Rather, people are becoming more and more unwise, ignorant. Our universities are not centers of learning, because no wisdom is contained there.

So Nanak's teacher himself took him home and acknowledged to his father that he was unable to teach him.

When Nanak reached the age of twelve, he was about to be initiated into the Hindu religion and receive the sacred thread. It was an important ceremony. Many people were invited and a band was arranged. When the priest had finished his incantations and was about to place the sacred thread on him, Nanak said, "Wait! What will happen by wearing this thread?"

The pundit said, "You will become a *dwij*," which is a member of the Hindu faith, literally a twice-born.

Nanak asked, "Will the old really die and the new be born? If that is so, I am ready." The pundit was concerned because he knew to the contrary, that nothing would happen, that it was only an empty ceremony. Nanak asked, "What if this thread were to break?"

"You can always buy a new one from the market and throw away the old," said the pundit.

"Then let this one go now," said Nanak. "Anything that breaks by itself and is sold in the marketplace for a trifling amount, how can it help me to find God? How can man's creation help to find God? For man's performances are always petty and inferior."

His father, Kalu Mehta, was convinced the boy was a total good-for-nothing. He had done his best to bring him round to doing something, but had failed. When there was no other way, there was a last resort that came in handy in the villages — he was sent to graze the cattle. Nanak went quite happily to the pasture and was soon lost in meditation while the cattle destroyed the adjacent fields. The next day he had to be removed from this, too. His father was now doubly convinced that the boy could do nothing and would amount to nothing.

Now it is an interesting fact that those people who have done the most for the world are denied this world completely; those who are the just claimants of the other world are almost unable to do anything in this world. It is not that they are not capable, but their whole quality of being and doing is different. They become only a means, a medium through which many things can happen.

What would Nanak have attained by grazing cattle? Many people do. What would Nanak have attained by running a shop well? Many do, and yet the world remains as before. This person has removed himself from the world of action and is drowned in the world of glory.

Glory means: "Thou art the doer. What can I perform?" No sooner do you begin to feel your worthlessness, expressed as, "What can I do?" than your ego begins to fall away, drop by drop. The day you feel this in totality — that you are unqualified, incapable, nothing happens because of you, you are helpless — the doors of liberation open for you.

> *Through your actions you receive this body,*
> *And by his grace the door to salvation opens.*
> *Nanak says: Know then his truth because he alone is everything.*
> *He cannot be installed in any temple, nor fashioned by any skill.*

The faultless one exists unto himself.
Those who serve him attain the glory.
Nanak says: Sing his praises, Lord of all attributes.

God cannot be installed in any place; therefore, how can you make temples? How will you consecrate his idols? He is complete in himself, so you have no need to create him. He was when you were not, and he will be still when you are no longer. Do not bother yourselves with the worthless task of creating his images. Rituals, temples, idols — these will lead you nowhere.

Then what will lead you to the goal? Those who have served him, those who have revered and worshipped him, have attained his presence. If he is everything, service is prayer; if he is everything, service is worship. The more you get absorbed in service, the nearer you will reach him. If the tree is thirsty, water it; if the cow is hungry, feed it. You are thereby quenching his thirst, and feeding him.

You need sensitivity in order to serve. Temples, big or small, serve no purpose. They are just devices to escape prayer. His temple is enormous and equally great should be your attitude of service — because that alone is He, the whole wide universe and all that it contains!

When Jesus was about to be crucified, his followers asked him, "What shall we do now?"

Jesus said: "Do not worry. If you quench the thirst of the thirsty, the water will soothe my throat. If you serve the poor and needy, you will find me hidden within them. If you have been angry or abused someone, there is no point in coming to the temple. If while you kneel in prayer, you realize your mistake, get up first and beg pardon of the person. For till then how can you pray? It is he who is spread everywhere." Therefore Nanak says: "Those who have served him have attained his glory."

What kind of worship? Service! This word is very significant, so allow it to go deep inside you. Remember to keep in mind that whomever you serve is God.

You can serve people in another sense also, which is very different. When you serve people knowing that they are poor, miserable or needy, it is out of pity; then you are above him and he is below. When you are being kind, taking pity, you are not serving. Then it is an ordinary social service and this service is not worship. You are a mere social worker, a member of the Lion's Club or a Rotarian flaunting the motto: "We serve." You are filled with arrogance. You build a small hospital but your publicity is enormous. Social service is not worship; you are throwing crumbs to the hungry, you are doing great kindness, obliging others. You are at the top, serving those who are way down at your feet and who should be grateful. This is not worship.

Service becomes worship when the one you serve is God. He is master, you the slave. It is not he who is indebted; rather you — that he gave you the opportunity. You have given a poor man bread and also thanked him.

There is an old Hindu custom of giving alms to the *brahmin* as well as a love offering, a gift as a token of gratitude for his having accepted the alms, that he accepted your service. Feeling indebted to the one you serve converts your service into worship; it is not social service but a religious act.

Understand well the difference: to be proud of what you do as a welfare worker, is not Nanak's idea of service. Service makes you humble. Service sees God in the lowly. Service makes you a servant. "He who is last becomes the first." And you will stand the very last. Service also presumes that you are indebted to him who gives you an opportunity to serve.

> *The faultless one exists unto himself.*
> *Those who serve him attain the glory.*

This glory is not of your ego because it is only realized when the ego is no more. Then these servants of the Lord became famous and buddhahood shone through them. Then the darkness of their house was banished and the lamp within shone full and bright.

> *Nanak says: Sing his praises, lord of all attributes.*
> *Sing and hear only of him; engrave him in your heart.*
> *So banish sorrow and suffering, and make bliss your abode.*

And this can only happen if you dedicate all your actions to him. When you sit in your shop and a customer comes in, see not the customer but God within him. Deal with him as if God himself has entered your shop. If you wish to be drowned in him all day long there is no other way than this. While eating feel it is he entering you in the form of food. Therefore the Hindus say food is Brahma. Do not eat thoughtlessly. Remember, it is he who bloomed on the plants; it is he who has become the grain. Accept him most gratefully. When you accept food as Brahma, when drinking water you feel it is he come to quench your thirst in the form of water, only then can you absorb him all the twenty-four hours. What other way is there for you?

You go to the gurudwara or church and pray, or chant, or sing hymns for an hour or so while your mind runs here and there. Even for this short period, you check your watch to see whether it is getting late, whether it is time to go to work. How can you worship him in bits and pieces? You try to pray a little in the morning and a little while in the evening while you remain your ordinary old self the rest of the day.

To be religious is a twenty-four-hour undertaking; the religious spirit should pervade you all day long. Religion doesn't exist in odd moments; there is no religious day or religious hour. All life in its totality is his. All moments are his. Religion is a very different way of living in which everything you do is in some way or other connected with God.

Nanak says: "Sing in praise of the Lord of all attributes. Sing only of him, listen only to him, let only him reside in your heart." As you sit listening to me you can hear in two ways: either as if someone is talking or as if it is God's voice coming to you. In the latter case you will feel a change coming over you. Keep him in mind always. Thus you will be rid of suffering and carry home the bounty of bliss. Thus after a full day's labors you will reach home carrying not sorrow but joy.

Now coming home you carry nothing but the pain of some customer who tricked you, or someone who picked your pocket, or whatever you ate that was not good; there is always cause for complaint. Your day is a collection of sorrows, but if you begin to see God all around you in whatever you do, you will reap a rich harvest of joy, says Nanak.

Not only will you live in happiness in your everyday home but at the hour of death when you prepare to leave for your real home, you will be overflowing, filled to the brim, saturated with joy. Then you will depart dancing, not crying. If death does not become a dance, know that life has gone to waste. If death is not an occasion of joy and celebration, know that your life was ill-spent, because you are returning home; and if going home is not a matter of celebration, then your whole life adds up only to sorrow.

So banish sorrow and suffering, and make bliss your abode.

Your suffering exists only because you are trying to steer your life without God. Having set him aside, you have trusted yourself too much and taken yourself to be too clever; there is no other reason for your unhappiness.

And the reason for your happiness is equally simple: you have set your cleverness and intellect aside, giving no credence to your abilities but experiencing him in everything; you have begun to live more in him and less in yourself. Ultimately you may dwell entirely in him.

Why should you see your wife as wife, and not as God? Why should you see your son in your son, and not God as your son? As your perception changes, happiness joins you. If your son dies you will be unhappy because your perception was wrong. You thought: "My son." Had you realized beforehand that he is God's son, you would have thought: "When he wished, he sent him to me; when he wished, he called him back. All is his command." And you would have accepted all conditions, knowing it was his son sent to you, and feeling grateful for the days he let you have him.

To whom to complain, and about what? He gave when he pleased, he took away when he pleased. You have no hand in it. All is his — everything! Then, where are the tears? Where the anxiety, the sorrow and distress? If he gives, you are happy; if he does not give, you are happy. His ways are unique. Sometimes he gives and thus creates you.

Sometimes he takes away and in so doing you evolve further! Sometimes suffering is necessary, because sorrow wakes you up, makes you conscious. In happiness you are lost and asleep! In suffering you awaken.

There was a Sufi fakir by the name of Hassan. One day as they were getting in a boat his disciple said, "That there is joy I can understand, because God is our Father, and it is but natural that he should give joy to his children; but why sorrow, why unhappiness?"

Hassan gave no reply but began to row the boat with only one oar. The boat began to turn in circles. "What are you doing?" the disciple called out. "If you row with one oar we shall never reach the other shore. We shall keep going round and round in this one spot. Has the other oar broken or is your arm paining? Let me row the boat!"

Hassan replied, "You seem to be a much more intelligent fellow than I thought!"

If there is joy alone, the boat will go only in circles and arrive nowhere. For it to work, the opposite is also needed. A boat moves with two oars, a man walks with two feet, and two hands are needed to work. In life you need night and day, joy and sorrow, birth and death; or else the boat keeps going round and round, reaching nowhere.

When a person begins to perceive correctly, knowing that he is in everything, he is filled with thanksgiving; even when sorrow comes he accepts it cheerfully. Then you accept his joy and you accept his sorrow equally. then joy is no longer joy, sorrow is no longer sorrow; the dividing line is lost. When you begin to look upon them impartially, your attachment to joy and rejection of suffering are both broken and you stand apart, free from both, having arrived at the attitude of *witness*. Then you shall be rid of sorrow and carry home joy.

> *Sing and hear only of gim; engrave gim in your heart.*
> *So banish sorrow and suffering, and make bliss your abode.*
> *The guru's word is the sound of sounds, and the Vedas too.*
> *The Lord abides in his words.*
> *The guru is Shiva, the destroyer; the guru is Vishnu, the sustainer;*
> *The guru is Brahma, the creator; he is the trio of goddeses —*
>   *Parvati, Laxmi and Saraswati.*

However well I know him, he cannot be described.
He cannot be expressed by words.
The guru is the secret that solves the riddle.
He is the benefactor of all. Let me never forget him.

Understand that Nanak has glorified the guru to a great extent. All saints have sung the glory of the guru, placing him above the scriptures. If the guru says something that is not found in the Vedas, forget the Vedas, because the guru is the living scripture. There is a reason why saints have extolled and treasured the guru's words so. First of all, the Vedas are also expressions of gurus; but these gurus are not present today. And the words have lost the purity they had when they were first uttered, because those who collected them, of necessity, combined and mixed them with their own thoughts — this they could not help. Though it was not done on purpose, it is certain that it happened.

If I tell you something with instructions to repeat it to your neighbor, you are bound to lose something and add something to what I said. The mode of speaking will change. Even if you use exactly the words I used, your preferences and your emphasis will be different from mine. When you speak, your experience, your knowledge, your understanding will creep into the words.

I give you a flower, and you take it in your hand to give to someone from me, but the flower will have caught some of your smell. Just as the flower's scent remains in your hands, the flower also picks up your scent. The flower is no longer the flower I gave you. And if the flower has passed through a thousand hands, it will carry the scent of all those hands. And if the flower were to come back to me, I would never be able to recognize it as the same flower. The essence of the flower I knew would be lost by the touch of a thousand hands. It will not look the same as when I gave it, but will have fallen into pieces, its petals scattered here and there. People will have to stick on other petals to complete the flower before they bring it back to me.

The Vedas are the utterances of gurus. Those who have known have spoken. But now it is thousands and thousands of years since these words were spoken. Much has been deleted, much added.

Therefore it is great good fortune to come across a living guru when the book has turned stale.

Another very interesting thing is: when you read a book, you interpret the words in your own way. It is you who reads and you who interprets, and your interpretation cannot be more than you; it cannot transcend your own understanding. You will attach your own meanings to the words.

So the book cannot become your guru; you become guru to the book! You have not learned the scriptures, rather you begin to teach the scriptures; thus you find thousands of interpretations. Look at the Gita — how many commentaries there are! Whoever reads it takes his own meanings from it. Krishna is no longer here to censor by saying: "Brother, this is not what I meant!" When Krishna spoke, he was definite about what he meant, but who is to say now what his intention was? Even Arjuna could not say, though he was the one to hear it; because whatever he says will have been changed by him.

The whole Gita has been written by Sanjay, who was no more than a news reporter of his day. It was his job to report on the battle being fought over one hundred miles away to Dhritrashtra, the blind king. He must have seen the whole thing on television. The deaf are listening and reporting to the blind! So the truth lies even further away. What Krishna said, even Arjuna could not have reported correctly, but only in the light of his own understanding. He could repeat only what he understood and not what Krishna actually said. And now we introduce Sanjay who is collecting the news. He is the reporter — the third person!

Then thousands of years elapse while we have all the commentators, each claiming to elucidate it out of his own understanding. By then each word acquires infinite meanings, and the Gita becomes meaningless. Whatever you put in has become a new edition.

Therefore Nanak and Kabir and others have stressed one point — seek a living guru. The scriptures had all become stale and secondhand, thirdhand, even at the time of these saints.

The guru's word is the sound of sounds, and the Vedas too.

The Lord abides in his words.
The guru is Shiva, the destroyer; the guru is Vishnu, the sustainer;
The guru is Brahma, the creator; he is the trio of goddesses —
  Parvati, Laxmi and Saraswati.
However well I know him, he cannot be described.
He cannot be expressed by words.

Those who have seen him with their own eyes, cannot describe him completely. He cannot be expressed through words. And you go looking for God in books? — the Gita, the Bible, the Koran or Guru Granth! Even a living guru cannot explain him thoroughly. About himself Nanak says: "Even if I had known completely, I would not have been able to give a complete description; because he cannot be expressed through words."

What cannot be expressed through words you are trying to understand through explanations and the printed word, but you can only get news of him through a living guru. And it is not that you will understand all that the guru says; you will understand what the guru *is*. The guru's presence will make you understand his very being. To be with him, to breathe the air around him, is to be in a different climate altogether! At least for that much time you are lost to the world; you reside in a different world, and your consciousness has assumed another form. Be ready and willing to look through the guru's window — there is no other way besides this.

The guru is the secret that solves the riddle.
He is the benefactor of all. Let me never forget him.

Gur means technique, method. He who gives the method is the guru. And the secret method, the technique according to Nanak is:

He is the benefactor of all. Let me never forget him.

He is the one creator of all, the maker. May I always remember this truth: that he is hidden behind all. He is the hand of all hands; he is the eye of all eyes. It is he who throbs; it is he who is life.

Let me never forget him.

May this remembrance remain every moment. By grasping this secret, you will gradually see beyond the beads of the *mala* and be able to grasp the thread that goes through them all. That thread is God and you are the beads. The stream of life that flows through you, is God; he is the thread on which turns the bead of your body, and this thread is the same in me as in you. It is the same that runs within the trees, the birds, the animals, the mountains, the plains. It is he living in the various forms, swelling in every wave, so catch hold of the constant remembrance of this thread and never forget it — and you have the secret at hand. All riddles will then be solved by themselves.

So what will you do? How will you guard this remembrance all day long? You will need terrible courage, for there are many difficulties to be faced. Had it not been for these obstacles the world would have become religious long ago. Pains and difficulties there are and will continue to be; because any attainment without trouble is almost useless. Without traveling you can never reach your destination; you are bound to wander. You will only appreciate and care for that which you acquire with difficulty. Besides, if you are out to attain the ultimate truth you will have to make some sacrifice!

Religion is to lose on one side and gain on the other, and so problems arise. If you begin to see God in the customer, how will you fleece him? It will be difficult. If you are a pickpocket, seeing God in your victim, your hand will be paralyzed. How can you do evil? How will you be angry? How will you make enemies?

If you see him in everything the structure of your life will begin to crumble from all sides. The house you have built stands against all he signifies, because you built it when you had forgotten him. If now you begin to remember him the house cannot remain.

One thing however is certain; though you cannot see it today, you will get a bigger house. Therefore we need gamblers on the path, people with the courage to leave whatever is at hand in order to realize something about which they cannot be absolutely certain. Therefore I always say, religion is not for the businessman, it is for the gambler! The gambler stakes his all with the hope of attaining twice as much. Whether he will or not, is never certain. He does not know which way the dice will fall — no one knows. It is that kind of gambler's courage that you need if you wish to walk along with Nanak.

All religions have become feeble because we have not the courage of the gambler, but stick to the mathematics of the businessman. Then it becomes very difficult to remember this sutra, which aims to change your life from its very roots; you will not be the same from even such a small sutra. It will start such a raging fire in your life that this life will disappear.

Kabir says: "Only he who is prepared to burn his house, need walk with me." Which house is Kabir talking of? The edifice you have created round yourself — the house of lies, deceit, anger, enmity, malice, jealousy and hatred — this is what your house is.

Grab hold of this sutra, only this:

He is the benefactor of all. Let me never forget him.

That within, the master of all, is one. For your life to change, you need nothing more. You do not need to do Patanjali's yoga *asanas*, nor have you to worry about the ten commandments of the Jews, nor concern yourself with the Gita or the Koran.

A small secret, such a tiny secret, to change your entire life! Through this secret Nanak attained and you can also.

But remember Kabir: "Only he who is prepared to burn his house, he alone need walk with me."

CHAPTER 4

Some Other Ganges

*If I have succeeded in attaining his pleasure, I have bathed
   in all the holy rivers.
And if I fail to please him, why should I bathe and adorn myself?
In this whole created universe, nothing is attained without actions;
but he who listens to but one teaching of the guru,
his understanding becomes like a precious jewel.
He is the benefactor of all.
Let me never forget him.
Were you to live through four ages, or even ten times more,
Were you known on all nine continents, and were to gain universal
   following,
Were you to earn fame and praise from all of mankind,
If you have not his grace, nothing will save you.
You are like the lowliest worm; even the worst of sinners may
   point the finger at you.
Says Nanak: He makes the worthless worthy,
And showers the gifted with more gifts.
None but God can bestow such excellence.*

Suddenly one night Nanak left his house and disappeared. Nobody knew where he had gone. They searched all the temples and dwellings of *sadhus* where he was likely to be, but he was nowhere to be found. Someone said he had been seen going towards the cremation ground, but nobody could believe it. No one ever goes to the burial ground of his own will. Even the dead man does not want to be there, so the question of a living person going voluntarily seemed impossible.

But when Nanak was nowhere to be found, as a last resort they had to look for him there. They found him sitting before a fire deep in meditation.

His people shook him and said, "Are you out of your mind sitting here at this hour, leaving your wife and children behind? Don't you know where you are? This is the cremation ground."

Nanak replied, "He who comes here has already died; death is no longer ahead. What you call your house is where you will die in due course. Then which one is to be feared? Is it where people die or where people never die? Besides, if some day you have to come here, it is most unseemly to come riding on four people's shoulders; therefore I came myself."

This incident is very significant. Nanak has no quarrel with what has to be. He accepts all that is. Death is to be. Death is welcome. Why trouble others? It is better to come on one's own. But we are always opposed to what will be. Our desire is for it to be different, but Nanak has no such desire. All is his wish! If he wills that Nanak should die, he accepts his wish.

That night, however, people persuaded him to come home. After he returned Nanak was never the same again; something within him had died and something new had been born. It is only by dying completely within that the new birth takes place. In the process of birth you have to go through the burning grounds, and he who passes through the burning *ghats* knowingly, voluntarily, attains a new birth. This is not the birth of a new body; it is the unfolding of a new consciousness.

You are full of fear; and where there is fear there can be no connection with God. All your prayers and worship are because you are afraid — not out of love for God. You visit the holy places, bathe in the holy rivers, perform sacred rites and worship — all out of fear. Your religion is the medicine of your fear; it is not a celebration of joy. You do all this to protect yourself. These are the precautions you take for your well-being. Just as you amass wealth, build a house, have a bank balance, take out an insurance policy, in the same manner God is also your insurance policy.

And who has ever arrived through fear? Fear is a way of

separating; love is a way of integrating. Fear creates distance; love brings closeness. Fear and love never meet. When fear is completely gone, only then does love arise. As long as fear prevails you can only hate. Though you may cover and decorate your hatred you cannot love.

How can you love one whom you fear? You fight the one you fear; you can never surrender to him. And even if you surrender, it will only be a new device for battle; futilely you hope to be rid of fear this way.

> *If I have succeeded in attaining his pleasure, I have bathed in all the holy rivers.*
> *And if I fail to please him, why should I bathe and adorn myself?*

People go to holy places and bathe in the holy waters, not as an act of joy but in the desire to be rid of sins. It is believed that by bathing in the Ganges all sins are carried away by the waters of the river. Now why should the Ganges wash your sins? How is it involved in your evil deeds? Besides, your sins come not from the body but from the mind. How can the Ganges wash your mind? At most it can clean your body and remove its dust and dirt; it cannot cleanse the dirt of your mind.

The Ganges is all right for washing your body, but not as a means of washing your soul. You will have to look for some other Ganges. There is an old story which says: One Ganges flows on earth, one flows in heaven. You will have to find the Ganges of heaven. The earthly Ganges can only touch the body, which is also of the earth. The Ganges of heaven will touch your soul and wash it. How is one to find the heavenly Ganges? Where is one to look for it?

These sutras direct you to the Ganges of heaven:

> *If I have succeeded in attaining his pleasure, I have bathed in all the holy rivers.*

That he should be pleased with you is as good as bathing in the heavenly Ganges. *Attaining his pleasure* is a very deep and profound saying. Try to understand it. You will gain his pleasure only when you do not stand against him. You will gain his pleasure only when you have completely dissolved yourself in him, when your sense of being the doer is completely annihilated. He is the doer, you are only a means; and that is enough to please him!

Right now however, there is a constant strain within you: I am the doer...I am the doer... When praying it is *you* who prays; while bathing in the holy waters it is *you* who bathes; when you do charity, again it is *you*. Everything goes to waste: your bath, your charity, your worship. All is in vain, and all because of your sense of doership. Until now you have been thinking only in terms of myself, mine.

There is only one difference between a religious person and a nonreligious person: for a religious person *he* is the doer; for a nonreligious person *I* am the doer. Everything happens through him — this attitude endears you to him, because this attitude is religion. You stand with your back towards him by your own will. It is your sense of doing that turns you away from God. The moment you give up this attitude you will stand face to face with him, and all opposition ceases.

What are your performances that you are so proud of? Neither birth nor death nor life itself is the outcome of your actions. Everything is done by him, but somehow you acquire this attitude of the doer. And with your sense of doing, when you commit sin it is sin; and even when you perform good deeds they too become sin. Remember! You are in the wrong. It is the sense of being the doer that is sinful! And nondoership is virtue! All good deeds become sinful if the sense of doership persists. Then whether you build temples, perform worship, observe vows, observe fasts, go to holy places — to Mecca or Kashi — all goes to waste.

The more you say *I* have done, the more you add to your sins. So sin relates not to the act but to the attitude. Any act performed in the attitude of nondoing cannot be sinful. But if your attitude is that of nondoing, all acts are sins.

In the Gita this is exactly what Krishna exhorts Arjuna to do. He tells him to abandon all sense of being the doer, to do only what God is doing through you. Let his will be done; don't put yourself in between. Make no decisions by yourself. Do not think: What is right?

What is wrong? How can you know what is right or wrong? What is the scope of your vision? What is the strength of your understanding? What is your experience? How much consciousness do you have? Don't try to see with your small lamp of consciousness when it cannot see more than four feet ahead — whereas life spreads into infinite space. Do what he makes you do; be a medium only. Just as the flute allows the flute player to play his tune, give way to him to act through you.

He who becomes his implement becomes his beloved. He who remains a doer becomes his foe; however, his love flows all the same, because it is unconditional. It makes no difference who you are, his love pours on everyone all the time. It is you who are unable to accept his love. Similarly, an upright pot gets filled with rain water, but if it is kept upside-down it will not fill. The rain pours all the same, because it is unconditional. It does not say: If you do this, or be like this, then only shall I rain on you.

This is important to understand, since, hearing Nanak's words, many people thought that "If I become this way he will love me." No, this is wrong! His love and benediction pour forever. If it were not so, what is the difference between temporal love and divine love? The very bane of human love is: If you do this I shall love you. If you become like this I shall love you. I shall love you only if you fulfill my conditions. This is what the father says to the son, the wife to the husband, the friend to a friend.

Nanak refers to an experience beyond worldly love. His love rains forever. If you fulfill the conditions you will be filled like the upright pot. Filled to the brim, you will overflow with his love and everyone around will receive the overflow.

The guru is one whose vessel is so filled with God's love that he can contain no more. As he begins to overflow other vessels are filled through him. The guru means one whose wants are all fulfilled, since all desires have died, and longing is silenced. His vessel is so full that now he is capable of giving. And what can he do but give? When the cloud is saturated it must rain. Then only can it become light. The flower saturated with fragrance must give it up to the winds.

In the same way, when your vessel is filled with his love, it will shower all around you. There is no end to his grace. Once you know that you will fill merely by keeping your vessel upright, the grace from above never ceases to pour. Then no matter how much you give out your vessel is always brimming. So remember, Nanak is addressing you when he says he has succeeded in winning his love by bathing in all the holy rivers.

Know that he lives! Otherwise how could you exist? Had he not wanted you to be even for a moment, you would have disappeared long ago. He resides in every one of your breaths. It is he throbbing within your heart. Existence has loved you, desired you, made you. It does not matter what you are like; it is still giving you life. You are already the loved one. But you turn your back to him, afraid of his love. You run away and hide just when he wishes to fill your being. When Nanak speaks of winning his love he means to become upright, stand facing him, and shed all fear.

It is only out of fear that you overturned your vessel, fear that it may be filled with something unwanted or wrong. It is out of fear you have closed all doors: for fear of thieves, for fear of enemies. Out of fear you have closed your heart on all sides. When you close your doors thieves cannot get in, but then the beloved cannot enter! For the door is only one, either for the thief or the lover. Avoiding the thief, remember, you have shut the door to the beloved too! And what is this life without the beloved?

You are so afraid of something entering that you have covered the opening and then cry that you are empty. You complain that no visitor ever comes to your house, no one ever knocks at your door, but it's your fear that has turned you away from your God.

It is interesting that your religions are only an expansion of your fears. Your so-called gods are concepts born of your own fears, and out of fear you have accepted them. You are afraid of doubting and so you raise no question, but real faith is not within you. If you are a believer out of fear, then faith is only superficial and doubt lurks within. How then can you meet the most mysterious, the most profound?

Mulla Nasruddin stood for election. He got only three votes: one his own, the second from his wife and a third from a stranger. When his wife heard this she cornered him: "So who is she?"

What lies hidden within surges up on the slightest pretext; it does not take long for superficial faith and love to break down. Any slight happening and doubt raises its head; a thorn pricks and you begin to doubt him, your head aches and your faith is gone; you lose your job and your love for God flies out of the window.

When the hidden doubt bursts out it is like an ulcerated boil; a slight knock and pus begins to flow. You may try to cover it with the ointment and plaster of faith, but it serves no purpose. Who is there to cheat? You can't even fool yourself, because you know very well that your faith is because of your fear, and you are filled with internal doubts.

You may bathe in the holy places or pray in the temple, church or *gurudwara*, but to no avail; unless the note of faith and trust arises within, you have not really called him. Also, when you go out of fear, you are bound to ask for something; fear always begs. If you get what you ask for you are satisfied; if not, the doubt becomes more intense. You are forever asking. Faith is only a form of thanks: "Already you have given too much. your grace, your compassion is so great." Faith is always filled with gratitude; and gratitude dispels all sign of doubt. Where there are demands, doubt is lurking. The demands are a form of test.

There is a story in the life of Jesus. After he performed the excruciating forty-day ordeal, Satan appeared to him and said, "Since it is said in the scriptures that when a prophet is born God always protects him, if you are really the son of God jump from this mountain and he will save you!"

Jesus said, "That is correct, but the scriptures also say that only those who doubt test him. I have no doubts. I am sure that the angels are standing there to protect me. I am thoroughly convinced. Had I the slightest doubt that perhaps they are not there, or that perhaps I am not the son of God, then I would have tested him."

As soon as there is doubt, the question of trial and investigation comes in and you make your demands. Your conditions are: "Fulfill my desire if you exist. If it is fulfilled then you are; if not, you are not." The faithful one makes no demands, makes no tests. Being always filled with gratitude, he never asks favors. The day you stop your demands, your fear will cease. As you are filled with gratitude, the demands will lessen and you will feel your face turning God-ward, straightening your vessel. And as your vessel becomes upright, drops of his grace will begin to fall in it and fear will vanish. Then you will find he is always pouring and you were unnecessarily frightened. Then you will open your doors wide because you know that even in the form of the thief, it is only he; in the form of the cheat, it is he. And until you begin to see him in all, you will not be able to see him at all.

And if I fail to please him why should I bathe and adorn myself?

If he does not like me, my bathing and adorning will only strengthen my ego. Have you ever seen a man returning from a pilgrimage to Mecca? He becomes the picture of arrogance. Had he really gone on a pilgrimage he would have returned a more humble person, a changed man who left his ego behind; but the reverse happens — he expects a loud welcome with great applause, and wants people to touch his feet and praise his action.

Even when you perform good deeds, you only want to fill your ego. You fast so that you may be feted. You secretly desire that bands should be playing and far and wide it should be known how much you have fasted. And as the ego gets stronger, you turn further and further away from him.

The more you are, the more you stand with your back to him. Understand that equation: the less you are, the more you are turned in his direction. And when you are completely not, he stands before you. Then the thief who enters is also him and all fears vanish, because he is everywhere.

> *If I have succeeded in attaining his pleasure, I have bathed in all the holy rivers.*
> *And if I fail to please him, why should I bathe and adorn myself?*
> *In this whole created universe, nothing is attained without actions;*

Whatever he has created and whatever is visible, nothing is attained without actions. Nothing is attained in this world without actions. This causes the illusion that we have to labor, to strive, in order to attain to God. Understand that although everything in *this* world is attained through labor, love is not attained thus — nor is prayer, nor worship, nor faith nor proximity to God.

Why? Because actions make the ego stronger. If you want to gain wealth, you will have to work hard. If you want to be known in this world you cannot afford to sit doing nothing. You will have to run about, plot and plan for or against others; you will have to carry many anxieties. Since effort, labor and work are the only ways to achieve anything in this temporal world, it is but natural for us to think it must require even more effort to reach the all-embracing, vast existence! And this is where we go wrong. The rules of that realm are entirely opposite to the rules of this world. To attain anything of this world, we need to have our backs towards God.

Understand that the more we ignore his support the more effort we have to make, because then we have to do what normally he would have done for us. We have to substitute our labor for his. To go out into this world is to turn your back towards him. His help is less, the flow of nectar is no more; although it keeps flowing, we do not receive it because our doors are closed in our desire to be self-reliant, to be in charge.

Thus, Nanak says again and again: "He is the master; I am the slave." The very endeavor to be self-reliant is because of the ego. The more we feel: "*I* shall do it," the more we deny the support of his power. It is like a man trying to row his boat against the wind. Nanak has given us the secret. Why use the oars at all? Go wherever the winds take you.

And Ramakrishna said the same: Why do you row the boat? Why do you not float along with the current? Open your sails and relax! The winds will themselves take you to the shore. You have to keep an eye on the right moment and the right direction — that is all. Do not go against the wind. If the wind is blowing towards the other shore, open your sails; if the wind is blowing towards this shore, then too, open your sails. Do not labor unnecessarily.

If you go against the wind or the flow of the river, you will have to struggle, and what will be the outcome? You will never arrive, you will only get tired. Observe the face of a worldly man after a whole life's labor — nothing but signs of fatigue. People are dead long before they die, so that at life's end they hanker for rest — at any cost! Why do you tire yourself so?

When man gets old he becomes ugly. The animals of the jungle do not become ugly but remain as beautiful as when young. So also the trees; though some are a thousand years old and near death, there is not a grain of difference in their beauty. With each year they grow a little more, and more and more people can rest under their shade. Their beauty increases with every year, and the pleasure of sitting under an old spreading tree is so much more than under a younger tree which has had so much less experience.

God knows how many seasons the old tree has seen, how many monsoons, how many springs, how many summers and winters; how many people rested under its shade; how much life passed under it, and the winds and the clouds that passed overhead; and how many sunrises and moonrises it must have witnessed, and how many dark, moonless nights. All is contained within it. To sit next to an old tree is to sit next to history. A profound tradition has flowed through it.

The Buddhists are still trying to save the tree under which Buddha attained enlightenment. The unique event that took place under its branches is still contained within its experience. It still throbs with its vibrations; the rays of the light of the supreme knowledge that Buddha attained are still contained in its memory. To sit under it is to feel a peace you have never felt before. Having known infinite peace, it allows you to share in its experience.

Old trees become more beautiful. Old lions become yet more majestic, because in the young there is still a kind of excitement, impatience, and longing that have become quiescent in the old. Man becomes ugly because he gets tired. The trees do not fight existence; they keep their sails wide open, and they are happy wherever the wind takes them. You are fighting existence; therefore you break. You become old and decrepit because your life is one long struggle.

All that is achieved in the object-world is attained through hard labor and toil, but you need no action to attain God. You need no worship, no prayer, nor yoga, nor austerities, nor the repetition of some mantra. He cannot be attained by deeds — but only through love! The direction of love and the direction of deeds are very different from each other.

Love is an emotion. Love is the only thing in life that never gets tired, because love is no work, no deed. The more you love, the more proficient you become at loving. As your experience of love deepens, you find your capacity to love also increases. Love keeps expanding. In the flood of love it is always high tide, never low. Love always ascends, higher and higher; there is no descent.

But love is a divine gift — not the fruit of your labor. In the right perspective love is your resting place; therefore, you always find yourself fresh when in love. You are calm, composed and relaxed. This is also true in what we ordinarily know as love. When you are in love with someone, beside him, all fatigue leaves you; you feel light and fresh. You are filled with cheer; all the dust of toil is shaken off.

Now imagine the condition of divine love! The day his love is born within you, what effort, what fatigue remains? God is attained not by labor but through his grace. Nanak speaks of the guru's gift. You cannot have a direct relationship with him, your eyes are not ready as yet. In order to look at the sun you have to start with a lamp. Concentrating on the flame of the lamp, you go on to a bigger flame, then to a yet more powerful light. Only gradually do you concentrate on the sun itself; or else, with your ordinary sight, the sun will make you blind.

The vessel has to be kept straight. First, it should be turned towards the guru, who is the preparation. When you are ready to be filled with the guru, when you become thrilled and happy and all your fears have left you, only then can you open towards God. A direct opening towards God can be dangerous, because you may not be able to contain him. To bring the goddess Ganges down from heaven you need a Bhagiratha, the king who achieved it through his penance. You will not be able to hold her up, since a small puddle is enough to drown you — as you are now.

Nanak lays so much stress on the guru, and this is solely because the guru prepares you. As you become more and more capable of learning directly what flows from the guru, you will become a Bhagiratha. Then you too will be capable of supporting the heavenly Ganges.

If God is attained but not through actions, then how is he attained? Nanak answers:

*But he who listens to but one teaching of the guru,
his understanding becomes like a precious jewel.*

It is very difficult to listen to even one teaching of the guru since you cannot hear anything with your present being. It requires a complete transformation of your life. For the guru's teachings you have to be eager and look up towards him, you have to learn the art of being quiet and serene in his presence. You must learn to leave your head behind at home, because if you bring it along with you, you will not be able to hear. Even if the guru teaches, your head will draw different meanings. You will be told one thing, you will hear another. Having come empty-handed, you will leave empty-handed.

The guru's teachings cannot be learned through the head, but heard through the heart. He has to be listened to with total faith. When the guru teaches, if you are thinking he is right or he is wrong, you are still sitting in the classroom and not yet in a gathering of seekers.

Coming to the guru means: I am tired of judging right and wrong. Now I can judge no more. It means: I am tired of thinking, I can think no more. It means: I am sick and tired of myself and I want to give myself up. In short, this is what is called faith.

You come to the guru only when you are completely tired of yourself. If you still think yourself to be very intelligent, there is no point in coming to the guru because you are still your own guru. You still need to wander a bit more, bear more hardships, incur more pain through doubts and indecisions. It is no use coming when you are still raw. More pain and suffering are needed to ripen you. The day that you are completely fed up with yourself, then go to the guru.

People often go to the guru when they are not yet ready; they still believe in their own selves. Thus whatever the guru says they sit and weigh his words, judging the right and wrong. What suits them they will believe; what does not they will not believe. In that case, you are obeying your own self and not the guru.

You cannot look upon this as faith, or call it surrender because you have changed nothing. There is only one secret in going to the guru: leave your self behind and go. Then whatever the guru says is right; there is nothing for you to decide. Only then can you hear his teachings, with the entire heart — then only can you learn. He who has heard the guru's teachings becomes a *Sikh*.

The word *sikh* is a beautiful word, coined from the Sanskrit word for student. He who is ready to learn is a Sikh. He who is ready to listen to the teachings is a Sikh. But he who is still full of ego and not prepared to listen is not a Sikh. To put on the turban and adopt all the outward signs of a Sikh does not make you a Sikh, because to become a Sikh is an emotional happening.

Nanak says:

But he who listens to but one teaching of the guru, his understanding becomes like a precious jewel.

By hearing a thousand things, nothing happens; by hearing just one, everything happens. And no matter how much *you* hear, nothing whatsoever happens. And no matter how much *you* have read, it brings no change within you — and the reason is clear: you have not heard from where you should have heard.

There are two ways to listen: with the intellect or with the heart. When the intellect listens, there is always a dichotomy: it thinks in terms of right/wrong, correct/incorrect, believable/unbelievable. The intellect never goes beyond the ego. It looks upon the heart as insane and never trusts it. The heart has almost been smothered because it cannot be trusted. You never know when it might make you do things you'd have to pay for later.

You are going along a street, you see a hungry man, and the heart says: "Give him something." The mind says: "Wait. First find out if he is a genuine case. He might be a fake out to deceive you. Besides, he seems fit enough to work, so why doesn't he?" The intellect will tell you a thousand things but if even one emotion arises in the heart the intellect suppresses it.

If love arises in the heart, the mind says, "That's a dangerous path. Love is blind and has ruined many. Open your eyes and gather your wits about you. The path of love is a footpath wandering into forests and glens: the path of intellect is like the royal path, wide and clear. Where are you going? Don't lose the main road. Go along with the crowd, because it is always better to go where others are and dangerous to go on one's own."

Love is the path that has to be trod alone; it needs privacy, seclusion, solitude. Love says: "Give!" The intellect says: "Wait! Make inquiries before you give." But then you never will give. Love says: "Surrender! Rest your head on someone's feet and forget about yourself." The mind asks: "How can that be? The world is full of deceit. God knows how many have taken advantage of gullible people!"

But what have you that anyone can take away from you? What is it that you will lose by giving? There is nothing but misery and miserliness inside you, yet you protect and preserve it with all your might.

If you live according to the dictates of your mind, your heart will gradually contract and break. There is such a distance created between you and your heart that no news of the heart reaches you. When the mind stands in between, then even if you love, you love with your mind.

Have you noticed that your love also comes from the head? Even if you say you love with all your heart, these words are but inventions of your mind. If you search your heart there is not the slightest stir there; there is no thrill, no dance, no song within you.

The guru's teachings can only be heard with the heart. When Kabir said, "If you can cut off your head and put it on the ground, come with me," which head was he talking about?

Bodhidharma, the Buddhist master, went to China. He sat facing a wall and said, "I will only turn my face when the true disciple comes. Why should I talk to anyone else? It is as useless as talking to the walls!"

And one day a man came by the name of Hui Neng. He stood silently behind Bodhidharma for twenty-four hours. Finally he said, "Bodhidharma, please turn this way," but Bodhidharma did not move. Hui Neng cut off his right arm and placed it before Bodhidharma, saying, "If you still persist, I shall cut off my head and put it before you."

Bodhidharma said, "Of what use would that be? Are you really prepared to cut off your head?"

Hui Neng said, "Yes, I am prepared for whatever you wish."

That was the first time Bodhidharma turned his face towards somebody; Hui Neng received this honor. When Bodhidharma had asked if he was ready to lay down his head, he was not talking of the head on his shoulders; he was talking of the ego. As long as there is an *I am* or *I am the judge*, you cannot be the disciple; you cannot hear the guru's words.

> *But he who listens to but one teaching of the guru,*
> *his understanding becomes like a precious jewel.*

His mind attains to such a cleanliness, such a transparency that he begins to see through things. Thoughts vanish, because they are not of the heart. As intellect is pushed away and its fog clears, what remains is a purity that is crystal clear, a freshness. It is this cleansing that is referred to as "bathing in the Ganges."

When Nanak speaks of bathing in the sacred rivers, it is an internal bath where the understanding becomes clear, where you think no longer, where the head is put aside. The head is a borrowed affair given to you by this world. When you were born the heart already was, but there were no thoughts — only innocence. One by one you were given words and society began conditioning your thinking to prepare you for what is necessary in the world. It gave you your mind. It had to crush anything that endangered the society. A dichotomy was created within; the heart and the mind were broken apart.

The heart was your own. But unfortunately, that which was truly yours was taken away and became not your own; and that which was created by society was made your own. What was implanted from above became your center, and you have completely forgotten the heart — the authentic center.

Only by removing the head can you hear the guru's teaching. And one teaching is enough; there is no need for a thousand. One lesson, one secret is more than enough, and what is that secret?

He is the benefactor of all.
Let me never forget him.

There are two states that require understanding: *smarana* means remembrance and *vismarana* means forgetfulness. The remembrance, smarana, is always flowing inside whatever you may be doing — walking, talking, sleeping, working.

A pregnant woman does all her daily chores — she cooks, she sweeps, she makes the beds — but all along she is extremely aware of the child she holds within her. A new life has struck root within her, a tiny heart has begun to throb. This awareness of the life she holds and has to protect is always with her; it results in a particular way of walking, so that from her walk you can tell she is pregnant.

Remembrance does not require a separate effort, because then you will keep forgetting. A thousand times in the day such a remembrance would be lost — while cooking, marketing or in the office. Similarly, it is not the remembrance of repeating a mantra. If you say, "Ram, Ram, Ram," all day, this is not smarana. Should you continue this, you could meet with an accident if you don't hear the car honking behind you. Any remembrance that is brought about by effort, rattling only in the mind, is not smarana.

That which permeates each hair of your body is what Nanak calls the unremembered remembrance. This remembrance has not to be repeated outwardly, because such a remembrance is superficial. Rather it saturates every pore of the body, every bit of you; whatever you do as his remembrance should reverberate like a soft melody within. Such remembrance Kabir called *surati;* therefore we have his "Surati Yoga." Surati also means remembrance.

Then there is the other state, vismarana: you remember everything — except one thing — you have completely forgotten who you are. And he who has no remembrance of his own self, what can he know of existence?

In this century Gurdjieff has put great emphasis on self-remembering. His method consisted mainly of one thing: to remember all twenty-four hours of the day that *I am*. By constant knocking, this remembrance becomes stronger and stronger. A crystallization takes place — a new flowing element forms within.

But there is a great danger in this method, as also in the method of Mahavira and in Patanjali's yoga. And that danger is that you connect this new element to your ego; because they are very close together. Gurdjieff calls this element the crystallized self, and there is every possibility that you will be superimposing the ego over it. You might become filled with arrogance. You may begin to say: I alone am. There is the real hazard that you might deny God. Then, having almost arrived, you will not arrive. Then you will almost have reached the other shore and turned back.

The same hazard lies in Mahavira's method, because there too you have to intensify the feeling of I am. This leaves no place for God. Mahavira says when the feeling of I am becomes total, through it alone will God reveal himself; the total I-amness becomes God. It is true and that is how it happened for Mahavira. However, the followers of Mahavira could not experience this; therefore, the flow of his method was stopped. The danger also exists in this method that the ego may begin to proclaim itself in the name of the *atman*.

This explains why we find no monks as egoistic as the Jaina *muni*. A Jaina monk cannot even fold his hands in *namaskar*, in greeting; he does not fold his hands at all. Again, the method is correct but hazardous. While every method has its hazard there is no such risk in Nanak's method, because Nanak does not tell you to remember *yourself*. He says: There is one benefactor of all living creatures — may I never forget him! The one resides in all; the one is hidden in the many — *Ek Omkar Satnam*. It is he that trembles in every leaf; it is he who wafts in every gust of the wind; it is he in the clouds, the moon, the stars, in every grain of sand. It is he! It is he! It is he! May I never forget him! May his remembrance within me become crystallized and solid.

It is difficult to find a sage more humble than Nanak, because if he resides in everyone, it is easy to fold your hands and bow to another. It is easy to touch the feet of another because he is in all.

If there is no risk of egoism in Nanak's method, there is another type of hazard: in the constant remembrance that he is in all, you may forget your own self. You may forget that *you also are* and fall into a deep slumber, and begin to live as if in a trance. You will see him all around you, except in your own self. All four directions will

Some Other Ganges ❧ 103

be filled with him. You will sing his praises. You will tell of his glory but you will remain untouched by his glory.

This danger is less than that of egoism, because he who is asleep can be awakened but he who is filled with the ego is in deep sleep, in a coma that is very difficult to break. The sleep of the devotee can be broken. Yogis have given this sleep the name of *yoga tandra,* which is not actually sleep; if you are in tandra and someone claps his hands the tandra breaks.

Nanak's path is easier than Mahavira's, but each method carries some risk of going astray and falling from the path. The path of Mahavira got lost in renunciation; the path of Nanak went astray in worldly pleasures.

Mahavira said to renounce the world completely, and to not allow an iota of enjoyment, but become the supreme sannyasin. As a result Mahavira's sannyasins lived as enemies of the world. But to develop enmity with someone is to become tied to the very foe. While Mahavira's renunciate is constantly fighting with the mundane world, the very struggle keeps the remembrance of the object-world always fresh within and the remembrance of soul pushed to one corner. He worries about where to sleep, what he will eat, his clothes, his food. So deeply involved is he in mundane things that he has gone astray.

Nanak has said just the opposite: Everything is he. Since he is present in all things there is no need to leave the world, so his followers went astray *within* the world. The Punjabis, the Sikhs, the Sindis — all followers of Nanak — center their lives in eating, drinking, clothes; they take the mundane world to be everything. This was not Nanak's intent. When he said there was no need to leave the world, he did not mean that the world alone is enough. We have to seek him in the world. The world need not be renounced nor is it everything.

Since there is a risk in every method, if you are not conscious and aware of it, ninety-nine times out of one hundred, you are bound to fall into the hazard. For your intellect never follows a straight course but is like a donkey walking: he never walks straight, but either sticks to the wall or goes to the other extreme. While a dull fellow can be called a stupid ass, intellect is true donkeyish-ness. Intellect never walks a straight line but is either at one extreme or the other; the wise person is always in the middle.

Most of the secrets of Nanak's path were lost. The Sikhs still exist, but they are not truly Nanak's Sikhs — those who have heard the teachings, those who have set aside their heads, those whose hearts are filled with faith and those who have remembered but one thing, one secret method that solves everything: that there is but one benefactor of all beings — *Let me never forget him!*

This knowledge should remain within constantly. If every act fills your very being with remembrance, then being in the world, you transcend the world — living in the middle of the world, you can reach *there*. There is no need to go to the temple, since the house itself becomes a temple. If the most ordinary task is filled with his special dignity, no work of yours will be ordinary; it will be extraordinary. Wherever you bathe, there will be the Ganges.

Whatever the hazard, it is all right. It makes no difference what you do; the real question is your own self. When *you* are different, the most ordinary stream becomes the Ganges; but if *you* are no different from the ordinary, then even the holy waters of the Ganges become ordinary. So it is a question of your being ordinary or nonordinary. And what is ordinariness but to live without his remembrance? Extraordinariness is priceless. It is to live with his remembrance. Accept losing everything but not his remembrance.

> *But he who listens to but one teaching of the guru,*
> *his understanding becomes like a precious jewel.*

Why talk of jewels? You will leave everything if need be, but not a jewel. If the need arises and you have money and a ruby in your pocket, you will part with the money, but not give up the ruby, because it has the most value. Remembrance is the precious jewel; let anything else in life drop away, because you know it is not worth a penny.

> *Were you to live through four ages, or even ten times more,*
> *Were you known on all nine continents, and were to gain*
>   *universal following,*
> *Were you to earn fame and praise from all of mankind,*
> *If you have not his grace, nothing will save you.*

Nanak says you may have a life of four *yugas,* extending from the *Sat Yuga* to *Kali Yuga.* Your life may become the life of creation — and ten times more.

All the people in the world and in creation may know you and go along with you, great may be your name and fame, yet if he is not pleased by you, all this is useless, worthless.

What is the reason? Have you ever come across a person who is satisfied? Even after attaining wealth is the millionaire ever contented? After achieving fame were Alexander the Great or Hitler satisfied? Instead of an atmosphere of well-being and fulfillment around the so-called successful man of the world, the reverse is the case. The nearer you approach these people, the more you sense their wretchedness. Their begging bowl has become bigger — they ask for more, and yet more! The nine continents of the world are not enough; life — four yugas long — is not enough. Infinite are their demands; they can never be filled because the more they receive the more they desire.

Desires always precede you. Wherever you may go, whatever you have, there is no sense of satisfaction and the ego won't let you retrace your steps.

Two beggars were resting under a tree when one of them began to complain. When even kings are unsatisfied, imagine the complaints of a poor beggar! "What a life! Is this living? Today we are in this village, tomorrow another. When they discover us traveling without a ticket they throw us off the train. Everyone preaches at us; if we ask for bread we get a sermon. They are always telling us we are fit enough to go to work. Nothing but insult and injury! Everywhere we are driven away. Every policeman is after us. Wherever we sleep they awaken us. It's impossible to get a good night's sleep."

The other beggar said, "Then why don't you quit this work?"

"What?" said the first beggar. "And admit I failed?"

If a beggar refuses to accept failure, how can a millionaire? How can a politician who is always proving himself accept his defeat? No one has yet been able to prove that he has accomplished anything real in worldly matters; if anyone had Mahavira, Buddha, Nanak would all be fools.

But the ego refuses to turn back; it forever goads a person forward. Maybe the goal is still ahead. Who knows? Perhaps just a few steps more and we may reach. The ego spreads its net of hopes before you, drawing you further and further on, preventing you from turning back. You have come so far without acknowledging that you are on the wrong path, how can you do it now? So you cover your weakness and hide your faults and go on, as if some day you are sure to succeed.

All your so-called successful men hide the tears within and don't allow them to show. Their public faces are different from their private faces. They are all smiling and laughing, but alone in their own rooms they cry.

Nanak says: After attaining all there is no satisfaction. You can be satisfied only if he is pleased with you. Even a naked fakir sometimes attains satisfaction whereas a man having everything remains unhappy. This means that satisfaction has nothing to do with what you have. It has everything to do with your connections with the supreme law — not your worldly attainments but your relationship with God. If you have established a relationship with him, if you have succeeded in turning your face towards him, having his grace, that decides whether you are fulfilled or not.

This is the meaning of attaining favor in his eyes. If he is not pleased with you, why did he give birth to you? He loves you, but alas, you stand with your back to him! To find favor in his eyes means to stand facing him, to have his grace. When you see his face in every face and feel his presence everywhere, then you find him throbbing even in a stone; and when you begin to see him everywhere, then you have found favor with him.

Nanak says: If I have attained his pleasure, I have bathed in all the holy rivers. Now the heavenly Ganges has truly descended on you, not by bathing in the Ganges that descends from the Himalayas and flows through Prayag and Kashi. His Ganges descends from on high, when you find favor with him.

Any worldly attainment is less than worthless; it is a loss in a deeper sense. All your fortunes are no more than misfortunes, since the only fortune worth attaining is to find favor in his eyes. When this becomes your only quest you become a sannyasin in the world. Then, whatever you do, your eye is on him. You keep busy in works great or small, but never for a moment is he out of your mind. He is always present within you. This smarana, this surati, this remembrance which is the unrepeated repetition, gradually carves a place for you within his heart. Finding favor in his eyes, receiving his grace, your life is filled with dance and celebration is everywhere. Then you have nothing — and you have everything.

> *You are like the lowliest worm; even the worst of sinners may point the finger at you.*

Nanak says that he who is bereft of God, even if he amasses all fortunes, is rated the lowest of worms, and even the worst of sinners heaps abuse on him.

> *Says Nanak: He makes the worthless worthy,*
> *And showers the gifted with more gifts.*
> *None but God can bestow such excellence.*

None but God can bestow you with good qualities. To miss him is to miss all. Remember, he is the target, the bull's-eye, the only attainment. If the arrow of your life does not reach him, no matter where it falls, you have failed.

Imagine how it feels to fall in love. The beloved accepts you, takes you to his heart, and your life thrills with the magic of love. Your feet hardly seem to touch the ground; you seem to fly in the air, as if you have developed wings. Unknown bells begin to ring in your life; you have never heard such a melody before. Your face lights up with a strange charm, your eyes convey something not of this world!

Therefore it is difficult to hide love. Everything else you can hide. If you are in love it will show in your face — in the way you walk, the way you talk — your eyes and everything about you will give news of it. Every pore of your body will be saturated with love, because love is a remembrance. If the love and acceptance of an ordinary person fills your life with such thrill, then when the whole existence accepts you, what will it be like? When the whole existence loves you, embraces you; when you are tied in the bond of love with existence...!

This is what Meera means when she says, "Krishna, when will you come to the nuptial bed? I have adorned it with flowers. When will you come? When will you accept me?"

The devotee is always thirsting for the lord, as the beloved is for the lover. When the partridge thirsts for the morning dew he calls out. Even a single drop satisfies; one drop becomes a pearl. When a person is so thirsty — the longing is so great — then ordinary water turns into pearls. When your longing is so great, a single teaching of the guru becomes a jewel. One drop is enough; one teaching of the guru can become the ocean. And what is the teaching? It is such a small sutra. If you understand it, grasp it, it is small; if you do not, you may take infinite lives more to understand!

So Nanak says one small secret formula quenches all your thirst, that is all: *He is the benefactor of all. Let me never forget him.* Such a small maxim – and it quenches all thirst, destroys all desires! And Nanak says: *He makes the worthless worthy* and fills you with qualities. When you face him you become worthy of all attributes. You always were worthy. You were always empty and as you turned towards him, Lo! You were filled. His glory has stirred you. The *veena* was always ready within. When you entrusted it to his hands, when his fingers have touched the strings...Lo! Music is born — the music that lay dormant all this time, awaiting his touch. It can only happen if you put your veena in his hands.

This entrusting itself is *shraddha*, disciplehood — to surrender, to be a Sikh. To entrust the veena is the meaning of sannyas. Then you say: Thy will be done. Your wish is now my life. All that is mine is to remember you; all else is yours. The only need in life is that he should fill your vessel for you not to remain a lonely wanderer in life, that he should be your friend and companion, or else you may seek him in many places but find him in none.

Some look to wealth to bring a comrade. Some look to a wife, a husband; but all these guests are imperfect. Until you seek him directly

Some Other Ganges

you will not attain him. All disqualifications and shortcomings vanish, as soon as he is attained.

Nanak does not suggest that you get rid of your defects one by one, because they are infinite. Avoid stealing, killing, anger, sex, greed, attachments, envy and what else? Nanak does not advise this. He says turn your face God-wards. Remember him! As soon as his gaze falls on you everything will change. When you have been accepted and have won his favor, then wrath will vanish and greed will fall all on its own.

Once he is attained — for what are you greedy? What is left for your wrath? Where is the sex? Where is the desire when the ultimate coupling has already taken place — the union with existence. After the ultimate nuptial there is no more search for the beloved. Kabir says, "I am Rama's bride." When you are in love with Rama, when you become his bride, what sexual desire remains?

In our lust we were really searching for him. We sought him in dirty gutters and were never satisfied, because the filth of sex could not satiate. It is like forcing the swan to drink from the gutter when it is used to the crystal-clear waters of Lake Mansarovar. The swan within asks also for Mansarovar. Nothing less than God can quench your thirst.

Wander where you will, no one besides him can satisfy you. You are wandering for lives on end without him, yet you have not come to your senses. You still hope to reach without him. Your ego stands guard behind, telling you not to let a full life's toil go in vain.

It is just as if a man builds a house on shaky foundations, perhaps on sand. When the house is nearing completion another man comes and tells him not to enter the house, because it is sure to fall and he may die. Then the mind says, "You have spent so much money, taken so many pains, gone through so much difficulty. Can you let so many years' toil go in vain? And who knows? It might not fall! Perhaps the expert is wrong. Besides, right now it is standing. Who can be sure it will fall?"

Such is your case too, like a man who has lost his way and has been told that he left the road far behind.

In reading the memoirs of a poet, I particularly liked one incident.

He writes that he lost his way in the valleys of the Himalayas. He stopped his car before a hut. When a woman opened the door he asked, "Am I on the right path to Manali?"

The woman looked at him keenly and said, "But I don't know which way you are heading."

The poet thought she was a mountain girl and perhaps not too intelligent, so he said, "Tell me, is the light of my car pointing in the direction of the road to Manali?"

"There is a light," she said, "red in color."

When you have traveled a number of miles in mountainous terrain and someone says your light points in the wrong direction, you feel a terrible blow. It means you have to retrace your steps and go back all the way you came. Your ego protests and says, "Go a little further; don't give up. Who knows, this woman may be wrong! She may be stupid, or mad, or lying, or trying to mislead you!"

To turn back is a blow to the ego. You wonder, "Could I have been wrong all this time?" Therefore it is easier to teach children than to teach older people. If they have already walked sixty or seventy miles can they admit to being wrong all that time? The child never resists, because the child has yet not walked. He will go wherever you take him. An old man never will. He will insist that the path he has followed is correct – because his ego depends on it.

You are all old! God knows how many lives you have been walking, and that is the difficulty. You haven't the courage to abandon the wrong path, because it involves so much effort through infinite lives...rather than to admit that all is in vain, that for lives on end you have been ignorant. Therefore, when you go to a sage you prepare a thousand devices to save your old self, lest his grace pour on you and your cloak of knowledge and experience come off!

Remember! You will have to turn back, because you have left the road way behind...far, far away. It is in this light that Jesus said: "Become like children once again." He is telling you to turn back, to be once again innocent as children. Once you move your intellect out of the way all attributes will shower on you. They always have!

Nanak was not a highly educated person, nor did he come from a rich family. He was born in an ordinary household. On the very first day he started school, schooling was seen to be useless, and yet the divine showers poured on him.

If it rained on Nanak, if it rained on Kabir, why not on you? The only obstacle is that you stand with your back to him.

One secret formula solves everything: *He is the benefactor of all living creatures. Let me never forget him.*

CHAPTER 5

The Art of Listening

*Through listening occult powers and saintliness are gained,
Heaven and earth are made stable,
And the world and lower worlds revolve.
Through listening death does not touch.
Nanak says: Through listening devotees attain bliss,
And sin and sorrow are destroyed.
Through listening Vishnu, Brahma and Indra came into being,
The most sinful will sing his praises,
And the secrets of yoga and mysteries of the body are revealed.
Through listening all the scriptures and teachings are known.
Nanak says: Through listening devotees attain bliss,
And sin and sorrow are destroyed.
Through listening all truth and contentment are attained,
And the virtue of bathing at the sixty-eight holy places is gained,
And through listening again and again honor is earned
Through listening spontaneous meditation happens.
Nanak says: Through listening devotees attain bliss,
And sin and sorrow are destroyed.
Through listening the highest virtues are acquired,
Sage, saint and king come into being,
And the blind find the path.
Through listening the fathomless is fathomed.
Nanak says: Through listening devotees attain bliss,
And sin and sorrow are destroyed.*

Mahavira has described four starting places from which you can reach the other shore. Of these, two can be understood: that of a *sadhu* and that of a *sadhvi,* a holy man and a holy woman. The other two seem more difficult: that of a *shravaka* and *shravika.* Shravaka means one who has learned the art of listening; he knows how to listen and understands what listening means. And shravika is used for the female.

Mahavira says that there are some who must keep on performing *sadhanas* in order to arrive. This is necessary for those who are not adept at hearing because if you can listen — totally — there is nothing more to be done to reach the other shore.

These sutras of Nanak depict the glory of *shravana,* listening, although on the face of it, it seems an exaggeration that everything can be attained merely by listening. We have been listening for infinite births and nothing has happened. It is our experience that no matter how much we hear, we remain the same. Our vessel is greasy; words fall on it but they slide off, leaving us untouched.

If our experience is correct, Nanak is exaggerating. But it is not true; our experience is incorrect, because we have never listened. We have many tricks and devices not to listen. Let us understand them first.

The first trick is: we hear only that which we want to and not what is being said. With great cleverness we hear what lets us remain as we are; nothing goes in which may cause a change in us. This is not only the observation of the sages; scientists who have carried out research on the human mind say that ninety-eight percent of what we hear we do not take in. We only hear the two percent that fits into our understanding; that which doesn't, cannot bypass the many obstructions.

Anything that synchronizes with your understanding cannot change you. It can only help to reinforce that understanding. Rather than transform you it gives yet more stones and cement to strengthen your foundations.

The Hindu hears only what strengthens his Hindu mind; the Muslim hears only what strengthens the Muslim mind; so also the Sikh, the Christian, the Buddhist. If you listen only to strengthen your

114   *The True Name*

own preconceptions, to strengthen your own house, then you will miss hearing completely, for truth has no connection with Hindu or Muslim or Sikh. It has nothing to do with the conditioning of your mind.

Only when you set aside your entire way of thinking will you be able to understand what Nanak means; however, this is a very difficult thing to do, because our concepts are invisible They are microscopic, or as transparent as a wall of glass; they cannot be seen. Unless you knock against them you are not conscious of their existence. You think that there is wide open space ahead, and the sun, moon, and the stars. You are not aware of the transparent wall in between.

Hearing a speaker you tell yourself that he is correct when what he says is consistent with your thoughts. To other things you say that it is not so because it disagrees with your thoughts. So you are not truly listening but only lend your ear to what agrees with you and strengthens your opinion. The rest, that you don't care about, you ignore and forget. Even if you do happen to hear something that is contrary to your understanding, you tear it to bits with your reasoning, because one thing you are sure of: whatever matches your thoughts is correct, what doesn't is incorrect, false.

If you have attained truth there is no further need to listen, but you have not attained truth so it is incumbent on you to listen. How can you still be searching for the truth if you have the idea that you have already attained it? Instead, you have to stand before truth absolutely bare, empty, void, naked. If your scriptures, your beliefs, your doctrines stand in the way you will never be able to listen; whatever falls on your ears will be nothing but the echo of your own concepts and you will hear only your own thoughts throbbing within you. Then Nanak's words will seem a preposterous exaggeration.

Another way to escape listening is to fall asleep when something significant is being said. This is a trick the mind uses to save itself; it is a very deep process by which, when something is about to touch you, you fall asleep.

I was a guest at the house of a very learned pundit. He was well-versed in the *shastras* and there was no one to equal him in reading the Ramayana. Thousands of people came to hear him. We were staying in the same room and as we put off the lights to prepare to sleep, I heard his wife come in. She spoke in a low tone but I could still hear. "Please say something to Munna. He won't go to sleep."

"How will my talking help?" asked the pundit.

"I have seen a number of people falling asleep when you speak at your meetings, so how could a small child resist your words! Come, say a few words to him," she answered.

People go to religious services only to fall asleep. Even those who suffer from insomnia sleep well in religious meetings. What happens? It's a trick of your mind. Sleep is like the soldier's armor; it protects you against all you don't want to know. So you look as if you are listening, but you are not awake; and without being awake how can you hear?

While talking you are awake; while listening you are not. And this doesn't happen only at a religious meeting. As soon as another person talks to you, you are no longer alert, but lost in an internal dialogue of your own. While he talks to you, you pretend to be listening, but you are really talking to yourself. Then to whom do you prefer to listen? Definitely to your own self, because the voice of the other person doesn't even reach you; your own voice is enough to drown out all the other voices. And then you fall asleep out of boredom with yourself, because what you are saying inside you have said and heard so many times before. Sleep is an escape from the repetitive talk that is going on internally.

He alone is capable of listening who has broken this conversation within. And that is the art of shravana. If the internal dialogue stops even for a moment, you find the whole expanse of space opening within you; all that was as yet unknown begins to be known. You find the boundary of that which was boundless; you become familiar with the unfamiliar. He who was a total stranger, with whom you were not acquainted at all, becomes your very own! And it all happens so suddenly. The universe is your home!

All gurus, all religions aim at one thing only: how to break the constant dialogue within. Whether we call it yoga or meditation or repetition of mantra, the aim is to break the constant internal flow of words in order to create an empty space within. If it happens even for a little while you will understand what Nanak is talking about.

Through listening occult powers and saintliness are gained,
Heaven and earth are made stable,
And the world and lower worlds revolve.
Through listening death does not touch.
Nanak says: Through listening devotees attain bliss,
And sin and sorrow are destroyed.

It is hard to believe what Nanak says — that by listening alone a person can attain *siddhis,* occult powers; or a person can become a *pir,* a saint; or a *devta,* a celestial being; or even Indra, the king of the *devtas;* that by listening, the sky and earth revolve and worlds and lower worlds exist, and death does not touch you.

It all seems a gross exaggeration, but it is not so in the least, because as soon as you learn the art of listening you learn the art of becoming acquainted with life itself. And as you begin to acquire the knowledge of existence, you find that the same silence you experience at the moment of shravana is the principle of all existence. It is the basis on which the sky and the earth are maintained; it is on the hub of this void that terrestrial bodies revolve; it is in silence that the seed breaks and becomes a tree, that the sun rises and sets, and moon and stars are formed and disintegrate. When words fall into silence within you, you reach the place where all creation is born and where it becomes extinct.

Once it happened: A Muslim fakir came to Nanak and said, "I have heard that you can turn me to ashes by your will, and that you can also create me by your will. I cannot believe this." He was an honest, genuine seeker who had not come out of idle curiosity.

Nanak said, "Close your eyes. Be relaxed and quiet and I will do for you what you wish." The fakir at once closed his eyes and became tranquil. Had he not been a serious seeker he would have been frightened, because what he had asked was very dangerous — to be turned into ashes and remade, because he had been told that creation and extinction lay in Nanak's hands.

It was morning, a day just like this. Nanak was sitting under a tree beside a well at the outskirts of the village. His disciples Bala and Mardana were also with him. They were very much perturbed, because never had Nanak said such a thing to anyone before. What would happen now? They too became alert and the very trees and stones also became alert because Nanak was about to perform a miracle!

The fakir sat, silent and tranquil. He must have been a man of great faith. He became absolutely empty within. Nanak put his hand on his head and pronounced the *Omkar*. As the story goes, the man turned to ashes. Then Nanak again sounded the Omkar and the man regained his body.

If you take the story at its face value, you will miss it, but this did happen within the seeker. When he became completely empty within, when the internal dialogue was broken and Nanak gave out the chant of Omkar, the *sadhaka* attained the state of shravana — there was nothing but the resonance of Om within him. And with this resonance the annihilation took place on its own. Everything within the man was lost — all the world and its boundaries – turned to naught, to ashes. There was nothing within, nobody. The house was empty. Then Nanak once again chanted the Omkar and the man came back to himself. He opened his eyes, fell at Nanak's feet and said, "I had thought this could never happen, but you have proved it possible!"

There are those who miss the point and believe that the man actually turned to ashes and Nanak brought him back to life, but this is a foolish interpretation. Internally, however, the annihilation and creation did take place. The fakir was capable of listening. When you develop the art of listening then it is not me you will hear. I am an excuse. The guru is just an excuse. Then you will be adept at hearing the breeze as it passes through the trees; in the silence of solitude you will hear the Omkar, the basis of all life. And in the resonance of Omkar you shall find that everything depends on the void. The rivers flow in the void, the ocean becomes one with it. When you close your eyes you will hear your heartbeat and also the faint sound of the blood flowing, and you will know that you are not these; you are also the observer, the witness. Then death cannot touch you.

For those who have mastered the art of shravana there is nothing more to know. All existence comes into being through shravana. All existence happens through the void; and when you are listening, the stamp of the void falls on you. Then the void vibrates in you and that is the basic resonance of existence — it is the basic unit.

By shravana death cannot touch you. Once you know the art of listening, where is death? Because the listener attains the knowledge of the witness. Right now you think and think, and then listen. The thinker will die because he belongs to the flesh. The day you listen without thinking you will become the witness. Then I shall be speaking, your head will be hearing, and there will be a third within you who will simply watch that listening taking place. When this happens a new element begins to unfold within you, the beginning of crystallization of the witness; and there is no death for the witness.

Therefore Nanak says that through shravana death does not touch. It is through listening that the devotee achieves permanent happiness; it *is* through shravana that suffering and sin are destroyed.

How is this internal dialogue to be broken? How can you become silent? How can the clouds be made to disperse so that the clear skies can be seen? This is what the process is all about. When someone is speaking, there is no need for you to keep on talking. You can be silent, but this habit dies hard, so you go on and on, talking away

I asked a little boy, "Has your little sister started talking?" He said, "Talking? And how! It's so long since she started to talk that now she won't stop. Now we are all busy trying to keep her quiet."

When you came into this world you were silent. Do you want to be talking away all the time till you leave it? Then you will miss life and even deny yourself the supreme touch, the supreme bliss of death. You entered this world in silence; prepare to leave it in silence, too. Talking is for in-between, and only in the mundane life is it useful, in relating to another person.

When sitting by yourself it is madness to talk since silence is the process by which we relate to our own self. If silent you will find it difficult to keep up outside relationships; if you talk, it will be difficult to relate to yourself. Talking is a bridge that is connecting us to others; silence is a bridge that connects us with our self. Somewhere, somehow, you err in your selection of the means.

If a person becomes quiet and talks to no one, he establishes no

The Art of Listening 119

relationships and gradually people will begin to forget him. Dumb people are the most miserable, even more so than a blind man. Notice carefully that you feel more pity for the dumb than the blind. While it is true that the blind man cannot see, he does establish relationships; he can have a wife; he can talk to his children; he can be a part of society; he can have friends. But the mute is closed within himself with no way out, no way for him to establish contact with others. You can sense his difficulty in the agony of his gestures. When you cannot follow him, how helpless and miserable he feels. There is no one more pitiable than a dumb person: he cannot talk, he cannot open his heart to anyone, he cannot express his feelings of love or joy or sorrow and unburden his mind.

As the mute is incapable of establishing contact with others, so you have become incapable of establishing contact with yourself. Where you should be dumb — absolutely silent — you keep on talking. The other is not there at all, so to whom do you talk? You raise questions yourself and then answer them yourself. This is nothing but a sign of madness. The only difference between a mad person and you is that the mad person talks aloud to himself while you talk silently. Some day you too may join their ranks and begin to talk aloud. Right now you manage to repress the insanity within, but it can erupt any moment, because it is a cancerous ulcer.

Why does this internal dialogue go on? What is the reason? It is out of simple habit. All life long you are taught how to speak. A child is born and the first concern of all around him is that he should speak as early as possible since this is considered a sign of intelligence; the longer he takes, the duller he is considered to be.

Since talking is a social art and man is part of society, how happy the parents are when the child talks. Also many necessities of life are fulfilled by talking: when you are hungry, thirsty, you can express your need. It affords a protection in life.

What on earth is the use of silence? It seems to be useless. It holds no meaning in our day-to-day life. How can you go shopping if you are silent? How will you satisfy the various needs of the body without communication? We are so habituated to talking that we talk even in sleep, all twenty-four hours of the day; talking is automatic.

We keep on talking and rehearsing. Before talking to someone we rehearse the dialogue internally; and then, after the conversation, we repeat over and over all that happened — what I said and what you said, and then what I said — and we gradually forget what we are losing by this useless talk. Externally you may be gaining something, but within you are certainly losing contact with yourself. You are getting closer to people while you are becoming further removed from yourself. And the more adept you become at this game, the harder it will be for you to go into silence. Habit! And habit cannot be broken just like that.

When a person walks he makes use of his legs; while sitting there is no need to move your legs. When you are hungry you eat; if a person keeps on eating when not hungry it is a sign of insanity. Similarly, if you try to sleep when you are not sleepy it is inviting unnecessary frustration. But we do not think the same way when it comes to talking. We never say that we shall stop all talk unless it is a necessity.

It seems as if we have completely forgotten that the process of talking can be begun or ended at will, which it certainly can, or else all religions become impossible. Religion is possible only through silence. This is why Nanak praises shravana so much, which is in praise of silence, to glory in silence so that you may begin to hear. But you go along merrily talking, carried along by your own momentum and even if it comes to your understanding it is very difficult to stop, since habits take time to leave and often require the development of opposite habits in order to break them. So you will have to practice silence. To stay in the company of holy men means to practice silence. In the presence of the guru there is nothing to say and everything to hear. You listen and sit quietly. You don't go to the guru for a chat.

A few days ago a friend offered to come for a discussion. I said, "In that case, *you* talk. I shall listen but say nothing."

He said, "But I want to exchange views with you."

I answered, "I have nothing to do with your thoughts. If you are prepared to be without thoughts I can give you something. Or, if you have something to give, I'm prepared to take."

We have nothing whatsoever to give, but we are eager to carry out transactions in thoughts. We say exchange of thoughts and what we mean is you give me a bit of your insanity, and I give you a bit of mine. As both are mad enough, there is no need of any give-and-take.

We do not go to the guru to exchange views but to sit quietly next to him. Only when we are silent can we hear, and that requires a little practice. How can you begin? In the twenty-four hours of a day you need to be silent for an hour or so, whenever it is convenient. The internal dialogue will go on but don't be party to it. The key to it all is to hear the talk within just as you would hear two people talking, but remain apart. Don't get involved; just listen to what one part of the mind is telling another. Whatever comes, let it come; don't try to repress it. Only be a witness to it.

A lot of rubbish that you have gathered over the years will come out. The mind has never been given the freedom to throw away this rubbish. When given the chance, the mind will run like a horse that has broken his reins. Let it run! You sit and watch. To watch, just watch, is the art of patience. You will want to ride the horse, to direct it this way or that, because that is your old habit. You will have to exercise some patience in order to break this habit.

Wherever the mind goes, merely watch; don't try to enforce any order as one word gives rise to another and another, and a thousand others, because all things are connected. Perhaps Freud was unaware, that, when he based his entire psychoanalytic method on this "free association of thoughts" as he called it, it derived from yoga. One thought comes, and then another, and each thought is linked to the other in a continuous chain.

Once I was traveling in a train that was very full. When the inspector came to check our tickets he looked underneath my seat, where there was an old man hiding. He said, "You, old man, come out! Where is your ticket?"

The poor man fell at his feet and said, "I don't have any ticket nor any money but I have to go to the village in connection with my daughter's wedding. I would be grateful if you let me go this time."

The inspector took pity on him and let him go; but when he turned to the next row he saw another man underneath the seat. This man was young. "Are you also going for your daughter's marriage?" the inspector joked with him.

"No, sir," said the young man, "but I'll soon be this old man's son-in-law, and I too am penniless."

This is how things are joined. Someone is the son-in-law; someone is the father-in-law. The connections are hidden and need to be brought out. There is a whole chain of them within you and you will often be shocked when you know how, and in what queer ways, your thoughts are interlinked. Sometimes you will also be frightened and think you are going mad.

This is, however, a very wonderful method. Whatever is happening, allow it to happen. If it is convenient and possible, speak your thoughts out loud so that you can also hear them, because within the mind the thoughts are subtle and there is the fear you may not be very conscious of them. Speak them aloud, listen to them, and be very aware and alert to remain well separated from them. Resolve to speak out whatever comes to mind, but be absolutely unbiased and neutral. If abuse comes — abuse! If *Ram, Ram* comes or *Omkar,* give voice to that.

It is absolutely necessary to empty the mind patiently for six months, because all your life long you have done nothing but load it with thoughts. If you persist patiently and diligently then only six months is enough; otherwise it might take you six years, or six lives! All depends on you, how wholeheartedly and sincerely you work at this method.

Many a time it will happen that you will forget to be a witness; you will ride the horse once again and set out on your journey of thoughts, involved once again. If you identify yourself with some thought, then you will have failed; as soon as you become aware of this, get off the horse and let the words, the thoughts, go where they will without riding them. Just keep watching.

Gradually, very faintly, you will begin to hear the footsteps of silence, and experience the art of listening. Then, when you are qualified to listen you no longer need look for a guru, because wherever you are, there the guru is. The breeze will stir in the trees, the flowers and the dry leaves will fall — you will hear all. Sitting on the seashore you will hear the waves. You will hear the river in spate, the lightning in the sky, the thundering of clouds. You will hear the birds sing, a child cry, a dog bark – under all conditions you will *hear*.

When the art of listening is mastered, the guru is present everywhere. If shravana is not known, all the masters sitting before you cannot make you listen. The guru is — only when you can listen.

Nanak says: Through listening the devotee is full of bliss,
And sin and sorrow are destroyed.

If you have learned the art of listening you will be filled with joy, because then you have become the witness; and the witness is joy itself. Shravana occurs, the mind is no more, and its extinction is joy. Bliss is to go beyond the mind. At the moment when listening takes place, the chain of thoughts is broken and there is bliss, there is transcendence. You are no longer in the valley of thoughts but on the lofty peak where thoughts do not reach — beyond the dust and grime, where there is only unbroken silence. On this lofty, silent peak there is nothing but the resonance of bliss and you reach the supreme blessedness.

Through shravana alone suffering and sin are destroyed. Where is sin for him who has acquired the art of listening? For sin is connected with thoughts only. Understand this a little. A car passes you on the road and the thought occurs: I should have a car like that. Now you have become glued to the thought. There is only one refrain within you: how to get such a car. By fair means or foul the car must be had. You cannot sleep nights, your days are equally restless; your dreams are filled with the car, your thoughts are filled with the car; the car surrounds you on all sides.

What actually happened? The car passed and a thought arose within you, because everything that you see is reflected in the mind. But once you are identified with the thought, you cannot stand apart.

A beautiful woman passes and a thought arises in the mind. This is natural, because the mind is only a mirror; its function is to reflect whatever happens around it. When the woman passed, the mind registered the reflection. When the woman is no longer there, the reflection must also cease. Had you been just a witness there was no way to sin. But once you became identified with the thought you wanted this woman at any cost. By love or by force, by violence or by nonviolence, you must have her.

Thus a single thought catches hold of you, possesses you. Had you allowed the thoughts to rise and fade, and been only a witness, there would be no question of sin. All sins arise because of your identification with thoughts. Then the thoughts get hold of you so badly that you shake like a leaf in a storm. Thoughts have brought you nothing but unhappiness and suffering, but you are not even conscious enough to realize that all suffering coincides with thoughts, and bliss occurs only in the state of no-thoughts.

Nanak says: "Through shravana suffering and sin are destroyed because the fruit of sin is suffering. Sin is the seed and suffering is the fruit."

When sin is gone suffering is no more. What remains when sin and suffering are no more — that state is *samadhi*, which is bliss itself.

Nanak says: Through listening devotees attain bliss,
And sin and sorrow are destroyed.

He who becomes an adept at listening is absolved of all sin. Such a devotee, says Nanak, attains bliss and his bliss develops more and more each day. The word *vigasu* is used, which is very meaningful; it contains both bliss and the idea of its continuous flowering and development. So *ananda,* bliss, is a flower that keeps on blooming. The moment never comes when it is in complete bloom: It just blooms and blooms and blooms – from perfection to more perfection. As if the morning sun rises and keeps on rising, and never sets. Such is this ananda. It is like a flower that never withers, like a sun that never sets.

When the void begins to crystallize in the heart and silence is born, the ripples of ananda rise and, having arisen, keep spreading more and more. Remember, ananda is not an object that you are done with once attained. It keeps on increasing constantly, limitlessly, once it is attained.

Thus we say: God is infinite. Thus we say: God is bliss. Because bliss is infinite, you can never attain it completely; every moment you feel it increasing and increasing, and each time it satiates you completely. This is a riddle that cannot be solved by the intellect, which argues: If once attained, what is left to be attained? Satiation is also not a goal but a live happening.

Ananda is not something to measure in kilos; you can't buy a kilo or two and be done with it, because bliss is infinite. Once you step into it, you drown in it more and more, and the delight is that each time you feel you have got it in full measure, yet each time it feels so much more than before.

Purna, the whole, the perfect, is also progressive; it is not a dead thing. It stops nowhere but keeps spreading more and more. Furthermore we have given existence the name of Brahma, that which is endlessly expanding.

The word also means that there is no limit to its expansion, that it is not just as much today as yesterday, but it spreads and spreads endlessly.

> *Through listening Vishnu, Brahma and Indra came into being,*
> *The most sinful will sing his praises,*
> *And the secrets of yoga and mysteries of the body are revealed.*
> *Through listening all the scriptures and teachings are known.*
> *Nanak says: Through listening devotees attain bliss,*
> *And sin and sorrow are destroyed.*

He who has heard truth in the guru's words has known fragrance in sitting quietly next to him. He finds that the happening flows towards him through such a person, and begins to penetrate him. Knowledge is contagious; bliss is contagious. If your doors are open bliss enters into you like a breath of wind from a person who has attained it. While you stand to gain he loses nothing since it increases and expands to the extent that it is shared. If you are silent a space is created within you. Remember, existence prefers a vacuum. No sooner do you become empty than existence fills your vacuum. As the river water rushes in to fill your empty jug, create a vacuum and air will rush in to fill it. Prepare to be empty and you will be filled, but as long as you are filled with yourself you will remain empty. Empty yourself and you will be filled with supreme energy. As you depart from one corner God will enter from the other.

Nanak says: "Even those who lead sinful lives, whose lips have never spoken a good word, whose tongue has always uttered abuse, whose heads are filled with curses, if even these listen but once, they are filled with glory. An infinitesimal glimpse of shravana can make you fresh, can bathe your entire being."

Nanak does not tell evildoers to stop sinning. He just tells them to listen and the isms will fall away. He doesn't tell them to improve first and only then can they listen, because that would be impossible and then there would be no hope for people to listen.

Nanak says: "Listen and forget about sin, forget about evil. And no sooner do you hear than a new sutra, a new path, begins to unfold in your life. A new spark will kindle a fire that will burn away your sins; your past turns into ashes as soon as you become silent."

What is sin? What have you been doing in the past? You have identified totally with your thoughts, constantly turning them into actions, and this is sin. Stand away from your thoughts; actions will crumble, the doer will be lost, and all connection with the past will snap. Then you realize that the past was no more than a dream. Through infinite lives everything you have done is because of the illusion of doing; the day that illusion is broken, all actions come to an end.

People will be unable to understand Nanak if they hold the common belief that each sin has to be wiped out by an equal virtue. For people of calculating minds this seems but fair — that for each sin you must atone with a corresponding virtue. But if this were so you would never be liberated; for infinite lives you have sinned and where is the guarantee that in the course of your equalization you will not sin further? Then this chain is impossible to break and liberation is impossible.

Your sins spread over infinite lives. If God is a shopkeeper or a magistrate who insists on the cleansing of each sin, when will it ever end? And even assuming that all present deeds are virtuous, it will still take infinite time to make up for the past. And how can you be sure you will perform only good deeds? Wise men follow a different method of calculation altogether, because they say that the question is not of sin but of the basis of sin, its very roots.

Say you have watered a tree for fifty years. Do you think you will have to starve its roots of water for another fifty years before it dies? The tree no longer depends on you for water; it draws its supplies directly from the soil. Cut off its roots and the tree will die today, but you can tear off the leaves one by one and the tree will not die even in fifty years; no sooner do you break one leaf than two new ones are born. No, by cutting leaves and branches you are merely pruning the tree. In the same way you cannot nullify sin by virtue. Eradicate one sin and four new others spring up.

Catch hold of the roots. Actions are the leaves, and the sense of doing is the root. Remove doing and the tree will dry up at once. All flow came from: I am doing. The art of eradicating doing is witnessing, and to witness means shravana.

Nanak sings of such unique and wonderful glory! He says, "Be silent and listen. In moments of such listening you are no longer the doer. Listening is a passive state since you have nothing to do in order to listen; it is not an action."

Now this is interesting. In order to see, one has to open one's eyes; whereas the ears are already open. You have nothing to do in order to hear. Therefore, there can be some sense of doing in seeing, but hearing does not involve doing at all! Someone speaks. You listen, sitting empty, motionless, passive; you are in non-action. Therefore that glory is not attained even by seeing which is attained by listening; hence the stress on shravana.

Mahavira speaks of *samyak shravana*, right listening, which Buddha also emphasizes. To Nanak it is a wonderful glory to hear. There is no doer there. No one is present at the moment of listening. If you are silent, who is there within? There is a solitude in moments of listening in which a voice resounds and passes away. There is no one within. If a thought comes, you come along with it; when thoughts are not, you are not. Since ego is the name given to a collection of thoughts, shravana also means the ego-less state.

Nanak says: "Through shravana alone you know the tactics of yoga and the secrets of the body." This is very significant. The

Western physicians have not been able to understand where and how the East acquired its knowledge of the human body and its secrets. Surgery developed in the West mainly because the dead are not burned by Christians and corpses were therefore available to be removed from their graves and taken for dissection.

Since Hindus burn their dead and no bodies were available for dissection, then how did the East acquire its knowledge of the human body? The East had no means: no corpses, no scientific development, no technique, no technology, and yet its knowledge of the human body is perfect. There is much research and discussion on the subject, but this sutra of Nanak provides an answer to the mystery.

Through shravana alone you know the knack of yoga and the secrets of the body. When you become empty and are established within yourself, you begin to see your body within. Right now all you have seen of your body is the skin. Until now you have gone round and round your house and know only the outside walls; you have no knowledge of what is inside.

From within you begin to see the entire network of the different systems. It is a unique experience to enter the palace and see all the grandeur within. It happens when you become silent and tranquil, when the mind poses no problems. The mind is a door to the world outside, and the moment you join it you move outward; whatever you think will be outside of you – wealth, woman, house, car, fame, status. All objects of thought are outside of you.

So as soon as you stop thinking, you withdraw from the outside and the energy is focused within. Now you sit on your own throne and see inside yourself for the first time. Then you know that this body is not as small as it looks; this small body holds a miniature universe within itself. It is a model of the vast universe, the vast existence. Therefore the Hindus say the whole of the universe is contained in an eggshell. Nanak says that he who becomes quiet, he who has become silent and learned the art of listening, and who has begun to hear his own body from within, comes to know the secrets of the body as well as the methods of yoga.

Whatever Patanjali has written in the Yoga Sutras derives from the experience of his own body and no one else's. His findings still stand totally correct even to this day. All the methods of yoga have been discovered with his own body.

I shall give you a few examples. If you become tranquil you will find that the rate of your breathing changes. As soon as thoughts stop, respiratory movements change; when thoughts start again the rate of breathing changes. If you begin to recognize the rate of breathing when you are tranquil, all you have to do is breathe in that rhythm and you will become tranquil. So you have learned one secret; you have the key to one mystery.

When you are absolutely peaceful, the spinal column becomes perpendicular to the ground you are sitting on. This happens on its own if the man is healthy and not ill or too old. Therefore, when you want to be peaceful, fix your spinal cord at a ninety-degree angle. Thus gradually a yogi comes to experience what is going on within him.

As you progress further you will feel energy rising upwards from your spine. You will feel it as a sharp warmth that flows through the spine. Ripples of electricity rise within, and as they climb higher and higher, you are filled with joy. Pain and despondency begin to vanish and a feeling of joy arises. As the electrical waves go even higher, all that is trivial and base in life falls away into the valley below and you are as if on a high mountain. The fog of the village, the talk of people and the mundane struggles of life are left far behind as you have risen.

This is why the spinal column is called the *Meru Dand*. Meru is a mountain in heaven; thus it is the Meru spine and it is said that he who climbs the heights of Meru Dand reaches the same height as Mt. Meru in heaven. The Hindu never shaves a tuft of hair at the top of the head; this is the last peak, the seventh door from which the energy then is absorbed into the infinite. When your energy begins to diffuse from this place you attain to *brahmacharya*, celibacy. You need do nothing to attain brahmacharya; whenever sexual desire arises you needn't actively suppress it. You have only to straighten your spine for all the energy to flow upward. The same energy that flowed into sexual desire becomes the energy of brahmacharya. It is the same whether it flows downward through the first door into nature, or upward through the seventh door to reach *paramatma,* the divine.

The person who develops the art of sitting quietly finds that his own body begins to provide a thousand experiences. You can know all of the Yoga Sutras through your own body. There is no need to read Patanjali. Actually, Patanjali should be read later on, only for corroboration, to show that you are on the right path. When you go within, many a time you will be frightened and not know whether the proper things are happening to you. By referring to scripture, it can be encouraging and reassuring to know that all who have attained have followed the same way. Such-and-such happened to them also and such-and-such will occur again in the future.

The scriptures are the evidence of the sages, but the authentic knowledge is attained only from within oneself and not through their words.

Nanak says:

> *Through listening all the scriptures and teachings are known.*
> *Through listening devotees attain bliss,*
> *And sin and sorrow are destroyed.*
> *Through listening all truth and contentment are attained,*
> *And the virtue of bathing at the sixty-eight holy places is gained,*
> *And through listening again and again honor is earned.*
> *Through listening spontaneous meditation happens.*
> *Nanak says: Through listening devotees attain bliss,*
> *And sin and sorrow are destroyed.*

To arrive at the ultimate freedom, Hindus require that a person bathe at sixty-eight holy places. These holy places are marked on the map of India, but in reality they represent sixty-eight points within the body through which one must pass to attain virtue. The Hindus have performed a wonderful task that no other race has equaled in discovering these points. However, places on the map are merely symbols; unfortunately, wandering in these symbols as if real, the Hindus have lost their consciousness of life. It is said: "Get the water of the Ganges and offer it at Rameshwara." These really refer to points within the body; the energy is to be taken from one point and directed into another, which is the holy pilgrimage. But what do we do? We actually carry water from the Ganges up to Rameshwara!

The external map is a symbolic translation of man's internal world. Everything within man is very subtle. To exemplify it, these external symbols were created, but in mistaking the symbols for reality we went astray.

Symbols are never truths; they only hint towards truth. They are pointers when Nanak says: through shravana truth is obtained, so also contentment and knowledge, and through it is attained bathing at the sixty-eight centers of pilgrimage. When you become silent you begin to find the holy places within the body. Then you do not have to ponder what truth is for you see truth directly. As long as you think, there is no truth — only opinions, concepts. Truth is an experience. And once you can see, why still think?

Contentment is attained. As long as you think, you are discontented, because thoughts lead to thousands of suggestions: do this, do that! Thoughts give rise to new desires and desires lead to discontent. It is very harmful to have thoughts as friends; they lead you astray. If there is any bad company worth giving up, it is that of thoughts. It is all right to use thoughts, but if you begin to obey them you are in for all kinds of trouble. They are like drugs; if you get addicted to them you go astray and will be so confused that you won't know what to do.

Mulla Nasruddin had so much to drink one day that he was afraid to go home. He knew he would have to furnish an explanation and he couldn't think of a plausible answer, so he wandered here and there aimlessly.

A policeman came upon him in the middle of the night, demanding to know, "What are you doing here at this time of the night? Answer quickly or I'll have to take you to the police station."

Mulla Nasruddin answered, "If I had an answer wouldn't I have gone home already?"

Thoughts are an addiction that has no answer. Had there been an answer you would have reached home long ago. Why are you roaming at such a late hour? You have no answer to explain your life. Thoughts have no answer. A real answer can only be found in the no-thought state.

Nanak says: contentment and truth through shravana; the sixty-eight holy places through shravana; and through shravana alone you attain the natural samadhi.

If you were only to listen, it becomes meditation. Without meditation you cannot hear. What is the meaning of meditation? Meditation exists only where mind is not; where the internal dialogue is gone.

> *Through listening the highest virtues are acquired.*
> *Sage, saint and king come into being,*
> *And the blind find the path.*
> *Through listening the fathomless is fathomed.*
> *Nanak says: Through listening devotees attain bliss,*
> *And sin and sorrow are destroyed.*

Through listening alone the blind find their way, the beggar becomes a king, and you reach the depths of the boundless! Thoughts are like a teaspoon, and you try to measure the ocean with it! Listening is to enter into the ocean. You will reach the bottom only by drowning in it and not by measuring it with a teaspoon!

Aristotle, the Greek philosopher, was walking along the seashore lost in high thoughts. Suddenly he came upon a man who was trying to empty the ocean into a pit he had dug, with the help of a spoon. He became curious and asked, "Brother, what are you doing?"

The man replied, "If you have eyes you can see. It is as clear as day. I mean to empty this ocean into this pit."

Aristotle laughed and said, "Is it not madness? Are you in your right senses? Can oceans be measured by spoons? Can pits be filled by spoons? Why waste your life in senseless tasks?"

The man laughed and said, "I thought it was you who is mad, because aren't you engaged in filling the infinite with your spoonful of thoughts?" It is said that Aristotle tried to locate that man later but he never found him.

The man was correct: how small is a thought, how vast existence! How will you measure this vast existence with your measuring spoon? Where will you keep it? Your head is so small, the universe so vast. Look at your arms, how short they are — how far can they reach?

You are engaged in a worthless task. Perhaps that man may have succeeded in emptying the ocean, because the ocean is finite. A spoonful of water does make the ocean less by a spoon, but the infinite you can never attain through thoughts.

Therefore, says Nanak, the beggar becomes a king as soon as he becomes silent. The depths of the depthless become known, the unknown becomes familiar, the stranger becomes the beloved, and the blind find their way — all through shravana.

> *Nanak says: Through listening the devotee is full of bliss,*
> *And sin and sorrow are destroyed.*

CHAPTER 6

Only Contemplating Can Know

The state of contemplation cannot be expressed;
Whoever attempts it will afterwards repent.
There is no paper, no pen, no writer,
That can penetrate such a state.
The name of the flawless one is such
That only contemplating can know it.
Through contemplation is remembrance born in mind and intellect,
And awareness of the universe acquired.
You cease to repent your words,
And gain freedom from the god of death.
The name of the flawless one is such
That only contemplating can know it.
Through contemplation the path is cleared of all obstacles,
And a man departs with dignity and honor;
One is saved from wandering astray,
And connection to religion is established.
The name of the flawless one is such
That only contemplating can know it.
Through contemplation alone the door to liberation is attained,
And the family can be saved;
Through it the guru is delivered and helps his disciples across;
They need no longer beg for alms.
The name of the flawless one is such
That only contemplating can know it.

Let us understand what *manan,* contemplation, means. Thinking and contemplation are both processes of the mind, but they are very different, even opposite.

When a man swims from one bank to the other he remains on the surface of the river. His position changes but not the depth. Now imagine a diver; his position in the water needn't change at all, but his course is downward, further and further into the depths. Thinking is like swimming and contemplation is like diving. In thinking we go from one thought to another; in contemplation we go into the depths of the one word. The position does not change; the depth changes.

The process of thought is linear; whether you think of your business or your spiritual liberation, thinking of God or of your wife, you remain on the surface. But in contemplation the journey inward begins; you plunge into the very depths of the word. Its deepest recesses resonate.

Contemplation is the only true revelation of the mantra.

Understand well this one word, and the entire sutra opens for you. The quintessence of Nanak's teaching is contemplation — contemplation of the one name, *Omkar. Ek Omkar Satnam.* Omkar is the one true name, the only truth. He gave the mantra to his disciples not to be *thought* about, but to submerge themselves in. As the one word *Om* keeps resounding, the resonance itself increases the depth of the experience.

There are three levels: in the first you pronounce the word out loud — *Om...Om...Om....* This is the level of speech. Making use of your lips, speech resounds outside. Then you shut your lips, not even allowing the tongue to move, and you pronounce the name in your mind —Om...Om...Om.... The second level is deeper than the first. You do not make any use of lips or tongue; you do not use the body at all — you use only the mind. On the third level even the mind is not used. Om is not even pronounced. You become silent and listen to the resonance of Om that is already within. The mind is no more; and when it is gone contemplation begins. Contemplation means the absence of mind.

The resonance of Omkar is with you from your very birth. Have you noticed how happy infants are without any apparent reason? They lie in the cradle and throw their little arms and legs about and make cooing sounds. Mothers in India think they are remembering something from their past lives, for there is absolutely no reason for their happiness. Lying in their cribs they have yet to start their journey in life. Psychologists are confounded with the child's joy, but take it to be the expression of their good health.

Yogis have discovered a different reason altogether, for the well-being of the body is not enough. Within, the child hears the resonance of Omkar, a soft melodious strain. The child hears it and is captivated by it, enchanted by it. Hearing it, the infant smiles and gurgles and feels happy. The child's health may remain good later on, but the melody within will be lost; this cheerfulness will be gone. Then it will become difficult for the child to hear the Omkar for the layers of words that surround it.

The resonance, *Ek Omkar Satnam,* is the first happening. In it lies the fountain of life. Then come the words brought about by our education, impressions, society, culture. Then the third level is actually pronouncing words in speaking, conversation and dialogues. While speaking you are actually farthest away from words. Therefore Nanak stresses the necessity of learning how to listen. For when you hear you are in between; you can go either way, towards speech or towards silence.

So there are three states: the state of Omkar, the state of speech, and the in-between state of thoughts and feelings. When you are listening you are in the mid-state of thoughts and feelings. If you begin to tell others what you have heard, you have descended into speech. If you begin to reflect, to contemplate on what you have heard, then you are in contemplation, and you go into the void. The distance is very subtle. Each person has to understand well the distance between the two within himself and provide for the equilibrium.

Contemplation begins as soon as you submerge yourself in any one word. Any word will do but no word is more beautiful than *Omkar,* because it is pure resonance. The words: *Allah, Ram, Krishna* can also be used, but there is no need to take big, big names. The English poet, Tennyson, repeated his own name and lost himself in its resonance.

As you enter into the depths of any word, the word gradually gets lost; and as it begins to fade, contemplation sets in. The word is always lost ultimately; all mantras are lost for they are of the mind. The supreme mantra, however, is forever resounding within. The first mantra only helps to bring you into silence, but not into the supreme mantra. Once you are silent you can hear the resonance of Omkar within you.

All mantras teach you to swim and then from swimming they teach you to dive. But how long will you insist on voyaging only on the surface? How long will you go on from one life to the next? How long will you merely keep changing your location, your situations? When will that auspicious moment arrive when you will take the plunge – from wherever you are? At that very moment contemplation will begin to happen. With this in view, now let us try to understand Nanak's sutras.

The state of contemplation cannot be expressed;
Whoever attempts it will afterwards repent.

Why is this so? First of all, contemplation cannot be talked about for there is no movement in contemplation – it is non-movement. The journey does not start; in fact, it ends. It appears like movement.

When you travel by train you see everything rushing past you. In fact it is the train that is moving, and all else is static. In a like manner, because of your habitual movement, when the mind begins to come to a halt, you feel it is a movement. But when the mind stops ultimately, you will suddenly find that everything has stopped, for nothing had moved.

He who is hidden within you has never walked — not even a single step. He has undertaken no journey, not even a pilgrimage. He has not stepped out of his house; he has been there forever.

It is the mind that has always been on the run and its speed is so great that everything around that has never moved appears to be running. When the mind begins to halt they also begin to halt, and when the mind comes to a stop, everything stops with it. While you can talk about movement, how can you speak about non-movement? It is possible to talk about a journey, for you can describe the different places in your travel from one place to another, but if you have gone nowhere what will you talk about? If there has been no happening, no change of situations, what is there to say?

You can write the life story of a restless man, but what can you write about a man of peace? It is the experience of novelists, writers, and dramatists that things come alive only around the bad man. The life of a good man is very dull and uneventful.

Don't be under the illusion that the Ramayana is the story of Rama; it really revolves around Ravana, the villain. Ravana is the actual hero of the story and Rama is secondary. Remove Ravana and what remains of the story? Sita is not stolen, the battle is not fought — everything is quiet and uneventful. How much is there to say about Rama? Can you write an epic on God? He is where he ever was. There has never been any change in him — the story just cannot take shape. Therefore there are no biographies or autobiography of God. For to write about someone, a journey is necessary.

You can write a great deal on thoughts; what will you write in connection with no-thought? Whatever you say about it will be false and you will regret it later. Sages always repent after speaking, for they feel they could not say what they wanted to say; and they have said what should not have been said. For what they tried to convey the listener could not follow, and what he understood had no meaning.

Lao Tzu has said, "Nothing can be spoken about Truth." And whatever is spoken becomes an untruth. The more you know, the more difficult you will find it to express yourself. Each word becomes a challenge to utter for now you possess a touchstone within by which you test; as a result all words seem too shallow and petty to express. A big event has taken place inside which cannot be contained by words, a vast space discovered within that cannot be filled with the capsules of words.

And even if you speak, the regret becomes greater, for by the time your words reach the listener their meaning becomes quite different. Everything that you said gets completely changed – you gave a diamond; it became a stone. The genuine coin you gave, in changing hands became false. As you look within his eyes and see that the coin has become a fake, then you are filled with remorse for this man will now carry it along with him throughout his life.

This is exactly how all sects run, how the crowds of thousands move. They carry the burden of what was never given to them. If Mahavira were to return, he would beat his chest and weep at the state of Jainism; if Buddha returns he will weep for the Buddhists; if Jesus returns the fight will start again with the Israelites, for what each of them said never reached the people for whom it was intended. Something very different was received and digested.

If Nanak were to return he would not be as displeased with others as he would be with the Sikhs, for you can be angry only with those to whom you gave the word; it is they who have distorted it into something quite different.

We are very cunning. When a person like Nanak speaks, we add our meanings to his words, as it suits us. We do not shape ourselves in Nanak's words; we fashion his words according to ourselves. This is our trick to bring things back to where they were. There are only two ways.

There once was a very rich woman. She was very artistic but also fickle and obstinate. Being fond of an ashtray that was very expensive, she had decorated her room so that it became the focus of the room and everything was made to match: the curtains, the furniture, the walls. The ashtray was the center of everything. One day the ashtray broke. She called the best craftsmen to make an exact replica of the ashtray but try as they would, no one could recreate the original color which was also reproduced everywhere in the room.

One day a craftsman offered his services. He asked for a full month to produce an ashtray to match the original one, but he laid one condition — no one was to enter the room during this month, not even the lady. In a month's time he invited her to inspect the room. She was completely satisfied.

When the other craftsmen asked him what the secret was, he said, "It was simple. First I made an ashtray as close to the original one as possible, then I painted the walls accordingly." Impossible as it was to get the exact shade in the ashtray, this was the only way out.

When Nanak speaks there are only two ways open to you: either you merge into Nanak's color and attain to satisfaction, or else you are bound to become restless. To be near a person like Nanak is like standing next to fire. Either you burn yourself as Nanak burned, you turn into ashes as Nanak did, you lose yourself as Nanak did — like a drop falling into the ocean; or, the only other alternative is to color Nanak's words in your own shade. This is very easy, for we never actually hear what is told to us, but hear what we want to hear. We infer meanings that suit us. We don't stand on the side of truth; we make truth stand on our side; we make truth follow us.

The difference between a genuine seeker and a false seeker is that the legitimate seeker follows truth wherever it might take him — whatever be the outcome — even if everything is lost, even if life is lost. He is ready to lose his all. The inauthentic seeker bends truth to follow him; but then it is no longer truth, it is falsity.

How can truth follow you? Only untruth can follow you, for you are false; your shadow is bound to be fake. You can follow truth if you desire, but truth can never follow you; it cannot be contained in your concepts, it is too big for your head. Therefore Nanak says whoever attempts it afterwards repents. There is yet another reason which you should note, that I have mentioned before. When you almost reach contemplation you come to the midpoint from which there are two choices, one of which is to start talking of it to others. In that case you will regret it; therefore, whenever the urge comes to tell others, first consult the guru. Do not trust in your own judgment to talk about it till the guru tells you.

The ways of the ego are very subtle. No sooner do you make one small step than it proclaims great triumph. It gets a fistful and claims to have attained all space! A little glimpse of light and it says the sun has risen. A drop has hardly fallen and you begin talking of the ocean. Then the talk leads to more talk and the result is that even the one drop vanishes, the glimpse dissolves. The result is that the person remains a shallow pundit, full of nothing but knowledge; he seems to know too much. He talks a great deal without any experience. If you observe him carefully you will note that his actions are completely inconsistent with what he says.

Once Mulla Nasruddin was trying to catch a train that had already started moving. He caught hold of the handle and one foot was already in the door when the guard grabbed him saying, "Don't you know it's an offense to climb a moving train?" The Mulla climbed down.

Then just as the train was leaving the platform the guard jumped into his compartment. The Mulla promptly pulled him down, saying, "Well, sir, doesn't the law also apply to you?"

This is exactly the state of the pundit. His statements apply to everyone else. He enjoys the taste of delivering discourses — bereft of the waters of life, unrelated to his own experience and this danger is always there.

When you reach the midpoint you arrive at two paths: one is the path of the pundit, the master of words; and the other is the path of the wise. The path of the pundit leads you to the world outside via words and pronouncements. On the path of the wise you leave the word and immerse yourself completely in no-word. Therefore without the guru's permission do not go on telling others.

There was a disciple of Buddha by the name of Purna Kashyap who had attained knowing but still followed silently behind Buddha. After a full year Buddha called him and said, "Why do you still follow me like my shadow? Go out into the world and tell others what you have known." Purna Kashyap replied, "I was awaiting your orders. For what about this mind? It might begin to take pleasure in preaching to others and then I might lose what I have attained only with so much difficulty! I know there is every possibility of the ego's returning."

It is very difficult to attain knowledge, very easy to lose it; for the path is very subtle and you can go astray any moment on the slightest excuse. So Purna Kashyap waited, knowing that Buddha would tell him when he was ready to preach to others. Do not set out to teach others before the guru tells you or else you will repent. And the repentance will be great for you were very close to the other shore when you went astray. The boat was just about to cast anchor when the shore receded. Wisdom and learning are the final temptations.

> *The state of contemplation cannot be expressed;*
> *Whoever attempts it will afterwards repent.*
> *There is no paper, no pen, no writer,*
> *That can penetrate such a state.*

Who is competent to express this state? For as contemplation goes deeper and deeper, the doer is lost, and the mind begins to end; contemplation is its death.

The mind can speak, the mind can tell. Its expertise lies in explaining what it knows, even telling of things you do not know; and frequent repetition leads you to the illusion that you know. If you keep explaining a thing again and again, you gradually forget whether you have known it or not and begin to feel and believe that you know. Just consider: do you say only things you know or do you also say things you do not know? Do you know whether God is? If not, do not tell anyone that God is. Have you known truth? If not, do not tell others about truth, for the danger is not that others will be deceived, but by constant repetition you yourself will be deluded into the certainty that you know.

This is a very subtle illusion. Once the thought takes hold of you that you know — when you have not known — your boat will never reach the other shore. A man who sleeps can be awakened, but he who pretends to be asleep is hard to awaken. The ignorant can be enlightened, but not a learned man who says he already knows all. Armed with this understanding, avoid the saints and scholars, only go to them when your knowledge gains sufficient strength to protect you. The pundit searches out the ignorant and avoids the sage. If Nanak comes to town the pundits will run away for they are frightened that such a man may lay bare their actual state. He might lift the veil and uncover their ignorance; and this veil is so weak and thin that it tears at the slightest touch.

Where there is no paper nor pen nor even writer, then the state of mind does not exist, and who is to ponder over contemplation?

The name of the flawless one is such
That only contemplating can know it.

That is how it is, but only you will know. Just as a mute cannot explain the taste of sugar, your lips will remain sealed. Every time you think of it there will be a lump in your throat, your heart will become full, so full; tears will flow, or laughter, but you will not be able to say a word. People will think your mind has lost its balance. Your inside will be so overfull that it will pour out of every pore in your body. You will dance, you will sing, but you will not be able to speak. So it was that Nanak sang and Mardana played. Whenever anyone asked Nanak about his state he would look at Mardana and nod. Mardana would pick up his instrument and begin to play, and Nanak would begin to sing. Nanak said nothing, he only sang.

When you hear a sage — if you hear him properly — you will find he is singing, not talking. You will find poetry in his words. Even as he sits he dances. You will find a kind of intoxication in the atmosphere around him, an intoxication that does not lull you to sleep or into senselessness, but rather awakens you. It takes you not into forgetfulness but into wakefulness. And if you are ready to flow along with it, it can carry you to unknown and wonderful shores. If you are really ready to dive down deep into the ocean it can take you on a long astonishing journey — to the ultimate.

The sage's tune is more melody than words. He speaks less, sings more, for what he has attained cannot be expressed in words. It will perhaps be transmitted by a tune, a low murmur; a slight glimpse and you may get carried away by it.

Gurdjieff defined two kinds of art. In ordinary art the artist, the singer, the sculptor expresses his feelings. Even a great painter like Picasso does no more than capture his state of mind in his work. Gurdjieff calls this subjective art. Objective art includes the Taj Mahal or the Ajanta-Ellora caves. In this the artist does not portray his feelings but creates a condition that elicits certain feelings in the viewer.

There is the statue of Buddha. If it is truly a piece of objective art – which it can be only if the sculptor has known what buddhahood means – then you will find yourself getting connected with it in a mysterious way as you keep looking at it. You will find that you have descended deep within yourself and the idol will become contemplation.

The idols in the temples were not put there without a reason. They are all part of this objective art. Music also was not created accidentally; those who went into *samadhi* first gave voice to music. Having heard the melody of Om within, in various ways they tried to capture the melody of this resonance in the realm of sound, so that those who know not the music within may get some taste of it. Little children invariably come to the temple in order to partake of the offerings made to the deity. Whatever your reason, there is value in going to the temple. The external sounds of the bells and devotional songs can become a divine gift if they touch off remembrance of the music within.

The deep pleasure in music is a glimpse of samadhi. Dance also is an objective art, thus the tradition of dancing before the deity. Witnessing the dance, your boat may suddenly leave the shore and sail off to distant lands!

One thing you must keep in mind about Nanak is that whatever he has said, he has sung; whatever he wanted to convey, he has conveyed along with music. For the real thing is the music — the *nada,* the sound. What he says is a mere excuse when his aim is to trigger the resonance within you. If it begins to resound in the right way your thought processes will break and you will find yourself on a different plane of words altogether. If you have gathered enough courage to flow along, if you are not holding on like mad to the shore, then the third happening — contemplation — will also occur.

> *There is no paper, no pen, no writer,*
> *That can penetrate such a state.*
> *The name of the flawless one is such*
> *That only contemplating can know it.*

It is like a dumb man tasting sugar; only he knows the taste. And then — this taste is never forgotten, not only throughout this lifetime but for infinite lives.

Once you get the taste, you find the taste is much more than you — you can never forget it. The taste is so enormous that rather than your containing it, you will be lost in it. It is like the ocean; you will be lost in it like a drop.

In truth how can you taste God? It is rather God who tastes you, provided you are ready. You get immersed in that taste and a harmony, a unison, is formed with the divine: such is the name *Niranjan,* the faultless one.

> *Through contemplation alone is remembrance born.*

As you get more and more involved in conversation, remembrance decreases. Perhaps you may have realized that. While you are observing yourself most of your troubles drop off; it is only when you begin speaking again that you land yourself in trouble. What happens? When you are speaking remembrance is at its lowest and awareness is almost nil, because in speaking your attention is on the other and not on yourself. Consciousness is like an arrow. When you talk, the arrow is pointed towards the other, so you are conscious of the one you are talking to, and your attention is diverted away from yourself. In this state of your non-awareness of your own self you say things you may regret all your life.

In a moment of non-awareness you tell a woman you love her although you had never thought about it before. On the spur of the moment words fall out of your mouth and now you are caught in the situation; one careless event gives rise to a thousand more. If you try to pluck one leaf, four more appear in its place, and you are propelled on a journey you least wanted.

Though it may never have struck you before, you will find that all your troubles have their origin in words. When one word has been uttered, the ego in its pride makes you fulfill your words. You are in love and you tell your beloved, "I shall love you for ever and ever." You cannot know what the next moment is going to bring for you. How can you make a promise for the morrow, when you do not even know what is going to happen tomorrow morning, let alone speak of the distant future or of lives to come? If you have even the slightest awareness you would say, "This very moment I am in love with you. About tomorrow I can say nothing." But then the ego would get no pleasure in that.

Mulla Nasruddin's wife said to him, "You don't love me as you did before. Is it because I have become old, or because my body has become sick and clumsy? Have you forgotten your promise before the clergyman that we shall be together in sorrow and in joy?"

The Mulla replied, "Aren't we together in sorrow and joy? But I had made no promise about old age!"

When today you say "forever" do you realize the implications? If today you declare your love, the rest of your life you will spend fulfilling this promise — a hard task! If you cannot fulfill your word, you will be full of regrets; if you do, you will be thoroughly miserable. For when love has flown away what will you do? Can you bring it back by force? Instead you must invariably weave a web of deceit.

While speaking, it is difficult to be aware of yourself, for on the plane of speech your attention is on the other person. Speaking is all right only for a Buddha, a sage, who by his *sadhana* has developed the double-pointed arrow, the consciousness that is aware of the other as well as its own self. This consciousness is called *surati*, remembrance or self-remembering. The mind is capable of looking in both directions simultaneously and it needn't be lost while talking. While speaking, the witness stands at attention all the time; then no word can possibly cause trouble for you.

There is a Sufi story: The guru sent for his four disciples to practice the sadhana of silence. The four sat in the mosque as evening fell and it began to get dark. No one had yet lit the lamp. As a servant passed by, one of the disciples called out and said, "Brother, light the lamp. Night is coming on."

The second disciple scolded, "The guru told us not to speak. You have spoken!"

The third could not contain himself, "What are you doing? You too have spoken!"

The fourth who had remained quiet now said, "I was the only one to obey the guru. I did not speak until now."

You may laugh at the story but it is really your own story. If you become silent for a while you will realize how much you long to talk, how you begin an internal dialogue. The slightest excuse and you lose your contemplation.

What is the meaning of the story? As long as no one was around they remembered to observe the silence. As soon as the servant came along, the other was present to attract their attention and all contemplation was lost.

Through contemplation alone is remembrance born.

Remembrance is a beautiful word. It corresponds with Buddha's right mindfulness. Whatever you do, do it mindfully. Be mindful when you talk, when you walk, even when the eyes blink. Do nothing senselessly, unconsciously; for whatever you do in such a fashion will lead invariably to sin. Whatever you do without awareness leads you away from your self. The only method of coming close to your self is to become more and more aware. Whatever the circumstances, whatever the situation, hold fast and never let go of your awareness – even should you stand to lose everything. Even if your house catches fire, move only with complete awareness.

Ishwar Chandra Vidyasagar, the philosopher and social reformer, has given the following account in his memoirs.

He was once invited by the viceroy who was about to confer an honor on him. He was a poor man, his clothes were old and threadbare, and he dressed in the Bengali style of *kurta* and *dhoti*. Friends advised him to get new clothes in keeping with the occasion. At first he refused but later thought better of it and let them order new clothes for him.

One day shortly before the event, as Vidyasagar was returning from his evening walk he saw walking in front of him a well-dressed Mohammedan in coat and pajamas, twirling a stick in his hand. He was walking at his own pace enjoying the evening. Soon a man — by all appearances his servant — came running and told him, "Hurry, sir, your house is on fire!" There was no change in the man's stride; he continued walking along as if nothing had happened. The servant, thinking maybe he hadn't heard, repeated loudly, "Sir, your house is on fire! Haven't you heard what I said?"

Even the poor servant, who stood to lose nothing, was trembling and perspiring with fear, but the master remained unaffected. "I have heard," he told the servant. "Should I change my habitual way of walking just because the house has caught fire?" Ishwar Chandra was shocked. Here is a man whose house is actually on fire, and he is not prepared to change his lifelong walk; and there he was, ready to give up his lifelong attire just to see the viceroy!

Ishwar Chandra was curious to know more about this unique man. As he followed, he saw him walking at the same pace twirling his stick; when he reached the house and saw the flames he calmly gave orders to put out the fire, directed it all, but himself stood on one side and watched without one iota of difference in his attitude.

Ishwar Chandra writes: "My head bowed in reverence to this man. Never had I come across the like of him." What is it that this man was guarding so zealously? He was guarding his surati, his awareness, and he was not prepared to lose it at any cost. Whatever happens, happens. All that was required to be done was being attended to; that is enough. On no account can contemplation be bartered away. Nothing is so precious in life that you can afford to lose your remembrance for it.

But you abandon your awareness for the slightest thing. A one-rupee note is lost and you go mad looking for it. You look for it even in places where it could not possibly be. A man has lost something and you find him looking in the tiniest box, much too small for such an object. You are always ready to lose your awareness, or is it better to say you have no awareness to lose — you are unconscious!

Nanak says: Through contemplation awareness is born within the mind and the intellect. As the Omkar settles more and more within, the external utterance stops first. The arrow now turns within, for now there is no one without to speak to; in other words, the external relations created by speech are no more. To speak is to build a bridge to reach others. It is the relationship between us and others. By not speaking, this relationship is broken; you have become silent.

To become silent means now the journey is reversed: the arrow has turned inwards, the journey within has begun. As soon as this happens, the first glimpse of awareness begins to appear, and for the first time in full awareness you know that *you are!* So far you could see everything except yourself. Only you were in shadow, as there is darkness directly under the flame. Now you will awaken. As the intensity of Omkar increases, contemplation settles on the word and awareness increases proportionately.

Take it this way: There are two sides to the scales; when one goes up the other comes down to the same extent. Proportional to your going inward, so awareness increases. On the third plane when even the word is lost and only the resonance of Omkar remains — pure sound — suddenly the awareness becomes complete. You get up. You awaken, as if the sleep of a thousand years has been broken. Darkness flees and there is light, and light alone. It is as if you were in a deep slumber through innumerable lives and dreaming away. Suddenly the dream is broken, and lo, it is morning. You see the dawn as if for the first time in your life.

> *Through contemplation is remembrance born in mind and intellect,*
> *And awareness of the universe acquired.*
> *You cease to bear the brunt of life,*
> *And gain freedom from the god of death.*
> *The name of the flawless one is such*
> *That only contemplating can know it.*

The day you awaken you realize for the first time the infinite space, the countless worlds, this existence, this *leela* — play of the gods. As long as you are steeped in your own desires, lost in the labyrinth of your own mind, you are blind and see nothing. The mind is another name for blindness; contemplation is the opening of the eyes, the restoration of sight.

Nanak says: "Through contemplation alone you become aware of all the worlds. All the heavenly bodies, the whole universe becomes visible. Life manifests in its complete and perfect glory. Then you see his initials in all things great and small. You will find his name on every leaf, his resonance in every hair of your body; you will hear his melody in the winds. Then the whole of existence unfolds his glory to you."

Now you ask: "What is the meaning of life? What is the idea behind it? Why are we born? Why do we live?" The great French existential thinker, Gabriel Marcel, has written that life has but one problem, and that is suicide. Why do we live? Why should we not commit suicide? The ultimate state of insensibility, of unconsciousness, is in suicide, where the priceless gifts of life are thrown away for you find nothing in them.

Just the opposite happens when you awaken into awareness; then the glory is boundless. World upon world opens before your eyes. Every stage abounds with mystery and wonder. Then you come to know the meaning of life, the bliss which we call samadhi. Then you know why life is.

In your present state you cannot know; however much you may ask, however much you are told that to attain God is the goal of your life, it does not solve your problem. No matter how much it is drummed into your ears that samadhi is the goal of your life, nothing strikes home as real until your remembrance awakens. You hear and you dismiss such talk as the words of those who are not very sound of mind. You trust your own understanding, but where has it taken you but to the brink of suicide? This valuable gift given to you is less than worthless, for you find no meaning in it. But no sooner do you become awakened than the mystery begins to unravel before you. A flower opens and each petal exudes nothing but joy — enchanting bliss!

Nanak is a simple rustic. He says: "Through contemplation you cease to bear the burden of. Life." He speaks plain village language, but what he says is significant and to the point. Through contemplation you need not spit out your words only to take them back again, bearing the insults and abuse, or even a slap on the face for whatever you said in your dullness. You speak through your ego-sleep, unaware of what you say, what you do, where you are going. Then it is only natural that you get slapped in the face.

Today you say you are in love; before morning dawns your love has flown away! One minute you feel like murdering someone and in a short while you rack your brains how best to please him. One instant you say one thing, the next minute you say the opposite. You cannot be trusted. You are as changeable as the seasons. There is nothing stable within you, nothing crystallized, so you have to bear a slap in the face every moment.

Nanak says: "Through contemplation alone you need not bear that slap on the face, and you no longer have to go along with the god of death. Everyone dies but all don't have to follow *Yama*, the god of death." Understand the symbol. Everyone dies, but once in a while a man dies consciously and then he need not follow Yama. As long as you live in non-remembrance you are a prisoner of Yama. The meaning of Yama is fear. One who lives in nonawareness, dies in nonawareness. He trembles and wails for someone to save him from death. He holds onto the very last breath of life, wanting to be saved from the jaws of death by any means. This state of fear, this dark face of fear, is symbolized by the god Yama astride a black buffalo.

But a person who dies in full remembrance and awareness is not obsessed by fear. Without fear he comes to realize that death is the culmination of life and not its end. Far from being fearsome, death is the gateway to his abode, an invitation to his dwelling, a process of merging into him. There is no need to weep and lament; rather, he enters into the faultless beauty of death, filled with joy and celebration — as if going to meet his beloved.

Nanak's last words are priceless. As he was about to leave the body he said, "The flowers are blooming, spring has come. The trees are vibrant with the songs of the birds!"

Which realm is he talking about? Some people thought it a nostalgic remembrance of his childhood, his village, where — that very season being spring — he imagined the trees in full bloom and the birds singing in them. It is a matter of coincidence that it was springtime, that the flowers were in bloom, and the birds were singing, and the air was filled with gladness. But this was not what Nanak had in mind. Nanak was seeing something else, but had to use familiar metaphors in talking to mortals. In the last moments he was entering into the supreme beauty, the incomparable loveliness where flowers bloom perpetually and never wither, where the birds sing eternally, where there is everlasting loveliness.

No sooner does a person become enlightened than he discovers death to be no annihilation but the ultimate flowering, the highest state of existence. He realizes that in death we lose nothing. One door closes; another opens. The sage enters dancing, singing; the ignorant man weeps and wails. If any man follows the emissaries of death, he himself is responsible, for there is no Yama, much less his emissaries. It is your fear that is your Yama; once you become fearless, God spreads out his arms for you.

Your actual experience of death depends on what you are. Death is the statement, the test, of how you have lived. If at that moment a man is cheerful, serene and filled with bliss and thanksgiving, know that his life was incomparable, for death is the ultimate offering to God. If he weeps and wails it is a sure sign that his life was a tale of anguish, a veritable hell.

Nanak says: Through contemplation you...

> ...*gain freedom from the god of death.*
> *The name of the flawless one is such*
> *That only contemplating can know it.*
> *Through contemplation the path is cleared of all obstacles;*
> *And a man departs with dignity and honor;*
> *One is saved from wandering astray,*
> *And connection to religion is established.*
> *The name of the flawless one is such*
> *That only contemplating can know it.*

All obstructions are within you and not outside of you. Obstacles are there because of your insensibility and they cannot simply be removed. The only way is to awaken within; then all obstacles vanish.

Now suppose your house is in darkness. As you enter, every corner of the house seems filled with danger; maybe there are ghosts or goblins, or burglars, or even a murderer. Everything seems so ominous; the house holds a thousand perils; there might even be snakes and scorpions around. How will you possibly overcome all these hazards if you set out to deal with them one by one? Who knows how many thieves, how many criminals, lurk within this darkness? You cannot deal with them individually. The only way is to light a lamp. One single lamp illuminates the whole interior and all fears flee. Once the house is lighted and you can see whatever danger there is, you can always find ways to deal with it.

The fact is as Buddha has said, "The dark house attracts the burglar." A thief avoids the house that is well lit. If the lamp is burning within and if the awareness stands guard, no obstacle or hindrance dare enter within you.

One day, early in the morning, Mulla Nasruddin came running to me. He held a paper in his hand and seemed terribly disturbed. He handed me the paper and flopped into a chair. The anonymous writer was warning Mulla that if he did not refrain from following his wife within the next three days, he would shoot him.

"What should I do?" asked Mulla.

"Why, that's simple," I said. "Just leave his wife alone!"

"But which wife shall I stop following?" he asked. "If it were only one woman I'd been following I'd know which one to stop!"

If there were only one hindrance you could get rid of it, but they are infinite. You are stalking an infinite number of women; your desires are inexhaustible. Destroy one, ten more take its place. If you keep grappling with each, hoping to eradicate them one by one, you never will succeed. A method is needed to finish it once and for all. And he who shows you this method, the *gur*, is the guru.

So Nanak says: Through contemplation all hindrances on the path are eradicated. Continue the repetition of Omkar and let it reach the non-repeating state, then you find your eyes have opened. Then there are no obstructions, for these are but your creations. There is no outside enemy to be vanquished. You are your own enemy. Your insensitivity is your enemy and because of it you are enmeshed in endless entanglements. No matter how cautious you are, you keep adding fresh hindrances at every step.

There are people in this world who regulate their lives with control and restraint. They must take each step carefully so as not to go astray. But restraint is not the end; awareness is the ultimate goal. The invitation to wander is always beckoning inside. However much you impose restraints, the raging passions will bring you down at the slightest opportunity. A person who practices self-denial and controls his every action must always be afraid, for within him the imprisoned passions continue boiling.

> *Through contemplation the path is cleared of all obstacles,*
> *And a man departs with dignity and honor.*

There is a different kind of honor that does not depend on others; it is the respect that arises out of internal dignity. He dies with majesty who feels death to be the union with God. He departs with joy and celebration in his heart, being grateful to existence for the life granted him. His air of thanksgiving for everything around is stamped on his face and in his every hair. Then it is not significant how many followed his coffin or where he died. None of this matters to his real dignity, his glory, his nobility, which are intrinsic qualities.

When death is no longer fearsome to you, you die with dignity; otherwise you cannot. For how can you be dignified when you weep and wail, entreat and beg? Then what does it matter how many people follow your funeral? All the pomp and ceremony cannot erase your anguish. All the flowers showered on you cannot smother the stink within you; the booming salute cannot overcome the uproar of sorrow and woe within you. Your death will be empty of honor all the same.

When Nanak says that through contemplation a person departs with honor, he talks of that internal honor, an internal reverence, a feeling of thanksgiving.

> *One is saved from wandering astray,*
> *And connection to religion is established.*

No matter how many scriptures you read, you cannot establish contact thereby with religion. No temple or mosque or church can connect you with religion. Slumbering, insensitive you go to worship; the same you who runs the shop, also goes to the house of worship. Your attitude should change, and once it is altered, everything else is transformed accordingly; otherwise you will keep on trying everything and yet remain your same old self.

Nanak went to Hardwar during the month of offerings to the dead. People were filling vessels with water, and then, facing East, were throwing them into the sky in order to reach their forefathers in heaven. Nanak picked up a bucket also, but he turned towards the West, and each bucket of water he poured, he cried out, "Reach my fields!"

After emptying a number of buckets, the people round him remonstrated with him. "What are you doing? You are turned in the wrong direction. You should face towards the rising sun! And why do you say, 'Reach my fields'? Where are your fields?"

Nanak replied, "About two hundred miles from here." The people began to laugh. "And you expect the water you throw here to reach your fields two hundred miles away? You are really out of your mind."

"How far away are your forefathers?" Nanak asked.

"They are infinitely far away," they replied.

"If your water can reach your ancestors an infinite distance away, why can't my water cover a mere two hundred miles?" asked Nanak.

What is Nanak trying to say? He is asking them to think a little, ponder: "What is this foolishness you indulge in? Become a little aware; what do you gain by such actions?"

Unfortunately all religion is filled with such stupidities. Some send water to ancestors, some bathe in the Ganges to wash away sins, yet others sit before idols without any feeling of worship or adoration, merely to ask for worldly things. A thousand foolishnesses prevail in the name of religion.

Therefore Nanak insists that religion is not attained through scriptures, nor through tradition and customs, nor through blind following. Contact with religion is established only when a person attains contemplation.

When a person awakens, awareness appears within him. When the resonance of Omkar first sounds, our relationship with religion begins. The day you are capable of hearing the resonance of Om within yourself, without any longer saying it, you are filled with joy, you are the witness, the observer. That very day you establish your connection with religion, not with some creed or sect. It is religion that Buddha calls *dharma*. It is religion that Mahavira and Nanak talk about.

Religion — dharma — means nature, the natural order of things. What Lao Tzu means by Tao, so Nanak means by religion. To be removed from one's nature is to be lost. To return to one's own nature is to return homewards. To be established in one's own nature is to be established in God.

The name, Niranjan — God, the spotless, the flawless one – is such that only he who contemplates his heart knows.

Through contemplation alone the door to liberation is attained;

And the family can be saved;
Through it the guru is delivered and helps his disciples across;
They need no longer beg for alms.
The name of the flawless one is such
That only contemplating can know it.

The gateway is within you, the wandering is within you, the obstructions are within you, the paths are within you. When once the lamp is lit you can see in both directions: what is truth and what is untruth. Under the light of the lamp all desire is seen as untruth, and to follow desire *is* the mundane world. As the light burns within, you will see that desirelessness is truth and also the gateway to liberation.

You are tied because of your desires. Desires are the chains that hold you. Each desire forms a fresh link in the chain, and God knows how long and intricate is your chain of desires. You desire and you enter the prison; you desire and you are tied down. And the more you desire, as you invariably do, the stronger become the shackles that bind you and the thicker become your prison walls.

Nanak says: "Through contemplation alone the door to salvation is attained. As soon as you awaken, your eyes are open completely and you see clearly. Cease desiring and the bonds are severed; there will be neither expectations nor attachments. When desire is missing there are no fetters; only then are the portals of liberation open. Desirelessness is the door to salvation."

And through contemplation alone the *family can be saved*. Which family is Nanak talking about? Certainly not of wife, children, brothers and sisters, for Nanak could not save them; nobody can. There is another kind of a family, that of guru and disciples, that is actually *the family*, for it is here that love occurs in its pristine purity. This love is born out of desirelessness; it happens without any reason.

You love your father because you are born through him. You love your wife because of your bodily desire. You love your son for you see in him a part of yourself or support in your old age. But what of the relationship with the guru? It is so difficult to find a guru, for you seek love without cause, without reason. With the guru there is love and love alone — no desire, no expectation. If you desire or expect something from him, you cannot be a part of his family. You will have to appear before him in all the simplicity and artlessness of a child.

Faith is called blind, and so it seems to those who are given to thinking. People come and say: Our parents ask, "Why are you mad about Osho? Are you out of your mind?"

As a matter of fact they *are* mad and their families are right, for the head that had managed the worldly affairs has really gone out of order. A new love is born within them that cannot be argued about. They cannot even plead a reason for this love. Even if they try, they find it impossible!

Nanak says: "Through contemplation alone can the family be saved." A family grows up around a guru; but when this family becomes a sect, deterioration begins. As long as it remains a family, it is different altogether. When a Buddha is born, thousands of people unite to form his family. Admission to the family of the guru is a very big event, for it signifies entry into a causeless world, a causeless love.

Nanak's followers are colored by him and drowned in his essence; his rhythm has caught their hearts and they are mad with ecstasy. But then Nanak will pass away and so also will those who joined his family of their own free will. When their children become Sikhs in turn, it has no genuine meaning, for the love that you have not chosen yourself cannot transform you. To choose Nanak is a great revolutionary act, but to be born into a Sikh household and call yourself a Sikh is no revolution.

A Mohammedan is born in a Mohammedan household; a Christian is born in a Christian household; so also with a Hindu or a Jaina or a Sikh. Your sect or faith is acquired through your birth, while family in this sense denotes what you have chosen yourself. A religious man always makes his own choice. An irreligious man is a sectarian; he identifies with the religion he was born into.

You are a Jaina by birth or a Christian or a Hindu, but how can you *be* a Jaina or Christian or a Hindu by birth? Birth gives you blood and bones and muscles; it does not give you your soul.

An insoluble riddle follows. When a guru is alive there is a light around him in which he floats and allows others to float also. When the guru is alive there is a live phenomenon, a happening taking place around him. When the guru departs, and also those who had offered their lives unto him, the children born into their families identify themselves with the sect of their parents and call themselves Sikhs or Christians or Buddhists; but they have no personal connection with the religion they profess.

One thing you must understand well: Religion is a personal decision. No one can be religious from birth.

Through contemplation alone the door to liberation is attained,
And the family can be saved;
Through it the guru is delivered and helps his disciples across;
They need no longer beg for alms.

As contemplation crystallizes, desires fall. What is the mundane world but an eternal round of begging for alms? Just observe yourself. What are you doing in your neediness? All twenty-four hours of the day you are wanting, your arms stretched out in desire. You are a veritable beggar. Nanak says through contemplation, your begging ceases. Remembrance makes a king of you, an emperor; it releases you from begging. Contemplation gives all and moves you beyond all desires.

Through contemplation God is attained. What else do you seek? Having reached the ultimate, there is nothing more ahead. Having attained all, what is still left to desire? You have reached samadhi. Having attained all, the need to beg disappears.

The name of the flawless one is such
That only contemplating can know it.

CHAPTER 7

The Journey Ends

Five are the tests and the ministers;
They gain shelter and respect at his door;
They decorate the king's court.
Attention is the guru of the five.
Whatever you will say, consider well first,
For the doings of the doer are impossible to assess.
Religion upholds the earth and is born of compassion.
Establish contentment and create the balance.
Whoever understands becomes the truth
And knows the burden religion bears
There are many worlds and many more beyond them;
What power assumes their weight?
Creatures of all forms and colors are created by his writ,
But only few know the rule to tell it.
Can anyone write the account of this mystery?
If it were written how great it would be.
What strength and power! How beautiful his appearance!
How great his charity; who can conceive it?
His single word creates this vast expanse —
Infinite mountains and rivers, the animate and inanimate.
How shall I think about it?
However much I offer myself could never be enough!
Whatever pleases you, O Lord, is best for me.
You are the formless, the almighty — you who abide forever!

The world begins when the one is lost, and it is natural that the journey ends when the one is found again. And this one can be found in many ways because it had been broken in many ways. When they pass through a prism, the sun's rays break into seven parts, the seven colors that form the spectrum; so also existence becomes fragmented.

The world is full of colors; color belongs to multiplicity. The color of God is white, the one being colorless. All *sadhanas* are only devices and techniques that seek out the one in the many — that reunite the fractions into the undivided, the integral. The Hindus contend that the one has broken into two: matter and spirit. If you get even a slight glimpse of the one within these two, your journey is complete.

There is another theory that the one has divided into three: truth, goodness, beauty. If you can see truth in beauty or vice-versa; if you see goodness in truth or in beauty; if you get a glimpse of the one within these three, so that all the three are lost and only the one underlying them all, *Ek Omkar Satnam,* remains, then your journey is over.

Nanak says the one is divided into five because of the five senses. If you seek the one within these five you shall attain, you become the *siddha,* the emancipated one. It is of no consequence in how many parts you divide the one, because it is already divided into infinite parts. The important thing is to discover the undivided, perfect whole within the fragments.

The senses are five, but within these five, meditation is one: to understand this is to grasp the sutra. Telling the beads in a rosary has no meaning, but if you can get at the thread that holds the beads together, then you will have taken refuge in God. Holding on to the beads is to remain in the mundane world; but to grasp the thread of the beads is to attain God.

There are five senses, but who is within these senses? When you look, who is it that sees through your eyes? When you hear, when you touch, when you smell, when you eat, who is it that experiences the perception, the experience? Nanak answers that *attention* lies at the center and unites it all.

There is an ancient anecdote: A sannyasin was sent by his guru to the palace of a king with the instructions, "The king may perhaps be able to make you understand what I could not." The disciple doubted this, but he had to obey the guru's order. When he reached the palace he found it flooded with light, wine was flowing and dancing-girls moved to sensuous music. He was terribly pained, thinking surely he had been sent to the wrong place; so he asked the king to allow him to go back, explaining that his search was something different. How could the king who was himself lost be of any help to him?

The king said, "I am not lost but you will understand that only after you remain here awhile. Just to see from the outside is fruitless. If you take the trouble to look deep inside perhaps you may grasp the key. Your guru sent you here only after great deliberation." The key is already hidden within, and not in the sense organs themselves.

The king persuaded him to stay overnight. He was put in a wonderful room that was the last word in comfort, but there was only one snag: from the ceiling just over the bed hung a naked sword on a slender cotton thread. The sannyasin could not sleep a wink because the thread was weak and the sword could drop any moment. He was dismayed by this cruel joke.

In the morning the king inquired whether he slept well. "Everything was fine," said the sannyasin with some sarcasm. "It couldn't have been better, but what was the big joke of dangling that sword over my head? I couldn't sleep a wink with my attention glued to the sword all the time."

The king said, "In exactly the same manner the sword of death hangs over my head constantly calling my attention. The girls dance but my mind is not in them; the wine flows but it gives me little pleasure; the tables overflow with all kinds of delicacies, but I can't enjoy the food with the sword of death always hanging over me."

The five senses are the five openings through which you contact the outside world. Without them you cannot relate to life, but the more you enter into them, the farther away from yourself you go. *Dhyana,* concentration, is hidden within each of the senses. When a particular sense points outward your attention moves outward through it. Therefore, when your attention goes out through one sense organ you become oblivious of the other senses. This happens because you know only through your attention, and not through your senses. Knowledge itself is attention. For example, you are sitting at a feast but a thorn has got into your foot and the pain is unbearable. You can never enjoy the taste of the food for the terrible pain engages your full attention, which flows only in that direction.

Another example: You have just been told that your house is on fire and your whole mind is on how to get home as fast as you can. Though you are walking on a road with many people you are aware of nothing around you. You don't notice the people rushing by, pushing one another, pushing you, or even that you are pushing others. You have no interest in what is being sold in the shops or what people are talking about. While your ears hear all, you hear nothing; while your arms touch the others you feel nothing. Your mind is entirely on the fire at your house.

The senses do not experience anything without your mind, their experiences rely entirely on your attention. When you pour your attention into a sense organ, then only is it motivated and gains strength. But if you withdraw your attention from all five senses, what remains is the one, because all the five will be lost instantly. And the real search is for this one alone. In these sutras Nanak has shown the method of removing the attention from the five senses.

Now let us try to understand the sutras:

Five are the tests and the ministers;

> *They gain shelter and respect at his door*
> *They decorate the king's court.*
> *Attention is the guru of the five.*

Dhyana, attention, is the one guru of the five senses. If you remain scattered among the five you are misled, but if you catch hold of the one you will arrive.

Looking at a woman grinding wheat, Kabir said: "No one can remain whole between the two slabs of the millstone." Kabir was telling his disciples that he who is caught in the millstone of duality is similarly ground to bits and cannot be saved.

Kabir's son said of this: "But there is something else in the millstone — the middle shaft. What if someone were to hold on to that?"

In his next couplet Kabir refers to this shaft, saying that he who takes refuge in it, he who seeks protection by holding on to the one amidst the two grinders, cannot be ground by them.

Whether you say two, like Kabir, or five like Nanak, or nine, or infinite, the meandering routes are many but the destination is one. On whatever path you choose to wander, the method of passing through will be specific for this path. Nanak's method means that when you eat you must be aware of your attention: the food is going in, various tastes are forming in the mouth, so experience it all with careful attention. If you taste your food attentively you will find that eventually the taste fades away and only attention remains. Attention and observation form a blazing fire which turns taste to ashes.

While seeing a beautiful flower, observe very attentively and you will find that the flower is gone and only observation remains. The flower is like a dream, attention is eternal.

When you see a beautiful woman and observe her without getting lost in a maze of thoughts, you will soon find that she is no more — like a line drawn on water — and only attention remains. If you thus remain alert and attentive with each of your senses, the forms of the senses fade away and the formless alone emerges. Once a person arrives at this dhyana, nothing can destroy it.

Nanak says there is only one master of the five senses, and that is attention. All the five senses, like five rivers, pour their waters into this very dhyana.

Psychologists also study this phenomenon: eyes see, ears listen, hands touch, the nose smells; but neither eyes nor ears nor hands nor nose can perform these tasks on their own. Then who is it that joins them all?

Someone is speaking, you are listening as well as looking. But how can you be sure that the person you are seeing is the same one you are hearing? Eyes and ears are different from each other. One indicates that it can see someone; the other indicates that it can hear someone. But how do you connect both of these? Who is it who combines the two experiences and conveys to us that they refer to the same person?

There must be a common ground where all the senses combine

their experience: the visions sent by the eyes, the sounds sent by the ears, the smells gathered by the nose, the touch felt by the hand. It is the focusing of attention that provides the common point determining the experience. Were it not so, life would be very jumbled and confused. You could never be sure whether you are seeing the same person who is talking, and whether the odors you smell also come from him. You would be broken into bits if there were not one to unite the five. All five paths must meet somewhere where their experiences are collected. This place is dhyana, attention.

Nanak says that attention is the guru of these five, who are disciples; but you have made gurus out of the disciples and forgotten the guru. You have turned the servants into masters and have no knowledge of the master at all. You heed your senses and don't give any thought to attention. You have completely forgotten that the senses are only superficial extensions of attention and you do not know what lies deep within.

If you want to lead a truly beautiful life, do not listen to the senses, because they are incomplete and only land you in trouble. In most cases people are slaves to one sense or the other. Some are mad after the sense of taste — food, food and food — they can think of nothing else. It is said about emperor Nero that he was a fiend for food. It was not just that he ate many times a day, but he kept on eating *all* day. Doctors were attending him permanently to make him vomit after each meal so that he could eat again.

You might say that he was mad, but this kind of madness exists more or less in all people. Some are addicted to sight — looking out for beautiful faces, beautiful bodies, even if they suffer in the process. They are slaves to their eyes.

You are blind if you are a slave to your eyes, because the authentic seeing organ is not the eye, which is merely a window. The one who looks out from this window is someone else. Do not ask questions of the window, but ask the one who peeps through it. People who are addicted to sounds and smells or to adorning the body, who are lost in music, or have the perversion of touching are all mad after their senses, and have accepted their slaves to be their masters. Listen rather to the owner who is the master within, because once he departs, the senses lie useless.

In 1910 the King of Kashi had to be operated on for appendicitis. Since the king had taken a vow not to partake of anything that induced unconsciousness, he refused any anesthesia. The doctors were in a dilemma, since the operation was absolutely imperative and so also the anesthesia. They tried to explain to him that it was a matter of opening his abdomen, but he persisted and asked only to be allowed to read the Gita while they operated, and that was enough. The doctors had to give in because delay in operating could be fatal. The king read the Gita throughout the operation, and when it was all over the incredulous doctors asked didn't he feel any pain. He said, "I was so engrossed in my Gita, I was not aware of what was happening."

You only know a thing when you apply your mind to it; you see only what you want to see. When your attention is diverted, everything changes. You are unaware of things that you really want to avoid. If you wander through the market, you will see only those things that interest you: a cobbler will concentrate on leather goods, a jeweler will have eyes only for diamonds. You only see those things that are illumined by your attention. All else remains in darkness.

The most profound art of living is to attain mastery over attention. If you are flowing towards God the world will be lost to you, and it is for this reason that sages call the world *maya,* an illusion. Maya does not mean that the world does not exist. It exists very much, but sages discovered that as their awareness flows God-ward, the world fades from perception. And where awareness is not, the existence or nonexistence of that place becomes irrelevant. Existence is born in the act of perception. It fades when the attention is withdrawn.

The sages say: "God is truth, the world is non-truth." Does this mean that the world we see around us is not there in actuality? It is very much there, but the sage no longer perceives it. If you are greedy wealth is real to you; when greed is gone, riches become like clay. Wealth is not wealth because of itself — but because of your perceptions. Or, with sensuousness the body becomes very significant; without sensuousness it becomes secondary.

Existence shifts with attention; it manifests only in the path of attention. Once you understand this you become your own master. Having discovered the master within, you no longer obey your servants, the disciples, because what is the sense in asking those who do not know themselves? Now you follow and do the bidding of the master within.

Nanak says one alone, dhyana, is the guru of the five. On the superficial level dhyana means attention; on the deeper level dhyana refers to meditation. It is meditation that leads to discovery of the master within. There is nothing more profound — nothing deeper — than meditation, so ponder over it and make no casual passing remarks about something so significant. But people are such that they talk about attention and meditation without any direct knowledge. People who do not know in themselves enjoy talking just for the sake of talking and they cause a great deal of confusion in the world.

We are experimenting with hundreds of different methods of meditation. Someone came to me saying so-and-so asked what is this thing that you are doing? Do you call that meditation? I told him to ask his friend whether he knows what meditation is, and if he does, to learn from him. For the question is not whether you learn from me or from someone else; the aim is to learn meditation. He went back and asked his friend, who replied that he had no experience with meditation and didn't know what it is. Now this same gentleman is very eager to advise his friend on what meditation is not. Not knowing himself what it is, he is ready to give his opinions. So irresponsible are we!

Nanak says ponder well before you speak. Be fully aware and say only if you know yourself. The world has gone astray not because of ignorant people, but because of those all wise and all knowing people who really know nothing, yet love to talk and advise others. Not being conscious of what they are doing, or why, they are just a plague with their opinions and views.

It is not difficult to gather fools around you; you have only to start speaking and continue speaking, no matter what. In a few days you will have gathered a whole band of followers, because there are always people more stupid than you in this world. To find disciples all you need is a little madness in you, some arrogance, and the strength to speak your loudest, and people will flock around you. As people begin to hang around you, many happenings will be attributed to you. The very people who are in total darkness, never having known the light, get caught in your trap when you begin to speak on light; because they feel there is certainly something in you.

Also, people are very imaginative: whatever they wish to happen, they begin to imagine. When the process of imagination begins, dreams are born. If someone imagines his kundalini rising, he may begin to see light or see colors, and when this happens, faith increases in the man who proclaims himself the guru. That is why we find so many gurus.

I know many such gurus who have no knowledge of meditation. When they meet me in private their question is the same: How does one meditate? What is meditation? And these persons have followings of thousands!

Nanak says whatever you say with regard to meditation, you must ponder well before you utter, because it is like playing with fire. Nothing could be more subtle, nor more valuable. The path that leads from the mundane world to God, the supreme spirit, is very thin and fine. You have to contemplate a great deal before you venture to express your thoughts.

Whatever you will say, consider well first.

"Do I know myself? Have I the experience?" If each person in this world were to take a vow to speak only of that which he has knowledge, all deceptions and misconceptions would end. When man is ready to acknowledge his ignorance of things he does not know and realize that he has no right to talk on such matters, then life will become simple and it will not be so difficult to realize truth.

But there is so much untruth all around, such a network of deception and false gurudom that you will not be able to find a true *satguru*, a perfect master. You will not come across a true Nanak, because there are so many impostors vying to be gurus. How can you discern among them? There are no criteria to go by.

Therefore Nanak says speak only after great deliberation, and only after you have known and experienced directly. Don't play with the life of others. This is exactly what you are doing when you advise others on things you are ignorant of yourself. There is no sin greater than misleading a person from the path of knowledge. Theft, murder, deception are nothing compared to it. When you steal you only deprive someone of some earthly possessions, which is hardly of any consequence. When you kill a person you deprive him of his body, but there is no shortage, since new bodies are obtained; you merely snatch the covering, not the *atman*. When you deceive someone what do you gain by it? Something very paltry, nothing of value.

But if you pose as a guru and lead your disciples along paths you have no idea of yourself, you can cause them to wander for endless lives. There can be no deception greater than this, no sin more heinous. There is no greater sinner than an ignorant guru.

Remember, a person can wander from guru to guru and, finding them worthless, his faith is shaken and his hope is lost. He begins to feel that there is nothing but hoax and hypocrisy in the name of religion. When ninety-nine out of one hundred are hypocrites how can one trust the one who is genuine? Such a person, even if he meets a satguru, a Nanak, will invariably be very wary of him, naturally suspecting him to be like the others.

A major reason behind much of the rank atheism in the world is the prevalence of false gurus. Atheism is not an outcome of science as is generally believed, nor does it get its impetus from the atheist philosophers. People have lost faith because of the impostors who masquerade as gurus. It is no longer possible to convince them that there is someone like a genuine master. They also refuse to believe that there is a power that is God.

When the gurus are fakes, how can God be true? This God, and these methods and practices, are merely devices to exploit gullible people — such is the experience of seekers, good people who have been so badly misled.

Thus Nanak exhorts us to speak only after due contemplation because it is like playing with fire, like laying a wager on other people's lives. Think well before you speak or else hold your peace.

Whatever you will say, consider well first;
For the doings of the doer are impossible to assess.

How can we say anything about God? For he has no beginning, no end, nor any limit. The only thing we can possibly do is to be silent about him. What will you say? What can you say about him? What can you say in connection with meditation? Then give it great deliberation and thought.

Understand that meditation is the method; and God, *paramatma*, is at the completion of the experience, the knowledge. You may be able to say something about the path if you have traversed it, but nothing about the destination, which is boundless; it has no limits, no direction. I cannot tell you what God is but I can certainly tell you how I have reached him; the path can be spoken about.

Buddha has said that a buddha can only give a hint and show the path, nothing more. Nanak has said again and again: I am only a physician who can prescribe the medicine. I know nothing about health. The doctor's knowledge is confined only to the treatment of a certain ailment; his medicine cures the disease but he has no knowledge of health, the well-being which fills a person with joy and gratefulness when the illness is gone – he knows nothing about that!

Whatever is spoken about God can only be negative. At most we can say, "He is not this. He is not that." As soon as you say, "He is this," you confine him within a boundary; because only that which bears an outline, a boundary, can be pointed out. The limitless cannot be pointed out. Therefore Nanak says: you can say nothing about God; therefore it is best to keep silent about him.

But nowhere in the world do we find people silent on the subject of God. In fact it is a constant topic of heated discussion. There are seminars and meetings where pundits debate on the existence or nonexistence of God. Busily proving their points, no one worries about the fact that God cannot be proved, much less disproved. God can be known, he can be lived. We can become God, but he cannot be proved nor disproved.

How will you prove that God is? Whatever you say of him will be wrong — absurd and wide of the mark. Or how will you prove that God is not? That will also have to be absurd and irrelevant. Whatever you say about him can only be absurdly incomplete, because God is the totality, the whole. The vast space that spreads all around you and far out into infinity is referred to in that simple word *God.* God is not a person sitting somewhere on high — God is an experience of being drowned, of being bathed in divinity, of being lost in it. God is a state in which you no longer are, and yet you are very much there.

It is a strange and wonderful contradiction; on the one hand you are absolutely annihilated, and on the other hand you are a perfect whole, the ultimate perfection! So God is neither an individual nor a conception nor a hypothesis. God is an experience, the ultimate experience! It is such an experience that you are absorbed in it completely, so lost that there is no one to return and speak about it.

So, says Nanak, nothing can be said about him. Only something can be said about meditation — but that too only if you have experienced it, and after due contemplation. Make it a rule for yourself to speak only of that which you know, and this small rule can transform your life. Forget about the rest of the world; worry only about yourself and don't budge from this rule.

We love to exaggerate. Say we know an inch of something, we want to give a mile's worth of information about it. We know only a grain and we set out to discuss a mountainfull. The state of mind is a state of exaggeration, because the ego revels in overstatements.

Mulla Nasruddin fell down on the road. He became unconscious and was taken to a hospital. When he was placed on the operating table, they found a piece of paper in his pocket on which was written in large letters: "I suffer from epileptic fits. Please do not operate on me for appendicitis. My appendix has already been removed many times."

The mind elaborates with great zest and alacrity. It gets a great kick out of it. A slight knowledge of something and you begin to elaborate, adding spice and color; and the more you color the falser your knowledge becomes till ultimately the essence is lost and only the color remains.

Always say proportionately less of what you know and that will harm no one. Beware of the urge to exaggerate. And this holds good not only in talking about god, but also about meditation, about life and existence. For existence is vast; whatever you have known of it is but an infinitesimal part, not enough to give you the authority to pontificate.

For instance, you are a shopkeeper. You have known only your shop, whereas existence is a vast thing in which there are infinite ways of living. You have not known life in its entirety. While there are thousands of shops dealing in thousands of things, you have only dealt in one particular kind of goods. Even as a shopkeeper you can at most claim to know only one kind of shop, and of the thousands of customers, you can claim to have known but a few; that is the sum total of your experience — a mere grain.

Newton has said, "People think I know a great deal. My own feeling is that the knowledge I have attained is like one grain of sand on the seashore. This one grain is my knowledge, whereas my ignorance is as much as the remaining grains on the shore!"

Direct your attention to what you do not know, what is as yet left to be known. This will make you humble; whereas if you concentrate only on what you know, your back will become stiff with arrogance, as your ego is strengthened. Always concentrate on what is yet to be known, what is yet to be experienced. There you will find endless vistas of knowledge yet to be explored and you will feel the futility of keeping count of the knowledge of things you know; because it will look ludicrous, almost nothing!

Therefore Socrates says: When the sage attains the supreme knowledge he finds there is only one thing that remains to be known — that I know nothing! This is the characteristic of a sage: he knows he knows nothing.

Therefore Nanak says to keep within limits, be simple, be humble. Say only what you know and, on the subject of God ,hold your peace! For what can you say about him? Whatever you say can be no more than gossip. Can an ant speak of the ocean? Who are you to prove his existence or nonexistence? Who has appointed you the judge? Does God depend on your arguments to make him or break him?

Keshav Chandra came to visit Ramakrishna to debate on the existence or nonexistence of God. He elaborated many points to prove that God does not exist. As Ramakrishna listened his heart thrilled with joy. He embraced him lovingly and said, "You have been very kind to come to me, a simple villager. I have never witnessed such magnificent intelligence, and looking at you now I am thoroughly convinced that there can be no greater proof that God is. How can a flower like you ever bloom if it were not for him?"

Keshav Chandra had come expressly to prove that God is not. His arguments were very lucid and clear, his reasoning so subtle. Such a great logician and genius is born only once in a thousand years. Though it was very difficult to answer him, Ramakrishna did not put forth even a single counter-argument! Ramakrishna was so filled with love and delight at the sight of Keshav Chandra, and was so genuinely convinced thereby of the fact of God's existence that Keshav Chandra was struck dumb by his pure ecstasy. Ramakrishna told him, "That *you* exist is proof that the world is not just material. If such a process of intelligence can be, if reasoning can be so subtle, then this world is not of matter alone; it is not as gross as the stone; there surely is a consciousness hidden within it. For me, your very being has proved that God is."

Keshav Chandra returned home and wrote in his diary that this man had won over him. It is difficult to defeat a religious man who offers no arguments. You can only defeat a person who reasons and argues, where all that is required is to be a better debater, a cleverer speaker.

A religious man gives you no ground for a debate when he refuses to compete with you. He says: I believe in God. I have faith in God. I have no opinion or decisions to make about him. God is my feeling, not my thought. God is in my heart and not in my head. And the heart keeps silent. A religious man is always silent when questioned about God. Ask him about meditation and he will speak, but only as much as he knows directly.

People in ancient times were honest. There is a beautiful story in connection with Buddha's search for truth.

For six years Buddha had gone from guru to guru. After each guru taught him all that he knew, he would move on to another. Then the moment came when Buddha knew all that the gurus knew. Buddha asked the last guru, "What shall I do now?"

"I have taught you all that I know," said the guru. "You will have to look for someone else."

This last guru of Buddha was Alar-Kalam. As Buddha took leave of him Alar-Kalam said, "I have revealed all knowledge that I have attained and have no more to give. Go forth and seek another who can direct you further, but do not forget to impart that knowledge also to me!"

This is the reason that many people of the past attained wisdom, for honesty was a part of their nature. In today's world who worries about honesty? If you can put forth your arguments impressively, it doesn't matter whether you really know what you are talking about, because people are bound to flock around you. It is a matter of how you advertise yourself, like any marketable commodity. If you advertise well, if you succeed in awakening the passion and the greed of the people, you are bound to attract a formidable clientele. It is so easy to become such a guru!

Therefore Nanak says to be very careful what you say about meditation, because it is religion that supports the earth. By even a few right or wrong statements you can upset the lives of thousands of people; one wrong statement can sow confusion for endless births. Religion is not a small matter; it is the basis of your life, the support of all existence. Only speak what you truly know about religion. To develop a false conception of religion is to lose all that supports and maintains your being. Religion upholds and maintains the earth. It arises out of compassion and pity, and the establishment of contentment forms its equilibrium.

Let the following lines go deep within you:

Religion upholds the earth and is born of compassion.
Establish contentment and create the balance.

Religion is the basis of all life, of all existence. Without it existence cannot hold together; the world would fall apart. It is the foundation on which stands the mansion of existence. All else is like the other building materials, like bricks, mortar, cement. Religion is the foundation, the innate quality of our nature. It is in the very nature of fire to give heat; without heat there cannot be a fire. It is the nature of the sun to give light; if it does not it will no longer be the sun, it will have lost its quality, its innate character, its dharma.

Jesus often said: If salt loses its quality of saltiness, how can you make it salty again? There is no way. Anything that loses its intrinsic quality is no longer that thing; it was what it was because of its very nature, its quality.

The sun is the sun because it gives light; fire is fire because it gives heat. And man is man because of meditation — that is his nature! The person who loses the quality to meditate is a person in name only. Though he still looks like a human being he is actually an animal, because he lives like an animal. We never criticize an animal who lives according to its nature. We never tell the dog he is behaving like a dog; that has no meaning to him. But we sometimes tell a person he is behaving like a dog or, "Don't be an ass!"

We can say this to a human being because he is not an actual human being unless he becomes properly established in meditation; that is his natural self. A Buddha, a Kabir, a Nanak are proper human beings. But the bulk of humanity has fallen so low that we call such special people *avatara*, "incarnates." Naturally we do not look upon them as human beings, for then what are we? We would have to rate ourselves lower, but to maintain that we are human beings, we have to create a special place for them just a little above us, that of the incarnate. It solves our problem, to call them godlike — no, gods — and remain human beings ourselves. But we are *not* human beings.

Manushya means man. It contains the root *mana*, which means mind. The words must be understood. When a person is deeply established in meditation, he becomes manushya, because consciousness and awareness as a higher state of mind is the nature of man. When you attain your own consciousness, you find that it is the portal to the consciousness of all of existence. So the only way for man to reach God is to discover the innermost basis of his own nature.

Religion upholds the earth and is born of compassion.
Establish contentment and create the balance.

Religion is the support, the nature, the basis of all life. It is the son of compassion. Establish contentment and the equilibrium is established.

Compassion, contentment are two very valuable words, because the whole life of the seeker can be contained within them. Contentment within and compassion without must be balanced on the scales. Be always satisfied within your own self and ever-compassionate towards others, never contentment based on others nor compassion for one's own self.

Understand that we do just the opposite. We see a man dying of hunger, or lying on the streets writhing with pain, and we say: Life is as it should be. You have to take it as it comes. Though we may have been taught that contentment is the satisfaction that things are as they should be, we misuse it. It should be contentment in what one has, but compassion for others. On the other hand, if I know that I am where I should be, and there is no need whatever to change, that whatever fate has given me is enough, then I am satisfied and fulfilled as I am.

Unrest and turbulence follows in the wake of dissatisfaction: when I feel things are not happening as I would wish them to happen, that I am not as I should be; that I have not been given what I am worthy of receiving; that God does not seem to be pleased with me; that there is some injustice; that I am not appreciated as I should be; that I definitely deserve more fame, more wealth... as soon as these thoughts of dissatisfaction begin to gather in your mind, you will feel the lack of things and your restlessness begins. Your mind will concentrate on all that you do not have and see only insufficiency and misery.

When there is satisfaction towards one's self, then you begin to feel and notice all that you have. And when you begin to realize all that you have, you are filled with thanks and gratefulness towards him who has given you so much, thinking surely I don't deserve all of this!

Contentment towards oneself, and *compassion towards others.* You must do whatever is possible for you to do for others — and more; give happiness and peace, whether they receive it from you or not, and don't worry or be discontented on that account — it is your own affair. So keep it to yourself if you tried your best and could not relieve a person of his pain or suffering. Let it not dishearten you; don't reproach yourself, but maintain your contentment.

But we tend to become contented about the lot of others and sympathize with ourselves. This is what has happened in India and caused its downfall, this is why India is poor, sick and miserable. Where others are concerned we say, God's will. But where we ourselves are concerned, we are not prepared to take what comes to us and fight to the bitter end. There we do not say: God's will.

Self-centeredness and selfishness lead us to proclaim: "Thy will be done! — as long as he has made me wealthy and the other poor. "Whatever is written in our destiny we get" — as long as I am the master and others are slaves. We are without pity for the lot of the destitute, having wasted all our feelings of compassion on ourselves.

The words *compassion* and *contentment* are priceless; only change their direction and they become dangerous. If we are satisfied with our own lot we enjoy infinite peace and tranquility in life; we become wholly fulfilled. If we can be compassionate and sympathetic towards others, we shall wipe out poverty and misery. Kindness and compassion develop into a sense of service to others that fills you with prayer and worship, because it then becomes the path that leads to God.

If you are kind to others but dissatisfied with your own self, you will end up a social worker; you will never become religious. If you are satisfied with yourself but have no compassion for others, you become a lifeless holy man. Having lost all that is precious and meaningful in life, such people run away to the jungles. They are satisfied with their own selves but without an iota of compassion. They succeed in finding their own happiness but they are the ultra-selfish people. If you look into their eyes there is no sign of pity, only a ruthless stare.

Ask the Jaina *muni*, who is busy accomplishing his own self-contentment, "What of kindness and sympathy for others?" "We all have to reap the fruits of our actions. What can I do about it?" he will reply. While he is cultivating his own satisfaction, his sadhana is incomplete; there is no balance.

Look at a Christian missionary. He cultivates compassion and kindness: he does not mind the jungles, or the *adavasis*, the poor primitive tribal man whom he serves with such fanatical zeal; no work is too mean for him. But he is dissatisfied within himself.

All these people are incomplete: the Christian missionary has compassion, the Jaina *muni* is self-contented, but there is no balance. If one side of the scales is heavier than the other, because of this lack of equilibrium, the instrument of existence cannot be tuned to resonate with the divine melody.

So Nanak says:

> *Religion... is born of compassion.*
> *Establish contentment and create the balance.*
> *Whoever understands becomes the truth...*

He who embodies both compassion and contentment — in their right proportion and the right direction — attains the supreme comprehension of life. He will then know what religion is; he becomes truth incarnate. The ideal is: satisfaction within and compassion without; meditation within, love and kindness without.

Buddha describes a similar ideal utilizing the words *compassion* and *wisdom*: wisdom within, compassion without. Until such time that both of these are present, whatever the knowledge, it can only be false. The lack of either leaves knowledge incomplete.

By merely being compassionate to others you do not reach anywhere; you have to do something within yourself also. No matter how many difficulties you endure to serve the downtrodden and the sick, if you do not cultivate contemplation within, awaken your remembrance and meditate, you can reach nowhere. If you have not found the one within the five senses, you yourself are still an ill person.

Just as you walk on two feet and birds need two wings to fly, just as you need two eyes to get a proper view of the world that surrounds you, so in exactly the same manner you need two wings for the ultimate journey. Nanak calls them compassion and contentment.

*Whoever understands becomes the truth
And knows the burden religion bears.
There are many worlds and many more beyond them;*

Scientists acknowledge that there are at least fifty thousand worlds within the limits of their discoveries, and how many more beyond these? Life does not exist on this planet alone but probably on tens of thousands of other planets. How can you perceive an expanse so enormous with your limited mind? You will have to put it aside.

As soon as the mind becomes silent the window falls away and you find yourself under the open skies. Then you begin to see how vast the expanse of existence is, how infinite! And when you realize the exquisite glory of existence, you wonder why you were lost in feeble nothings all this while: someone abused you, someone insulted you, a thorn pricked your foot or you had a headache — such is the story of your life! While the magnificent phenomenon of existence is taking place every moment around you, you are involved in futile matters. Your calculations were all of the wrong kind; while infinite wealth was raining around, you were counting shells.

*There are many worlds and many more beyond them;
What power assumes their weight?
Creatures of all forms and colors are created by his writ,
But only few know the rule to tell it.
Can anyone write the account of this mystery?
If it were written how great it would be.
What strength and power! How beautiful his appearance!
How great his charity; who can conceive it?
His single word creates this vast expanse —
Infinite mountains and rivers, the animate and inanimate.
How shall I think about it?
However much I offer myself could never be enough!
Whatever pleases you, O Lord, is best for me.
You are the formless, the almighty — you who abide forever!*

As soon as you step aside from your silly involvements you will see your present state. It is as if it were raining rubies and diamonds outside while you have shut yourself inside your house, holding your rubble and stones tight against your chest for fear you might lose them.

Where in your thoughts do you abide? What engages your attention? What discussions and arguments are going on within you? If you examine these you will find them very petty and insignificant, so trivial as to be unworthy of any consideration, but you have wasted all your life in them.

And Nanak says: "When the mind is set aside, when you are in the no-mind state and the sound of Omkar begins to vibrate within you, you begin to witness the glory of existence, its vastness; you see the infinite life, the overflowing boundless nectar, the limitless beauty and the unaccountable power that has no beginning, no end. All this you see when you enter his court. And then you realize you can never even imagine such vast existence o guess at its wonderful taste. But alas, how foolishly we are frittering away all chance of this wonderful experience."

Nanak asks: "How shall I think about it? It is to stand dumbfounded, the eyes filled with surprise and wonder. The trouble is we never lift our eyes upwards, having kept them firmly focused on the pebbles and stones."

How is one to think of nature? Even if I offer myself in sacrifice a thousand times it is but a paltry gesture. And how shall I repay the limitless phenomena that happen every moment, the infinite nectar that showers incessantly? I cannot, I cannot, even if I offer myself on the sacrificial fire a thousand times. Such a feeling of gratefulness is born; and such thanksgiving is the real prayer.

The words Nanak uses in prayer are priceless: "What pleases you, O Lord, is best for me. Thy will be done!" In such moments your desires and wishes will drop off and there will be only one prayer on your lips: O Lord, do not fulfill my wishes; let only your will be done! For whatever you ask is bound to be mean and insignificant. Children always ask for toys and foolish people ask for foolish things.

Then you will say to him: "Let not my desires be gratified, O Lord, because what you have ordained is best for me. Who am I to decide what should be and what should not? Whatever you will is always the best. What does not come to pass is surely not for my good. There is only one criterion, one proof — whatever you will is forever the best. You are the formless, the almighty, the birthless one!"

The Lord is forever. It is I who exist at specific times and become nonexistent at others. My being is like a bubble of water. He is the ocean. I am a wave. And what can a wave ask? It lives but for a moment, then how can its desires be real? The last words of Jesus are truly priceless — "Thy will be done, O Lord!"

Whatever pleases you, O Lord, is best for me.
You are the formless, the almighty — you who abide forever!.

Doubt raised its ugly head even within the mind of Jesus when he was being hung on the cross. At the very moment that the nails were being hammered into his limbs and the blood began to flow there was a moment — just a single moment that is so very valuable because it demonstrates how weak man is. All of humanity manifested its complete helplessness through Jesus. And Jesus said in that moment, "What are you showing me? What is this you are doing unto me, O Lord?"

The question arose, and though Jesus did not really doubt his Lord, even so there is a slight suggestion of doubt. It is a very personal question which Jesus asks, "What is this you wish to show me?" And doubt lurks behind the question. One thing is certain, that Jesus was not happy about what was taking place. He did not approve of the cross, the hammering of nails. Something was happening which should not be happening.

So it is a complaint, all right; and the complaints of all humanity manifested in the words of Jesus. You will also experience these moments in your own life when all your faith will be shaken and your mind will cry out, "What is happening?" You will doubt the bonafides of God; you placed so much faith in him and is this the result? But this in itself proves that you have not trusted him wholly; or else you would accept whatever happened. If your acceptance bears even a little hesitation within, it is not perfect acceptance. If you accept complainingly, your acceptance is incomplete; your faith must be wholehearted — whatever he wishes.

But Jesus pulled himself together. For just one single moment the entire race of mankind trembled through Jesus, for only one moment, then Jesus raised his head and said, "Thy will be done, O Lord! Thy will, not mine." At that moment the man faded and Christ was born. Jesus disappeared and Christ manifested in his place. So small is the distance between Jesus and Christ, the distance of a single moment. How great a difference lies between ignorance and knowledge, between Buddha and you, between Nanak and you! No matter how high you ascend, one fear always nags at your heart — is my wish being gratified? The devotee also always keeps an eye on God: is he doing his bidding? If not, he complains. No matter how tender the words he uses, a complaint is a complaint, and the thorn keeps pricking within.

The perfect devotee has no complaints; his confidence in him is complete: Whatever you will is best for me. You are my protection. You are the eternal, the formless, the almighty. I am but a wave; where is there any question of my will? Thy will be done. Thy will is my will. The wave's desire cannot be different from the ocean; the leaf's desire cannot be different from the tree; the limb's desire cannot be different from the body's. In this manner one should let go of one's self like a drop in the ocean.

However, this is possible only when you discover the one behind the five. As you are now, you do not exist; then whom shall you seek? Right now you are so divided within yourself that there is a crowd within, not one whole integrated individual. Then how will you take the jump when some parts are going right and some left, and others in other directions? You do not exist as one individual. Scattered in many fragments, your being has no meaning.

So the first thing Nanak says is: "Seek the one behind the five — seek attention, awareness, meditation!" And the second thing is: "As meditation grows stronger, let there be contentment within, compassion without. As compassion firmly takes root, contentment will become more profound, and you will experience the dawning of the feeling of gratitude and thanksgiving, and you will say, 'Thy way, not mine, O Lord!' This is the ultimate, the culmination of perfection."

CHAPTER 8

Countless Ways

There are countless ways to repeat his name and express devotion,
Countless ways of worship and purification.
There are countless scriptures and countless mouths to recite them,
Countless ways of yoga to make the mind dispassionate.
There are countless devotees who contemplate his virtues and
  knowledge,
Countless who are virtuous and generous.
There are countless brave men who risk their lives because him,
Countless who vow to silence and meditate on him.
Nanak says: how shall I praise him?
However much I offer myself could never be enough!
Whatever pleases you, O Lord, is best for me.
You are the formless, the almighty — you who abide forever!
There are countless ignorant fools and countless who are blind,
Countless thieves and shirkers.
There are countless numbers who ruled by force before they
  departed,
Countless murderers who earn only by murder.
There are countless sinners who commit nothing but sin,
Countless liars who live by their lies.
There are countless barbarians eating only filth because food,
Countless fault-finders who fill their heads with scandal.
Thus Nanak ponders on the wicked and the low.
However much I offer myself could never be enough!
Whatever pleases you, O Lord, is best because me.
You are the formless, the almighty — you who abide forever!

Countless are the names and the places where you dwell,
Countless worlds that have never been reached.
To say countless is to burden the mind.
Through the letter comes the name, and all the prayers.
Through the letter is all knowledge and songs in his praise.
Through the letter is all writing and speaking,
Through the letter are all events destined.
All destiny has already been written,
But he who writes is beyond destiny.
All creation is his name;
There is no place that is not his name.
Nanak says: How shall I praise him?
However much I offer myself could never be enough!
Whatever pleases you, O Lord, is best for me.
You are the formless, the almighty — you who abide forever!

There are infinite paths open to the seeker. Which one should he choose? And on what basis? Is there some criterion because choice? Not only are there infinite paths to truth, but there are equally infinite paths to non-truth. What protection is there from taking wrong paths, to escape futile wanderings? The greatest problem because a seeker is how to choose the right path and distinguish the wrong ones. Once we recognize that a path is wrong, we begin to steer away from it, because how can one continue along a road which is known to go in the wrong direction? You are bound to shun it. The knowledge of non-truth is in itself freedom from it. But how is one to decide among such infinite choices?

The moment of recognition of truth is also the first leap into experiencing it. No sooner is it recognized than it imparts its color to you and you develop wings and the flight begins. But again — there are innumerable truths. Infinite paths have been discovered in the course of centuries — so numerous, so very complex and involved as to defy any solution. So Nanak asks what is the seeker to do? These verses deal with this problem.

There are countless ways to repeat his name and express devotion,
Countless ways of worship and purification.
There are countless scriptures and countless mouths to recite them,

Countless ways of yoga to make the mind dispassionate.
There are countless devotees who sing his praises and contemplate the knowledge,
Countless who are virtuous and generous.
There are countless brave men who risk their lives because him,
Countless who vow to silence and meditate on him.

What is the seeker to do? How is he to choose his path? "Which path is right because me? Since I am truly ignorant, therefore I seek; and in my ignorance I have no way to test what is gold, what is dust. What can my best be worth when I am so ignorant and uninformed?" A person who has never seen gold, though he possess a touchstone will never know the value of gold. He who has known only mind all his life, will also take gold to be an aspect of mind. We can only recognize what is within our field of experience. We have not known God; we have not reached that far. Which way will lead up to him?

There seems to be only one way, what scientists call trial and error. Seek, experience, wander again and again, and with constant trial and error you will find the right path.

But if we follow this trial and error method we may never arrive, because life is so short and the paths so numerous; we can barely complete a simple path in the course of one lifetime. How is one to gather experience? Who is the guru? How is one to know and recognize him so that we may follow him?

The problem gets more and more intricate. Were it only a question of choosing one among many right paths, it would not be so hazardous, because whichever one we chose would ultimately lead to reality. But there are so many false paths for every right path, that only one in a million attains truth. The rest wander about blindly creating their own paths, writing their own scriptures.

Things were easier in ancient times when the Vedas were the only texts on spiritual science; then there were no Mohammedans or Christians or Buddhists. Whenever there was a question the Vedas provided the answer. It was so convenient to have only one single book of scripture offering the gospel truth. Now there are infinite Vedas, infinite scriptures. It is impossible to thread your way through them. Which scripture will you consult? The Jainas have their own scripture, so also the Mohammedans and the Hindus, the Catholics, the Jews. And they do not have one but many. The *Guru Granth Sahib* is a scripture that has been added to many times. As the number increased, so also our problem of deciding on a path.

Perhaps this is why mankind has turned atheist. It is well nigh impossible to choose a path, or even to believe in God, under the influence of so many philosophies running at cross purposes, each trying to disprove the others.

Ask the Jainas, they say Vedas have nothing in them. Ask a Buddhist, he will say Vedas are meaningless. Ask the Vedantist and ne proclaims that everything besides the Vedas is useless and trivial and leads a person astray. Ask the Hindu and he says: Buddhists and Jainas are atheists. If a single word from them enters your ears, you are lost. The Hindu says the Vedas are the oldest scriptures and hence worthy of our trust. Ask a Mohammedan and he says: the Koran is the latest scripture and therefore the most authentic, because when a new order comes from above, all old orders are automatically superseded.

The Hindu says that once only did God send down the Vedas. There is no need for any new scripture since God is not a human being who errs or needs to improve upon his work. He is the ultimate knowledge, the Vedas are his only true words, and therefore all else is false. God, having once made his order known, all else that follows is merely a device of man. The Christians and the Mohammedans however say that the universe undergoes perpetual change; since man changes, God must change too. Orders change because situations change. Therefore believe in what is new, not in what is old and outdated.

Whom will you heed? Whom will you believe? You are ultimately left with your own understanding. You stand with legs trembling in the midst of this vast entanglement.

Man has turned to atheism because it is becoming infinitely harder to have faith in something. Some way has to be found by which a simple, innocent human being can believe, can again become a theist. While the greatest of philosophers have failed to decide on the choices, what is a simple human being to do? He has neither the means nor the time nor the armor of reasoning and logic. Which path is he to choose and how?

Nanak's suggestion is priceless: It is futile to wander in these infinite paths. I know of only one solution and that is:

Whatever pleases you, O Lord, is best for me.

Therefore I leave myself entirely to your pleasure. I cannot choose for myself for I am ignorant and stand in darkness; I am blind. I have nothing on the strength of which I can set out to seek. I have no means to test the authenticity of my path. What shall I do? I surrender myself at thy feet — thy will be done.

Thy will be done: I sit at your command, I stand at your command; whatever I do is your command. I do not bring myself into it at all. If you make me wander I shall wander; if you make me reach the destination, it is your will. I shall not complain if I wander, nor shall I pride myself if I arrive, because all is your will. I shall not be the decider. This is exactly what Krishna means when he says to Arjuna in the Gita: "Leave all religious duties aside and surrender unto me." These are words spoken on behalf of God.

What Nanak says are the words of the devotee: "What pleases you is best for me. The path you choose is the path for me. In your will lies my salvation. I shall not care to choose, lead me where you please. If it is your will that I should wander, then that is the path for me. If it is your will to leave me in darkness then I shall take it to be the light for me. If you make the day into night, I shall accept it as night. Thy way, not mine, O Lord!"

This is very very difficult, because your ego will keep interfering time and time again. Your mind will keep asking what is all this? Could it be that God has made a mistake? Am I wrong in placing my faith completely in him? When things are going well, you will put your trust in him, but when things do not go as you wish, trouble starts; and that is the true time of test, that is the time for your practice.

For instance when there are flowers spread everywhere before you, you will say with Nanak: "Your will is my will." But when you are caught in the midst of suffering, when there is nothing but insult and failure all around, then is the real time to test your faith, your practice. In sorrow and pain also, you should be able to say with Nanak: "Thy way, not mine O Lord! I am happy in whatever you choose for me!" In sorrow and suffering you must also accept what he gives.

But this acceptance must not be a pretended show of contentment. Keep in mind that sometimes we assume a false sense of contentment when we find ourselves helpless. When there is suffering and unhappiness with no way out, then the easiest thing is to say, Thy will be done. But our dissatisfaction lies hidden behind our words. Outwardly we accept but inwardly we feel that it should not have been! What we wished for did not come to pass, we could not do anything about it either. We are helpless, powerless, impotent — so the best thing is to accept his will.

Had you uttered these words of Nanak in a state of helplessness and resignation you would not have understood the real meaning of these words. Contentment is not a pitiful state; it is the state of the highest blessedness. These are not words spoken for consolation when nothing else can be done, but as the manifestation of truth. Understand well that it should not be an act of deceiving and consoling one's own self.

Generally this feeling comes about after a person has tried his very best to get out of some trying circumstances. Having made full use of his sense of doing, he finds himself defeated on all sides, and then he turns to him in desperation, leaving everything to him; but this is no real surrendering. From the very beginning you should not make any effort to change your circumstances, but leave everything in his hands.

Nanak's concept of supreme surrender is the ultimate spiritual path, the highest practice of a devotee. Then you needn't worry about choosing a path or method or scripture. You needn't worry about logic or proof of any philosophy; you have no use for any of these. The devotee rids himself of all these in the one stroke of surrender. He leaves everything at one time and cries out: "Thy way, not mine, O Lord! Thy will be done!"

Experiment a little and you will understand. Nanak is no philosopher. He has not written a scripture, his words are the expression of his inner feelings. He is giving voice to his own experience. You will have difficulty at every step because of the ego, whose very cry is: *I know what is right and what should be.*

There is a short story by Tolstoy: The god of death sent his angel to earth as an emissary to bring back the soul of a woman who had just died. The angel found himself in a dilemma because the woman had given birth to triplets. All three were girls: one was still sucking milk from the dead mother, another was crying and the third was so exhausted that it had fallen asleep. Such was the state — three little babies, the mother lying dead and no one to look after them, since the father was already dead and there was no one else in the family.

The angel returned without the woman's soul and told the god of death: "Forgive me, I did not bring back the woman's soul. You can't be aware of what I have just witnessed: there are three little babies that this woman has given birth to, one still suckling at her breast. There is no one to care for them. Can't you allow a little time to the mother so that the girls are big enough to look after themselves?"

"So you have become very clever and wise, it seems," said the god of death, "perhaps wiser than he who wills both death and life to all mortal beings. You have committed the first sin for which you shall be punished. You will have to return to earth and, until such time as you laugh three times at your own foolishness, you shall not return."

Understand this: laugh three times at your foolishness. The ego always laughs at the nonsense of others. When you can laugh at you own absurdity, the ego breaks. The angel readily agreed to undergo the punishment. He was quite certain he was right under the circumstances, and wondered how he would find an opportunity to laugh at himself. He was ejected from heaven.

It was almost winter. A cobbler, who was on his way to buy warm clothes for his children, came upon a poor man, bare to the bones and trembling in the cold. It was none other than our friend the angel. The cobbler felt sorry for him. Instead of buying the children's clothes with his hard-earned money, he went and bought clothes and a blanket for the naked man. When he also came to know that he had nothing to eat and nowhere to go, he offered him the shelter of his own house. However, he warned him that his wife was bound to get angry but he should not be upset, everything would be all right later on.

The cobbler arrived home with the angel. Neither the cobbler nor the wife had any idea who he really was. As soon as they entered the door the wife fired off a volley of abuse at her husband for what he had done.

The angel laughed for the first time.

The cobbler asked him why he laughed. "When I have laughed again I shall tell you," he answered, knowing that the cobbler's wife was unaware that the very presence of an angel who was her unwanted guest would confer a thousand benefits.

But how far can the human mind see? For the wife it was a loss of warm clothing for the kids. She can only see the loss, but not what had been found — and free of cost, at that. So he laughed, because she didn't know what was happening around her.

Within seven days he learned the shoemaker's trade, and within a few months the cobbler's fame had spread far and wide. Even kings and noblemen ordered their shoes here, and money began to flow in an endless stream.

One day the king's servant came to the shop, bringing special leather in order to have a pair of shoes made for the king. "Take care you make no mistakes, for this is the only piece of leather of its kind," said the servant. "Also, remember, the king wants shoes and not slippers." In Russia, slippers are worn by a dead person on his last journey. The cobbler gave special instructions to the angel to be extra careful with the king's orders, or else they would be in trouble.

In spite of this the angel made slippers for the king. The cobbler was beside himself with rage. He was certain now he would be hanged. He ran to beat the angel with his stick. The angel laughed out loud at the very moment that a man came running from the king's court, saying, "The king is dead. Please change the shoes into slippers."

The future is unknown; only he knows what is to be. Man's decisions are all based on the past. When the king was alive he needed shoes, when he died he required slippers. The cobbler fell at the angel's feet and begged forgiveness. The angel replied, "Don't worry. I am undergoing my own punishment." And he laughed again.

The cobbler said, "What makes you laugh?"

The angel said, "I laughed for the second time because we do not know the future and we still persist in desires which are never fulfilled, because fate has different plans. The cosmic law works, destiny is set out, and we have no say in the matter. Yet we raise a hue and cry about things as if we are the makers of our destiny. The king is about to die, but he orders shoes for himself! Life is drawing to a close and we keep planning for the future."

Suddenly the angel thought of the triplets: I did not know what their future was going to be. Then why did I intervene unnecessarily in their affairs?

Soon the third event took place. Three young girls, accompanied by an old rich woman, came into the shop to order shoes. The angel recognized the girls as the daughters of the dead woman who had been the cause of his punishment. All three girls were happy and beautiful. The angel asked the old woman about the girls, and she said, "These are the three daughters of my neighbor. The mother was very poor, and died while nursing her newborn babies. I felt pity for such helpless babies and, since I had no children of my own, I adopted them."

Had the mother been alive, the girls would have grown up in poverty and suffering. Because the mother died the girls grew up in riches and comfort, and now they were heirs to the old woman's fortune. They were also to be married into the royal family.

The angel laughed for the third time.

He told the cobbler, "My third laugh is because of these girls. I was wrong. Destiny is great, while our vision is limited to what we can see. What we cannot see is so vast. We cannot imagine the enormity of that which we cannot see and of that which is to be. Having laughed at my foolishness three times, my penalty is completed and now I must leave."

What Nanak says is that if you stop putting yourself in the middle, and stop getting in your own way, you will find the path of paths.

Then you needn't worry about other paths. Leave all to him and be thankful for whatever he has caused to happen for you, for whatever he is making you do this moment, for whatever he will cause you to perform. All praise unto him! Give him a blank check of gratitude. Whatever he has chosen for you and through you, whether you liked it or not, whether you were praised or blamed, whether people called it your good fortune or misfortune, let there not be even a trace of difference in your thankfulness.

Nanak sees only one path and that is: "You are the formless, the almighty, you who abide forever. I am too small, like a wave in the ocean. I leave everything to you. You have given me so much. Your bounteous grace pours all the time everywhere; so much so that if I were to give myself as an offering a thousand times, it would be too insignificant. He knows only one path: Whatever pleases you is best for me."

> *There are countless ways to repeat his name and express devotion,*
> *Countless ways of worship and purification.*
> *There are countless scriptures and countless mouths to recite them,*
> *Countless ways of yoga to make the mind dispassionate.*
> *There are countless devotees who contemplate his virtues and knowledge,*
> *Countless who are virtuous and generous.*
> *There are countless brave men who risk their lives for him,*
> *Countless who vow to silence and meditate on him.*
> *Nanak says: How shall I praise him?*
> *However much I offer myself could never be enough!*
> *Whatever pleases you, O Lord, is best for me.*
> *You are the formless, the almighty — you who abide forever!*

On the one hand is the congregation of saints and philosophers who have with great deliberation devised untold methods for finding truth; but unfortunately, just because of the countless methods, truth was lost.

> *There are countless ignorant fools and countless who are blind,*
> *Countless thieves and shirkers.*
> *There are countless numbers who ruled by force before they departed,*

Countless murderers who earn only by murder.
There are countless sinners who commit nothing but sin,
Countless liars who live by their lies.
There are countless barbarians eating only filth for food,
Countless fault-finders who fill their heads with scandal.
Thus Nanak ponders on the wicked and the low.
However much I offer myself could never be enough!
Whatever pleases you, O Lord, is best for me.
You are the formless, the almighty — you who abide forever!

On the other hand, there is the crowd of the wicked, the sinners, the murderers and the lustful. They too, with all the skill of their egos, have found countless paths to circumvent truth. They are creative innovators of lies. They are great discoverers who have uncovered delightful untruths, created beautiful tantalizing dreams. Anybody can be caught by their hypnosis and led astray.

One can go astray either by choosing a wrong path or by remaining undecided about which right path to follow; in both cases you will fall into error. Says Nanak: "I care for neither. Whatever you choose is best for me. I care not what the virtuous say, I care not what the sinners say. I choose neither sin nor virtue, neither the right path nor the wrong. I choose nothing; I leave all to you. Whatever you make me do is auspicious. Wherever you take me is favorable for me. Whichever path you indicate is the path for me. It matters not whether the goal is reached or not reached.

Understand this: if the desire for attainment lurks within, you will not be able to leave everything to him. Then all your attention will remain on the goal and you will always be anxious about your progress. Your surrender will be incomplete and half-hearted, which is worse than no surrender at all.

No! There is no question of either reaching or not reaching the destination, because there is no longer any destination. To abandon all thought of destination is the destination itself. Surrender is the ultimate quality for the devotee. Nothing remains after this. Then if he makes the devotee sink to the lowest depths, the seeker feels himself raised higher and higher. If he throws him in the darkest pit, the devotee feels the sun rising from a thousand directions. The question is not where you are going, nor what you are attaining, but what is your innermost feeling?

Nanak's method is totally a method of surrender.

> *Countless are the names and the places where you dwell,*
> *Countless worlds that have never been reached.*
> *To say countless is to burden the mind.*
> *Through the letter comes the name, and all the prayers.*
> *Through the letter is all knowledge and songs in his praise.*
> *Through the letter is all writing and speaking,*
> *Through the letter are all events destined.*
> *All destiny has already been written,*
> *But he who writes is beyond destiny.*
> *All creation is his name;*
> *There is no place that is not his name.*
> *Nanak says: How shall I praise him?*
> *However much I offer myself could never be enough!*
> *Whatever pleases you, O Lord, is best for me.*
> *You are the formless, the almighty — you who abide forever!*

His name! There have been almost as many discovered as there are people in the world. Each makes his choice. There is a Hindu scripture, *Vishnu Sahastranam*, which is nothing but the names of God. Mohammedans have their own names. It is both a Hindu and Mohammedan tradition to name their children after some name of God: we find Rehman, Rahim, Abdulla, which are all Islamic names of God, and Ram, Krishna, Hari, which are Hindu names of God.

If we were to consider all the various names, we would find them to be as varied as there are people in the world. And yet there is a way out: no matter how many names we coin, they are all the product of the human mind. He is without name. Therefore, whatever name we give him, that will do.

So Nanak says: Which name of yours shall I repeat? Which name shall I call you by? Which name should I take that will reach you. The seeker is always worried about which name would be best. It is common knowledge that when we write a letter you have to write the address and so we pay the utmost attention to the name and address.

The True Name

It happened once that Mulla Nasruddin was working for a man who had a weakness for writing anonymous letters. He sent them to ministers, newspaper editors, and also to the intellectuals of the town. One day he wrote a letter and gave it to Nasruddin, who promptly went and posted it.

"Where is the letter? Have you posted it?" he asked Nasruddin.

"Yes", said Nasruddin.

"But I hadn't yet addressed the envelope. Couldn't you see that?"

"I did notice it," said the Mulla, "but I thought this time you wanted to keep the address anonymous as well."

If you keep the address secret how can the letter be delivered? How will you address a letter so that it reaches him? Thus his name is essential. There is a constant search for a name befitting him, which would evoke a response from him. Says Nanak: Either all names are his or no name is his. The *akshara*, the letter, *is* his name. Akshara means the letter and also that which cannot be erased. A, B, C, D can be rubbed out after they are written. And the reason for calling the letters akshara is very meaningful. It implies that which is meaningful, that which is authentic and inexpressible; what is written is only the reflection thereof.

It is like this: there is the moon in the sky, and there is a lake below in which the moon is reflected. Disturb the water and the reflected moon breaks in a thousand pieces, because it is perishable. But no matter how much you try to stir things up, it has no effect on the moon, which is indestructible. Our language is only an echo of the language of God. Whatever we write in books and on boards is mere reflection which can be erased at any moment. But the source from which the words come is beyond extinction. You who are speaking are destructible, but that which speaks through you is beyond extinction.

So Nanak says akshara is his name, and the letter can be neither written nor erased. Other than akshara, all is man's creation. What is this akshara, this letter, the word?

We do have a very close echo of akshara in Omkar. The whole philosophical system of Nanak is based on this one focal point, *Ek*

Omkar Satnam — that is all. Know these three words and you will know the whole *Japuji;* you will then understand Nanak in his fullness, because that is the essence of his verse. Akshara, according to Nanak, is Omkar — there is one resonance that vibrates even without being expressed or written. And this resonance is beyond annihilation, it is the very music of existence; therefore there is no way of destroying it. When everything else is destroyed, it will still go on.

It is said in the Bible, what is invariably repeated in all scriptures: *In the Beginning was the word.* What is referred to as the word, the *logos* in the West, is Omkar. In the beginning was the word; all the rest followed later, and when all else is no more the word will still resonate; everything will be absorbed in it.

India has developed various methods of *Shabad yoga,* the yoga of the word. The practice consists only of the word. Its significance is to make oneself wordless so that the speaker is silenced, and then what is heard is the voice of God. This is what the yoga claims.

Nanak says: *Countless are your names and the places where you dwell, and countless the realms where no one has yet been.* What is the sense in saying countless when it only increases the burden on your mind? In truth, to speak about God is only to increase the load of words; because whatever you say only magnifies the burden on your mind, because whatever you say will be basically wrong.

Suppose a man stands at the shore of an ocean and pronounces: "This ocean is boundless." If he has not tried to measure the ocean and is only making a statement, what is the use of it? The Pacific Ocean is said to be five miles deep, yet you cannot say it is boundless, because that means that which is truly without a boundary.

If we ask him what he meant, he may say, "I was just standing at the shore and made the statement." Then he has used the wrong words. If he says, "I dived down but could not find the bottom," then too it would have been incorrect, because only as far below as he dived was there no ground. Perhaps if he had gone a little deeper he might have reached the ocean bed. In that case what he should have said is, "I went five miles below the surface but did not find the bottom of the ocean." If he had said he went all the way down and still there was no ground, it is a lie. When you go the whole distance you are bound to hit the sea bed because then nothing is left of the sea.

What can you say with regard to God? For you to say he is boundless you must know him in his entirety. But at that point all words become meaningless, for the depth has been reached, the ultimate attained. Or you might say you went very far but you did not reach the depth. There, too, you should not use the word *boundless*. For who knows? — had you traveled a little more you might have reached the destination.

How can you say innumerable? Is your counting over? If so, no matter how imposing the figure, it is still not beyond counting. If you say that you are still counting, then wait; don't be in a hurry to make statements because, who knows, your calculations still may be completed.

So to call God innumerable is to call the innumerable by its own name; you merely add to the weight of your thoughts. Whatever you call him — fathomless, infinite, boundless — makes no difference. It is useless and meaningless to say anything about God. Whatever you say is only a statement about yourself. The man who says God is fathomless is only admitting that God is beyond his capacity for measuring.

Different people have different measures of determining the innumerable. There is an African tribe whose counting does not go beyond three. When there is no numeral beyond three, all things after three become countless. In fact this tribe only counts up to two. Three became too many, too much. Beyond three — which is already too much — comes infinity.

Is God really countless or does our counting come to a stop? Is he immeasurable or do our measuring devices run out? Is he boundless or do our legs give way so we can go no further? Whatever we say, we are saying about ourselves; we cannot say a single thing about him. It would be better to limit our talk to speaking about ourselves, because that can be the truth.

We become absolutely incapable and incompetent before him; none of our methods or approaches work. We fail, having been vanquished completely; in our complete defeat we call out: "Thou art boundless, infinite, fathomless!" Then we are speaking of our inability to fathom him; if we feel we have said something about him, we only increase the load of our thoughts.

You cannot — just cannot — say anything about God. You can only remain silent with regard to him. Complete silence alone gives an inkling of God. Therefore, says Nanak, even calling him countless, unfathomable is only increasing your load of words. Say nothing — absolutely nothing! Become something. Do not say a word. When your personality undergoes a transformation, you come nearer to God. A labyrinth of words merely adds to your confusion and you are nowhere near God.

When Nanak was admitted into the school the first question he asked of his teacher was, "Will your teaching help me to know God?" The teacher was taken aback because he never expected such questions from children. He replied, "By learning you shall come to know a great deal, but this learning will not enable you to know God."

"Then show me the method through which I can know God. What shall I do with knowing so many things? If I know the one I shall know all. Have you known this one, teacher?"

The tutor must have been an honest person. He took Nanak back to his house and told his father, "Forgive me, but there is nothing I can teach this child. He already knows so much that he asks questions to which I have no answer. This boy is superhuman and is destined to be great. We cannot teach him anything. It would be better for us to learn something from him."

How do we explain this? In India we have a specific philosophical explanation for just such occurrences: Nanak's body is that of a child, but the consciousness within the body is ancient. Through innumerable births his consciousness searched and struggled until he came to understand that He cannot be known by knowing. You cannot establish contact with him through words. Only through silence can you hope to communicate with him. What the child Nanak says is the outcome of knowledge attained by his consciousness over infinite births.

No child is completely a child, for no child is born with a blank slate. He brings along with him the impressions of all he has gathered through infinite births. So give the child his due respect; who knows, he may know more than you! Your body may be older than his, but the age of his experiences can be greater than yours. Many times we find children asking questions that baffle us, and we have no answer; but because we are older and stronger, we think we should know, and therefore we smother their curiosity with a heavy hand.

Nanak was fortunate that his tutor was an honest person, so they went back to Nanak's house, because it became absolutely clear to him that what the child said was true. He realized that if all the scriptures had not made him wise, what was the sense in teaching the same useless things to this child? It would only increase his burden.

In knowing the one all burdens drop. To know everything is only to overload the mind; to say countless is only to load the mind. The word, the letter, is the name.

The word is his name. *Omkar* is his name and that alone is his praise and the prayer. Say nothing — just nothing. Just fill yourself with the resonance of Omkar and the prayer has begun! Do not say anything. Do not say: I am a sinner, I am lowly; you are the redeemer! There is also no sense in kneeling, falling to the ground, crying and wailing — that is no sign of prayer.

Man has devised such prayers for God as he would use to praise and flatter an egotistic person. Go to a king, fall at his feet, join your hands and call him your redeemer, call him your savior and he is very pleased with you. So you have made up prayers for God accordingly.

Nanak says: This is not prayer. God is no egotist. Then whom are you trying to flatter? Whom are you trying to deceive? You must be trying to get something out of him by singing his praises, or else what reason lies behind all this praise? No, prayer does not mean praise. What value has praise? Therefore Nanak says again and again: What is one to say of creation or nature? How is one to express the wonder that is? There are no words to describe it.

What else can be meant by prayer? The only meaning is to be filled with Omkar. There is no prayer, no worship besides the resonance of Omkar. Temples have been so designed that the cupola reechoes with the resonance of Om and throws the vibrations back to you. Special attention was given whenever a temple was built so that if you pronounce Om in the correct manner a single resonance bounds back to you a thousandfold.

The West has recently introduced a new scientific technique, biofeedback, which may prove very useful in the future. It is a training method that can help calm the mind by showing it what is happening inside. When the mind is very very busy and excited, electrical currents are produced that reflect the level of activity. By means of small wires this current can be transmitted to a biofeedback machine, whose job is to show you how busy the mind is by measuring the current and turning it into a sound that you can hear. When the mind is filled with thoughts and the body is tense a high pitched tone is repeated very rapidly. When the mind becomes more quiet, the sound slows down and drops in pitch. Slowly, slowly, it helps you to become more and more aware of the changes that are happening within, until eventually you are able to control the sounds, and thereby you produce a state of total relaxation and quietness within. Finally, when the body is trained to hear itself you don't need the machine any more. This biofeedback technique can also be used for training in meditation.

The East was well versed in biofeedback techniques for ages. The vault of the temple is one proof of it. It collects the resonance of Om and sends it back to the center of its origin. The sound is created by you and it showers on you. Then as the resonance of Omkar begins to approach nearer and nearer to the actual Omkar, the speed of the feedback will increase as well as its intensity. As you become more advanced, you will feel the resonance forming within you; then your Omkar will be more from the heart than the throat. Simultaneously there will be a change of tone of the echo resounding in the temple. You will find its quality to be more tranquil.

As the resonance of Omkar sinks deeper into your heart you will feel more pleasure in the echo of the temple. When the sound comes only from the mouth it will seem like so much noise at first. When the utterance begins to come from the heart you will begin to sense the music in the resonance. When it becomes absolutely perfect you will find the resonance taking place by itself; you are no longer producing it. Then will every atom of the temple shower its bliss on you.

The temple is like a small pool for you to practice. It is just like learning to swim in shallow waters. When you have completely mastered the art of uttering Omkar, step out into the vast ocean of space. The whole world becomes one big temple for you, with the cupola of the blue skies above. Wherever you stand and pronounce the Omkar, the vast vault of the skies will respond to your utterance and bliss will shower from all sides.

Says Nanak: From the letter, from the word alone can he be praised. From akshara alone all knowledge is attained. From akshara is all writing and speaking. From akshara all destiny takes place.

This is a very subtle point to understand. Nanak says through the letter alone are all events destined. As the word opens within you, your destiny changes. The key to changing your life lies within in the form of Omkar. The further away from Omkar you go, the deeper you plunge your life into misery. As your coalition with the sound, the word, the name develops, good fortune comes your way accordingly.

To be removed from Omkar is to be in the seventh hell; to come nearer to Omkar is to approach closer to heaven, and to be one with Omkar is to realize salvation. These are the three directions your destiny can take, and there is no other way to change your fortune. No matter how much wealth you attain, if you are in hell you remain in hell — only your hell will be the hell of the wealthy. If sorrow is your lot it will remain so even if you build a palace for yourself; you succeeded in changing the hut into a palace, but not your misery into happiness. Your suffering remains the same. Your destiny does not change because the wavelength of the vibrations that determine your destiny have not changed.

There are two types of people in this world. There are some who constantly strive to change the conditions of their lives: a poor man strives to get rich, a small-time clerk struggles to become the head of his firm, a man living in a tenement wants his own house, another wishes for a more beautiful wife — and so on. They try to change the situation, but the wavelength of their life currents remains the same; there is no change in them whatsoever.

The other class of people are the seekers. They do not care to change the conditions around them, but get down to changing the wavelength of their life vibration. No sooner does the wavelength change, whether in a shack or a palace, the person finds himself in the highest kingdom.

Throw him into hell, he experiences only heaven. The resonance of Omkar fills him with bliss and celebration. You could not take his happiness from him even if you throw him into the fire!

There was a woman who was a Zen fakir. Before she died she told her disciples: "I want to sit on my pyre while I am still alive. What way is it to go on other people's shoulders? I don't want it said of me that I had to be carried by others. All my life I have never taken anybody's help. The One alone is my only help. To whom else should I now turn, and why?" She would not listen to reason. Her disciples had to construct the pyre. She sat on it and ordered that it be lighted. People ran away, the heat was so unbearable; but she sat unperturbed. "How do you feel?" someone called out from the crowd. She opened her eyes and said, "Only such as you can ask such a foolish question."

The expression on her face never changed. Whether a bed of flowers or a bed of flames, it was all the same to her.

Once the inner wavelength is adjusted, no fire can burn it, no flowers can increase it. It is this inner current that Nanak calls destiny. Your fate is not written on your forehead; rather it is written in the wavelength of your life current, your vibration. And the pursuit of this life current is possible through Omkar alone.

> *Through the letter is all writing and speaking,*
> *Through the letter are all events destined.*
> *All destiny has already been written,*
> *But he who writes is beyond destiny.*

There is no destiny, no fate for God. God has no desires, no motives. He is beyond destiny. He has nowhere to go. He is in no search of a destination. Therefore the Hindus speak of God's *leela*, which means God's play. God plays with his creation as a child plays with his toys; a child has no other motive than to play for the sake of play. He is happy and cheerful always.

Flowers bloom — what for? The moon shines and the stars twinkle — what for? What reason is there to love? Why do rivers and streams flow? God is. He goes nowhere. The day your life current gets adjusted to the right wavelength, you will find all purpose disappearing from your life. This is why we refer to the lives of Rama and Krishna as leela and not as biography. Their lives are a play, a sport, a frolic, a festival!

He who writes is beyond destiny. We receive only what he orders. All creations are his name. Therefore why search for his name? In the trees, in the plants, in stones and pebbles, is his signature. Jesus used to say pick up a stone and you will find me pressed under it. Break the branch and you will find me hidden within it. Everywhere is his name; he vibrates in every sound, and all vibrations are forms of the one — Omkar. Its intensity and subtlety give birth to all sounds.

The one is hidden in the many. All creation is his name. There is no place where his name is not...in what way shall I praise him, the creator of creation? Nanak is overflowing with wonder. Again and again he is filled with gratitude and awe — how should he express nature?

> *Nanak says: How shall I praise him?*
> *However much I offer myself could never be enough!*
> *Whatever pleases you, O Lord, is best for me.*
> *You are the formless, the almighty — you who abide forever!*

Leave all to him. The only grip you have to loosen is the grip on yourself, and everything is solved. Your only trouble is that you listen to your own advice. You have accepted yourself as your guru. The solution is also only one: make him your guru and stop meddling in your own affairs; step aside, let him take over the reins of your destiny. Then whatever happens, do not judge or draw conclusions, because nothing happens against his will. Whatever happens, happens for the best. What pleases him is the most auspicious. *Thy will be done!*

CHAPTER 9

Dyed in His Hue

If the body is covered with dirt,
Water can wash it away.
If the clothes are soiled and polluted,
Soap and water can wash them clean.
Even if mind is filled with evil,
Love for his name can dye you in his hue.
Saint or sinner are no empty words;
All our actions have been recorded.
Man sows and he himself reaps the harvest.
Nanak says: By divine order are some saved and others reborn.
By visiting holy places, austerities, compassion, and good deeds,
You may gain respect from others;
But he who listens to God and meditates on his name,
His heart is filled with love and he is deeply cleansed.
All virtues are yours, O Lord. Nothing is in me.
Without virtuous actions, no true devotion exists.
Yours is the only true word. You are the sound.
You are Brahma. Your power is magnificent and self-directing.
What was that time, what date, what season,
What month when you assumed form and creation began?
The pundits knew it not,
Or they would have written it in the holy books;
Neither did the kazis know,
Or they would have put it in the Koran;
Nor did the yogis know the day, the time,
The season and month when it happened.

The creator who creates all creation,
He alone knows.
How should one praise him and express his greatness?
How can one know him?
He is supreme. His name is great.
Everything happens as He ordains.
Whoever credits himself as worthy,
Gains no honor before him.

Religion is an internal bath. When we travel from place to place our clothes become dirty and collect dust. This is easily removed by washing. But as we travel through time, dust gathers on the mind, which is not as easy to remove as the dust in the clothes. Because the body is external the water required to cleanse it is available outside; since the mind and its dust are within we have to acquire some cleaner within.

Every moment the dust keeps gathering within, even if you do nothing but sit. A man may indulge in no activity, yet his body requires a bath each day. The mind is never inactive, but always doing something or other; a tranquil mind is rare. So dust is gathering on your mind every moment, which, no matter how many times you bathe during the day, cannot be cleansed by the outside water.

This sutra relates to water within. It is priceless. If you understand it well enough to recognize the lake within, you will have acquired a key to transform you life. Whatever keys you hold now, none is effective. Had even one worked, there would be no further need to understand Nanak. Though you have many keys, your ego will not allow you to admit that they are useless.

Mulla Nasruddin was a servant in a rich man's house. One day he told his master, "I wish to retire. I can serve you no longer. After all there's a limit to one's endurance. You have no faith in me, and I cannot bear it any longer."

"How can you say, Nasruddin," the master asked, "that I do not trust you? Aren't the keys of my safe always lying on the table?"

"Yes," said the Mulla, "But none of the keys fits the safe."

You also have many keys; so much information have you gathered.

When your information works, then knowledge is attained; otherwise you are merely burdened with it.

Carrying the burden of so many keys, it is necessary to ask yourself whether any of them works. Does the gate of life open with it? Do lights come in? Do I experience bliss? Have I heard the enchanting notes of divine music? Or, for that matter, do I express joy and gratitude to the Lord who has given birth to me? Do I cry out: "Your compassion is great. You have given me life!"

Our complaints are many, our thankfulness nil. And how can you be thankful when no key fits? Throw away these keys and listen to Nanak who speaks of the key that works, and it is not Nanak alone who has spoken of this key but also Mahavira, Buddha and Jesus. Isn't it strange that you carry a load of useless keys and leave out the one key that works? It is also not correct to say the key that works because it is a master key that can open all the doors of life. Since time immemorial man talks about useless keys and never bothers about the one that really matters.

The reason behind this is very clear: the keys that you are willing to use do not require you to undergo any transformation. You remain as you are. There is no danger of your changing or losing yourself. Besides, the pleasure of jingling keys and making loud noises is very enjoyable, so you are satisfied to have the keys and yet save yourself from the difficult process of transformation.

You do not listen to Nanak or Buddha or Mahavira, because the key they offer is dangerous — it works! And once it is set in place the lock will open and you will no longer be the same. You have invested heavily in yourself as you are, so a lot is at stake; if you change, all your work till now will have been in vain. The mansions you raised will fall like a house of cards; all the boats you set sailing will capsize. Whatever you have treasured within your mind, the dreams you dreamed, will all prove false.

Your ego refuses to accept this. Your ego says it may be that I am not a super-wise man, but I am wise. Maybe I have committed some errors, but it can't be that everything I have done is wrong! And it is but human to err sometimes – who doesn't? You put forth all these old sayings and console yourself. To err is human, you say.

The one thing, however, that you are not prepared to admit under any circumstances is that you are ignorant. If you erred — it just happened. Don't the wise sometimes make mistakes? A well-informed person can also go astray, or fall into a pit, or knock his head against the wall. You are not prepared to own to being blind.

Try and understand this: whenever you make a mistake you say something bad has happened. You protect the doer and blame the action. You get angry and say what a terrible thing to happen that I got angry, as if the anger happened to you — that the conditions were such that it was necessary — you don't acknowledge that you are an angry person. If you hadn't been angry someone would have suffered, or you were angry for someone else's sake, never admitting the violence in your temperament. Or you admit that sometimes you tend to get angry though you are aware that it is a mistake. You somehow manage to save the doer and blame the action. You admit the wrongness of the act, but never of the person behind it.

Exactly that is your ego. Because of that ego you guard yourself against the genuine key, because as soon as the master key turns and the lock opens, the first thing to fall away is your ego. You become an insignificant nobody. Whatever you had earned and amassed suddenly proves to be meaningless rubbish. All this falls and the you with it. When the ego is annihilated, then you know that the key has worked; therefore, keep miles away from the key.

Rabindranath Tagore has written a beautiful poem. He says: "Since infinite births I have been seeking God. I do not know how many paths I have trodden, how many religious orders. God only knows how many doors I knocked on, how many gurus I served or how many yogas and penances I performed. One day, however, I ultimately succeeded in reaching his door. I used to get glimpses of him, though; but that would be as near as some distant star. By the time I reached there, the star had long gone by.

"But today? Today I stand before his gate. I read the name outside — it is his. I climb the steps so overjoyed that the destination is reached. I hold the knocker, I am about to knock, then....

"Then a fear catches hold of me! What if the door opens? What will I do then? And if I do meet God — what then? What will I do next? Till now there was only one aim in life — to attain God. Then there will be no more goal to work for. Till now there was only one obsession, one occupation — it will all be destroyed! And what when I have met him? Then there will be nothing left to do, no future to look forward to, no journey to undertake — nothing for the ego to work on.

"Fear made me tremble. I quietly put the knocker down. So gently did I let it go for fear lest a slight jerk may cause a sound and the door might open! Then I removed my shoes so that I could go down the steps noiselessly. Then I ran! I ran for my very life, so to say, and never even looked back once!"

In the last verse the poet says: "I am still searching for him. You will find me searching for him on different paths though I know full well where he abides. And yet I ask others where can I find him?" And I know where he stays. I seek him even now. Far away near the moon and the stars I catch a glimpse of him. But now I am confident because I know he will have gone far, far away by the time I arrive. Now I seek him in all places save one – where he abides; and I never go anywhere near it. I guard myself...only from him!"

This poem is a very significant statement, and it describes exactly your condition. Do not ever say you don't know where God is. He is everywhere; then how can you not know where he is? Do not ever say the lock is closed and you don't know about the key, because the key has been given to you a thousand times, but you always forget where you kept it. You leave it somewhere; your unconscious self tries to run away from it. Until your doubts are cleared away you will be seeking him on one hand and losing him on the other. You will be raising one foot to step in his direction and the other in the opposite direction.

You keep alive the myth that you are a seeker, because it satisfies you and appeases your conscience. It gives you a sense of importance to feel that you are not an ordinary base person who seeks wealth or position. You feel yourself above them because you seek God, truth, religion. While others are involved in lesser things, you have opted for the vast universal existence.

So you keep claiming that you are seeking him, while secretly from within you are trying to escape him. Unless you understand and confront this duality within you, you will never be able to seek him.

Your state at present is like that of the man who builds a house during the day and destroys it at night. He repeats the same process day after day. Or, you might say, he lays a brick with one hand and removes it with the other; or he may employ two workers, one to lay the bricks and the other to remove them. When will his house ever be completed? For infinite lives you have been trying to build your home and yet it is not yet built. Surely something is basically wrong that makes you do two opposing things at the same time!

You carry your false keys that do not work. You bathe in the sacred rivers but your mind remains unwashed. You offer rituals in temples, but that is no worship. You offer flowers; you do not offer yourself. You give in charity, you feed the poor, you do these little religious deeds and take cover behind them.

Remember, you will be purified only if you are prepared to be annihilated; therefore you need waters that will make you extinct, that destroy every bit of you. Here we are discussing these waters. Try to understand:

> *If the body is covered with dirt,*
> *Water can wash it away.*
> *If the clothes are soiled and polluted,*
> *Soap and water can wash them clean.*
> *Even if mind is filled with evil,*
> *Love for his name can dye you in his hue.*

The hue of love. No word is more significant, more meaningful than the word *love*. After the names of God, love is the next most significant word, so try to understand.

We all know the word. You might say we all know love. What is so special to make it the key? Though we already know the word, mere acquaintance with words will not do. You have learned your words from the dictionaries of language but not from the dictionary of existence. The dictionary gives various meanings, but love has nothing to do with any of them. When love arises in your book of existence, the experience suffuses the word with life — so different from the lifeless words in the book. Now for instance, the dictionary describes fire as a thing that burns, but this fire does not burn you, any more than, similarly, the water in the dictionary can quench your thirst. If you try to understand love in a like manner, your sins will never be washed away.

Love is a fire. Gold is purified by passing it through a fire in which all but the gold is burnt away — only that remains which is worth preserving; so also, when you pass through the fire of love, all that is worthless and useless in you goes up in flames. All sins are burned away and only the purposeful you, the meaningful you, remains. You become purified, perfect virtue.

So understand love well. First and foremost you must clearly distinguish love from sin, then only can you eradicate sin. Perhaps you have not recognized the relationship between these two very deep-seated conditions within you: You can sin only when love is absent. Sins are born in the absence of love. Where love is, sin is impossible.

So it is that Mahavira says nonviolence. Nonviolence means love. Buddha says compassion. Compassion means love. And Jesus' words are direct and clear. He says that love is God!

Someone asked St. Augustine, "What is the essence of religion? Please tell me as briefly as you can. How shall I save myself from sin? Sins are so many and life is so short."

The significance is that since life is short and sins are many, could he rid himself of them one by one in the short span of a lifetime? So he pleaded for a master key that opens all locks.

You can steal only if you have no feeling of love towards the person whose possessions you are coveting. You can kill only if you have no feeling of love towards the person you kill. You can cheat, you can deceive, you can commit all other sins — only when love is absent within you. Sins are born only in the non-presence of love. Just as an unlighted house attracts thieves, robbers, snakes and scorpions — and spiders weave webs within it and bats make it their home — but when light is brought in they all make a hasty retreat.

Love is light. No lamp of love has been lit in your life — therefore the sins. Sin has no positive energy of its own. It is a negative, a non-presence. You can sin only when that which should be within you is absent.

Understand a little: you get angry though all religious books exhort you not to. But if your life energy does not flow towards love, what else can you do but be angry? You will have to be angry, for anger — if you understand it well — is that very love that has lost its direction. It is the same energy that could not become a flower but instead became a thorn. Love is creation. If there is no creativity in your life, your life energy turns destructive.

The difference between a saint and a sinner is only that the life energy of one is creative and the life energy of the other is destructive. Thus, whoever creates can never act satanic. And one who creates nothing can never be a saint, no matter how much he deludes himself. The energy within has to be utilized one way or the other, for energy cannot remain stagnant; it has to flow. If you can love you dig new channels for your energy to flow towards love. If there is no love within you, what will your life energy do? It can only disrupt and destroy. If you cannot create you will destroy. Virtue is the positive state of the life energy; sin is the negative state of the same energy.

People come to me and say there is so much anger within them, what should they do? I tell them to stop thinking about anger. The more you think of anger the more energy you supply to your anger. Energy begins to flow in the direction of our thoughts. Energy flows and thoughts are its channels. Just as canals direct water from reservoirs to the fields, the canal for life energy is attention. Wherever your attention is, there your life flows. If your attention points in a wrong direction your energy flows in the wrong direction. If it is directed towards the right direction, your life flows in the right direction and the right attention is love.

Nanak says the day your love is directed towards his name you shall be dyed in his hue; you shall be cleansed. Not only will your past sins be washed away but also future possibility of sin; you will be washed and cleansed before you can even get dirty. You are bathed and cleansed every moment.

You must have had this feeling when in the presence of a saint — a sense of freshness of the morning dew, as if he has just come out of his bath. The reason is simply that the presence of love does not allow dust to gather on him. Love incessantly washes away all dirt — even before it can touch him.

So the first thing regarding love is for your life energy not to become destructive. Destruction is sin when it occurs for its own sake. There is another kind of destruction: a man tears down a house in order to build a new one. This is not destroying but a part of constructing. When you break for the sake of breaking, it becomes a sin.

If you have a small child whom you love very much, you sometimes give him a whack or two — because of your love you have beaten him for his good, to improve him. You hit him because you care. If you did not care for him you would not have bothered what he did and what he didn't do; you would have been indifferent. But you love him enough not to allow him to go on doing what he pleases. You will stop him from going near fire; you will even hit him if he does not listen. This hitting is not sinful, but creative. You want to make something of him.

When you hit an opponent, it is the same hand; the slap is the same, the energy is the same. When the feeling within you is that of enmity, when you are hitting to destroy and not to create, it becomes a sin! An act in itself is not a sin. If the feeling within you is positive and creative, no act is a sin; if the feeling within is destructive, the same act becomes a sin.

There is a Sufi story: A Sufi came to a village on his way to a temple hidden somewhere in the nearby mountains. He went to a tea stall on the roadside and asked, "Can you tell me who is the most truthful man and the most untruthful man in this village?" The stall keeper gave him the two names. In a small village everybody knows everything about everybody else, so it was not difficult to guide him.

The Sufi went to the most truthful man and asked him for directions. The man looked at him and said, "The easiest way is through the mountains." Then he gave him detailed directions in order to reach the temple.

Then the Sufi went to the untruthful man and asked him to show him the easiest way to the temple. The Sufi was shocked when this man showed him the same route as the truthful man. He did not know what to believe! He went back to the village square and asked if there was a Sufi in their settlement.

The traveler was directed to a Sufi saint. A truthful person and an untruthful person are two extremes. When a person reaches sainthood he goes beyond both. The fakir heard the problem and responded: "The answer is the same but the angle of vision is different. The truthful and righteous man directed you across the mountains, although it is easier to cross the river to reach the other side. He took into consideration the fact that you have no boat, nor any means of going through the river. Since you have a donkey on which you ride, how would you carry him across? In the mountains the donkey would be useful to you, in the boat he would cause you problems. Seeing all this, he suggested what was best for you under the circumstances.

"The unrighteous man pointed out the same path, but his intentions were dishonorable. He wanted to cause you trouble. He took delight in the fact that you would be harassed." The answers are the same, the intentions are different. Actions can be similar, therefore they tell you nothing; it is the feeling behind them that is the deciding factor.

Therefore we never keep count of the number of times a child gets punished by his father or mother. The truth is, say the psychiatrists, if a mother has never beaten her child, there cannot be any deep connection between the mother and child; it shows she does not truly recognize him as her own; there is a distance, a gap, between them.

A son never forgives the father who complies with all his demands. Later on in life, he realizes that his father has injured him. The child is not experienced, so his demands have less value. The father has to think and decide what would be good for him because he is more experienced in life. If he really loves his child he will decide on the basis of his own experiences rather than the child's demands. If a man gives his child full freedom, the child will never be able to forgive him.

Nowhere in the world has a child been given so much freedom

as recently in the West. During this century Western psychologists have been teaching people to give total freedom to their children. The result has been an unbridgeable gap between the parents and the child. In former days sons feared their fathers; in the West today, the father is afraid of the son. In the past parents were revered and respected. In the West today, the child knows no respect for the elders, not an iota of love or caring. What is the reason? It is only this: as the child grows up he begins to realize the harm his parents have done to him by letting him loose to do as he pleased. He should have been stopped when he did anything wrong. It was their duty to prevent him from going astray since they were experienced, and he was not. They should not have listened to him; they should not have given in to his wishes. This revelation comes but, alas, then it is too late.

Remember this: love cares! Love cares that your life should be good, beautiful, truthful, and attain the highest glory. Indifference is a sign that there is no relationship, that your being born to your particular parents is a mere coincidence for all of you. There is no give and take. There is no feeling of oneness or belonging, with the result that in the West all intrinsic relationships are breaking down.

Love can also punish, because love is so strong and so self-confident that it can bring about creation through destruction. The important thing is that the aim is always creation. If destruction is necessary, there is bound to be a creating aim behind it.

The guru kills the disciple — completely! He kills him outright — no father's blows that fall only on the body. Just as water cleanses the body from outside, the father superficially cleanses the life of his son, but the guru hits hard and deep within. He bores inside you to your utmost depth, and will not rest until your ego is completely melted. Until you find such a guru, know that whatever master you follow you will never be able to forgive. Sooner or later it will dawn on you that this man has been wasting your time.

The mark of love is creativity. As long as you are creative in your relationships, you cannot commit sin. How can I sin when I am filled with love? The love gradually spreads and you find yourself hidden in each living being. Then whom will you rob, whom will you cheat? Whom will you deceive, whose pocket will you pick? As love increases you discover that all pockets are yours, and when you harm someone you find you have harmed yourself.

Life is an echo: whatever you do comes back to you. He whose love increases becomes aware that there are no strangers in this world. It is common knowledge that when you love someone, you feel one with him.

You will not want to harm your wife when you realize that by harming her you ultimately harm yourself; because when she is unhappy you also become unhappy. You would wish her to be happy when her happiness increases your potential happiness. One day you comprehend that the sorrow we give others makes us equally sad; the joy we give others makes us equally happy.

But we think in opposite terms — saving joy for ourselves and wishing sorrow on others. And we feel, perhaps, that in that way our own quota of happiness will be greater. The end result is that you find your own life filled with sorrow because whatever you give returns to you. If you have sown thorns for others, your own life gets surrounded by thorns. And if you go about sowing flowers unconcerned with what others are doing, your life becomes filled with flowers. You reap what you sow. But we do not seem to understand this formula of life.

A woman came to me wanting to divorce her husband. I will never forget what she asked of me. She said, "Show me a way of getting a divorce so that my husband remains miserable for all time to come." She knows very well that her husband will be the happiest person in the world the day she divorces him; she has pestered him endlessly. Now she wants that he be made miserable even after she leaves.

When we are together we wish to give sorrow; when we are apart we wish to give sorrow. Together or apart, if our aim in life is to create sorrow and pain for others, then it can only gradually create a painful wound within ourselves. The wound is of our own making. It comes out of constant attention to provoking pain.

This is what we call karma, the process of actions. Fate, destiny, only mean that whatever you do comes back to you. Though there may be a certain lapse of time, eventually it is bound to bounce back to affect you. Therefore do only what you want to obtain for yourself. If you find yourself in a veritable hell, it is of your own making — the fruit of what you have been doing for countless births.

People come to me and say, "Bless us so that we may attain happiness." There would be no problem if it were so easy, if one man could just bless everyone and they would find happiness. How could my blessings wash away your misery? Try to understand me and not ask for blessings; that would be mere deception. You have given pain and suffering to others, now you must reap the fruits of your actions; and you come to ask for blessings? And your attitude is that you suffer because I do not give you my blessings. No blessings can remove your suffering. If somebody's blessings help to improve your understanding and sow seeds of love within you, that is more than enough. Sins can be washed away only with love, and suffering can end only when you give happiness to others.

Nanak says: "If the mind is filled with sin, only the love for his name can purify it." When you begin to love a person, you find it impossible to harm that person, because then the other's happiness becomes your happiness; the other's sorrow becomes yours. The barrier between your life and your beloved's exists no more; you flow into each other.

When that phenomenon takes place between a person and God, it is called prayer, worship, devotion; it is the ultimate form of love. When it gives so much joy to make someone happy and so much pain to make someone unhappy, the same holds true in the case of you and God. If the relationship is one of love you are in heaven; in the absence of love you find yourself in the depths of hell.

God means totality. You have to love this vast expanse, the whole universe, all that is, as if it were a person. All your sins will be washed away when you fall hopelessly in love with all that is. Then whom will you deceive? Wherever you look he is there; in whatever eye you look you will find him seated.

Devotion is a revolutionary process. It means now there is none but He. Your life has suddenly become simple, uncomplicated. Now there is no more need to sin, no more need to deceive. Do not think that devotion implies going to the temple to offer worship. Reciting the Japuji early in the morning is not devotion; nor is going to the mosque or church. This will not lead you anywhere.

These are the false keys. The genuine key is to fall in love with the infinite. Now every particle of dust on this earth is entitled to your love. Every inch of this earth is my beloved; every leaf bears the name of my beloved; through every eye he looks at me. Everything is his, everywhere.

When you reach this recognition, however you live your life will be through devotion; it will transform your very way of life. You will sit differently, walk in a different manner, because everywhere you see him present. You will speak differently if whomever you speak to is he. Now how can you annoy or tell lies about someone; how can you insult someone? How will you escape serving others because in the feet of others you find him hidden!

When this knowledge dawns on you, you will be in a perpetual ecstasy – what Nanak refers to as being dyed in his hue. You will possess nothing yet have everything. You will find yourself absolutely alone and yet all the world is with you. There will be a rhythm, a harmony between you and existence; you will have established an intimate contact with existence. Nanak says only such a love can cleanse you of sin. All worship and recitations, all sacrifices and incantations are of no avail for the basic factor is missing.

I was once traveling on a train. A woman got on at a station with about ten children, who immediately ran from one end of the compartment to the other, upsetting everyone's luggage, getting into everybody's way; there was complete chaos. At last one passenger could bear it no longer when the kids had overturned his bag and torn his newspaper. He turned to the woman and said, "Sister, it would be much better if you didn't travel with so many children. If you have to travel it would be more comfortable for all of us if you left half of them at home." The woman flared up, "Do you take me for a fool? I have left half of them at home!"

When basic understanding is missing, it doesn't matter how many children you leave behind. If the woman did not use her discrimination while producing twenty children, how can you expect her to use her understanding when traveling?

Sins there are thousands, virtue is only one; illnesses are thousands, health is only one. It is not that you have your kind of health and I have mine. You can be ill with tuberculosis, cancer or some other complaint; there can be differences in illnesses. There can be originality. An illness can carry your individual stamp because illness is part of your ego. For different egos there are different illnesses, but health is one. Virtue is one, because God is one. You cannot be different in this context.

What is this health, this well-being, that is one? It is the feeling of love. Try to drown yourself in life, immerse in it little by little. When you get up from your chair, do so as if the beloved is present. Even when you enter a vacant room, do it as if God is present all around.

There was a Sufi fakir by the name of Junnaid. He would tell his disciples, "When in a crowd remember your aloneness, then the remembrance of God will be with you. When you go into solitude, go as if God is present all around."

He is right. If you can remember your aloneness in a crowd you can maintain the remembrance of God; otherwise the crowd will seize hold of your attention and you will be led astray. And if you do not maintain the remembrance of God when you are alone, you will lead yourself astray.

There are two hazards: you can either lose yourself in others or get lost in your own self. God is beyond both. If you remember your aloneness in a crowd and are aware of his presence in your solitude, you will never go astray.

Nanak says: "He who is dyed in the hue of love becomes pure within. He has undergone an internal bath."

> *To be saint or sinner are no empty words;*
> *All our actions have been recorded.*
> *Man sows and he himself reaps the harvest.*

To claim you are trying hard to be virtuous brings about no change within you. By thinking or by speaking about it nothing ever happens. It is not strange that we talk a great deal about virtue and good deeds, whereas we never think or speak about sins, we only do them. If you are told to hold yourself back for a minute when anger comes, you will say it is impossible, anger cannot be postponed. How can you withhold anger when the withholder is not present when anger comes. Where are we when anger comes?

If you are told to meditate you say: "Not today, I have no time." Besides, you feel what's the hurry? We still have such a long way to go in life and these things are intended for the end of life when death is about to come. Remember you can never feel death coming; not even the dying man feels death.

A politician died and Mulla Nasruddin was called upon to make a condolence speech.

The Mulla said something noteworthy: "God's kindness is so great. Whenever we die, we die at the end of life. Imagine what disaster it would be if death came at the beginning or in the middle of life!"

And we keep putting off the end. It never seems to come until it actually arrives. Others come to know when one's end has come; the one who dies has gone before he knows it!

So, if you understand correctly, you never die. You remain always alive in your thoughts. The occurrence of death you do not know — others know it. You are weaving fresh plans for life even in the moment of death. You put off death for the morrow. All that is auspicious we keep putting off; all that is not we do immediately.

The day you do the opposite, you will be dyed in the color of his name. Then you will put off the inauspicious and carry out the auspicious immediately. When the feeling to give arises, give immediately. Don't trust yourself too much; your mind will devise a thousand tricks in a second to make you forget.

Mark Twain wrote that once he went to a convention to hear a minister speak. After five minutes, being very impressed and moved, he decided to donate the hundred dollars he had with him to the minister's cause. After ten minutes, he wrote, the thought arose in him that a hundred dollars was too much; fifty would do equally well. As soon as the thought of the hundred dollars appeared he lost all connection with the clergyman, because the internal dialogue had taken over. Before half an hour had elapsed he was down to five dollars. When the lecture was over he thought: "No one knows I intended to give one hundred dollars. And who gives so much? People don't even give one. I think one dollar is more than enough." By the time the collection plate came to him, he writes, "The dollar didn't come out of my pocket. Instead I picked up a dollar from the plate...who was watching? No one. No one would ever know."

Don't trust yourself too much about doing the right thing; it is often rather difficult. At certain moments, when you are on the peaks, the impulse to do good arises within you. If you lose that opportunity it may never come your way again. Never indulge in righteous thought, because the auspicious is the very thing which is not to be thought about but acted on. When you feel like giving, give! When you feel like sharing, share! When you feel like renouncing, renounce! When you feel like taking sannyas, take it! Do not lose a moment, because nobody knows when that moment will come into your life again, or whether it will come at all.

And when the inauspicious, the evil, arises within you — stop! Defer it for twenty-four hours. Make it a rule: if you want to harm someone, do it a day later. What's the hurry? Death is not standing at your door; and even if it is, what is the harm? At the most, the enemy will not have been damaged, that's all!

If you can put off a negative act for one day you will be incapable of doing it, because the frenzy to do harm is momentary. Just as the impulse to do good comes in a moment, so also the frenzy for evil is momentary. If you can bring yourself to desist at that moment, you will realize how futile your action would have been. Restrain a murderer for a moment, and he cannot kill. If a man is about to jump into a river to drown himself, interrupt him for a short while and he will no longer try to kill himself. Certain acts are possible only in certain moments. Within you are moments of both dense insensibility and intense awareness.

At times of heightened awareness you are filled with love and creativity. In moments of intense insensibility you are overwhelmed with senseless destruction. In your frenzy you wish to destroy, then later you repent, but this is empty and worthless. If you must repent, repent after doing some good. What is the sense of repenting after sin? But that is what you always do — first sin, then repent. And good deeds? Since you never do them, the question of repentance doesn't arise.

Nanak says nothing happens by thinking, nor by saying. Sin and virtue have nothing to do with words, but with acts. Your account before God is not in words but in deeds. He judges you by your actions, by what you are. What you have said, what you have learned, what you have thought, has no relevance here. The final outcome rests on your actions. Nanak says man sows and reaps the harvest himself.

Generally we say others cause our trouble, but success we achieve for ourselves. Failures are due to obstruction by others; all that is good is my own attainment. This way of thinking is absolutely wrong. Whatever happens in your life is part of the chain of your actions, part of your karma; you are responsible for all that is good or bad, auspicious or inauspicious, flowers or thorns. The day a person accepts and experiences total responsibility for himself a transformation begins to take place within.

As long as you blame others, there can be no transformation. If others are the cause of your misery, what can you do? Until such time as they all change, your misery must continue unabated. And how can you change others? There is no other way but to bear your sorrow. There is no other alchemy than religion to transform misery.

It takes time for seeds to bear fruit; and because of this, you completely forget that you had sown the seed when the fruits begin to appear. Because of this forgetfulness, you attribute your woes to others. Remember, nobody is worried about you. Each is worried about himself: others are plagued by their own ills and you are plagued by your own. Each person must seek out the thread of his own actions. Recognize well this fact and only then is a profound transformation possible. As soon as you understand that you are responsible, something can be done. The first thing you must do is recognize and accept quietly the reactions and results of your past actions. It makes no sense to produce fresh turmoil while reaping the fruit of your past actions. Only this way can your past actions be neutralized.

A man spat on Buddha. Buddha quietly wiped his face with his cloak. The man was very angry and so were Buddha's disciples when it happened. After he left Ananda could not contain himself. "This is sacrilege!" he exclaimed. "Moderation doesn't mean that anyone can get away with doing whatever he wants to you. That way would inspire others to do likewise. Our hearts are burning! We cannot bear the insult."

Buddha answered, "Don't be unnecessarily excited, lest that become a link in your chain of karmas. I must have hurt him sometime and now he has cleared the debt. I may have insulted him somehow and now we are quits. I came to this village expressly for him. Had he not spat on me I would have been in a quandary. He has solved my dilemma. Now my account is closed. This man has freed me from some past action of mine. I am grateful to him.

"And why are you all so excited? It had nothing to do with you. If your wrath is stirred up and you do something to this man in your excitement, you will have created a new link in your chain of karmas. My chain is broken, yours will be made anew — and for no reason. Why are you intervening? I have to reap the result from the one I have troubled. Before my total, highest annihilation, before I merge completely with the infinite, I must settle my account with all people, all things, all relationships formed in anger, insolence, hatred, attachment, greed, etc. For only he whose actions have been equalized is a completely liberated being."

So remember, let your past actions be discharged peacefully. Accept them cheerfully and be contented. Remember, you are settling your accounts and do not create fresh links; then gradually your connection with the past is loosened and disintegrates.

Now the second thing to remember is: do not do any fresh harm to others or else you will simply be binding yourself to your actions. We create the fetters within ourselves. So remember that you have to break the old links and not create new links.

For this Mahavira used two very beautiful words: *asrava* means do not allow the new to come in, and *jirjara* means allow the old to fall off. By and by a moment comes when nothing of the old remains and nothing new is being formed; you are free. Ultimate bliss occurs only in this state.

> *Man sows and he himself reaps the harvest.*
> *Nanak says: By divine order are some saved and others reborn.*
> *By visiting holy places, austerities, compassion, and good deeds,*
> *You may gain respect from others;*
> *But he who listens to God and meditates on his name,*
> *His heart is filled with love and he is deeply cleansed.*

All outward ablutions bring no transformation. At most you may gain a little respect in the eyes of others. But this reverence can be dangerous because your ego will try to make a mountain out of it; it won't stop recounting how many pilgrimages you undertook, how many fasts you have observed.

Bodhidharma went to China from India. The Emperor of China came to him. This king had become a Buddhist and then had constructed thousands of monasteries, ashrams and temples. He had printed and distributed thousands of treatises on Buddhism. He fed millions of beggars every day. All this he recounted to Bodhidharma. He also told him how many images of Buddha he had had made. In fact there still remains a temple constructed by him which bears ten thousand statues of Buddha. He had whole mountains dug up for this purpose. His charity was immense, and all this he made a point of telling Bodhidharma.

Bodhidharma listened completely unmoved. The king could wait no longer. "What will be the fruit of all these good deeds?" he asked.

Bodhidharma replied, "Nothing. You will rot in hell."

The king was dumbfounded. "What is this you say? I in hell?"

"The deeds in themselves are not the problem. They are indeed good deeds, but your feeling of having done them is the difficulty. The good deeds have happened; leave them at that. Don't take upon yourself the doership of them. If you presume that you have done them, all virtue in your actions turns to dust; the medicine will turn to poison. As it is, medicines are made from poisons."

In the days when rupees, annas and pais were still in use Mulla Nasruddin went to the doctor because his wife suffered from insomnia.

"Help me please, doctor," said the Mulla. "She keeps bickering all night long, as if it wasn't enough all day."

"Take this powder," said the doctor, "and each evening give her as much as would cover a four-anna bit."

After about a week the doctor came upon Nasruddin on the road. "Say, how's the wife?" he inquired.

"Your medicine worked wonders, doctor. She is still fast asleep!"

The doctor was worried. "How much of the powder did you give her?" he asked.

"Well," said the Mulla, "I did not have a four-anna bit so I took four one-anna coins, covered them with the powder and gave it to her — so much peace in the house! What wonderful medicine."

Medicine can become poison if you aren't careful about the quantity. Virtue can also become poison beyond a certain proportion. Remember, as long as virtue remains simply an action it is all right. When the doer is involved the proportion can become dangerous. If good deeds are performed to counteract one's evil deeds it is all right. But if good deeds are performed with the idea of earning or accumulating virtue, it is dangerous. You may gain some respect, but that is all. Don't take this to be religion.

I was once traveling with Nasruddin on a bus.

Suddenly Mulla got up in the moving bus and cried out, "Brothers, has anyone lost a bundle of notes tied in a string?" Many people claimed the bundle was theirs; they vied with each other to reach Mulla.

"Peace, Peace!" exclaimed Mulla, "So far, I have only found the string."

Religion is like the bundle of notes; good deeds are like the string. Don't pride yourself on them. The string in itself has no value, only when tied around the rupee notes does it assume value. What worth has a string that is tied around a stone? When good deeds unite with a selfless attitude they become the boat that takes you to the other shore. When good deeds are tied to the ego, they become like a rock on your chest that invariably drowns you. So there are people who are drowned in their evil deeds, and people who drown in their good deeds.

This is why it often happened that a sinner arrived while the virtuous man lagged behind. An evildoer more easily becomes egoless because he knows he is a sinner; he knows it is well nigh impossible for him to reach God. He is convinced he has no good qualities and is only a storehouse of evil. He doesn't even dare to think that his voice could ever reach him. In the absence of ego, even the sinner can reach; but when ego is present even the virtuous person drowns.

> *By visiting holy places, austerities, compassion, and good deeds,*
> *You may gain respect from others;*
> *But he who listens to God and meditates on his name,*
> *His heart is filled with love and he is deeply cleansed.*

Such should be your attitude. Don't allow pride to creep in over being a renunciate, or giving charity, or doing this or that. Don't let the pride of the emperor find a foothold in you, or, as Bodhidharma says, "You will rot in hell."

> *All virtues are yours, O Lord. Nothing is in me.*
> *Without virtuous actions, no true devotion exists.*

I am not even worthy of worshipping you. I have no eligibility, no capacity.

Therefore, Nanak says: all things are obtained through his grace. What is our capability? All devotees have said the same. It is always through his grace whatever you attain, since you are not capable of attaining by yourself.

To feel yourself capable implies that he has to give. If he does not give in spite of your capability, then we have reason to complain; and if he gives, what reason to be thankful? You have attained by your own merit. Within you a complaint arises out of considering yourself capable yet not having achieved.

On the other hand the devotee's mind is always filled with gratitude, because he always feels unworthy of all he has attained. His whole way of thinking is different. By singing and chanting one doesn't become a devotee; rather your attitude toward life should be: Unworthy I am, he has given me so much! The devotee's prayer is always filled with thanksgiving and gratitude — never with complaint.

Nanak says: I have no talents and without talent I cannot perform worthy actions, so how can I worship you? All I can do is sing your praises, O Lord. All glory be! That is all I can say. I can only sing your praises, O Lord. I am unworthy, I deserve to get nothing. I am so worthless that all I can do is sing your glory — that is all.

> *Yours is the only true word. You are the sound.*
> *You are Brahma. Your power is magnificent and self-directing.*
> *What was that time, what date, what season,*
> *What month when you assumed form and creation began?*
> *The pundits knew it not,*
> *Or they would have written it in the holy books;*
> *Neither did the kazis know,*
> *Or they would have put it in the Koran;*
> *Nor did the yogis know the day, the time,*
> *The season, and month when it happened.*
> *The creator who creates all creation,*
> *He alone knows.*

And I? I am devoid of all talent. The pundits don't know, nor the *kazis*, the Mohammedan priests. The scriptures give no information; if all the wise men don't know who you are, where you are, how you assumed form, how you fashioned creation, then how can I, a poor ignorant fool, know what to do?

The devotee never bothers about what he is; the pundit, the learned man does. The knowledgeable man tries to seek him by analysis; he tries to lay everything bare in order to get at him. The devotee remains blissful in his grace, because his contention is: How can anyone besides you know how all this came about! You alone can know, all else are foolish surmises. So the devotee never claims that he knows. His only claim is love. Remember, to claim knowledge is the claim of the ego; the claim of love is ego-less.

> *How should one praise him and express his greatness?*
> *How can one know him?*

Nanak says: "You alone know; how shall I call out to you? I know no form of greeting! What words shall I use? I am afraid of using wrong words. Which aspect of yours shall I glorify? What praise will be fitting? What words would be worthy for you? I know not. Clever people have expressed praises in your honor, and each has striven to outdo the others."

But all expressions are incomplete. The really intelligent person has realized that he cannot be expressed because any name will fall short of him and seem hollow and insignificant when compared to his glory.

> *He is supreme. His name is great.*
> *Everything happens as he ordains.*
> *Whoever credits himself as worthy,*
> *Gains no honor before him.*

Whoever considers himself to be something invariably misses him, because there can be only one: either you or he. In one scabbard there is room for only one sword, not two.

There is a very well-known poem by the Sufi poet Rumi: The lover went and knocked at the door of the beloved. A voice asked "Who is it?" He said, "Open the door. It is I." There was no answer, all was silent within. The lover knocked again. He called out again and again, "Open the door. It is I, your lover," but there was no response. Finally a voice came from within, "Two cannot be contained in this house. This is the house of love, it cannot accommodate two." Then again there was silence.

The lover turned back. He wandered for years in the jungles. He undertook many fasts and practices; he performed many rites and holy works. He purified himself and thus cleansed his mind. He became more aware; he began to understand the conditions. After many, many years he returned once again and knocked at the door. The same question came from within, "Who is it?" But this time the answer that came from outside was, "You alone are."

And, Rumi says, the door was opened.

If you go to the gates of God as somebody — then even if you appear as a sannyasin, a renunciate, a wise man, whatever, you will fail. The gate opens only for those who are nothing, nobody, who have annihilated their selves totally.

In ordinary life also, love opens its doors only when you are not, when you are completely merged in the other and the voice of I has stopped. Then when this I becomes less important than you, and when you becomes your whole life, then you are capable of destroying yourself for the beloved; you willingly and happily enter into death. Then only does love blossom. In everyday life we thus get a glimpse of the one when two are no more.

When the ultimate love arises, there should remain no sign of you; your name, your designation, your very self should turn to dust. Only when you annihilate yourself completely can this happen. Remember the words of Jesus: "He who saves himself will be lost; he who loses himself will be saved. In his kingdom he who destroys himself attains everything and he who saves himself loses everything."

Nanak says he who considers himself to be something is unworthy before him. The truth is, he never even reaches him.

Proud eyes are blind eyes. He who has even a single thought of being someone, his personality is deaf, inert; he is already dead. He cannot appear before God. God stands ever before you but as long as you are, you cannot see him. You are the obstruction, the obstacle. When this hindrance drops, your eyes become pure and open, devoid of I-ness. You are as if you are nothing, a mere emptiness. And in such emptiness he enters at once.

Kabir has said the guest arrives in the house of one who is empty. No sooner do you become empty than the guest arrives. You miss him as long as you are filled with your own self. The day you empty yourself he fills you.

CHAPTER 10

The Lure of the Infinite

There are millions of underworlds
And infinite skies above.
The Vedas say millions have searched and searched,
Only to end in exhaustion.
The holy books claim eighteen thousand worlds
But only one power behind all creation.
If anything could be written we would keep the account,
But all estimates are destructible.
Nanak says: He is the greatest of the great.
He alone can know himself.
Those who worship praise him,
But have no remembrance of him,
As rivers and streams know not the ocean
Into whose vastness they fall.
Even kings and emperors of great domains,
Who possess enormous treasures,
Cannot compare with the lowly ant
With remembrance of God in his heart.

An incident occurred at a research institute where they were investigating various types of poison. The institute became infested with rats, their number increasing every day. Every possible method was used to kill them, but to no avail. Whatever poison they set out the rats ate merrily. The rats had learned to feed and thrive on poisons, because that was all that was readily available to them there, and they had become immune.

Then someone suggested the age-old method of setting traps, as for mice. So traps were brought and fitted with pieces of bread and cheese, but the rats ignored them completely! So accustomed to poison were they that they did not like anything else. Not a single rat was caught.

Finally someone came up with the obvious solution and covered the bread and cheese bait with poison. The rats immediately were caught in the traps.

This strange sounding story is nevertheless true. It actually happened at a research institute. Man's state is almost the same. He has become so habituated to words that even if silence is offered to him, he has to seek respite in words — just as the rats went only for the food covered by poison.

When the infinite is to be explained we need the help of pitiful words. Even when man is to be led into the void, the base language of words must be used. When explaining the ocean, one can speak only of the drop, and discussion of a drop cannot even hint at the ocean. It is not possible. Look at the mighty ocean, and look at the insignificant, tiny drop. Similarly, where are words compared to the void, where the intelligence of a lowly human being and where the immeasurable expanse? There is space and space, there are worlds and underworlds, all without end.

But these have to be measured in terms of men's feeble understanding, because man has become so addicted to the mind, and it is very difficult to break out of any addiction. Truth is not so far away; only our habits are the hindrance. Truth is very near, even closer than one's own heartbeat, closer than one's very breath. God is closer to you than your own self. But we have woven an intricate web of habits, and because of them it is difficult for us to see. The mind is nothing but a collection of habits. Therefore all saints have striven to eradicate the mind, to bring about the state of no-mind.

As soon as you let go of the mind, let go of the shore, you enter the ocean. There is no other way of knowing the ocean than to become the ocean — nothing less will do. While standing on the shore, no matter how much you speculate or expound on the ocean, it is all useless babble. The very fact of your standing on the shore shows that you are not directly acquainted with it. Once you are really acquainted, why remain on the shore? Once a person becomes familiar with the infinite, no power on earth is strong enough to chain him to the shore. The attraction of the infinite will pull him away. There is no power more magnetic than the lure of the infinite; all other attractions fade away when it pulls.

But we sit and just talk. We remain closeted in the room and talk of the open skies...outside! We lock ourselves within our own cages and talk of freedom. We are imprisoned by the web of our own words and we talk of the formless.

These verses of Nanak are very valuable:

There are millions of underworlds
And infinite skies above.

There is space...and space...and nothing but space. It is one sky that becomes infinite, because there is no boundary to space. It is one boundless space. Says Nanak, "There is the sky, and the sky, and only the sky...infinite times infinite."

There is not just one single infinity; there are infinite infinities. Wherever you go you will find space. Whichever direction you may take, you will find boundless space; whatever you touch you will find it is space. The boundless abounds everywhere.

In the midst of this boundless you are trying to trap God in your tiny cage of words? You try to imprison him in books like the Vedas and the Koran. It is just like trying to imprison the vast skies within your palm. The wonderful thing about this is, when your palm is open there is space in it, but the moment you close your fist, whatever space was in it evaporates. The tighter you make the fist, the emptier it is.

Use words like an open fist, not like a closed fist; but words that are like an open palm no longer remain logical. The more logical you want to make an expression, the more you have to enclose it. The greater the definition, the more constricted the expression. Whenever a thing is well defined, it becomes limited; you create a wall around it.

The more rational the words, the less are they indicative of God. It seems as if they tell you a great deal but they really tell you nothing; the palm is closed. When words are free of reason they seem to tell little but they tell all. Keep in mind this difference.

The words of Nanak are not the words of a logician; they are the words of a poet, a bard. They are the words of a lover of beauty. Nanak is not giving any definition of God through his words. They are like the open palm – hinting at something, not telling anything. They point towards something that cannot be said. Don't hold on to the words or else you will miss Nanak's message altogether.

If I point to the moon with my finger and you catch hold of my finger and refuse to look beyond it, how will you see the moon? The finger means nothing in itself; it is only a means to point at the moon. You have to let go of the finger to look at the moon, but people are such that they cling to the finger.

This is why books are worshipped. Some worship the Vedas, others the Koran and yet others the Guru Granth. They directed their attention towards the book, and miss what the book points to. The harder you hold on to the book, the further away from the truth you go – the fist gets tighter. For then words become more important; whereas the greatness lies not in the words but in the silence. For through silence alone you can know.

> *The Vedas say millions have searched and searched,*
> *Only to end in exhaustion.*

Man is incompetent when he seeks through his intelligence. All who set out to seek his depths were themselves dissolved, while he whom they sought remained undiscovered. The Vedas are one long story of man's incapacity. All scriptures agree that whatever man does, his field of action is so small that God cannot be ensnared in the web of his maneuvers. The harder you try to catch him, the emptier you find your hands.

The way of attaining God is different. Your method of grasping will not work; rather, you have to let go of your hold completely. Nor will your thinking and pondering help; you must discard these too. Your reasoning and logic will be a hindrance rather than a help, and your intelligence will act more like a wall than a stepping stone. On this path the more you rely on your understanding, the further astray you go. You have to leave it all to him.

To trust one's intelligence is the way of the ego. It means that you have taken upon yourself the task of finding him. Have you ever realized that whatever we set out in search of must be less, smaller than ourselves? Whatever you attain or acquire must be small enough for your fist to hold. And if God comes within your grasp, he can no longer be God.

Then how is one to attain God? It is quite the opposite way: he who is ready to lose himself attains him. The only way is to put yourself in the palm of his hand. Our usual attempt is to tie him in a bundle and bring him home to show off to others: See we have attained him! The attempt must fail. Such a vast expanse can't be tied into a bundle. Space cannot be wrapped up in a packet. The packets and the bundles will reach home, but the space will not. Leave yourself in his hands if you wish to attain him.

Nanak never tires of saying: "Endless sacrifices of myself are too little", "Whatever pleases you is best for me," "Whatever you make me do, that is the path," "Whatever you show me, that is the truth."

All these statements suggest only one thing: I have removed myself. I shall not intrude myself on you. I have no wish, no goal, no motive. I shall flow within you.

Therefore I say, faith is priceless, reasoning is fatal. To reason means: I shall decide, I am the judge. Faith means: you are the judge.

There are millions of underworlds
And infinite skies above.
The Vedas say millions have searched and searched,
Only to end in exhaustion.

Veda does not mean only the four books of the Hindus; rather it means the words of the sages, of all who have known. The word *veda* is derived from *vid* which means to know. It refers to the words of those who have known — the Buddhas, the Jainas, the *rishis*, just as the original Vedas, the *Rig Veda*, the *Atharv Veda*, etcetera, were the words of ancient rishis, people who have known. Whenever a person attains, knows, his words become Vedas, as will your words when you arrive. There is no limit to Vedas; the words of all those who have known in the past, all those who know today and all those who shall know in the future, are Vedas. Vedas are the quintessence of knowledge, of truth.

Nanak says: "The Vedas declare that all those who set out in search ultimately give up, exhausted and frustrated." It is important to understand this, because exhaustion and fatigue bear great importance in the life of the seeker. You will not be prepared to annihilate yourself until you are completely drained and depleted from exhaustion. The time comes finally when you realize that all your efforts are meaningless, that whatever you try to do you know that nothing will come of it. When your attitude of doing reaches the last stages and you realize the uselessness of whatever you do, whatever you find, whatever you attain turns out to be meaningless. Desire goads you on but even success proves flat and useless. Then you are filled with deep sadness and melancholy because all the endeavors turned to nothing. This is the point you must reach before you can let go of your ego; not before that.

How could you let go as long as there is still the hope of attaining something — either a little more effort and it will happen, or the direction is wrong, so you change the method or the guru, and abandon temple for mosque, or church for *gurudwara*. Until you are completely exhausted and thoroughly frustrated, until your dejection is complete, you cannot let go of the ego.

Buddha searched for six long years. Perhaps never has a human being approached the quest with such intensity. He staked his all in each trial. Whatever he was told he did to the last dot. No guru could say that he was lacking in effort or resolve.

One guru told him to eat only one grain of rice per day for three months. Buddha carried out his instructions. He was reduced to skin and bone, his back and abdomen became one; he could hardly breathe he was so weak. Yet he did not attain knowledge, because knowledge is never attained by doing anything.

Buddha did all that he was told, but the sense of I-ness persisted.

He undertook fasts, repeated endless mantra, did penance, worked diligently at other practices, but deep within the subtle ego kept repeating: I am doing it. The fist was closed, the I was present.

The only condition to attain him is that the I must drop. What difference does it make whether you are running a shop or offering prayers? In both cases the ego is involved; it is you working or worshipping. They are both the shop because you remain at the shop as long as the ego exists; there is a vocation, a job — that is the everyday working world of *sansara*. When the ego drops God begins; as you fall away and disappear he appears. You are out, he is in. Both cannot exist together; duality has no place here. There is room for only one — either you or he.

At last Buddha tired of it all. He had done all that was humanly possible — all to no avail. The hands were as empty as ever. He stepped into the river Niranjana to bathe. He had become so weak that he couldn't even wade out of the river. The current began to drag him away and he hadn't the strength to swim. He caught hold of a tree branch that was bent over the river; and there, while hanging onto the branch, he realized the fruitlessness of all his efforts. He had done everything that could be done, but gained nothing. In the bargain he had lost all bodily strength, and was so weak that he couldn't cross even a river as small as the Niranjana. Then how was he going to cross the ocean of existence? "All my efforts have brought me only to this. The world has become useless to me — the palace, all the wealth of the kingdom is like dust to my eyes. Now I am so terribly tired and disheartened that the spiritual search has become meaningless; even liberation is useless." At this point Buddha came to the realization that there is nothing worth achieving either in the mundane or in the spiritual world. All is a sham; all the running about is meaningless.

Somehow he got himself out of the river and went and sat under a tree. At that very moment he gave up all trying, all endeavor, because there was nothing to attain. All lesser attainments had led to frustration and hopelessness. His frustration became total; there was not an iota of hope. As long as there had been hope, ego persisted. Buddha slept under a tree that night. After endless births this was the first night when there was nothing to look forward to, nothing to attain, nowhere to go; nothing was left. If death had approached Buddha this moment, he would not have requested it to wait a while, because there was no need; all hopes were dashed to the ground.

In total tiredness all hues of the rainbow of hope have been rubbed away, all dreams are broken. That night Buddha slept soundly; no dream disturbed him. Dreams stop when there is nothing left to be attained, for dreams follow on the heels of desires. Desires walk ahead, dreams follow like shadows, because they are the slaves of desires. No desires, no dreams.

Buddha awakened when the last star was about to fade. But today was different — there was nothing to be done. Everything had become meaningless. Until the previous day there had been all that feverish activity — to find his soul, attain religion, God, so many things. And today, nothing! He just lay there. What else was he to do? He was looking at the fading star and, the story goes, at that moment he attained realization.

What happened at that moment? What happened that night that had not happened while he was straining every fiber of his body for six long years? What unique event brought about the realization of the ultimate knowledge to Buddha that morning? The answer lay in that complete exhaustion that Nanak was talking about. Buddha could do no more. He had reached the end of his body's strength, and with no result. The ego was crushed. All activities left him.

As soon as all effort ceases, grace descends; as soon as your hopes are shattered and all activities drop away and all struggling ends, the ego falls and the palm opens.

Do you realize it takes no effort to open your palm, though it does require work to close the fist? When you do nothing, the palm opens of its own accord, because that is its natural position. You needn't do anything to open the fist. Just don't close your fist and the palm remains open. That morning Buddha did nothing — and the palm opened.

Kabir said, "Things happen without being done." That moment Buddha did absolutely nothing — and everything happened! He was so tired, dead tired; he was frustrated. He had given up — and the ego fell away. As soon as the ego dropped God appeared.

Nanak says all the Vedas proclaim that those who set out to fathom His depth ended in utter frustration and exhaustion. And only when they were completely exhausted did they attain enlightenment. When you are completely tired then only will you attain him.

Therefore the aim of all yoga is to tire you out. God is not attained through yoga; only the ego is tired out. No methods lead to God — just to exhaustion, so that you reach a state of perfect relaxation; so that when the fist opens there is no strength to close it again.

Many have been exhausted and disillusioned in their quest. The Vedas say that effort must lead to this state and then realization takes place. The *satgurus*, the perfect masters, say that God is attained by grace alone and not your endeavors. He would be small compared to you if He could be attained by your endeavors. He is infinitely greater. No sooner are you empty than you are filled.

When the rains come it rains equally on the mountains as in the valleys. The valleys get filled; the mountains remain dry. The mountains are filled and have no place for water, but the valleys are empty, so they fill with water and form lakes.

God showers on all alike. He shows no discrimination. Existence is the same for everyone, without any differentiation. There is no question of the worthy or unworthy, sinner or saint. God's grace showers on all alike just as the skies cover everything beneath. But those who are filled with themselves miss his grace, because there is no room within. Those who are empty inside become filled, because there is enough space.

When the *I-ness* falls he himself comes, and the *I-ness* persists as long as there is hope for attainment.

> *The holy books claim eighteen thousand worlds*
> *But only one power behind all creation.*

In this infinite expanse with infinite forms, there is only one hidden behind the many. If you concentrate on the many, you will wander in the world; if you concentrate on the one, you will reach God.

Take it this way: there is a *mala* with many beads but the string that holds them together is one. If you hold on to the beads you will wander, but if you catch hold of the thread you will attain God.

There are infinite waves on the surface of the ocean. If you do not concentrate on the ocean but get involved with the waves, you will keep wandering. For the waves will form and disintegrate endlessly; one wave will lead you to another, then another...and another. You will be like a fragile little paper boat, jumping from one wave to another, drowning in one then in another, suffering here, suffering there. You will not reach the destination because the waves have no destination; there is only change. The destination is eternal, ever-abiding. You cannot rest in the waves. You can rest only where all waves become tranquil. There you attain that which never changes.

Do you realize that the more changes there are in your life, the greater is your restlessness? This explains so much of the agitation in the world today, because there is constant change. Scientists say that as much change took place in the course of the first thousand years after Christ, as took place in the five thousand years before Christ. Within the next two hundred years as much change took place as in the previous thousand years. By the time we reach the present century the rate of change is fantastic — in five years the changes equal the five thousand years before Christ! And by the time this century draws to a close, the same change will occur in five months. It happens so quickly that you can hardly reach one wave before another comes.

Ask an old villager; he will tell you his village is almost the same as when he was born. But look at the towns; they are the blueprints of the future; nothing is the same on two consecutive days. In the West the change is reaching a frightening pace.

People don't remain in one place in America. The average occupancy there is three years. Since this is the average, actually half the people stay longer, and there are others who change places every two to four months. Imagine every second month a change of place, change of atmosphere, of food, of clothes. With each change of season there is a change of cars, of clothes. The waves are increasing at a frightful pace, and they believe that the greater the change the more the enjoyment. In fact the greater the change, the greater the suffering. It is just as if you would uproot a plant every second day and plant it elsewhere. You do not have time to find your roots before you move again.

The greater the change, the more hellish life becomes. Therefore hell has become more intensified in the West. In the olden days the East was very tranquil because change was almost nonexistent; everything was static. In such stability it was easier to descend into the ocean, because the roots were well consolidated and each person could muster up the courage to dive deep.

Remember, if you keep floating with the waves you are a worldly person. If you begin to search for the ocean within the waves, by and by you become a sannyasin. To seek the eternal in the changing is sannyas. To grasp the unchanging within the changing is the art of sannyas. That alone is religion.

Nanak says that the writers of the holy books said there are eighteen thousand worlds. There are eighteen thousand existences, but the power behind all is essentially one. It depends on what you choose; both are open to you. You may choose the changeable that comes and goes; or you may choose that which is unchangeable, which never comes, never goes, but always is — on whose breast all change occurs, but which remains forever unchanged.

He who catches hold of this one, finds his life showered with bliss. He who grasps the infinitely changing finds himself passing from one suffering to another. He is never happy; he experiences merely a shadow of happiness in the process of change between two states of suffering.

How many times have you changed houses? How many times have you changed your car? When you exchange your old car for the new, the process of change gives you a momentary happiness; but this is how you felt when you bought the old car before, and this is how you will feel when you sell the present car for a newer model. And these are the same glimpses you feel when you change this wife for another, or one husband for the next. There is a momentary ray of hope.

When people are carrying a dead body to the burning grounds they keep changing shoulders when the weight is too much for one shoulder. For some time they feel relieved but the weight is the same, and soon the other shoulder tires and the weight has to be shifted again.

You are merely changing shoulders, as you change one wave for another. The way to attain happiness is to slip into the ocean through the wave. The waves are many; the ocean is one. There may be multiple existences, but the power is one. The one hides within everyone. The entire art of life lies hidden in this small verse — seek the one, grasp the string within the mala.

> *If anything could be written we would keep the account,*
> *But all estimates are destructible.*
> *Nanak says: He is the greatest of the great.*
> *He alone can know himself.*

Nothing can be written about him, because anything written can be erased whereas he is forever. How can a perishable thing give evidence of the imperishable? All writings get lost. How many scriptures have already been lost? And those that exist now will be lost. How many words have been born and how many have dissolved into the emptiness? But truth has remained the same forever.

So the quality of the two is different. What can be written can be erased. If you learn the art of reading that which is not written — if you learn the art of reading a blank paper — you will be able to understand God.

It happened once in the state of Maharashtra in India, there were three saints: one was Eknath, and there was Nivruttinath, and a woman fakir, Muktabai. Eknath sent a letter to Nivruttinath that was only a blank sheet of paper; nothing was written on it. Nivruttinath opened the letter and read it with great interest, then handed it to Muktabai. She, too, read it with one-pointed attention. Then both were lost in ecstatic bliss. Nivruttinath handed back the same letter to the messenger saying, "Take this reply back to Eknath."

The messenger was very puzzled. When he had brought the letter he had not known the contents. He certainly didn't suspect a blank piece of paper. Now seeing the same blank paper sent then returned in answer left him confused. He folded his hands and turned to Nivruttinath: "*Maharaj*, before I leave would you be so kind as to satisfy my curiosity? When nothing was written, what did you read? And not only you, even Muktabai read that letter with interest, and you were both overjoyed. You read so intently that it seemed you did read something. What did you read? And now you are returning the same piece of paper without writing a single word!"

"Eknath sent word," explained Nivruttinath, "that if you must read him you will have to read a blank paper. Whatever you read on a written paper is not him. We agree with him. We have understood his message, and this is our message — that we have understood. What he says is absolutely correct."

Books have been written but God cannot be written. How will the books tell about him? You wish to read the unwritten. Read the Vedas, the Guru Granth, the Koran; leave the written words and attend to the unwritten. Read the space between the lines, between the words, and remember what you have read.

If you read and concentrate on the written word you will become a pundit or a priest. If you read the unread, you become a sage. If you concentrate on the written word you will acquire a lot of information ; if you remember the unwritten, you will become like a child — innocent, artless. Remember, the unwritten is the door.

Therefore, asks Nanak, is there a record or an estimation of him that can be written? Has anyone ever known something about him that he can tell? No information can be his information. Those who know become silent. If ever they say anything it is always an arrow pointing towards silence. If they have written anything it is always with the intent that you may read the unwritten.

No account of him can be written. Whatever is written will disintegrate one day. No matter how much you may protect the books, they are bound to be lost. After all, they are made of paper and the words are ink. What can be more perishable than these? Regard them as paper boats. Those who ride the boat of the scriptures and attempt to reach God are sailing in paper boats that are bound to capsize and drown them. Don't ride paper boats. They are all right for children to play with, but not safe for undertaking a journey. And this journey is a great journey, perhaps the greatest of journeys that man ever embarks on, because there is no ocean greater than the ocean of existence.

No, scriptures will not do. Understand their message, the hint they give. It is only this: become empty.

But there is no end to man's foolishness. We promptly fill ourselves with that very person who tells us to be empty, cramming our skulls with such people, once again starting the cycle of changes. Our hopes, our expectations, our intelligence, offer no wisdom or understanding.

I must tell you a well-known story from the life of Alexander the Great. It is said that he was in search of the elixir of life, which once taken keeps death away. His plan to conquer the whole world was mainly in order to find this nectar.

The story goes that he ultimately found the spring of the immortal waters in a cave. Alexander entered the cave filled with joy, that now his lifelong desire was about to be fulfilled. He rested his eyes for a moment on the bubbling brook in front of him. Just as he was about to take the water, a crow that was sitting in the cave called out, "Wait, don't make that mistake!" Alexander looked at the crow. His condition was pitiful. It was difficult to make out that he was a crow. His wings had fallen off, his eyes could see no more, his whole body was in a state of disintegration. He was just a skeleton. Alexander asked him, "Who are you to stop me? What is your reason?"

"Listen to my story first, O king, then do as you see fit," said the crow. "I too was in search of this spring. I too discovered the cave and drank this water. Now I cannot die and I want so much to die. Look at my state: my eyes are blind, my body is old and withered, my wings have broken and I cannot fly, my feet have disintegrated, but alas, I cannot die! Look at me just once and then do what you please.

"Now I beg that someone should kill me, but alas I cannot be killed because I have drunk this nectar. Now I pray to God night and day to grant me death. I want to die somehow, anyhow!"

It is said that Alexander stopped and pondered, then he silently left the cave without touching the water.

If your desires are fulfilled you find yourself in as much difficulty as when they are unfulfilled. You do not wish to die. If you were to find this cave and you drink the water from the spring, then you will find yourself in a dilemma — what will you do with your life now? When life was in your hands, when you could have really lived, you were busy looking for the nectar to escape death. You cannot live with the elixir, you cannot live with death, you cannot live in poverty, you cannot live in riches; you cannot live in hell, you cannot live in heaven, and yet you consider yourselves wise!

Bayazid was a Sufi mystic. He told God in his prayers, "O Lord, do not listen to my prayers; do not fulfill my prayers, because where have I the wisdom to ask for what is good for me?"

Man is absolutely without intelligence. He gets himself caught in the web of his desires and then wanders about within them. If his desires are not satisfied he is in difficulty. If they are satisfied he finds himself again in difficulty. Ponder a bit, go back into your own past and take stock of your life. What have you desired that has even partially come to pass? Has it given you happiness? Some of your desires that have not been fulfilled – have they given you happiness? In both cases you have had nothing but sorrow and suffering. You become involved with your desires, some that were fulfilled; and you are still involved with the unfulfilled desires.

What is understanding? What are the characteristics of wisdom but to ask for that which when attained, all sorrow and miseries end? On that basis nobody in the world except a religious person is wise. Only he who desires God never repents; whatever else you ask for ends in regret.

Keep in mind that all your desires end in regret and repentance, except to desire God. Less than that will not do, because that is the goal of life.

Can you attain him through the scriptures? Nanak says you will not find him there. You will find mere words and doctrines, not truth. Where will you find truth? The answer Nanak gives is: "He is the greatest of the great and he alone can know himself. It means that you cannot stand away from him and know him. When you drown yourself in him, then only can you know him. The only path to truth requires that you become one with God."

We can obtain information about matter. That is the basis of science. The scientist examines and investigates matter from the outside and obtains knowledge of it. But nothing can be known about God in this manner. You have to go within, so deep within yourself that the boundary between him and you is lost. You become his heartbeat and he yours. Where there is such oneness, there wisdom resides.

How can this come about through scriptures, through mere words? It can happen only through love. Therefore Nanak declares: "Love is the key. If love for his name arises within you, if his melody begins to play within you, and you go mad in his love, then only can you know."

In the scriptures you will find a lot of material to discuss and debate. Don't confuse this with wisdom or you will miss the real thing. You will know neither God nor yourself, because the way to know both is the same. To know your own self, be one with God; then alone the wisdom to know is attained. To know God, then, become one with him. You have to taste him; that is the only way. All your debates and discussions without this experience will be childish and foolish.

When Nasruddin reached the ripe old age of eighty, he sent for his eldest son, who was about sixty. He told him that as it was quite some months since his mother had died and he could no longer stay without a woman, he had decided to remarry.

The son was worried – marriage at this age? He asked Mulla, "Whom have you decided to marry?"

"The girl next door," replied Nasruddin.

The son burst out laughing, "What a joke! Are you crazy? That girl is not more than eighteen years old!"

"Call me crazy?" the Mulla shouted at his son. "You fool! Your mother was barely eighteen when I married her. How does her age make a difference?"

All reasoning of man in connection with God is like that. It is always outside of the facts. For all purposes the girl is of a marriageable age, but the Mulla forgets his own age. Likewise you try to catch God from the outside with the help of reasoning and doctrines, but you do not give any thought to the fact that you have to go within yourself; you have to become a part of the doctrine.

The pundit, the learned ecclesiast, always remains outside. Knowledge is the goods he gathers, but he remains outside of it. He is very clever, very cunning. He does not risk the disruption of going within; he calculates from outside. But this cleverness ultimately proves to be great foolishness, because there is no other way to know him.

It is just as if someone were to read treatises on love and assume that he knows what love is. Someone else reads about the dawn and feels he knows the beauty of day breaking. Yet another reads about flowers and considers himself an authority on them. This is no more than information. But the real encounter is with the rising sun or the dew-filled flowers! Then the sun is not outside of you; for just that moment you and the sun are one, when your hearts beat together.

And when you meet the flowers — when their fragrance and your very existence are intermingled — you are lost in each other, you are one. Oh, the bliss! This is the moment when your being and that of the flowers dance together, sway in the breeze; can you ever get this moment from a book? Impossible! When the experience with an ordinary flower cannot be obtained from books, how can the experience of God, who is the highest flower of life?

How can you establish a relationship with him through doctrines? You will have to go within. Only those who are mad can enter, not the intelligent; they are left out. For your intelligence, your cunningness is not genuine. It has always been true that lunatics have attained and the wise have lagged behind.

Nanak says there is only one way and that is to know him. He is great and he alone can know himself. You can never know him unless you become one with him and merge in his omnipresent power. To know God you must become God! There is no other way. Reach those very heights, those very depths, then only can you know. You have to be one with him.

Those who praise, praise him, but this does not bring about awareness. No matter how much you sing his praise, you still remain outside of him. The distance persists. He will forever remain God and you the devotee. You will be repeating words and words, but never bridge the distance, which will only be increased. Prayers should not be said, they should be heard. Listen, do not speak. Be silent so that he may speak and you can hear him.

Instead you keep on talking — not only talking, but shouting! Kabir had to say, "Is your God deaf? Can he not hear, that you have to shout so much? Does he not have ears? For whom are you shouting? Will your voice reach him quicker?"

> *Those who worship praise him,*
> *But have no remembrance of him.*

The word *surati*, remembrance, is the quintessence of Nanak's practice. All saints merge into surati. The word comes to us from Buddha, who uses the Sanskrit word *smriti*. Gurdjieff calls it self remembering, and Krishnamurti refers to it as awareness, a state of complete consciousness.

Remembrance is very subtle. It needs to be explained with an example. A mother is very busy cooking. Her little child is playing around. For all purposes it looks as if she is engrossed in her cooking, but her surati is in the child — lest the child fall, or go too near the staircase, or pick up something wrong to put into its mouth. She is busy in her work, but in everything that she does there is a persistent remembrance of the child. While the mother sleeps at night, no thunderclap can disturb her asleep, but let the child so much as stir her sleep is disrupted and her hand goes out to the child. Surati persists even in sleep — remembrance of the child.

Surati involves a continuous remembrance, like the thread in the beads. Do everything that the world demands of you, but let your mind stay always with him. Sit, sleep, walk, eat; no purpose is served by running away from the world. Go to work, go to the office or the shop or the factory. Dig pits, because money has to be earned; worry about your kids. All these webs of the material world are there, but through it all keep alive remembrance of him. Let life go on outside as usual, but within let there be only he! Keep your relationship with him always fresh and alive.

Nanak says there is no need to run away from the world. Attain surati and you become a sannyasin. Once remembrance is found, everything is in order. Of what use is your running to the woods if your surati is filled with the world? But this is what usually happens. People leave the world and flee to the forest — and think of home! It is the mind's way not to worry about where it is, but focus on where it is not. When you are here you think how wonderful it must be in the Himalayas. Then you go to the Himalayas and start thinking: Perhaps I could have been in Pune. Maybe I have gone astray. The rest of the world stayed where they were. They can't all be wrong. What am I doing sitting under this tree?

Even in the wilderness you will count your money and keep your accounts. The faces of wife and children will hover around you. You will be in the Himalayas all right, but your surati will be in your home with your family.

Nanak says: Stay where you wish, but let your remembrance be in God. Nothing is achieved by singing praises; everything is achieved by surati. All singing of praises is superficial, whereas remembrance is within. There is no need to shout aloud: "You are great, O Lord, I am a sinner. You are the redeemer, I am a beggar." Why shout like that? Whom are you telling? There is no need to ring bells and sing praise; what is needed is remembrance. Keep his remembrance; do not forget for a moment. Nurture his remembrance.

If you were to find a diamond, you would quickly put it safely away in your pocket. You might even tie it in a handkerchief lest it fall somewhere. Whether you go to the market, make your purchases or meet your friends, your remembrance will always be with the diamond. A faint low sound repeats again and again saying, "The diamond is in the pocket, the diamond is in the pocket..." Every now and again you will feel it with your fingers to see whether it is still there.

Nurture the remembrance of God within in the same manner. Now and then touch it inside to be sure it is there. While walking on the road, stop and look inside. Is the thread of remembrance intact? Is the flow continuous? While eating stop for a second and check; close your eyes and watch if the remembrance is flowing.

Gradually the experience will go deeper and deeper. Then the flow of remembrance continues in your sleep too. When it flows all twenty-four hours of the day, you will have made the bridge between yourself and him. Now you can close your eyes and merge into him whenever you please. The road is now made; the instant you close your eyes you are lost in him. And when you return to the world from your meeting with him you will be refreshed, filled with absolute energy, as fresh and light as if you have just had a bath. Therefore Nanak says that bathing in thousands of holy places takes place in surati.

> *Those who worship praise him,*
> *But have no remembrance of him,.*
> *As rivers and streams know not the ocean*
> *Into whose vastness they fall.*

The rivers and the streams fall into the ocean, but that is not enough to know the ocean. The rivers and canals have no consciousness; therefore, though they fall into the ocean they are not aware of it. We also are falling into God all day long, but we are not aware of it. We move round and round and about him but we know not. Again and again we fall into him. In every death we fall into him, in every birth we arise from him, but we lack remembrance.

So we are like the rivers and rivulets. We fall into the ocean but are unconscious of the event. Without awareness we are unfeeling, unconscious. We move as if in a trance, as if under the influence of drugs, or in sleep, or caught in a deep weariness. The rivers and streams fall into the ocean but remain inferior, because they are unaware of what has happened.

We are going in and out of him every moment. If you observe carefully and as your remembrance becomes stronger, you will realize how each breath you take goes into him and comes back to you from him. When the breath goes out of you, you go into God; when the breath comes in, God flows into you. In every moment, with each breath, he spreads all over you. And your joy can know no bounds.

With this experience you will get your first feeling of gratitude, of thanksgiving. Then only will you be able to say, "Your grace is unbounded." Then only will you be able to say, "Blessed am I," and then for the first time the light and splendor of faith in him will descend. Singing the Lord's praise does not make one a believer in God, but remembrance does.

Even kings and emperors of great domains,
Who possess enormous treasures,
Cannot compare with the lowly ant
With remembrance of God in his heart.

The greatest of kings possessing wealth as vast as the ocean and whose splendor is untold, cannot equal a tiny, lowly ant who has acquired the alchemy of remembrance, who always thinks of you. The lowliest of the lowly became the greatest of the great on acquiring surati; whereas the greatest of kings remains miserably destitute without remembrance.

There is only one wretchedness — to forget God. There is only one wealth — to attain his remembrance. He whose surati awakens has acquired all that is worth acquiring, achieved all worth achieving. Then it doesn't matter if he has no cloth to cover him, or roof to shelter him. It doesn't matter how much wealth you possess, how many palaces, how many titles, if in the absence of surati you feel a miserable beggar within. The pain, the anguish of poverty will always gnaw at your heart.

Nanak says the only kind of wealth is his remembrance. The only kind of poverty is to forget him. Ponder well over this. Are you rich or poor? Don't think of your bank balance, which is a deception, but open your internal account and see the entry labeled remembrance. You are rich to the extent of your remembrance. If there is none, then you have not yet begun to acquire wealth. What you amass in the outside world makes no difference.

When Alexander the Great was about to die he told his ministers that his hands should be left hanging outside the coffin. When they complained that this was not the custom and wanted to understand the reason, he said, "I want people to see that in spite of all my conquests I leave this world with empty hands."

People like Alexander die as paupers. The most powerful turn out to be impotent; but if even an ant is filled with remembrance, all the Alexanders pale in insignificance before it.

Who was Nanak? What was he? He had no wealth, no status, no kingdom, but how many kings faded into insignificance before him?

Nanak became precious because of his surati. Kings will come and go but Nanak will remain forever. Fame and honor are made and destroyed, it is not possible to destroy Nanak, because he who takes shelter in him who is indestructible cannot be destroyed.

Even if you are a lowly ant it does not matter; only let his remembrance forever be. Do not indulge in the madness of acquiring vast kingdoms, because it always happens that the more you are engaged in piling up outside wealth, the more you forget to remember him; how else could you succeed? If you remember him all outside wealth will be as dust to you, then the world's honor and fame will be of no consequence.

When little children gather colored stones, try to explain to them that they are worthless pebbles; they will still smuggle them home. The mother finds their pockets filled with this junk. These same children, once they grow up and their understanding develops, no longer collect these stones; they in turn tell their children not to indulge in this foolish game. But what about all the useless things they continue to collect?

Whatever you gather in the world holds significance and value for you as long as your understanding or remembrance has not awakened. As soon as remembrance awakens in you, you become mature. Then a flame of understanding is kindled. By its light you come to know that all you hold precious was mere rubble. You wonder why in heaven you went after it, why you were so mad about it. What have you attained by gaining this you ask yourself.

Suddenly it all becomes meaningless and worthless in your eyes. Life is transformed the moment surati awakens. A revolution takes place within you. Your old personality dies and a new one is born.

The quest for this new birth is religion. Think about this. Seek within — is there a place, ever so slight, for surati within you? Some little corner? Is there a temple in you where remembrance vibrates? Do you hear some little melody inside singing his remembrance? Is that remembrance always inside you or do you keep forgetting? Or do you remember him at all?

If you begin to contemplate these lines the very thinking will provoke the birth of remembrance within, because as you begin to think, you will naturally start thinking of him. The very thought that there is no remembrance of him inside me will awaken his remembrance.

As the remembrance appears more and more frequently, as the hammer strikes again and again, the mark goes deeper and deeper. Constant hammering writes a mark even on a stone; and so with your heart the mark is bound to be intensified.

Kabir said that the rope rubs against the well as it goes up and down in drawing water and it forms a mark on the stone. As the rope of surati rubs against your heart, surely it will form a mark; and the mark develops soon, because nothing is more tender than the heart. All that is required is for the rope to keep rubbing against you.

CHAPTER 11

Fear Is a Beggar

There is no end to his virtues,
Nor to their narration.
There is no end to his works and his bounty,
And endless what He sees and hears.
There is no knowing the secrets of his mind;
There is no beginning or end to it.
So many struggle to know his depth,
But none has ever achieved it.
No one has ever known his limits;
The further you look, the further beyond He lies.
The Lord is great. His place is high,
And higher even is his name.
Nanak says: One only knows his greatness
When raised to his heights,
By falling under the glance
Of his all-compassionate grace.
His compassion is beyond all description.
The lord's gifts are so great He expects nothing in return.
However great a hero or warrior, man keeps on begging.
It is difficult to conceive the countless numbers who go on asking.
They indulge themselves in desires and dissipate their lives.
And others receive, yet deny it.
They go on suffering from their hunger,
Yet will not take to remembrance
O Lord, these too are your gifts.

252   The True Name

Your order alone gives freedom or bondage.
Nobody can debate this fact.
He who indulges in useless babble
Realizes his folly when struck in the face.
He alone can know himself,
And only the rarest can describe him;
He bequeaths the quality of his state to whomever He chooses.
Nanak says, He is the king of kings.

There is no end to his grandeur. Whatever we say about it is so little as to betray our utter incompetence.

Rabindranath Tagore lay on his deathbed. An old friend sitting by his side said to him, "You can leave this world satisfied, you have accomplished whatever you wanted to do. You have attained great respect, you wrote many songs, and the whole world knows you as the divine bard. Really nothing is left undone."

Rabindranath opened his eyes, looked sadly at his friend and said, "Don't say such things. I was just telling God that all I wanted to sing is still unsung. What I wanted to say is still unsaid. My whole life has been spent merely tuning my instrument!" He felt he had not yet begun to sing his praise and already the moment to leave had arrived.

Rabindranath had written six thousand songs, all in praise of God. Yet he felt he hadn't sung a single word of his glory. Nanak also says the same thing and this is the experience of all the *rishis* who have known. Whatever is said about him is only like adjusting the instrument; his song can never be sung. Who will sing it? How can one limited personality contain the boundless expanse? How can you hold the skies in your fist? All our efforts prove futile and only after trying totally can we realize our incompetence.

Only when you realize how insignificant you are can the understanding of his greatness take root. Fools always think themselves great; wise men are aware of their smallness. As understanding increases the feeling of being too small, too insignificant, parallels the sense of his vastness and all-pervading presence. A moment comes in this quest when you are completely lost, and only he remains.

The speaker is lost — what is there to say? Only he remains: his glory, his grandeur, his endless resonance. The seer is lost; only the seen remains. You are extinct, completely annihilated; then who will give tidings of him? Whatever discussions men have had about God have been hopeless. When a tremendous event occurs we are struck dumb; when a person reaches God he becomes speechless. Not only is speech lost, but the very breath stops. You stop completely at the moment of knowing him: neither thoughts move, nor words, nor breath, nor does the heart beat. Even a single heartbeat would deprive you of his sight, that slight trembling can produce a separation.

In just such a moment of speechless silence, Nanak has uttered these words. They are not to teach others, but to express his own helplessness.

> *There is no end to his virtues,*
> *Nor to their narration.*
> *There is no end to his works and his bounty,*
> *And endless what He sees and hears.*
> *There is no knowing the secrets of his mind;*
> *There is no beginning or end to it.*
> *So many struggle to know his depth,*
> *But none has ever achieved it;*

As long as you feel you have known God, you are under an illusion — you err. For whatever you have known cannot be God, whatever you have measured cannot be God, whatever you have fathomed cannot be God. You must be diving into some lake; you are nowhere near the ocean. You have gone into some insignificant valley; you have not known the abysmal depths where falling is endless. You must have climbed some nondescript hill on the outskirts of your village; you have no knowledge of his Everest where climbing is impossible. We have succeeded in climbing the Everest of the Himalayas, though with great difficulty, but to scale his Everest is unthinkable.

Why is it impossible? Try to understand how inconceivable it is to gauge or understand God....we are a part of him. How can a part know the whole? I can hold everything of this world within my hand, except myself. How can I hold myself in my own hand? My eyes can see everything under the sun, but how can they look at me? They cannot see me completely for the simple reason that they are a part of me, and the part can never know the whole; it may get glimpses but not the complete picture.

The difficulty is that we are a part of this vast expanse. Had we not been a part of God we would have known him; had we been distinct and separate from him, we could have gone around him and investigated. But we are a part of him; we are his very heartbeat, his breath! How can we go around him? How can we grasp him? Man is but a particle of sand in this vast expanse, a drop in the ocean. How can this one lonely drop contain the whole ocean? How can it know the entire ocean?

This is very interesting: the drop is in the ocean and the drop is the ocean. So in a very profound sense, the drop knows the ocean, because the ocean is not different from the drop. And yet in another sense it cannot know the ocean because the ocean is not separate from it. This is the biggest paradox of religion: we know God and yet we do not know him at all. How can this be when he throbs in us and we in him? We are not far from him; in fact there isn't the slightest distance between him and us.

So in a sense we know him well; and yet we do not know him at all, because we are a part of him. How can a part know the whole? We dive in him, we float in him, live in him; at times we forget him and sometimes we remember him. Sometimes we feel ourselves very near him and sometimes far. In clear moments we feel that we have known him. When the heart gets over-filled, we know that we have known, because we have recognized him. Wisdom comes, then again it is lost and there is deep darkness. Then we falter again. But this very state of knowing and not knowing is the basic condition of a religious person.

When anyone questioned Buddha about God he would keep silent. What could he say? Contradictions cannot be spoken about. If he were to say, "I know," he would be making a mistake, because who can say that he knows? And if Buddha were to say he did not know, he would be making a false statement, because who knew more than he!

Early one morning a very learned pundit came to Buddha to ask about God. Buddha remained silent. Soon the pundit left. Ananda asked Buddha why he had not answered, since the pundit was a man who knew a great deal and deserved an answer. Buddha said, "Just because he is deserving, it is all the more difficult to give him an answer. If I said I have known him, it would be wrong, because without knowing him completely how could I claim to know him at all? I said I did not, that too would be false. All claims derive from the ego and the ego can never know him. Since he is deserving and intelligent and understanding, I had to keep silent. He understood. Did you not see him bow before he left?"

Then Ananda remembered how the pundit was so grateful that he bowed reverently at Buddha's feet. "How wonderful! Did he really understand? That never occurred to me."

Buddha replied, "Horses are of three types. The first type you hit with a whip and they will move, inch by inch. The second type you need not whip; just threaten them and they move. For the third, you need not even crack the whip; just the shadow of the whip sets them going. The pundit belongs to the third type. I had only to show him the shadow and he started on the journey."

Words are the whips; silence is the shadow. Words are needed, because it is the rare horse that responds to the shadow of the whip. The condition of one who knows is such that he cannot say he knows, and he cannot say he does not know. He is in between knowing and not knowing.

Nanak says he is without end. Whatever you say of him is too little. You keep on saying and yet you find that there is so much to say that you have hardly said anything. All expressions regarding him are incomplete. And all scriptures are incomplete; they are meant for the horses who don't respond to the shadow of the whip.

> *There is no end to his virtues,*
> *Nor to their narration.*
> *There is no end to his works and his bounty.*

As religion penetrates a person more and more profoundly, he begins to see his various works and also his beneficence.

His works are manifested all around us but most people are blind to it. They say, "Where is God? Who is the creator?" Seeing the creation around them, they are blissfully unaware of the creator! They persist in asking, "Is there a hand behind all this creation? Who could it be?" They are stone-blind, they cannot visualize the hand that has produced this vast creation. The irony is that in other respects they accept and believe blindly.

To date no one has seen the electron with the naked eye. Science says that the electron is the last particle of electricity. As the basis of the world of matter, its various combinations have given rise to the earth. But so far no one has seen the electron, nor is there any hope of seeing it. Then how can scientists believe in the electron? They say that its effects, its results, prove its existence.

The cause is subtle, the effect is gross. We cannot see the hand of God, but we can see his works. We believe in the existence of electrons because we see the results. Yet we deny the existence of God whose proof lies all around us. The flower opens; some hidden hand must make it bloom, or else how can it? The seed breaks but someone must break it; when the hard shell cracks the tender plant appears bearing delicate flowers.

Everywhere we see his handwriting, but the hand cannot be seen. The hand is not visible because there is a balance between the subtle and the gross. The cause is always subtle; the result is always gross. We cannot see the cause. God is the highest cause, but his handiwork is evident all around us.

So there are three types of people — the three types of horses according to Buddha. First are those who cannot even see his handiwork, they are so blind! They ask: "What is God? Who is the creator? What proof is there?" If the vast creation all around us is not enough for them, if they cannot see his hand behind all creation, what else will make them understand?

What greater proof is there than that life moves in a consecutive and balanced order? There is no disjunction anywhere within this enormous *leela*, this play. It is a continuous flow. Night and day the music of creation plays its enchanting melody. Everything happens as it should. The universe is not a chaos, but a cosmos; it is not happening by chance but by a well-determined law working all the time.

This law is referred to as *dhamma* or *dharma*. Lao Tzu calls it *Tao*, the way; Nanak calls it *hukum*, divine order. When Nanak says hukum do not imagine that he is standing somewhere issuing orders. Hukum means the universe is an order, not a chaos. Things do not happen here haphazardly. An ordering hand is in everything, providing a purpose behind each event. All happenings are directed towards their ultimate development.

If you have no eyes for creation you are totally blind. There are many who cannot see the hand behind creation. When you see a small picture or statue and you ask who made this, you never for a moment think it may have been formed by chance. But such a vast painting hangs all around you, each leaf a work of his genius, and you cannot see him behind all this? You must simply have made up your mind not to see him; you have resolved to turn your back towards him as if you feel there is some danger and you are afraid.

Certainly the fear is there. No sooner do you recognize his hand behind the canvas of this vast creation than you are a changed person; you cannot remain the same. Whoever hears even the faintest murmur of the divine music in creation has to alter his life, because once you begin to see his hand behind everything, you cannot continue to do what you have been doing; it all appears wrong.

As long as you pretend he doesn't exist you can sin, misbehave, mistreat others, and give yourself full freedom to indulge in any evil; as soon as his hand appears to you that freedom is lost. Then you have to think twice before you act and pay more attention to remembrance, to remembering God, because now you know that he sees, that he is present. He is in and around everyone, everything. Whatever you do to anyone, you do to him. If you pick someone's pocket, it is his pocket you pick; if you steal, you steal from him; if you kill, it is him you kill.

Most human beings turn a blind eye towards him. Once aware of his presence, you can no longer remain as you are; you will have to change at your very roots. This change is so sweeping that many prefer to avoid all the trouble, so they deny God and remain as they are.

A hundred years ago Nietzsche declared: "God is dead. Now man is totally free." It is exactly for this freedom that you deny God, because then you are at liberty to do as you please. There is no one to decide for you. You are unrestrained, independent. He who is self-willed and independent persists in denying God no matter how much you try to convince him. It remains easy to deny him because the gross handiwork can be seen, but the subtle hand remains invisible.

So people say: "Creation happens by itself; everything happens on its own." But this is the definition of God: he who happens on his own, who is *swayambhu*, the self-created.

The second type of man sees God's handiwork and also accepts the hand behind it, but his acceptance is only mental. He is intimidated and frightened, so you will find him in temples and mosques, in churches and *gurudwaras*. He goes there because he is frightened, having suffered the lashes of the whip of life. Out of fear he comes to pray, to beg protection and to seek solace in wealth, position, name. He has come to beg. Fear is always a beggar, always asking for something or other. He has an inkling of the hand behind creation and a slight feeling for the presence of God, but only because of his fear. He is totally oblivious to God's munificence, or else he would not beg.

The third type is what Nanak talks about, the devotee. He sees his handiwork all around; he also sees his bounty and his grace in everything. To see his grace is subtle, like seeing the shadow of the whip. The devotee can see at every moment that he showers us with his gifts. What is left to be desired? You can only thank him, therefore the devotee goes to the temple in thanksgiving, not as a supplicant. He has nothing to ask for.

Were God to appear before him and say, "Ask whatever you wish," he will instead reply, "You have given everything. It is already more than enough, more than I deserve. To ask for anything would imply a complaint that you haven't given enough, but I have been filled to the brim. What more is there when you have been given life?" But you attach no value to life.

It is said that a great miser's life was coming to an end. As is usually the case his whole life had been spent gathering wealth which he was hoping to enjoy someday in the future. When death knocked at his door he was frightened that all his endeavors had been in vain. In working untiringly to gather enough wealth he had postponed living.

He told death, "I shall give you ten million rupees; give me just twenty-four hours, because I have not yet enjoyed life."

Death replied, "There can be no bargaining."

The man persisted, "I would give fifty million, a hundred million, just for one day." Ultimately he offered all his wealth for twenty-four hours more.

A whole lifetime lost amassing this fortune, and now he was begging to give it away for just one day more. He had never breathed freely; he had never sat beside the flowers; he had never seen the sun rising at the break of day, nor had he ever talked with the twinkling stars. He had never lain on the green grass and seen the clouds pass by nor heard the birds sing. He had had no time to see life as it passed by. All along he had deferred that moment. "Now I shall work, later I shall enjoy." That moment never came.

Death said to him, "This is no transaction. Your time is up. Get ready to leave."

The man said, "Give me a few moments. I ask not for myself but for those who come after. Let them know how I toiled all these years and let life pass me by in the hope of enjoying it someday. Let me tell them that day never came." He wanted this inscription put on his grave.

All graves bear this inscription. If you have the eyes, go and read them. And the same will be inscribed on your grave too, if you do not sit up and take notice. If only you could see — you would find that what life has given you is limitless and beyond comparison.

How do you value life? For a moment more of life you are willing to give up everything, but during the years you have lived you were not at all thankful to God. If you were dying of thirst in a desert, you would be ready to part with all you possess just for a mouthful of water, but have you ever looked with gratitude at the rivers that flow, the clouds that bring rain? If the sun were to become cold we would die this very moment, yet did you ever get up in the morning and thank the sun?

Actually man follows a strange logic: what is near him he cannot see, what is not there at all he sees. When a tooth falls out, the tongue goes time and again to the empty space in your mouth. When the tooth was there the tongue never once stopped in that spot. Now no matter how much you try to stop your tongue, it keeps exploring the empty place.

Man's mind always searches out empty places. He is blind towards all the filled places, but has eyes for all that is empty. Have you ever taken account of all you possess? Unless you do, you will never become aware of God's gifts; they are infinite.

God's bounty is infinite but try to be aware of what he has given you. All around his grace pours. Just as each handiwork bears his signature, so behind each handiwork his grace lies hidden. All existence blooms only for you, all existence is his gift — to you. When a person becomes capable of seeing this, a new kind of devotion is born.

There is the atheist, stiff with pride; there is the believer, trembling with fear. Both are irreligious. The really religious person dances and sings in utter gratefulness; he is filled with ecstasy.

There is no end to his works and his bounty,
And endless what He sees and hears.
There is no knowing the secrets of his mind;
There is no beginning or end to it.
So many struggle to know his depth,
But none has ever achieved it.
No one has ever known his limits;
The further you look, the further beyond He lies.
The Lord is great. His place is high,
And higher even is his name.

What does it mean for his name to be high? For travelers on the path, it is only through his name that we reach him. His name is the bridge; if it got lost the bridge is gone. For us the path is more significant than the destination for the simple reason that the goal cannot be reached without the path.

Therefore, Nanak says, he who knows the name has found the key. The key is more important than the treasure-house. To look at, it is only a piece of iron; but this piece of iron will open the doors to infinite treasures.

His name, which Nanak refers to as *Omkar*, is the key. This key opens his gate. When this "remembrance" begins to crystallize in you, you will also have cast the mold of this key inside. The key is not such as can be given to you; you have to cast it yourself; you have to become the key. Gradually you will find yourself turning into a key through the resonance of Omkar. Then you yourself will open his gates.

Man can find himself either in the state of thoughts or in the state of no-thought. In the first state, storms of thoughts are raging inside you; the mental skies are filled with clouds of argument, debate and discussion. It is as if there is always a crowd gathered in your head, as in the marketplace; it is a schizophrenic state.

The other state is of no-thoughts; the bazaar has cleared, the shops have closed; the market is deserted, there is silence and stillness all around. All thoughts have gone. As long as you are united with the thoughts, you are one with the world; as soon as your mind is freed of all thoughts, in this no-mind state, you are one with God. No sooner are you empty than the door opens.

The key that takes you from thoughts to no-thought is called the name, the resonance of *Omkar*. The first stage is the *japa*, the repetition of Omkar. Get up in the morning or in the stillness of the night, sit in your room and repeat Om, Om, Om as loudly and quickly as you can, so that it resonates all around you. The Omkar has a very lovely melody. It is not music created by man, it is the rhythmic melody that resounds in existence. As you progress, taking the name louder and louder, its impression will begin to form on you. This is the state of japa, repetition.

Then, slowly slowly, close your lips and begin sounding Om within, as you did without. This time the resonance will be only in the mind. This is the intervening state between japa and *ajapa*.

Let the resonance increase deeper and deeper within. You must repeat the Omkar as well as hear it; articulate the name and be aware and listen to it also. Gradually you must decrease articulation of the name and concentrate on the resonance within. Then a moment comes when you will stop pronouncing the japa but the resonance continues. Then you only listen. This is the *ajapa-jap*, the unrepeated repetition.

When the resonance arises on its own, the Omkar has manifested. This is the sound of the stream of life that flows within you. The day you are capable of hearing it, you will discover you can hear it all day long. It is already there so you don't have to bring it about. You merely close your eyes and you will hear.

When anxiety, tension, restlessness or anger take hold of you, just shut your eyes for a moment and hear the resonance within. A moment's touch of Omkar and anger flees. A slight contact with the music within, a faint remembrance of the name, and the mind that made you so restless is no more.

Light a torch in a dark house; at the appearance of light darkness flees. Thus, a slight spark of Omkar and all darkness fades.

So it is that Nanak lays so much stress on Omkar — *Ek Omkar satnam*. All of his practice aims at attaining the resonance of the authentic Omkar. He refers to it as *sabad*, the word, or *nam*, the name.

> *The Lord is great. His place is high,*
> *And higher even is his name.*
> *Nanak says: One only knows his greatness*
> *When raised to his heights,*
> *By falling under the glance*
> *Of his all-compassionate grace.*

Nanak is saying: Greater than you is your name. You are endless. For us the name is our only clue, through the name alone are we joined to you. Whether you are or you are not, we do not know. It is the name alone that brings tidings of you. Through the power of the name shall we be drawn gradually towards you. When the resonance sounds by itself you are drawn towards God.

Scientists speak of the force of gravitation. We remain on the ground because of gravitation. If the earth were to lose this power of gravitation we would be flung up into the skies.

Simone Weil, a leading thinker in our century, has written a book called *Grace and Gravitation*. She says, "Just as we cannot see the force of gravitation that pulls us to the earth, there is another force at work, which is called grace."

Only yesterday it appeared in the newspapers that scientists are worried because the force of gravitation is becoming less. Though it has decreased only minimally, if this continues the earth will disintegrate, because it is gravitation alone that holds things together. It is this invisible magnetic force of the earth that keeps the trees rooted in the soil, allows man to walk and birds to fly.

Simone Weil has asserted that the force of grace also exists, and it too is invisible. She is talking precisely about that which Nanak calls his gift — that is, his compassion or his grace. As gravitation binds us downwards to the earth, grace pulls us upwards — to him. As the resonance of Omkar intensifies inside you, the pull of gravitation diminishes, and the pull of grace increases proportionately. Then a moment comes when you become absolutely weightless. Yogis often experience this.

Some people intensely practicing meditation here have experienced this sudden feeling of weightlessness. No one can perceive this phenomenon from the outside. If the meditator were to open his eyes, he would find himself seated on the ground just as before; but as soon as he closes his eyes and feels the resonance inside, he experiences a sense of weightlessness. The physical body remains on the ground but the inner body separates from the earth and rises. If you continue in meditation one day you experience two bodies, not one; the body that has risen can see the body sitting on the ground, a thin thread of light connecting them.

Therefore remember, if someone practicing Omkar is deeply lost in meditation, do not shake him or bring him back too suddenly. This can be dangerous, and cause an imbalance between his physical and subtle bodies, which can be irreparable because the balance is very delicate.

In a deep stage of meditation a person steps out of his body, then comes back. When you become perfectly fluent with this art of stepping in and out of your body, you will know how to enter into and emerge from God. Then you see no difference between the material world and God himself. You stay in your body but your remembrance becomes uninterrupted; the thread of your thoughts is connected with him.

> *The Lord is great. His place is high.*
> *And higher even is his name.*
> *Nanak says: One only knows his greatness*
> *When raised to his heights,*
> *By falling under the glance*
> *Of his all-compassionate grace.*

It is rather intricate and complicated. There are only two systems of *sadhana* — of spiritual practice. The basis of one system is resolve, and that of the other is surrender. Both lead to the same goal but they are diametrically the opposite of each other.

The methods of Mahavira and Patanjali and Gorakh are based on resolve, on effort. All life-energy is devoted to the effort. When there is absolutely no energy remaining outside that effort, when you have given yourself up to it wholly, that very day the event will occur; when you have left nothing for yourself, your resolve will be complete and perfect.

Nanak, Meera and Chaitanya have followed the second path, the way of surrender. It is entirely different; the seeker believes that nothing happens through one's own effort — only through his grace do we achieve. Now this does not mean you make no effort, but don't put too much faith in your prowess. Try you must, but remember that the outcome will happen only through his grace.

This is very, very important. If you rely only on your own labors, you will strengthen your ego. Therefore it is easy for a yogi to be proud, because he begins to believe that things are happening because of him.

Once this ego develops it is very difficult to be rid of it. It is easier to be rid of the arrogance of wealth, it is not difficult to renounce the pride of position, but it is very difficult to be rid of the ego of one's own endeavors. There is every possibility of the seeker feeling that whatever is happening is because of him; the I becomes primary and God secondary. Because of this danger,

Mahavira, Patanjali, Gorakh and others who follow this path lay great stress on the annihilation of the ego.

Make the effort, put your all into it, but renounce your ego is what they stress so emphatically. If the ego functions along with the effort, it will get stronger and stronger. Then you feel in whatever you do, I am doing it: I have done japa, I have done penance, I have attained occult powers. And if this arrogance is not eradicated in good time, you will have opened many doors but not the last. All your efforts will have been in vain.

Therefore, Nanak says: Try with all your might, but remember, his grace alone can bring about the happening. With this precaution, the risk in the method of resolve is removed. But there is a different risk in the path of surrender, which arises at the very beginning.

The danger is in feeling that there is no need to do anything. If the happening occurs only through his grace, what can we do? It becomes an excuse for not doing anything. So you remain involved in all the useless daily activities of life. You may assume it is not yet his will that you should set out on this path — and so you wait. Meanwhile you indulge in all that is most contemptible in life; you wander in the maze of the material world. Thus the danger in the path of surrender lies at the very onset — you might become lost in laziness and inertia.

So try you must in the fullest measure, while remembering that the fruit of the endeavor is attained only through his grace. Therefore Nanak repeats over and over: his grace showers only on those within the gaze of his compassionate vision. On whom does this compassion descend but those who prepare themselves for it through their efforts?

Understand that in everyday life the meaning of a compassionate look is quite different. Does he too show partiality? Is he kind to his own but lets the rest be? Does he select a few to shower with his grace while he leaves others to suffer? We cannot associate God with such injustices. Things would become meaningless if a sinner might receive his grace while a saint is deprived of it. There would be no sense in doing anything.

No, this is not the meaning of the compassionate look. It is not that he chooses someone that suits his whim or fancy, or that he favors those who flatter and sing his praises. His grace showers on all, but there are some who have turned their pots upside down, so that they never get filled. If your pot is upright, it is bound to be filled. And don't imagine that your upright pot caused the grace to shower! Grace showers all the time.

Nanak says the filling takes place by his compassion, but some effort you have to make — by placing your vessel in the proper position to receive. And you will have to see that there are no cracks or holes in it, that it is not lying upside down or slanting so that the grace cannot reach the mouth of your vessel and enter it.

His grace pours on everyone incessantly. It is you who are not standing upright to receive it or in your twisting and turning, it slides off you.

There is an apparent contradiction: if you are deprived of grace you have only yourself to blame, but if you attain grace it is only because of him. You attain through him, lose through your own self.

When following the path of surrender it is imperative to remember that if I am losing, it is I who am wrong; if I am gaining, it is entirely by his grace. This way the ego cannot be fattened, because there is no space within for it to expand — or even to exist. He who has no ego finds that God is within him.

> *His compassion is beyond all description.*
> *The Lord's gifts are so great He expects nothing in return.*

Understand the meaning of *dana*, charity. You too give in charity, but behind your gift hides some desire. If you give two *paise* to a beggar you do so with the hope of a return in heaven – if not in heaven, at least your neighbors or your friends should be watching so that you rise in their esteem, or gain some respect from them.

There was a blind, deaf man who attended church regularly although he couldn't see what was going on, much less hear the hymns or sermons. What motivation could he have had but to show how deeply religious he was?

Now you may have eyes, but your reason for coming is just the same; you have ears, but your reason is no different. Going to the temple or church or gurudwara has become a social obligation, a duty to be performed. And when you give a single paisa you expect a return. You know nothing of charity, everything is a business deal.

This is the difference between a charity and business. When you expect a return it involves bargaining, it is a business. Then it turns out you have never given in charity, you have only invested for future gains. And those who exploit you know very well that you are striking a bargain, so they explain to you: "Give one paisa here, you will get a million there." Whatever you offer will be returned a millionfold, that is the promise. Every exploiter knows for certain that you are a businessman, a trader — that you cannot truly give as charity.

Will you ever donate to a temple when it is proclaimed that you will get nothing in return? It will be difficult to find a donor for such a temple; it will never last, nor even get constructed.

When you think of God's charity, do not think in terms of your charity. He does not give the way you do. Nanak says, "He gives but expects nothing in return. And what do you have that you can give him? His charity is pure, unconditional."

What have we given in return for all that we have received? You were given life and in this life you found love; you had faint glimpses of well-being and health, of beauty and of truth, and what have you done in return? It is astonishing that we never think of repaying him.

Once aware of all that you have received, you would dance in celebration forever, singing his praises not out of fear but out of gratitude. All that was given you was too much, and without any motive. We neither know the way nor have the ability to repay. We can repay the debt owed to our parents, but never can we repay God for all that he has given us, for his gift is unconditional.

> *His compassion is beyond all description.*
> *The Lord's gifts are so great He expects nothing in return.*
> *However great a hero or warrior, man keeps on begging.*

Not only beggars, even our warriors beg. There is not much difference between a beggar and a king, only a matter of degree. Remember, when your neediness ends you begin to see and experience his gifts. The smoke of your demands prevents you from seeing what you have already received. The need to beg hides the gratitude. The day your demands drop, the false form of prayer drops and the correct form of prayer takes shape.

It is difficult to conceive the countless numbers who go on asking. They indulge themselves in desires and dissipate their lives.

Nanak has made the important observation that your demands are so blind and thoughtless that if you attain them you destroy yourself. Your asking is for the wrong things. Nanak is right; observe your life carefully and you will see that all the ills you suffer are the result of your own desires.

If you wish to rise in status, it entails anxiety and sleepless nights and restless days. In the West they say that if you do not get a heart attack by the time you are forty you are not a successful man; if you do not have a stomach ulcer you are a poor man. These are the signs of success and prosperity.

After all, what does a successful man gain by desiring more success? Whatever a man wishes for, he attains something or other. It may be early, it may be late, but you will find that your desires are fulfilled. Therefore be very careful in what you ask for, so that you won't regret it later. First you waste time in asking, then in repenting and regretting.

Analyze your own life carefully and you will find that you alone have got yourself in the state you are in. You got enmeshed in your desires. You wanted riches, you got it; but along with it came all the worries and anxieties, because they are very much a part of wealth. With wealth comes a constriction of the soul; with wealth comes a thousand kinds of illness; with wealth come pride and arrogance. They are all very much a part of wealth and cannot be separated from it. Then you repent.

They indulge themselves in desires and dissipate their lives.
And others receive, yet deny it.

Some are destroying themselves through their desiring. Others receive and yet deny. They offer no gratitude.

Every morning at prayer time Mulla Nasruddin would call out loudly to God: "Remember one thing, I need a hundred rupees, not a paisa less. Whenever you feel like giving, remember ninety-nine will not do."

Mulla's neighbor used to hear him every day. He decided to play a joke on Mulla. He filled a bag with ninety-nine rupees and dropped it from the roof into the room where Mulla was praying aloud as usual. He was sure Mulla would not accept the gift for one rupee was missing. As soon as Mulla saw the bag he forgot his prayers and began to count the coins. When he found there were ninety-nine he said, "Well done, Lord. You are a businessman all right: you deducted one rupee for the bag."

Man is not prepared even to acknowledge and offer thanks. He still finds room for complaint — one rupee deducted for the bag!

A wealthy man was returning home after a long sea voyage. A heavy storm overtook them and the ship was in danger of overturning at any moment. Everyone began to pray, including the rich man. At first his prayers were very vague, but when it became a question of life and death he called aloud to God and said, "If you save us today Lord, I shall sell my castle and distribute the proceeds to the poor." As it happened the storm abated and the ship reached shore safely. Then the rich man was filled with remorse. He thought the storm would have abated anyhow, and he had unnecessarily opened his loud mouth. Now that everyone had heard him, he would have to make good his pledge. This is why people pray silently, so that no one knows what bargains they strike with God.

Everyone on the boat had heard the rich man's prayer, and as soon as the ship landed the news spread like wildfire. He thought and thought, until finally he announced his decision to sell the castle. Many buyers came, because it was the largest in the area. Although it was valued at a million rupees, the owner had imposed a strange condition. He tied a cat before the house and said he would sell the cat for a million and the house for one rupee. Whoever buys must take both offers together.

At first people were surprised at such madness. Had anyone ever heard such a fantastic price for one cat — a million rupees? But buyers came all the same. What difference did it make to them about the price of the cat if they would be getting the property? So the deal was struck. The rich man pocketed his million rupees and distributed one rupee among the poor — that being the price of the house.

People establish a business or legal relationship even with God. Even there they are still trying to get off as cheaply as possible. So as Nanak says, there are many who have their wishes fulfilled, yet deny it outright. They say it was a coincidence, that it was about to happen anyhow. Many others don't even say that much; they coolly forget that they had asked for what was given, let alone are grateful.

There are many who keep asking and who keep receiving, who never rise above this tendency of asking and receiving. They keep enjoying, but it never leads anywhere; they only waste their time. Eat whatever you may, what will you get out of it? Wear whatever you want, what is the gain? Decorate yourself with gold and precious stones, how will that profit you? While you are doing this the priceless moments of life are slipping by, moments when you should have prayed and attained the wealth of meditation. Life is just passing you by, wasted in the gathering of pebbles and stones.

Nanak says there are many who are suffering from their hunger, yet do not take to remembrance. We suffer in desiring yet we do not awaken to the fact that we suffer because of our desires. Our woes are the fruits of desires and our hells arise from our longings, but we never connect the two. Always pleading for happiness, can't we see that the longing itself leads to suffering?

It is just as if a man were to walk with his back to the sun then wonder why he cannot see the sun. You could see the sun here and now, but your desire-ridden mind goes towards suffering. Then you color your prayers with the hues of those desires. In his prayers, the devotee offers up all his desires as a libation to be burned; whereas you dedicate your prayers to the service of your desires.

Nanak reminds us that many suffer and go on suffering and yet do not awaken. For how many births have you been bearing the weight of misfortune? Buddha said there are three types of horse. This is not correct. I say there are four. The fourth type do not stir an inch no matter how hard and how long you beat them; they are really obstinate creatures. The more you hit them the more stubborn they become.

In spite of your misfortunes you are oblivious to your sufferings. You have become used to them, so much so that you feel that is what life is. You have forgotten — no, you are unconscious of — the fact that life is supreme bliss, one long celebration; and if you are unhappy it is because of some error of your own.

O Lord, these too are your gifts.

People keep asking, and the Lord keeps giving. Remember, you will get whatever you ask for. Existence does not discriminate or judge. Ask for the right things and you will get them; ask for the wrong things and you will get them. Existence gives unconditionally. God puts no obstacles to your freedom, he lets you choose whatever you like. You may wander in the maze of *sansara*, or you may set out to attain him. He leaves you free to make your own choice.

This brings up a question: since God knows everything, what is right and what is wrong, why does he comply with our wishes that are wrong? If he were not to fulfill your desires you would lose your freedom. You would be no more than a puppet on strings. Then he would give you whatever he chooses and your wish would no longer matter. Then the whole dignity of man is lost; it lies in the fact of his freedom — freedom even to go wrong. There is the possibility of freedom, you are not entirely tied to chains. You have the opportunity to make a conscious choice. You can go whichever way you please. He does not oppose you or stand in your way; he leaves all paths open to you.

If you choose, you can fall into the deepest hell and he will not stop you. You can rise to the highest heaven, he will not obstruct you. You get his power under all conditions; his grace is unconditional. His gift does not make you dependent in any way. He gives — you may use his gift as you please. He does not question.

O Lord, these too are your gifts.
Your order alone gives freedom or bondage.

But it is we who ask to be enslaved, and slavery results. The order is his, the command is his, the law is his, so also the rule.

For instance, if you jump from a high tree you are bound to break your bones. The same gravitational force that holds you to the earth becomes the cause of your fractured bones. If you walk straight this force helps you to walk, but if you sway and stagger you are bound to fall and hurt yourself. The force at work in both cases is the same.

Energy is neutral, impartial; God is absolutely impartial, unbiased. If you use the energy well you can attain the highest experience; use it ill and you can fall into life's deepest abyss. Says Nanak: "All comes through you — heaven as well as hell." But our desire is behind these. It is your law that works, but it is we who ask and ask and exhaust ourselves.

A great politician died. When he reached the door of heaven he announced that he would first inspect both heaven and hell before deciding where he would stay. He was taken around heaven and found it too quiet and insipid for his liking. A politician used to living in Delhi with all its excitement is bound to find heaven rather dull. People are relaxed and peaceful; there is no noise, no tumult, no chaos; there is no fighting, no processions, no blockades; in fact, nothing is happening there.

He asked for a newspaper and was told there was none. A newspaper can only be printed when there is news. News requires disturbance and trouble. If you want to be in the news you have to cause some kind of commotion. If you sit under a tree like Buddha, no reporter will come your way.

He said he didn't enjoy such a dull atmosphere and he would like to pay a visit to hell. He reached hell and was immediately impressed. It was more lively and gay even than Delhi; there were lots of newspapers, lots of processions — everywhere there was noise and movement. There was gaiety and mirth all around, with hotels and bars and cinemas. He was very pleased and wondered why people on earth had the opposite impression of heaven and hell.

He asked Satan, who stood at the gate to welcome him, "Why is such a wrong account of hell given on earth? Had I accepted it without looking for myself I would have suffered in heaven. On earth when a person dies it is good manners to say he has left for his heavenly abode. Actually, this is the place to come. There is so much more life here."

Satan answered, "There is a reason for all this false propaganda. The opposition party has campaigned against me. They are always publicizing heaven and who listens to me? Whenever I try to tell someone the actual facts, they warn him, 'Beware of Satan!' See for yourself how unjust this is."

The politician went back to the gate to tell the escort from heaven to leave because he had made his decision to stay in hell. No sooner did he say this than the doors of hell closed suddenly and the conditions inside changed drastically — just like in the films. He found a crowd of people attacking and manhandling him. When he shouted in protest and demanded to know what was going on, Satan answered, "Before you were on a tourist visa. Now you are an immigrant. What you saw was meant for visitors only. Now you will get the real taste of hell."

People choose hell all the time, because the initial stage of every desire is "for visitors only." Every desire seduces in the beginning. It is the display window, not the real thing — only an advertisement. Once you choose a particular desire the real hell starts. You alone select your particular path to hell.

Heaven is dull at first glance. Bliss is bound to appear uninteresting, because it is the supreme peace. Suffering appears much more interesting and exciting in the beginning because it is provocative. And you choose excitement; you succumb to its provocation, and then suffer. Once you choose tranquility you will attain bliss. Everything happens by his order, by his rule; but his order shapes to your desire. He is neutral. He does not impose his will on you. Even were he to do so, you would not be ready to accept his will.

If heaven were given to you by force, it would seem worse than hell; and if hell is chosen by your free will, it seems like heaven, because your independence is whole and challenged.

A subtle philosophical question is involved: how can man's freedom and God's independence exist together? On this basis

Mahavira denied the existence of God, because if the will of God is supreme man cannot be independent. And if there is no independence, what value has the soul? Therefore Mahavira insists: There is no God, there is freedom! Others have disagreed: There is no freedom! Only destiny is, God is.

Nanak's concept is between these two. He says man is free and God also exists. Man has the freedom of choice; he can ask for whatever he desires. He can work towards attaining his desires, but he succeeds only through his compassion. Ask for joy or ask for sorrow — you will get it.

Now this is interesting. Why do you go on asking for suffering? The fact remains that if you do not ask for happiness, try as he may, God cannot give it to you.

Junnaid, the fakir, used to say that you cannot give happiness by force, you cannot force tranquility. He would say, "I am eager to give joy and peace to others, I have tried many times, but it is impossible. The more you urge upon a person, the more you startle him and he becomes suspicious. You cannot give bliss to anyone, because no one is ready to take it."

One of his devotees said he could not believe this and he would like to try an experiment. He chose a pauper as the subject, and told Junnaid: "The king is your devotee. Ask the King to give him ten million *asharfis*, then let's see if he still remains a pauper." Junnaid agreed. On the day fixed for the experiment the asharfis were placed in a pot which was placed in the middle of the bridge that the pauper crossed every afternoon. All traffic on the bridge was closed for that day. Junnaid and his followers and the king stood on the other side and watched from their hiding place.

Now the man came along. The bridge was empty. There was not a soul to be seen and there was the open pot with the golden coins shimmering in the sun. But wonder of wonders, the man passed the vessel without so much as looking at it and crossed the bridge. Junnaid and his followers ran up to him and asked, "Couldn't you see the pot filled with coins?"

"Which pot?" he asked. "For such a long time I wanted to cross the bridge with my eyes closed, but as there was always such heavy traffic I couldn't do so. Today when I saw the bridge empty the thought came to me that I should take this opportunity to try my skill. I succeeded in crossing the bridge with closed eyes. I am sorry. I didn't see the pot you are speaking about."

Junnaid told his disciples, "Do you see this? He who is going to miss will fail by some means. He will create a thought that will make him fail. He who is bent on missing the opportunity cannot be helped under any circumstances."

Even God cannot give you what you are not ready to take. If you are ready for suffering you get suffering, if you are ready for happiness you get happiness — you get only that for which you are prepared. And you receive it only through his grace, whereas you attain through your own effort. His grace is forever showering on all but you are filled only when you are ready and eager to be filled.

> *O Lord, these too are your gifts.*
> *Your order alone gives freedom or bondage.*
> *Nobody can debate this fact.*
> *He who indulges in useless babble*
> *Realizes his folly when struck in the face.*
> *He alone can know himself,*
> *And only the rarest can describe him;*
> *He bequeaths the quality of his state to whomever He chooses.*
> *Nanak says, He is the king of kings.*

There are many who indulge in this prattle in the sphere of religion. In no other field is it so easy to say whatever you please, because the whole field of religion is mysterious and there are no proofs, therefore anything passes.

Thus there are three hundred different religions. Could there have been so many otherwise? And in these three hundred religions there are three thousand sects — both big and small. A lot of useless junk has been introduced in the name of religion. Besides, there is no way to judge what is true and what is untrue. And the one who sermonizes is usually so glib!

Mahavira used to speak of seven hells. There was an opponent of Mahavira by the name of Makkhali Gosal. When his disciples asked him whether he knew about the seven hells that Mahavira spoke of, he said, "Mahavira doesn't really know. There are really seven hundred hells."

What are we to do now? Is Makkhali Gosal stating the truth or Mahavira? Who is right? What is the truth?

In the life of Makkhali Gosal it happened exactly as Nanak would predict. Having made far-fetched statements his whole life, he repented at the time of death. As death approached he began to tremble with fear. He called his disciples together and said to them, "Whatever I have told you is a lie. Drag my body along the road when I am dead and tell people to spit on my face, because with this mouth I have uttered nothing but falsity."

This man Makkhali Gosal must have been a man of courage and honesty, or else he would have kept quiet a few moments more. Having spoken lies his whole life, he could have remained silent and died quietly. Then perhaps there would have been a sect or a religion following after him, because there were many who believed in him. He was one of the greatest opponents of Mahavira, though he started as Mahavira's disciple. As soon as he learned something he began to create his own new order, because he was clever and able and a good orator.

When Mahavira came to the village where Makkhali Gosal was staying he insisted on meeting him. "He is my erstwhile disciple. I will ask him why he is indulging in this foolishness." When they met, Makkhali Gosal pretended he was seeing Mahavira for the first time. One can never trust a liar. Mahavira said to him, "Have you forgotten completely the years when you were with me?"

Makkhali replied, "You are mistaken. The soul that stayed with you left long ago. Now the soul of a *tirthankara* has entered this body. This body may have been with you — I have heard so — but I am not the same one who was with you. He who was your disciple is long dead. Now don't ever say that Makkhali Gosal was your disciple."

Mahavira must have remained silent. What could be said to such a man? And he had a large following and was very influential. However, he must also have been a good man, because at the time of his death he owned up to his hypocrisy.

Nanak has spoken of just such examples. He who preaches false sermons will realize his foolishness when fate slaps him in the face, when death confronts him and life ebbs away. Then he realizes the utterly useless nonsense he spoke about heaven and hell, when in fact he knew nothing. Now life has passed out of his hands and he had laid no firm foundation. All life long he floated paper boats, now when the time has come to sink, alas, it is too late!

Beware! When it comes to religion, speak only if you know, or else hold your peace! For the mind endlessly investigates and makes discoveries; it is a skilled explorer. Once the mind begins to search and debate, a discussion begins and a web of thoughts and words is woven that expands on its own. Then you have nothing to do. Automatically one word gives rise to another, one theory expounded leads to another, and then another....

It once happened: A well-known priest came to a rest home. He tied his horse under a tree and went in to rest. Mulla Nasruddin happened to be looking on. The priest was known to be attached to his horse, which was a fine animal and very valuable. Everywhere he went to preach, he would go on his favorite horse.

The Mulla went up to the horse and began to rub its neck gently. At that moment a man came along and asked, "Is that your horse?"

Now such a fine animal — it was a shame to admit it did not belong to him. So the Mulla said, "Yes, it is mine."

"Do you want to sell him?" the man asked.

Things were now becoming complicated. "Have you the courage to buy him?" the Mulla asked. The horse was worth a thousand rupees, but Nasruddin was looking for a way out so he asked for two thousand, thinking it was too stiff a price and the man wouldn't pay. But the man agreed. Now the Mulla was in a fix. He could not go back on his word. Then he thought, "What is the harm? I'm making two thousand rupees, and besides, the priest is sleeping."

Just as he pocketed the money and the buyer had left with the horse, the priest came out. The Mulla thought fast. There was no time to run. He quickly tied the rope around his neck and shoved a bit of straw in his mouth.

The priest was frightened. He began to tremble. But he put up a brave front and asked the Mulla, "Where is my horse? And what are you doing here?"

"Your horse and myself are not two," replied the Mulla. "I am your horse."

"What? Are you mad or are you drunk?" demanded the priest.

"Neither," replied the Mulla. "Please hear me out. Twenty years ago I committed adultery. God was angry and he turned me into a horse — your horse. Now it seems my sentence is over and I have become a man again. My name is Nasruddin."

The priest now was really frightened. Such divine wrath — a man turns into a horse! He went down on his knees and implored God to forgive him for all his sins. So many sins had he committed, he pleaded for his compassion.

Then he spoke to Nasruddin. "Brother, it is all right. What has happened has happened. I have to go ahead to the next village. You go home, and I will go to the market and buy a new horse."

He went to a horse-dealer, and there he saw his horse. He was beside himself with fear. He went up to the horse and whispered in his ear, "Nasruddin, how come?...And so soon?"

Once the mind starts a lie, they sprout like leaves on a tree. One lie gives rise to four others, and these in turn produce more lies. To save one lie we have to tell a thousand more. Then the number of lies becomes so astronomical that you even forget they are lies. Frequent repetitions gives them the garb of truth, and these very falsities then hypnotize you.

Thousands of such untruths prevail that have no bearing on truth. With religion this is very easy because there is no way to test, no institute where one can investigate, no criterion by which to judge. Religion lives on faith; no scientific research can help.

Therefore remember: do not ever utter an untruth, or else you will repent. The habit of lying is very deep-seated in the mind.

People come to me and say, "I have been doing Vipassana

meditation for the past ten years." When I ask if something has happened I see from their expression that nothing has changed, but they say, "Yes, a lot has happened."

Then I talk of other things and ask again, "Tell the truth, have you experienced anything? If something had been happening there would have been no need to come to talk to me in the first place, so make up your mind and say nothing has happened so that I can take your case in hand."

Then they admit it, "Nothing has happened."

Now a few minutes before, this very man was claiming so much success. The mind refuses to admit that ten year's effort has yielded no result. The mind is very deceitful. Beware of it. The more you fall into its trap the more you will regret. Life will pass away and death will stand at your head; then you will repent and wonder why you wasted yourself in all these lies.

God alone knows himself. God alone gives. Knowing is his; giving is his. For us it is enough to be the recipient. Knowledge is his. Existence is his. We shall receive both when we are open and eager to receive them, when we have our gaze turned toward him.

There is no need to fall into the mind's trap. The mind can give neither knowledge nor existence; it can only give untruth. He who listens to the mind falls into falsity.

In an old story, the gods were once so pleased by a man's devotion that they gave him a magic conch shell that would fulfill any wish expressed to it. You say a palace and immediately a palace appears. You say a banquet fit for a king and there is a great feast laid out before you. The man was very happy as he began to enjoy all the good things in life.

One day a priest who was passing through the town halted at this man's palace for a night's rest. He had heard about the magic shell and wanted to possess it. He too had a conch shell which he called *Maha-shankha*, great conch shell. He said to his host, "Your shell is nothing compared to mine. I too practiced many austerities and the gods favored me with this Maha-shankha. You ask one thing of it, it gives two."

Now as is human nature, the man's greed was awakened. He said, "Show me the magic of your conch shell."

The priest took out the Maha-shankha and placing it before him said, "Brother, make a palace."

The conch said, "Why one? Why not two?"

The host was impressed. He gave his conch to the priest and took his Maha-shankha in return. The priest then soon left. Almost immediately the man tried frantically to find him again, because the conch only spoke but did not perform. You say two and it will say, "Why not four?" You say four, it will say "Why not eight?" This was all it could do.

The mind is a Maha-shankha. Whatever God gives it says, "Why only this much, why not more?" The mind is only a babble of words. It is all lies. It can produce nothing. But we are such that we have let go of God and cling to the mind. For the mind talks in a duplicity that sets fire to our greed. Just think, has the mind ever given you anything? Have you ever attained anything through the mind?

> *He alone can know himself,*
> *And only the rarest can describe him;*
> *He bequeaths the quality of his state to whomever He chooses.*
> *Nanak says, He is the King of Kings.*

One last priceless thing in this sutra. Dhun-nun was an Egyptian fakir. When he realized God he heard a voice in the skies which said, "Dhun-nun, before you set out in search of me, I had already chosen you. Had I not, you would never have set out in search of me."

Nanak says that he ordains the one he chooses with the quality to sing his praise. The fact is, you set out to seek him only when he has knocked at your door. How can you set out on this tremendous quest all by yourself? How can you arrive at the idea of the quest, how can you acquire his remembrance, how can his praise be born within you, if he does not will it?

Then no matter how long it takes in the quest, the fact is that he has already chosen you. Your search has begun; he has already entered into your life. He has awakened the thirst within you and Nanak says:

It is he alone who awakens the thirst for him.

Nanak's method is: leave all to him. Keep nothing in your hands because the arrogance of the ego can arise very subtly. You may begin to say, "I am a seeker, I am in quest of God." But Nanak, so that this I does not take root anywhere, says it is his grace that confers the quality to sing his praise. We can only sing your praise if you will us to do so. How can we sing your praise without your direction? We cannot even raise our eyes towards you unless you give support to our vision. Our feet can never walk along your path unless you direct them. We cannot think of you, or dream of you, or ponder over you, unless you have already chosen us.

Nanak plucks out all roots of the ego. Where ego is not, there his doors open to us; where ego is not, the resonance of Omkar starts on its own. Only because of the tumult and noise of your ego, can you not hear the faint resonance within.

CHAPTER 12

Steeped in the Wine of Love

Priceless are his qualities, and his trading, too;
Priceless are his salesmen, and his storehouses;
Priceless is he who comes to take, and what he takes;
Priceless his feelings, and his samadhi, too;
Priceless his divine justice, and his courts;
Priceless the weights and balance to judge man's actions;
Priceless his bounty, and the symbols which distinguish it;
Priceless his grace and his order, too;
He is the priceless of the priceless; He cannot be described.
Many fall, lost in meditation, even while reciting his attributes.
The Vedas talk of him, and puranas study him;
And learned ones describe him; so also Indra and Brahma;
The gopis and Krishna speak of him, and Vishnu and the siddhas;
And many, many buddhas; and demons and deities too.
Men and sages and those who serve, they all sing his praise.
Many there are who can express it, and many die before completing the task.
He will bring even more to this existence.
No one can predict his actions.
Whatever He feels — so it happens.
Whoever knows this, he himself is truth.
If someone boasts of knowing him, then he is the fool of fools.

Nanak speaks in praise of God not as a pundit, but as if inebriated. His words aren't those of a scholar, but rather they express a person completely steeped in the wine of love; therefore the repetitions. They are words spoken in a state of ecstasy, just as you see a drunkard going along the road repeating himself over and over and over again. Nanak is completely inebriated with some profound intoxicant, so he also indulges in repetition.

Babar, the Moghul, invaded India. Taking Nanak to be of doubtful character, he had him imprisoned along with others. But gradually the news began to reach Babar that there was a unique prisoner who created around him a strange atmosphere, a spirit of intoxication, and he kept singing happily all day. Babar thought such a man cannot be imprisoned who has an internal freedom that cannot be put in chains, so he sent Nanak a message to come and see him. Nanak replied, "You will have to come and visit, O king, for Nanak is in that realm from which visiting people is out of the question."

So Babar himself went to the prison to see. He was very impressed by Nanak's personality. He brought him to the palace and offered him the choicest wine. Nanak laughed and sang a song in which he told the king that Nanak has already tasted the wine of God, now no other wine can affect him. The king would do well to drink from Nanak's wine instead of the ordinary wine.

These are songs of a drunkard. Nanak sings away like a small child or like a drunkard. He is not guided by any rule or conditions, nor has he tried to beautify his language. His poems are like uncut stones. When a poet writes, he writes and rewrites and makes a thousand changes. He worries about the grammar, he worries about the rhythm, the meter, the words. He makes many changes. Even a poet the caliber of Rabindranath Tagore used to do this. His diaries are full of cuts and rewrites.

Nanak's words are different. They are not changed and arranged. They are just as Nanak uttered them. These are words that were spoken and not written; therefore no account is kept of the rhythm or the cadence or even the language. If it has a meter, it is the meter of the soul; if there is any grammar, it is not of man, but of God. If you find any rhythm in it, it is the rhythm of the ecstasy and intoxication within. This is why whenever anyone asked Nanak a question he would say, "Listen!" then Mardana, his close disciple, would pick up his instrument and Nanak would sing.

Remember this, otherwise you will be confused at Nanak's constant repetition. You will wonder why he keeps saying his attributes are priceless, his worth is priceless...again and again. These are words spoken in ecstasy, not words repeated from somewhere; these are words that hummed within him. It did not matter if others heard. If you keep this in mind, Nanak's words will reveal countless depths.

> *Priceless are his qualities, and his trading, too;*
> *Priceless are his salesmen, and his storehouses;*
> *Priceless is he who comes to take, and what he takes;*
> *Priceless his feelings, and his samadhi, too*
> *Priceless his divine justice, and his courts;*

First, he is priceless, everything of him is priceless. There is no way to evaluate, no scale by which to weigh him, nor yardstick to measure him. There is no way in which we can surmise how much he is, what he is, how far he extends.

Whoever sets out to measure him finds that not only do all yardsticks fall short and break, but the mind that has set out to measure also breaks.

The Sanskrit word, *maya*, refers to illusion. This word is derived from the same root word as *mapa*, which means measure. The English words *meter* and *measure* also come from that same root.

Maya signifies that which can be measured or weighed. That which cannot be weighed is Brahma. Whatever you can measure, know it is maya; whatever can be evaluated or defined, know it is maya. When you approach that which cannot be defined, which defies all measures and cannot be weighed, when you come near to this immeasurable, that is the beginning of religion.

Science can never know God for the whole scientific method is based on measure. The weighing scales are the symbol of science; to measure is its way. Therefore science will never come anywhere near God and will always maintain that there is no God, because it only believes in that which can be measured, which can be investigated. Marx has said, "If God manifests in the research institute, then only shall I believe in his existence." But such a God cannot be God.

Do you not feel the presence of something that is immeasurable all around you? He is even within your measuring devices. Now, for instance, take a flower: you can analyze it in your institutes. You can weigh it, you can measure it, you can discover its chemistry; but one thing in the flower cannot be measured. When you will have completed your full analysis you will suddenly realize that the flower is no more. With all your investigations you could not locate the beauty of the flower. Therefore scientists do not accept beauty as such.

Isn't it strange? The very first response to looking at a flower involves its beauty, yet this is completely lost in scientific research. What is destroyed by the first stroke of science is the very thing that first affects you when you see the flower; the first feeling, the first ray of consciousness reflected on your mind at the sight of the flower, is of its beauty. The feeling is unspoken, unsung, but deep within a cloud of beauty encircles you. Science is unable to grasp this.

You see a child dancing, playing, laughing, and your first feeling is of life — energy flowing. If science is asked to analyze this child it will do it thoroughly. The scientists will list the percent of iron, phosphorus, calcium; how much water, how dense is the child's body; but that life will be no more.

Once a scientist was walking along the road with his friend. A beautiful girl passed by and the friend stood still, mouth agape. "Forget it," said the scientist. "She is ninety percent water." Man is ninety percent water and ten percent matter. It is said that the total value of the substance of a human body is not more than five rupees. That is all the minerals within the body are worth. Therefore the human body is burnt on death, for it has no more value.

Science will measure everything and then say that there is no such thing as a soul. How can they find the soul when it is immeasurable? When we cannot locate it through any means of measurement, then we claim that it doesn't exist. If we were wise we would say that all our ways of measuring take us only up to maya and no further. Therefore we must devise some other means than measurement to know him.

The method of science is measuring, investigating, examining, defining. The method of religion is absolutely different; it is not to measure or examine or define — but to drown in it, be immersed in it. The scientist stands apart from his quest, the religious man becomes one with it; he drowns in the very thing he is seeking.

Nanak once went to Lahore. The town's richest man came and bowed at his feet. It was the custom in those days that a man who had ten million rupees could fly a flag over his house. Seth Dunichand, that was his name, had many flags flying. He touched his head to Nanak's feet, then with folded hands he said to him, "I wish to be of service. By his grace God has given me enough. Whatever you wish I will fulfill."

Nanak took out a sewing needle from his cloak, and giving it to Dunichand he said, "Keep this very carefully, and return it to me after your death."

Dunichand was so engrossed in the pride of his wealth that he did not realize what Nanak was saying. "As you wish," he said and left. Arrogance makes a person so blind at times that he does not realize some things are impossible. Finally, on the way home Dunichand thought about what he had been asked and realized he could not return the needle after his death.

So he went back to Nanak and said, "You have entrusted me with a difficult task. I thought nothing of it at the time, but now I feel that you might have been joking with me. What need is there to take care of a needle? Since I presume that the ways of a saint are mysterious, there must be a reason for it. Forgive me, but take back the needle for I shall not be able to clear the debt later. How could I take the needle with me beyond death?"

Nanak said, "You can give back the needle since it has served its purpose. That is the very question I was going to ask of you. If you cannot take such a small thing as this needle when you die, what will you take of the millions and millions of rupees you have amassed? If you cannot carry a puny little needle, what else do you have that you think you can take? You are really a poor man, Dunichand, for only he is rich who can take something with him after death."

Anything that can be measured cannot be taken beyond death; only the immeasurable can be taken.

There are two types of people in this world. One type is always anxious to measure, always searching for things to count and weigh. The other type is always looking for what is immeasurable. The first type are not religious but worldly; they belong to *sansara*, the world of illusion. The second type are the religious people, the sannyasins.

The search for the immeasurable is religion. He who has found the immeasurable conquers death; he has attained the nectar, the elixir. What can be measured is bound to disintegrate; whatever has a boundary is bound to rot. Whatever can be defined is here today and gone tomorrow. Mountains like the Himalayas will disappear one day; so also the moon, the sun and the stars. We call the mountains stable and immovable, but they too are movable and unstable. Everything is unstable, as far as measure goes; all things that can be measured are like individual waves. Where all measure ends, where all boundaries fade, that is the beginning of the Ocean of Brahma, the beginning of God.

Therefore, Nanak says, his qualities are invaluable, and his trading too. You cannot set value on him — that is the difficulty. You can evaluate Napoleon and Alexander, for their wealth and kingdoms set their value. But how will you estimate the value of Buddha? What is the worth of Nanak and the likes of him? We can judge the worth of those with wealth and position, for their possessions are their very souls: one man is worth a million rupees, another is worth ten million. But how can we gauge the value of someone who has nothing except God? Thus many a time we fail to see a Nanak. Many a time Buddha crosses our path but we have no eyes to see him, for we are only conversant with the art of measuring; it is only things that we see. If Buddha held a diamond in his hand we would have seen the diamond, but not Buddha — whereas the diamond is worthless and Buddha is beyond value, beyond price.

Our eyes, our vision, our way of thinking, our minds — take stock of these. Outside is the world of measure, inside is the mind. The mind and maya, the world of illusion are one. Outside lies the measure, inside is the measurer — the mind. The immeasurable that is outside is Brahma; it has no connection with the mind, but is related only to the soul, the *atman*; for the atman is also immeasurable. You can only relate yourself with that which you are within. The mind has its boundary, thus through it you can only know the limited. The soul has no boundary, so through it you can know the boundless. What is the worth of God? Nothing!

It is said that Judas sold Jesus to his enemies for thirty pieces of silver. We are shocked. A man like Jesus who comes only once on earth after hundreds of years, and Judas trades him off for a few pieces of silver? We find it hard to imagine. But you would have done the same. Perhaps you would have taken thirty thousand instead of thirty, but what is the difference? A measure is a measure. Note one thing: after staying with Jesus for years, Judas could not recognize Jesus, he could not see him. When someone bribed him with thirty pieces of silver, he promptly told him where Jesus could be found. The coins seemed more valuable than Jesus.

We see only what we can evaluate. We are trapped by the price of things. People come to me and ask what they will gain by meditation. How will they benefit by it? It is not that they do not know that meditation will lead them to God. They do know, but they see no profit in God. They know meditation leads to bliss, but bliss has no market value. If you try to sell it who will buy? In their own language people want to know the value, the price, of what can be attained through meditation.

They are not wrong in inquiring, for the economics of life is based on value. For one hour of meditation, how many rupees could you have earned in your shop? If you attain something of equal value or more, then meditation is worthwhile; otherwise it is poor business and useless.

Unfortunately, what you get in meditation has no value. As long as you ask the price of things you will be unable to begin meditation, for you are held in the grip of the world of values, *sansara*. Whereas God means to enter into pricelessness and non-value.

Priceless are his qualities, and his trading, too;
Priceless are his salesmen, and his storehouses.

Who are his salesmen? Those whom we call saints, realized men, buddhas. They have come to sell you something that you have not the courage to buy. They want to give you something priceless, but you aren't ready to take it. You feel that which is given free is bound to be worthless. God is given free, so you aren't interested. If a price were set on him, you would think twice. Buddha, Nanak, Kabir are his tradesmen, but their business is rather confusing and beyond your understanding. They do not appear as traders or salesmen to you.

Finding Nanak useless for any kind of work, his father began to worry what would happen to him. He exhorted him time and again to do something and not be so utterly useless. Nanak's father didn't have the eyes to see what was invaluable in his son. People came to tell him what a priceless son he had, but he would answer, "Priceless? My foot! He hasn't the sense to earn a *paisa*. He only knows how to lose money!" What is earning in this world is losing in the other.

Nanak's father told him that if he could do nothing else at least he should take the cattle to graze. If someone is angry with his son he tells him to go and graze cattle; it is considered the meanest of jobs for the dullest of people.

So Nanak's father said, "Go and take the cattle to graze. Sitting as you do the whole day long with your eyes glued to the skies, how else can you make a living?" The father was a totally worldly man who worried about his son's future.

Nanak agreed happily, but for different reasons: he found more peace and tranquility in the company of animals than man, for at least animals aren't constantly talking about economics. They are not always hankering after wealth and possessions. So Nanak was happy to find that work. He loved to be with animals; having no ego, the animals would quietly leave him to himself.

Nanak went along with his cows and buffaloes. But such people always land in trouble. He let the animals loose and said, "Graze to your hearts' content, my friends," and he closed his eyes and was lost in his ecstasy. The animals moved into the adjoining field and destroyed it completely. The farmer came shouting, "What have you done? You'll have to pay to the last paisa. My whole harvest has been destroyed by your animals."

Nanak opened his eyes and said, "Don't be disturbed, brother. The animals are his, the field is his. It is he who let them loose in your field. Don't worry. Good fortune will rain on you."

"Shut up!" raved the man. "Good fortune indeed! Stop your babbling. I am ruined."

He ran to Nanak's father and dragged him to the village head. He demanded the value of the full harvest. The village head was a Muslim by the name of Shah Bullar. He was a devotee of Nanak. He said, "Let's see what Nanak has to say." When Nanak was questioned he said, "All happens through his will. It is his order and all is well. It is he who sent the animals, it is he who grew the harvest. And if he has grown it once he will grow it a thousand times again. What is the need to panic? No loss was incurred."

The farmer said, "Come with me to the field to see for yourselves. My field is destroyed and this man says everything is all right."

As the story goes, all of them went to the field and what did they see? A golden harvest was swaying in the breeze! The adjoining fields paled in comparison. Such a harvest had never been seen before.

The story may be true or not, but it carries great meaning. What is one to say of the field of someone who leaves everything entirely in his hands? The harvest that bloomed in the life of Nanak has perhaps rarely been seen in anyone's life. But the courage to leave all to him...!

The owner of the field could not believe his eyes. The greatest miracle in the world is to leave everything to God, then things begin to happen every day of your life for which you will have no rational explanation.

The moral of the story is that he who leaves everything to God finds such wonderful things happening for which there are no logical explanations. when the immeasurable enters your life, riddles begin. Mystery means only one thing: you have turned your eyes away from the world of measure and directed your vision towards the immeasurable, from limitations towards the unlimited, from the known to the unknown. As soon as you create a little place for the unknown in your life, the harvest of miracles begins to bloom.

Nanak is a salesman of the other world. This world has always treated such people very badly. Jesus was hung on the cross. Socrates was poisoned. Even when we did not maltreat them quite so drastically, we avoided listening to them. Whenever we worship it is only a device to keep ourselves as we are. We pray: you are great, O Lord, how can we attain you? We offer these flowers at your feet, but we shall remain as we are.

You offer worship to appease your soul — and stay the same. Your worshipping is false. If it were genuine there would be one sure test — you would be a changed person. If you truly revered Nanak, you would be transformed. But you remain the same even if you pretend to revere Nanak; then your reverence is only an escape device. You say, "You are great. All you say is absolutely right, but the time is not yet ripe for us. When the time comes we will set out on this path, but there are so many duties in life to be done first. What's the hurry?"

We keep postponing it. Our reverence is filled with such cunning. Remember, reverence can be a very cunning device. To poison someone is a straighter and simpler way to get rid of him; in Greece they poisoned Socrates, and the Jews crucified Christ. India is more cunning, for they are past-masters at it. We neither poisoned nor crucified Buddha, Nanak, Mahavira or Krishna — we worshipped them.

Remember, the Jews haven't yet been able to shake off Jesus after crucifying him. Jesus still haunts them; the feelings of guilt and sin for his crucifixion continues to torment them. They cannot brush aside his memory.

But we Indians are clever; we have rid ourselves of them and are not tormented by thoughts of them. We are indeed very, very clever. We have fixed days to remember them: their birthdays, the anniversaries of their deaths. We remember them with full fervor, with drums and conch shells and flowers and processions — but only on these days. The rest of the year we beg them to leave us alone to carry on our work, our trade. We are not yet ready to deal with the other world. We didn't have to take the trouble to remove our great men bodily, because we know so many tricks to bypass them, so why take the trouble. And besides, killing them would mean we had taken them too seriously.

We shall worship you, give you the status of God, and call you guru, saint, whatever — but let us remain as we are! This is a non-violent device to be rid of them. We place them on the altar in the temples, and remain in the world of sansara ourselves. When we need something we call on them. We use them but we aren't prepared to change ourselves for their sake.

We are a clan of clever, cunning people with an old history. Old people are very clever, for life's experience has shown them ways and means of evasion. Why crucify or poison? Why all the plotting and planning? Put them on a pedestal and you are rid of them! Thus we have placed all our salesmen of the other world on the altar and settled the issue: "You are God, we are your devotees, your worshippers," and so the matter ends.

The real thing is to become Nanak yourself, and not to worship Nanak. The real thing is to become the Guru Granth, the Sikh holy book, so that your utterance starts the resonance of Omkar. But then you have to undergo a complete transformation.

Priceless are his salesmen...

Therefore, we cannot recognize them. We feel that whatever they say doesn't fit our sense of reason, doesn't touch our understanding. Then we raise a wall between them and ourselves, and we make separate compartments. When you are in the gurudwara you are a different man from when you are in your shop. In the temple you shed your tears of adoration and sway with emotion. In the mosque you are different from the marketplace. There seem to be two different persons, not one; it is also a skillful evasive trick.

We have made separate compartments in ourselves. Religion is our Sunday-corner. We go to church on Sunday morning, and as we come out, that corner is left behind in the church and we forget all about it for the next seven days. As if religion implies only going to church! What about the rest of the time? We spend that as we please. In churches and gurudwaras we hear the words of God's salesmen — but do we hear? We only pretend to listen as a social obligation.

Nanak says: his salesmen are priceless. If you want to move

towards him, try to understand his salesmen. You will be unable to gauge his tradesmen; your intellect will be sorely taxed in the attempt, for none of your yardsticks work here. Whatever way you try to measure them, they always turn out to be more.

Priceless is he who comes to take, and what he takes.

Here everything is dealing in the priceless, the immeasurable and the inestimable. Here the customer, he who buys the goods, is also priceless; for the only thing on sale here is: Ek Omkar Satnam.

Priceless his feelings, and his samadhi, too

If the feeling of God is born within you, you enter a different realm. Then you are not here, you are somewhere else.

If anyone mentioned the name of God, Ramakrishna would stand up at once. His eyes would close and torrents of tears would begin to flow; his body became inert, and he was lost to the world. The mere mention of his name transported Ramakrishna to another world, which opens before you as the doors of this world close.

Nanak speaks of his feelings, mere remembrance, *surati* — the slightest recollection and you are transported elsewhere. When his feeling becomes total, *samadhi* results.

Understand the difference between feeling and samadhi; feeling means a glimpse, a ripple — being immersed in him for a moment, but the you is present. You dived inside him but you did not cease to exist. Like a person diving under water, how long can he remain under water? He has to come out in a moment. Besides, he was very much there as he dived.

Shaikh Farid was a *siddha*, an enlightened one. He lived almost at the time of Nanak. One day he was going to the river for a bath when a seeker questioned him, "How is God attained?" Farid said, "Come along with me. Let us bathe first. Then I will show you; and if I get the opportunity I shall show you while you bathe."

The seeker was rather frightened. He is asking about God and this man takes him for a bath, and offers to show him during the course of the bath! He was troubled, but having already asked he couldn't back down. And Farid was a well known saint, so there was the possibility of being shown something in the river. His curiosity was great as he stepped into the river. No sooner had he dived in than Farid jumped astride him. Tiny and thin though he was and Farid a hefty person, he mustered all his strength and succeeded in throwing Farid off of his back. When he came out he screamed, "You are not a saint but a criminal. What way is this? You must be mad. If you didn't know why didn't you tell me in the beginning?"

Farid replied, "Later we shall settle this problem of my sanity or unconsciousness. Now I have to ask you before your weak memory gives way, when I pressed you under water, how many thoughts were there in your mind?"

The seeker said, "What thoughts? Surely you are mad. How could there be any thought other than how to save my life? The only idea was to shake you off and get a breath of fresh air."

"That will do," said Farid. "You have understood. The day your mind is empty of all thoughts, and there is only the idea of God within you, you shall know all that is to be known. And remember, unless you risk your all in life, it is difficult to know God."

The word *bhava* is used for feeling or idea in the deepest sense, where there is no thought, only his remembrance. Had you been in place of the seeker, you too would have come out of the water.

Samadhi is the complete state of bhava, of feelings. Once you go you are gone! It is a point of no return. Then this feeling stays with you forever, you become one with it. It is not a dive, it is complete immersion, complete absorption. You also become water with the water. Now who is to come out? Who is to go in? It is as if you were a doll fashioned out of salt or sugar; you jumped into the water and were dissolved! Now whoever tastes the water also gets a taste of you. In bhava you are still separate; in samadhi you become one. The glimpse is now eternal.

> Priceless his feelings, and his samadhi, too
> Priceless his divine justice, and his courts;
> Priceless the weights and balance to judge man's actions;
> Priceless his bounty, and the symbols which distinguish it;

Try to understand the value of his symbols. There is such complexity and confusion associated with idols and images. Hindus have thousands of sacred places and carved images. They are all symbols.

The Muslim cannot understand what there is in the idol. He destroys them, and when they break he thinks that if the image could not protect itself, how could it protect its devotees? This also happened in the life of Swami Dayanand. He was at the temple of Shiva on the night of Shiv-Ratri, when Shiva is worshipped. As is natural all the devotees who were supposed to keep vigil fell asleep. Dayanand however, who was still only a child, happened to be awake. He saw a small rat climbing all over the Shivalinga and nibbling at the offerings. Then the thought came to him: What use is it worshipping this image which cannot even drive away a rat? The Muslims miss the point, and so did Dayananda, for a symbol is a symbol and not God.

It is with the aid of a symbol that you set out on a journey; it is not the end in itself. Suppose your beloved makes you a gift of a handkerchief worth four *annas*. If you try to sell it in the market you will not even get two annas for it. Who will buy an old hankie? Perhaps it might fetch a small price in a secondhand shop. But for you it bears a different significance; you couldn't set a price on it. You even keep it locked away in a favored place in your cupboard. For you it is not only a handkerchief, but a symbol. Through it you are connected with your beloved. So that no one may know, you use this insignificant article. For you, in a very deep sense, your beloved lies entwined in its threads. This very cloth has touched her hands, she has filled it with kisses and has given it to you. In a profound way your beloved has become one with it. For others it is just a piece of cloth; for you it has immeasurable value.

What is the difference? For you it is a symbol, for others it remains a mere handkerchief. The images of the Hindu are his symbols when he has filled them with his bhava; for the Muslim it is only a piece of stone. The image of Buddha is a symbol for the Buddhists, that of Mahavira is a symbol for the Jainas; and for each, the other's symbol is of no value. A symbol has no general value. It is a very personal and private thing. Whoever knows this, knows; he is connected with it.

Therefore how could you ever criticize someone else's symbol? For you it may be ordinary — you are right! But for someone else it is extraordinary — and that, too, is true. You are right when you ask what is there in a mere handkerchief that you should hold it to your heart? And what if it is lost? There are so many more available in the market. But for the right one it has great value, great meaning; it is a symbol, and, as such, cannot be replaced at any price. It is unique and personal.

Nanak says: Even his symbols are unique. He is unique — that goes without saying, but if you have attained a glimpse of him through some medium, that medium also becomes priceless. Every symbol must be respected, for who knows which one will light the way to him? And never make the mistake of branding a symbol wrong, for a symbol can never be wrong. A symbol is a symbol for some and not for others; there is no right or wrong.

The Muslim insistently believes that images are useless — but the stone of Kaaba? This stone he kisses! No stone in the world has been kissed so much — by millions and millions of people in the last 1400 years. The Muslim takes the Kaaba as a proper symbol and finds this stone worth kissing, but he thinks the Hindu's images fit only to be broken.

A religious person must understand enough to realize that what is not a symbol for him could be a symbol for someone else. There is no need to prove it to be a commonly held symbol, for it is a personal matter that deals with deep intrinsic feelings.

For some the fig tree is holy. Would you say, "Are you mad to worship a mere tree?" The question is not at all what you worship, but worship itself. Any excuse, any means, is good enough if it inspires worship. All means are correct and all means are wrong. If you see with a scientific eye, a *Peepul* tree is a Peepul tree, a stone is a stone, a handkerchief is a handkerchief; but what has science to do with religion? Religion is the kingdom of love and not of the intellect and logic. Isn't it strange that every man reveres and guards his symbols but creates a thousand difficulties around the symbols of others? If you can hold your beloved's hankie to your heart, let the others keep theirs also; they are the mementos of their beloved.

Let the hint come from anywhere. For instance, if a man is interested in the God of the Peepul Tree and he is lost in samadhi while dancing and entertaining his God, the real question has nothing to do with the tree, but his going into ecstasy. Wherever this dance occurs, whatever the means that brings his remembrance, that thing is priceless.

> *Priceless his bounty, and the symbols which distinguish it;*
> *Priceless his grace and his order, too;*
> *He is the priceless of the priceless; He cannot be described.*
> *Many fall, lost in meditation, even while reciting his attributes.*

This is the very intent of singing his praises – understand it! Again and again Nanak says one cannot describe him, we cannot enumerate his attributes, for there is no way to do so. And yet Nanak keeps on recounting his attributes. What is he doing? If he can't be described what is the need for so many words? They do nothing but express his qualities. We are faced by a metaphysical riddle.

People come to me and ask if the Buddha says that nothing can be said about him, then why does Buddha speak? They also tell me, "You say nothing can be expressed in words about him, and here you are talking every day! It seems so inconsistent."

Try to understand. Nanak says he cannot speak about him and he speaks constantly of him; for while recounting his attributes, the speaker slips into samadhi. He is not done with praising him, he cannot praise him enough, but oh, it is so lovely to talk of him! The talk is never complete; having said so much, nothing has been told. Everything seems unsaid. But it gives so much joy to talk about him, that one slips into meditation recounting his ways. No amount of talking conveys anything, but in the course of speaking the speaker is lost.

> *Many fall, lost in meditation, even while reciting his attributes.*
> *The Vedas talk of him, and puranas study him;*
> *And learned ones describe him; so also Indra and Brahma;*
> *The gopis and Krishna speak of him: and Vishnu and the siddhas;*

And many, many buddhas; and demons and deities too.
Men and sages and those who serve, they all sing his praise.

To speak of him is not for the sake of speaking, but as a method of meditation. To discuss him is a way to be lost in him. To talk about him is to be ready for him. Even to sit where he is being discussed and listen — perhaps a drop of this rain may fall on you. Perhaps your parched throat may be relieved; perhaps some word may pierce your deaf ears and enter within; perhaps your blind eyes may get a ray of light; perhaps your thoughts may for a little while be soaked in the color and melody of his music; and perhaps you may fall silent for a while and your internal dialogue may be interrupted.

Nanak sings of him, for while singing of him he is lost in him. Not only the singer, but even the listener is lost in him. Therefore Nanak did not speak, he always sang. It is easier when you sing. He used singing so that the internal chord may be tuned. In the rhythm of the song you may perhaps touch the fringe of that profound silence; then you will never forget it.

Nanak also stresses the importance of associating with saints. Associate with people who talk of him, sing of him. By and by, with constant hearing, the color will begin to spread over you too. When you walk through a garden, your clothes pick up the fragrance of the flowers without your knowing it. If you stand out in the morning sun the warm rays will cause the blood within you to flow faster. And if you lie beneath the starry sky and watch the moon, its cool light is bound to find a place within you.

Association with holy men and saints means to be where he is discussed, where he is being praised. The Hindus have said, "When he is criticized, close your ears. Where he is being talked about, listen with all attention; become all ears!" Therefore Nanak says time and time again, "Listen!" He talks about him and he sings his praises. But he also reminds you again and again that however much you describe him, you have made no headway, you have only just begun. No words can describe him or enumerate his attributes. Don't think that whatever Nanak has said has become his measure. It is just a slight beginning, a feeble effort. Therefore Nanak praises him while also saying he cannot be expressed.

> *The Vedas talk of him, and puranas study him;*
> *And learned ones describe him; so also Indra and Brahma;*
> *The gopis and Krishna speak of him, and Vishnu and the siddhas.*

The *gopis* and Krishna never spoke of him at all; they just danced. But in their dance they expressed him. Krishna never sat down and talked of God to his milkmaids; he danced with them under the light of the full moon. Nanak says through dance they were expressing their praise of him.

So many different ways there are: some sing, some dance, some keep silent — but all are expressions of him. Whoever has realized him expresses him in each action, each indication, each gesture. If Buddha raises his hand, it is an indication towards him. Whether Buddha opens his eyes, or keeps silent, he is still expressing him.

Each person's way is different. Buddha could not dance. It was not in him. It would not have suited him. He would have looked very awkward dancing, but he looked so beautiful under the *Bodhi* tree. The posture he assumes as he sits is his dance. He does not move, there is not a tremble. Like a statue he sits; that is his way!

Buddha's image has been the reason for all statues or images being referred to as *But*. In Arabic and affiliated languages, *But* is the corrupted form of Buddha. Buddha sat so statue-like that had you seen him alive you would have thought it was a marble statue. There was a reason for this. Buddha used to be that way, so tranquil, so cool, so still. That was his way and that is how he expressed him.

Krishna dances. His way is just the opposite of Buddha. You can never imagine Buddha with a crown of peacock feathers on his head. He would look so clumsy. But if you make Krishna sit cross-legged under a Bodhi tree, like Buddha, he would look equally comic. This is not in keeping with his nature. He looks right only with a crown of peacock feathers and the gopis surrounding him and music and dance happening.

Nanak is saying that the dance of Krishna and the gopis is another unique way to express him. This is a lovely statement of Nanak. In a thousand ways the awakened ones have spoken of him. There are thousands of indications, and he towards whom all fingers point is one — Ek Omkar Satnam.

And learned ones describe him; so also Indra and Brahma;
The gopis and Krishna speak of him, and Vishnu and the siddhas;
And many, many buddhas; and demons and deities too.
Men and sages and those who serve, they all sing his praise.
Many there are who can express it, and many die before completing the task.
He will bring even more to this existence.
No one can predict his actions.
Whatever He feels — so it happens.

These words are worth pondering over. He cannot be expressed fully, for God is not an event that is completed; if it is still in the process of completion you cannot give a full account of it.

A man's biography, to be fully written, must wait till he dies. Until then his story is incomplete, some chapters still remain. How can we write God's life story? He will never die nor grow old. He will never reach the point where you can say this is the end.

God keeps on happening. He is a constant occurrence, an eternal manifestation. He is a flower that is eternally blooming, but the petals of the flower will never reach the point where we can say it has fully grown. It has been blooming always, it is blooming now, and will keep on blooming always.

Because his power is infinite, all descriptions fall short of him; all the images we have made of God and descriptions we have given of him remain incomplete. It is just as when we make children's clothes, they soon outgrow them. Only when they reach an age when they stop growing and their measurements remain constant can the tailor take the measurements once and for all.

God always keeps growing, therefore all the clothes we make for him soon become inadequate. All scriptures fall short and become old and outdated; therefore new religions manifest in the world, and new sages bring out new explanations. But these explanations remain valid for some time, then soon they begin to fall short and need to be replaced by new explanations, by newer sages who now sing his praises according to the needs of their times.

Every new song is popular and applicable only for a very brief time. Its relevance does not last even until we finish the song, for in that brief time God has gone even further ahead. Before we put the final touch to his image, he has become something else. Everything remains incomplete.

The Hindus are very wonderful people. Only they have made images of God that have no features. Everywhere else in the world the images have definite features. The Hindus pick up a stone, smear it with vermilion and lo! it becomes the image of Hanuman, the Monkey God. It has no features; it is just a small boulder. The Hindus say: What is the sense of giving it any shape? By the time we give the image its features, God will have moved further on. This stone will do just as well.

The image of Shiva, the Shivalinga, is egg-shaped and has no features. It is an eternal symbol. Whatever form God takes, this symbol will not be affected, while others become outdated.

Nanak says: "He has done so much up to now and he will keep on doing. Were he completely evolved, we would have been able to say something, we might have drawn some conclusions; but he keeps expanding further and further. He is unpredictable. We can make no inferences about what he will do next – neither about God nor the world — all is hidden in the unknowable."

> *He will bring even more to this existence.*
> *No one can predict his actions.*
> *Whatever He feels — so it happens.*

His wish — and the happening occurs! For the Christians and Jews, God said "Be!" and the world came into existence.

With our limited energy, there is a distance between our feelings and our actions. If today the desire arises in you to build a house, the house will come into being in two years. This is because our energy is limited. If we had a little more energy, perhaps it could be constructed within a year; with yet a little more, perhaps in a day. And if your energy were total, as abundant as that of God, then there would be no gap between the wish and the action.

Therefore, time exists for us but not for God. It is an event in man's world because of his weakness.

If you but think back you will find that the weaker you were the longer time seemed to you. For instance, your wife has a fever of 104 degrees. You run to the doctor and are back with the medicine within five minutes, but your wife complains you took too long. Time seems so long in fever.

There is evidence that time seems longer in illness. Not only the patient, but those who sit by his side feel it. Sitting next to a dying man, the night never seems to end. When you are well and happy time seems to have wings; when you are unhappy it seems to drag. It all depends on your energy.

God is omnipotent. For him time does not exist. Whatever he thinks, wishes, feels, becomes immediately a realized act. Nanak says, "Whatever he wills or thinks, or feels, so it happens, and at that very instant, without a moment's hesitation." The willing and the happening are simultaneous. His desire is the act. Nanak says, "He who knows this is himself the truth." This utterance has two meanings:

> *Whatever He feels — so it happens.*
> *Whoever knows this, he himself is truth.*

The first meaning is that he who realizes the truth of the omnipotence of God, that his idea and its realization are identical, becomes truth himself.

The second sense involves Nanak saying he alone can know himself. A man of truth can only know himself. We cannot know him, for we know not his future nor his past and he will never be complete. He goes from one completion to another — not an incomplete happening proceeding towards completion. His completion moves to further completion, to further perfection.

The first meaning sees the man of truth as he who recognizes God's all-pervading power. In the second meaning, the man of truth recognizes that he can only know himself, since God is never completed and can never be known completely.

If someone boasts of knowing him, then he is the fool of fools.

To make a list of fools, the very first name is the man who boasts of knowing or describing God.

Nanak talks about him, for to speak of him is enchanting, it drowns us in ecstasy, it is meditation itself. Talking of his will, the heart begins to bloom, joy is born within and nectar begins to flow. But if someone thinks He can be described, he is the biggest of fools. He is a wise man who knows he cannot be described.

Nanak talks of him for his very name is a source of bliss. He mentions him at the slightest excuse, for it gives much joy. It seems he has nothing else to talk about. To introduce the subject is to knock at his door and when you talk of him, the door opens. Have you ever noticed how a mother is always talking of her newborn child? Whether she talks to the neighbors, to her visitors, to the shopkeepers, the topic is always the child.

The lover constantly tells his beloved how much he loves her, how beautiful she is, how unique, unparalleled. He tells her again and again, that there will never be another like her. How lucky he is to have her! The beloved doesn't realize why he keeps repeating the same things over and over. Constant repetition increases love. Love intensifies by constant repetition. Like the buzz of a bee as it hovers around the flowers, love begins to hum around the beloved.

What happens in ordinary life is the same as in divine love, only on a different scale, but the substance remains the same. So Nanak goes on and on telling the same things about him. If you have not loved, you will find this very jarring and foolish. The Japuji can be told in three small words: Ek Omkar Satnam. Then why does he go on and on? There is so much pleasure, so much joy in talking about him! And if the feeling takes birth within, you too will find how sweet, how tender is his name.

A child was taught to say his prayers before going to bed. One day his mother observed him closely to see whether he really prayed. The child muttered one word and pulling the blanket up, lay down on the pillow. "What is this?" she asked, "Are your prayers over so soon?"

The child answered, "Why should I waste my time saying the same things every day? So I say to God, 'Ditto!' and I'm sure he is intelligent enough to understand."

The intellect gives you such advice: Why repeat yourself? But the heart wants to repeat over and over. The heart has never heard the word *ditto*. And while the heart keeps repeating, it is immersed in the nectar of his name. The more the heart repeats, the more we are lost in ecstasy. This is like the humming of the bee, but it can only be understood if you have had the necessary feelings.

At the very end Nanak reminds us not to indulge in boasting of knowing him or being able to describe his attributes, for that can only prove you to be the chief among fools. If by constantly singing his praises your ego is lost, you shall be the wise among the wise. If, however, talking of him is strengthening your ego, if you think: Who else but I could know what I know? — then you are the fool of fools!

CHAPTER 13

Birds Don't Go to College

*Where is that door? What mansion is it
Where you sit and overlook your creation?
Infinite sounds are ringing, and infinite are the players;
Infinite the singers, and infinite the melodies they sing.
Water, fire and wind sing your glory,
And the God of death sings at your door;
Chitragupta, Shiva, Brahma, Devi — all sing your glory;
And Indra on his throne and all the deities,
And holy men in meditation, and realized beings in their
  samadhi,
And ascetics, chaste women, contented people and warriors,
And pandits, rishis, and their Vedas through the ages,
And beautiful maidens of heaven, and fishes that dwell in
  the depths,
And the fourteen gems created by you, and the sixty-eight sacred
  places,
Heroes and great warriors, and creatures of the four kingdoms
  sustained by you,
All continents, all spheres, and the entire universe,
Those in your favor and deeply immersed in you, such delightful
  devotees,
They all sing your praises! And how many more, I cannot
  conceive or infer.
He and only He is the true lord. He is truth — Satnam.
He is and always will be. Though all vanish his reality will
  never leave.*

> He created Maya — things of various colors and emotions and dispositions.
> He creates all things and watching over them, He also gives them greatness.
> He does what pleases him. None can interfere with his order.
> Nanak says, He is the King of Kings. Abide by his will.

There is a Sufi tale: Becoming angry with his prime minister, a king had him confined in a very high tower with no way to escape; if he tried to jump he would surely be killed. The king did not know it, but on his way to the tower the prime minister had whispered something in his wife's ear. On the very first night she came and left an ordinary insect on the tower wall. She applied a little honey to its antennae and the insect began to climb up the tower in search of the honey, but she had also tied a thin silk thread to its tail. Slowly the insect climbed the three hundred feet of the tower where the minister was waiting for it. He grabbed at the silk thread to which the wife had tied a string, and to the string she had tied a cord, and attached to the cord was a strong rope. The minister pulled till he had the rope in hand, and with its help he climbed down from the tower.

The story states that not only did the minister escape the prison, but he also discovered the means to escape from life's ultimate prison. If even the thinnest, weakest thread comes to hand, there is no difficulty in attaining liberation. The weakest thread can pave the way to beatitude, but the thread must come to hand. A slight ray, once recognized, can lead to the sun.

All religions, all gurus, have reached God by catching hold of one thin thread or other. These threads are many, and can be tied to many kinds of insect. It isn't necessary to smear the insect's antennae with honey; you can apply anything that tempts the insect to climb to the prisoner. The thread becomes the bridge.

The thread that Nanak caught hold of is so crystal clear, but since we are both deaf and blind, we cannot hear him.

If you observe life closely, you will find that the most outstanding thing in existence is song. The birds have always been singing; each morning at the break of day they herald the coming of the sun with their song. The wind brushes against the leaves of the trees, and there is music. The waterfall has a melody all its own. The clouds clash with tumultuous sounds. The sound of the rivers as they flow, and the waves as they lash against the shores, have a quality of their very own. Look at life all around and listen! Existence sings from every corner.

Nothing in existence is clearer than music. It stops at death when life has become silent. Life is full of resonance, but man is deaf; therefore, though the thread is clear and within our hands, we do not grasp it. If life is so full of song, then it is certain that God's hand is behind it. God is somewhere hidden behind the song. If we could sing, if we could lose ourselves in the rapture of his song, the thread will be grasped. To be absorbed in the song is the thread that leads to him. Then it will not be long to escape the prison of *sansara*, this everyday world, and reach liberation in God.

Nanak made his *sadhana*, his practice, out of song. Sometimes you must have felt the intoxication creeping up on you in the exhilaration and ecstasy of singing. But people are afraid to sing. Birds do not care whether their voices are sweet or not, but man is very careful. Only a few people sing, those with good voices; the rest sing only in the bathroom where no one can see and no one can hear. Singing makes you feel fresher than a bath, for bathing only touches the surface while the song sinks deep within. He who cannot hum has lost connection with God; he retreats further and further from existence, like a living corpse.

Kabir has said about this country: "This is the land of corpses, for the song of life does not play here. No one dances in celebration, no one sings with a full heart, and no one loses himself in song."

It doesn't matter whether your voice is sweet or not, for song isn't a commodity to be sold in the marketplace, but rather an expression of gratitude and happiness. A song is made meaningful and beautiful by you being enraptured by it, not by the quality of your voice. You can be so immersed in your song that you are no more, only the song is — the singer is lost, the song remains. It can happen so simply, and there is no easier thread. If birds can sing, plants hum, and the waterfall babble, are you so useless that you can't stand amongst them? Are you so incapable that you can't compete with the stream or with the birds and the trees?

The fact is that you are frightened since song has been made into a sellable commodity. As a result, it is no longer a natural act in life but a product for the market, and you worry about making time for it and whether your voice is adequately trained. No stream stops to learn music; it is as natural a flow as a river. Music is already within, so it needn't be learned.

All you require is the courage and daring to be a little mad, and then the song will spurt out of you. Birds don't go to college to learn music; they don't worry about who says what; they are not anxious whether their song will sell; they sing with joy and abandon. Why not you?

Since we started selling our songs in the bazaar another calamity took place; we stopped singing and became listeners. We are passive: if someone sings we listen, if someone dances we look. Think of how impoverished and wretched we have become. The time will come when someone will be happy and we will be the audience. What a difference between watching someone's happiness and being happy yourself! Imagine looking on while someone is making love, and you don't make love yourself. Do you see the difference? Can love be known by watching? No, it can only be known when you yourself love.

If you listen to a person singing, no matter how melodious the voice, and how great the artist, you will not know what it is to sing. This is borrowed pleasure; you sit like a corpse and listen, not connected with the music at all. You must actively enter into the music. Dance can only be known by dancing, not by watching. Watching is a mere substitute; it is false, inauthentic.

Slowly, slowly man is leaving everything to others. Some few perform, most watch; some dance, the rest watch; some sing and many gather to listen. If you neither sing nor play nor dance what is the purpose of being alive? Is life to be carried on by a few specialists?

Neither spectator nor performer gain anything from this, for the latter's attention is totally into making money. The dance comes not from the soul; it is merely superficial skill. The dancer is actually not dancing at all, since the dance doesn't penetrate enough for him to lose himself in it; his mind remains apart, involved with the money he is making.

Birds Don't Go to College

It happened this way: The emperor Akbar told Tansen one day that he would like to meet and hear his guru. He said, "Last night when you left, a thought came to my mind that there has never been a singer greater than you, nor will there ever be. You are the ultimate in music. But then it occurred to me that you must have learned from somebody. You must have had a guru, and perhaps he is even better than you. So I would like to meet your guru and hear him."

Tansen replied, "That is very difficult. I do have a guru who is still alive, but you cannot call him to the court for he does not sing on request. His songs are like the songs of the birds. A cuckoo will never sing at your request. The more you plead the more silent he will become, for it will begin to wonder why the request. You can hear my guru only when he chooses to sing. If you are that eager we shall have to go and hide behind his hut and listen secretly. If we approach him directly he might stop singing."

Tansen's guru, a fakir named Haridas, stayed in a hut on the bank of the river Jamuna. At three o'clock every morning, before dawn, he would sit by the river and sing in ecstasy. His singing was like the song of the birds; his songs had nothing to do with anybody.

Akbar and Tansen reached the hut at two o'clock. At three the singing began. Akbar listened as if hypnotized, his eyes raining tears. When they rode back he could not utter a single word to Tansen. In fact he totally forgot that Tansen was there.

As he stepped down from the chariot he told Tansen, "I was under the impression that you had no equal, but today I see the your guru far surpasses you. Is there some reason for it?"

Tansen replied, "Is there really any need to ask? I sing for you, but my guru sings only for God. When I sing my eye is on the gift you will give me, for singing is my business. My guru doesn't sing to get anything. In fact, it is the other way around; he sings only when he receives, when he is so filled with the emotion of God from the grace he received from above, when his throat is full, when waves of ecstasy arise in his heart. When he is flooded with his grace he sings, he flows, he bursts into song. Singing is like his shadow to him. But for me, I sing first, then receive. My eyes are always on the fruits of my effort, therefore I am lowly. You are absolutely right: how can

I stand next to my guru? No matter how skillful I become, however practiced my hands or competent my voice, my soul will never be able to enter into my song. I am a specialist, not so my guru. His song is like the song of the birds. I am nothing before him."

The singers you hear today are professionals. The listeners sit passively while they do their jobs, so far have we come from the song of God. Whoever is making love on the screen is a professional doing his job. He acts and viewers watch, nothing more, just glued to their chairs.

The realities of life can only be known actively; you must enter into these realities. Just to see a person swimming, how can you enjoy the pleasure? If seeing gives so much pleasure, how infinitely joyful must be the act of being and doing.

Sing, dance, but forget the world for it is the thought of the world that prevents you from singing and dancing. Dance, sing — and you stand in the footsteps of God. Nanak says it in such poetic words:

> *Where is that door? What mansion is it*
> *Where you sit and overlook your creation?*
> *Infinite sounds are ringing, and infinite are the players;*
> *Infinite the singers, and infinite the melodies they sing.*
> *Water, fire and wind sing your glory,*
> *And the God of death sings at your door;*
> *Chitragupta, Shiva, Brahma, Devi — all sing your glory;*
> *And Indra on his throne and all the deities,*
> *And holy men in meditation, and realized beings in their samadhi.*

Nanak asks? Where is his door? Where is his abode? And he provides the answer that infinite melodies play and infinite are the players. Nanak is saying: There is your door, hidden in the sound. You are looking after the world, and Omkar is your door.

If even a part of the song comes within your grasp, with the help of this thin thread you can reach to his door. When the music, the Omkar, begins to sound within you, when you lose yourself in the sounds, that very moment you find yourself before his door.

He says: So many ragas and their variations, so many melodies, so many sounds, you singers! They are all your door. From morning till evening, from evening till morning, infinite melodies play.

Begin to recognize these melodies in life. Man's music is derived entirely from existence. All his musical instruments, all his melodies are derived from sounds of nature: the song of the birds, the sound of the waterfall, the sighing of the wind.

Try to recognize the melody in the world. Early in the morning when you wake up direct your attention to the sounds around you. Once you catch these melodies you will keep hearing them all day long, for they are continuous; only you are deaf.

Sit in the silence of the night and listen to it. This sound of stillness is very close to the ego. When Omkar begins to sound within you, at first you will hear only the sound of stillness: its echo is like the chirping of a cricket in the silent night. You can hear it all day long, anywhere — in the market, at the office, in the shop. The resonance is everywhere. It may be faint or seem to get lost in the noise of the marketplace, but it is very much there. Once you grasp it you will recognize it more and more often. All day long there is a festival of melodies at his door.

Whoever has known him has called him *satchitanand* — truth, consciousness and bliss. When a person is filled with joy he is filled with song. Joy and song are so close. Except in films no one sings in sorrow; tears flow, not song. Whatever you do in moments of happiness will be filled with song; even if tears flow it will have the tinkle of music in it. In your sitting and standing, in your gait, in your very breath, music will play; your heartbeats will lend rhythm to your song. Truly music is his door, for within resides the supreme bliss.

Ultimately the music stops, for it is only a door; once you pass through it the music stops. A moment comes when your music becomes a hindrance. Then only his music sounds. Infinite melodies play within you, but you have no music of your own; you are like an empty house.

Our temples are designed for sound to reverberate inside, their construction based on it. The temple is always absolutely empty. This signifies the ultimate state of a seeker; it is a symbol. When the Omkar sounds, we shall be empty within — absolutely empty. A bell is hung at the temple door; whoever comes first rings the bell, for the *nada* is at the door.

These are all symbols. No one should enter the temple through that door of doors without ringing the bell, for only through the sound itself can you enter. The uniqueness of a bell is that it keeps resounding long after you ring it, so the resonance keeps sounding as you enter the main entrance. In that sound alone is the key to your entry into the temple.

Through the sound, as it were, you enter into God's abode. The temple is a symbol of God's dwelling. When it is sounding constantly you need not ring the bell, but we have formulated a method with the symbol. When you return from the temple ring the bell again. You have to journey back amidst the reverberating sound. All worship, all prayers start with the ringing of the bell.

Nanak says infinite nadas are ringing and infinite are the players. He does not speak as an observer. He describes it as one standing at the door; therefore, his words are straightforward and simple. As if this is happening before his eyes he says:

> *Where is that door? What mansion is it*
> *Where you sit and overlook your creation?*
> *Infinite sounds are ringing, and infinite are the players;*
> *Infinite the singers, and infinite the melodies they sing.*
> *Water, fire and wind sing your glory,*
> *And the God of death sings at your door.*
> *Chitragupta, Shiva, Brahma, Devi – all sing your glory;*

Understand that Dharmraj, the god of death, signifies the zenith, the climax; he is the deity of virtue and ethics. To investigate what is good and what is not good in its finest subtlety is the work of Dharmraj. Nanak says that even he sits at your door and sings.

There can be no one of a more serious nature than Dharmraj. His very name implies one who has a very grave and weighty temperament, for he thinks in the minutest detail: what is right, what is wrong, what should be done and what should not, what is worth doing and what is not? Nanak also finds such a person singing in ecstasy.

Chitragupta's job is to note down and keep an account of the sins and virtues of people. What can he sing? Even high court judges are only minor Chitraguptas, and just visualize how they carry themselves, sitting stiffly in their chairs in black clothes and white wigs – such grave faces! Laughter is taboo – in contempt of court – and singing is out of the question. Imagine, this is the state in the lesser courts, and Chitragupta sits in the ultimate court!

Nanak says: "I see even Chitragupta singing at your door. All his seriousness has vanished, it would seem; his door is the door of celebration."

Understand that your attention should not be concentrated on keeping an account of good and bad deeds in your life, for in so doing your life becomes cold and heavy with solemnity. He who becomes grave, loses. Do not be lost. Do not become dry. Don't contract in the constant anxiety of what is good and what is bad, for there is no entry to his door for such dehydrated, unfeeling, long-faced people. Dejection and melancholy cannot gain entrance here. Only those who dance and sing have access. Therefore it invariably happens that your so-called "holy men" remain distant from him, for they have become so very grim.

Remember that gravity is a part of the ego. A solemn person can never be egoless, and an egoist is invariably conceited and arrogant. There is no sign of the simple, the childlike, the artless in him. Nanak's full name was Nanak Nirankari. The very name Nirankari means egoless.

Mardana sits at Nanak's side, always ready with his instrument to play. Ask Nanak the most serious question and he answers with a song. To all solemnity he responds with cheerfulness. Ask him a profound question, his answer is filled with festivity and rejoicing. Do what you will, Nanak always sang in answer while Mardana played his instrument. There was a special reason why Nanak chose to do that: to bring home to us the fact that music plays at his door.

Rejoicing is characteristic of the truly religious man; whereas an ordinary so-called "religious" man has just the opposite disposition: stiff with arrogance, his eyes filled with scorn and censure. The constant thought of good and bad reduces them to this state. They kill themselves this way. When do they have time to sing? They are forever worried: what to eat, what not to eat; whether to get up this time or that; whether to dress this way or that — or not to dress at all. All their time is taken up in the boredom and insensibility of rules and regulations.

It is true that rejoicing also has its regulation, but it is not superimposed, it arises from within, it is an inner discipline. Solemnity has its own rules that are superimposed: whatever is inside, wear a solemn expression on your face! The body becomes lifeless. This is not the characteristic of a religious man. In fact, these are the ways of a frightened man. He is so frightened that he dare not laugh for he fears that laughter may lead him to some sin. So laughter has become sinful, and a grim, long face a symbol of virtue.

In Nanak's method there is song and festivity. Holding on to this sutra of celebration and festivity one can reach his gate.

> *And holy men in meditation, and realized beings in their samadhi,*
> *And ascetics, chaste women, contented people and warriors,*
> *And pandits, rishis, and their Vedas through the ages,*
> *And beautiful maidens of heaven, and fishes that dwell in the depths,*
> *And the fourteen gems created by you, and the sixty-eight sacred places,*
> *Heroes and great warriors, and creatures of the four kingdoms sustained by you,*
> *All continents, all spheres, and the entire universe,*
> *Those in your favor and deeply immersed in you, such delightful devotees,*
> *They all sing your praises! And how many more, I cannot conceive or infer.*

Nanak never tires of saying that his song sounds in all of creation. From all sides existence is a celebration. God laughs; he does not cry, nor does he like crying faces. Melancholy has nothing to do with existence. In fact, to be grim and sad is to be cut off from existence, to be turned away from God.

If sadness and sorrow overtake you in life, you must have taken some wrong step; when you suffer, know that you have gone astray. The suffering is only a pointer, don't make it your life style; don't become masochist, for masochism is a disease from which many people suffer.

Sacher-Masoch was the writer after whom this illness is named. He described whippings, pricking with thorns till one bled; he described fixing nails to the soles of one's shoes so that they made wounds with each step. Such masochists are everywhere. You will also find them lying on beds of nails in Kashi. There are ill people who revel in self-torture. You will find them fasting, you will find them rotting, decaying in various temples and hermitages — and common people worship them!

Why? There is yet another parallel illness, sadism. The sadist revels in others' torment and agony. The sadist and masochist are paired; one loves to see the other in agony, and the other delights in having pain inflicted on him. Keep in mind whenever you revere a sad, suffering, self-tormenting individual, you suffer from the other's illness. Since these illnesses are complementary, sadists gather around masochists. They say, "How wonderful you are to lie on a bed of nails. Such self-sacrifice." Thus their egos are inflated and they are coaxed into tormenting themselves even more.

Keep it well in mind not to support a man who is in suffering or troubled, for that is a sin and equal to inflicting pain on him. It is a very subtle device. Should I want to pierce you with a dagger it would be a sin. But if you thrust a dagger into your chest and I say, "Wonderful! What a sacrifice! You have become a martyr!" it is sinful and I am partner to the act. A man lying on a bed of nails is a sinner all right, but those who come and offer flowers and coins at his feet are also partners in his sin. They are offering him encouragement by calling him a saint. These are two types of sick people; both suffer from a perverted state of mind. Beware of them both.

A healthy man troubles neither himself nor others. As a person becomes more and more healthy, he becomes more and more cheerful, and begins to share his joy with others. He always respects joy and cheer. When you see a man singing and dancing with joy, offer flowers at his feet. But you have never done this, or else the ashrams and temples in this world would have been quite different: they would have been filled with celebration.

Unfortunately, our ashrams and temples are filled with sick and diseased people, with people who are mentally ill, who should be treated by psychiatrists. And they are that way because of you. You have revered them and encouraged them. Have you ever honored a man who is cheerful?

Only yesterday a sannyasin told me of a strange event taking place. As her meditation is getting deeper and deeper, she experiences more and more joy. But with this, she is feeling that something wrong is happening, some transgression, as if she is following a wrong path. This is bound to happen to you when bliss enters, for we have all been groomed for suffering since childhood – not for happiness. If the child sits in the corner, dull and despondent, the parents say, "Good boy." But if the child dances and prances about with joy, the whole household gets after him, "Keep quiet! Don't make so much noise." Whenever he shouts in glee there is someone to reprimand him. He is made to feel that he has committed some error whenever he is happy, but that everything is all right when he is sad and dejected. Gradually the feeling penetrates the subconscious that it is wrong to be cheerful, but to be sad is a sign of virtue.

Whenever a person progresses in meditation the opposite process begins, he moves towards happiness and song. The closer he approaches the door of his abode, the more pronounced the celebration becomes. As the internal festivity begins, suppressed desires, the gaze of the outside world, and a sense of guilt raise their heads and stand in the way. The need to suppress it finds a thousand and one ways to thwart your happiness.

A friend comes and says he is making progress in his meditation but one thing plagues him: when all the world is plunged into suffering and sorrow, isn't it just plain selfishness to seek happiness for oneself?

Now he has devised a rational device to express the deep fear of his own joy. Six months earlier he came to me saying he was so unhappy, so miserable. All he wanted was to be happy. Then he wasn't concerned with God at all. Now that he is coming closer to joy, when the first chink has opened and the first tune has begun to play, he is seized with fright! He switched off his mind at once. He said, "I have stopped meditating. It seems too selfish." I told him, "Be sad and unhappy to your heart's content. To feel that way will be a great service to others. Cry aloud, beat your chest, torment your body, kill yourself — and you will deliver the world!"

Now how can your suffering deliver the world? Your misery will increase the suffering of others; it raises the ratio of suffering in the world. If you are happy you make suffering that much less in the world. One single person's happiness and joy raises currents strong enough to make those around him happy.

If a single house has a lamp, it helps make the neighbors conscious that their houses are in darkness. When one lamp is burning it is not difficult to light others with it. One lamp can light the lamps of the entire world.

But the mind is trained only for suffering. The whole world is divided into two kinds of unhappy people: there are those who wish to be made to suffer, and others who are always looking for someone else to oppress and torture. Neither group has any bearing on religion; for neither can ever hope to hear the music within. They are the two sides of the coin of sorrow, and sorrow has no relationship to God.

When your connections are broken you become unhappy and you suffer. Illness means your connection with nature is broken. Suffering means your connection with God is broken. When the body conducts itself against the principles of nature, illness results; when it flows along with nature, there is health and well-being. When the mind follows paths away from God, suffering is the result. When the soul moves in the footsteps of God, when it flows with the universal principle, there is bliss.

Nanak says there is music at his door. No, music *is* his door. Celebration, festivity are his practice. The whole of existence is filled with song. You are deaf. That's what the matter is. You cannot see, you cannot hear. On every leaf, on every flower this message is written. He has filled the universe with so many colors and it is his music that vibrates in the rainbow of infinite hues. All creation is always celebrating this festival.

Those in your favor and deeply immersed in you, such delightful devotees,
They all sing your praises! And how many more, I cannot conceive or infer.
He and only He is the true lord. He is truth — Satnam.
He is and always will be. Though all vanish his reality will never leave.
He created Maya...

Nanak has very skillfully removed the sting from the word *maya*. He has deleted the feeling of contempt that is associated with maya. The mystery that Shankara himself could not unfold, Nanak has revealed. Shankara was a very rational thinker who founded a whole philosophical school. His sole aim was to explain the whole universe through logic and reason. He found himself in great difficulty over maya and Brahma.

On the one hand, Shankara knows that maya is a myth; it does not exist, for maya means that which is not. Maya is visible to the eyes but does not exist in actuality; whereas, that which is not visible, but which *is*, is Brahma. Maya is forever changing, kaleidoscopic, like dreams. Brahma is forever, the eternal truth, the creator.

Shankara represents the *Advaita-Vedanta* theory that is non-dualistic. It faces the question: "How is maya born?" If it is entirely nonexistent, then how could there be any problems? Then it would be foolish to tell a person: Why are you involved in the illusion of maya? How can a person be entangled in that which does not exist? Then it is mere nonsense to exhort people to shun maya — something that is nonexistent.

And if maya does exist how can it be without God? His support is absolutely necessary. The dream arises only when there is someone to see it. So Advaita-Vedanta is concerned with this problem: If it is God who has created maya, then all the mahatmas who preach against maya are preaching against God. And if God himself is holding on to maya, how are we expected to leave it? It is not within our power. When it is by his will, then his will is supreme and cannot be wrong.

Where does maya come from? If it arises out of Brahma, then

how can that which is born out of truth be an untruth? What is born out of truth can only be truth. Or, if maya is an untruth, the Brahma from which it is born must be an untruth, too. They must both be of the same nature: either both are real or both are false. Shankara could not solve this problem.

But Nanak can resolve it. What philosophers cannot unlock devotees easily unravel. For Nanak, maya is the festival of colors and music that goes on at his gates continuously. The multitude of colors in the flowers and the trees, in the birds and the bees are all an expression of his bliss. He manifests himself in so many forms; he blooms in so many flowers and delights in all the forms he assumes. It is all an expansion of his supreme energy. So maya and Brahma, the creation and the creator, are not the opposite of each other. All creation is a festival, a dance of Brahma, the creator — his song.

Shankara's concept of Brahma is very dry, for he eliminates maya entirely. His is a mathematical concept, devoid of all music and color, all joys and sorrows. It is like the void, an emptiness. How can you love the Brahma of Shankara? How can you make love to a mathematical theorem? That two plus two equals four is correct, but why should one fall in love with such figures? Anything mathematical is dry and feelingless.

Nanak's Brahma is absolutely different. It is not the concept of a mathematician, but of a poet who adores beauty. Nanak is a poet, not a philosopher. And what a philosopher cannot solve, a poet can. The philosopher is caught in his logic, the poet doesn't concern himself about it. He can afford to be illogical. His imagination makes incongruous things become consistent. All conflicts and contradictions become harmonious in his love and his devotion.

Keep it well in mind that to Nanak maya is God's festivity. Therefore Nanak never advised his followers to leave the world. How is one to leave, and why should one shun anything that is his?

He would tell his disciples, "Stay right in the world and seek him there, for the world also is his. Seek out your path from this very *sansara*, the material world that is part of the wheel of birth and death. Don't be afraid of maya, it is only his play."

One thing is certain and imperative: don't lose yourself in this play. Always keep your mind on the player — this is "remembrance." Don't get lost in the dance. Keep constantly in mind him who directs the dance. Look at the trees, hear the song of the birds, but do not be so lost in them that you forget the one who is behind them all! Maya means the manifest Brahma. Keep seeking the unmanifest within the manifest, the invisible within the visible.

> They all sing your praises! And how many more, I cannot conceive or infer.
> He and only He is the true lord. He is truth — Satnam.
> He is and always will be. Though all vanish his reality will never leave.
> He created Maya — things of various colors and emotions and dispositions.
> He creates all things and watching over them, He also gives them greatness.

What a wonderful thing Nanak has said. He says God makes the creation, and having made it, he looks at it, just as a painter paints a picture, then steps back a little to view his work. He observes it closely, he steps to the right and looks, steps to the left and looks again. Then he views it from a distance, then he takes it up to the window to scrutinize it in the light and in shadow. He examines it in a thousand ways, as does a sculptor.

> He creates all things and watching over them, He also gives them greatness.

Thus he gives prominence and importance to his creation. So God is not against *sansara* or else why should he create it?

Nor is he maya's enemy, or why should he bother with it? So the difficulty encountered by logic had no ground with the devotee. Nanak says not only does he create but he admires his creation and looks at it exultantly, thus giving it honor and importance.

Remember, God has created you and having created you he has examined you from all sides, and he is still looking at you constantly as a part of his own handiwork, giving you dignity and importance;

and on its own all sin will fade away from your life. If you remember this you will move about as a creation of his. You will speak and hear, fully conscious of the fact that you are his creation. In all your dealings you will be conscious of the fact that you are his and he is looking after you all the time.

He watches over you constantly. He provides you with comfort and care. He looks at you lovingly, again and again. He never tires of looking at you. He is pleased with you for it is he who has made you. He is neither disappointed nor disheartened by your ways or else he could destroy you so easily. No matter how bad and sinful you become, his flame of hope for you never burns out. No matter how far you wander away from him, no matter how completely you forget him and turn your back on him, his loving gaze is still fixed on you. For he knows that if not today, tomorrow you are sure to return. Sooner or later the prodigal must return, his coming back is certain, for the further you go away from him the more unhappy you will become, like a little child who has run away from home.

A little child, barely four years old, ran away from home. He took a small bundle of clothes and set out. A policeman found him going back and forth along the side of the road a number of times. He approached him, thinking he needed help, and asked, "Where do you want to go? Where have you come from?"

The child said, "I have run away from home but mother always said not to cross the road, but to stay on this side. Now I don't know what to do, since I can't cross over."

How far can a small child stray? Even if he does, mommy has always set a limit and how can he disobey her?

How far will you wander from God? Even if you are angry with him for some reason, you will keep shuttling between home and the road crossing. How far can you go and where will you go? Wherever you roam it is within his boundaries. Wherever you are will be within him. Your anger is the anger of a little child; it is nothing but a part of love. He is never displeased by your displeasure.

Nanak says: "He gives you importance and glorified you. What he has created he surveys, and he likes what he surveys."

He does what pleases him. None can interfere with his order. Nanak says, He is the King of Kings. Abide by his will.

One must remain well within his order and abide by his will. If you go outside his rule, he will not be displeased or annoyed, only you will have suffered unnecessarily. The suffering is not a punishment by him, but the direct result of going against his will.

If you try to pass through the wall instead of going through the door, and injure your head in the process, the wall cannot be blamed. You are totally responsible for not using the door.

That door is his will. When the door is available why should you want to pass through the wall? You will only break your head. Remember, too, God is not breaking your head. You suffer because of your own foolishness. Existence feels only compassion towards you even when you break your head; again and again existence tends to your wounds. No matter how much you wander, no matter how much you injure yourself, existence sets you right again and again, ad infinitum. For infinite births you have been knocking your head against the wall, and still you are well and whole! Nothing is broken in you. The soul cannot be broken. The only thing is that you have unnecessarily caused yourself suffering by your own hands.

Therefore, Nanak says, remain within his order and abide by his will.

How is one to know what he wills? How to be sure what his order is? Even great thinkers have not found an answer. Granted one should abide by his will, but what is his will? How will you be sure that in the medley of thousands of voices the voice you hear is his and not your own, or someone else's?

There is a way to know his wish, but not through the medium of thoughts. The way unfolds as you drown in his melody, as your ego disintegrates, as you are immersed in meditation and *samadhi*. At once his voice becomes audible. Usually the noise and tumult of your ego prevents you from hearing his voice. As the ego abates and the tumult of thoughts dies out, you will be able to hear his voice. He is forever calling; his voice has never left you.

An inner self lies within man. Just as you see with your eyes and hear with your ears, so the soul is also the mechanism within you that catches the voice of God. The eyes catch the rays of light; how, the scientists don't as yet fully know. How the eye grasps the light from outside objects and reflects it in the mind is still a mystery. The hands touch, but how does the mind get word of the touch, whether the hand is rough or smooth, tender or velvety? The touch happens at the tip of the fingers, but how does the brain get the right message, and at that very instant?

As there are five sense organs to ally us to the world of objects, so also is there a sixth sense organ called the *antah-karana*, the "inner voice." This inner voice is not the conscience; it is not the sense of right and wrong you were taught in childhood. It is not the voice that punishes you for what you did or what you thought. It is the wordless voice of understanding — of consciousness — deep in the heart. It is the sense — deep, deep within — of knowing. It is tuned to God, tuned to the order in the universe. In that sense it knows what is right. But it only speaks to you when all other voices inside have been stilled.

But you are preoccupied with other things. The milling crowd of thoughts within suppresses the voice. When there is complete silence within, you suddenly experience the existence of this voice and realize that it was always there.

Nanak says abide by his will! But first you have to seek out his will, and this is not difficult. Right and wrong cannot be decided by your mind. Stop thinking, eradicate all thoughts, and you will hear what is right. Then there is no more anxiety, no more responsibility for which you are answerable. Everything is his will. You do his bidding.

"His will" is Nanak's path. Therefore he refers to the supreme thread of life as the divine order. And you have a device to relate to him. You were born with it, but have never made use of it. Meditation leads you up to your antah-karana, which then joins you to God. It is the cord that keeps you connected with God, telling you at each moment what you should do and what you should not.

Nanak says, when you begin to hear the voice of consciousness, remain within its field. Then sorrow cannot touch you and life becomes one long downpour of festivity and celebration.

Kabir has described this moment: "When bliss is born, clouds thunder and nectar rains." As soon as you establish contact with your heart, with the voice within, you are directly joined to God. This contact always is — from God's side — but it is missing from your side. To be silent is the art of establishing this contact. Only silence is the way.

CHAPTER 14

Posture Is a Template

Oh yogi, assume the posture of contentment and modesty.
Pick up the carrying bag of dignity and honor,
And apply the sacred ash of meditation.
Establish death as your bedroll; make a maiden of your body.
Let experience be your staff of liberation,
And consider the unity of all as your first principle.
To conquer the mind is to conquer the world.
If you must bow, bow to him.
He is the primal being, pure, without beginning or end.
He is the unstruck sound.
He is immutable through all time.
Make knowledge your pleasure and compassion your storehouse.
Make a conch shell of the eternal music playing in every being.
He alone is a master in whom all beings are intertwined,
While the search for supernatural powers is a false path.
The law of union and separation governs all things,
And destiny determines our just inheritance.
If you must bow, bow to him.
He is the primal being, pure, without beginning or end;
He is the unstruck sound.
He is immutable through all time.

Try to understand on the deepest level every word of these incomparable verses:

Oh yogi, assume the posture of contentment and modesty.

Pick up the carrying bag of dignity and honor,
And apply the sacred ash of meditation.

There are certain fundamental errors of the human mind that are repeated again and again; it has always been so and will continue in the future. Whenever a religion is born many methods, many devices, and many experiments are conducted in the quest for God.

Close to the original source of a religion there are symbols and signposts that help. As that fundamental source recedes further and further away and the religion becomes a tradition, the symbols are no longer alive. They become inert and their meaning is lost. Then people drag the religion along like a dead body, with dead symbols. Religion becomes a duty to be performed, as a social obligation.

For instance, I give you sannyas and you put on the orange clothes. After a few days the meaning of the orange clothes will be lost. The further you go from me the more will the clothes become a mere external symbol. Dyeing your clothes orange doesn't change the soul within. The orange robe is only a signal for remembrance — now the soul has to be dyed.

When someone wants to remember something during the course of the day he might tie a knot in his handkerchief as a way of remembering. The knot itself isn't to be purchased, nor does it have any meaning in itself. However preoccupied he is all day, every time he touches the handkerchief he will be reminded that he has to buy something. Now maybe his son has noticed that he often leaves home with a knotted handkerchief. He is intrigued; there surely must be something to it. So when he goes to the market he knots his handkerchief, but he has no notion of the significance of the knot. It has no further relationship to remembrance but has become an idle custom as the son does what he saw his father doing; and so the tradition can go on for thousands of years.

In this household then, tying a knot before setting out from home becomes a sacred custom. Whoever observes it honors his forefathers; whoever doesn't observe it will be branded a rebel, an irreligious person. But neither the one who ties the knot nor the one who doesn't is able to tell why the knot is there.

This sort of confusion is natural in all religions. The mind grasps what is shallow and superficial and forgets what is deep and profound; it has no depth, thus is unable to grasp the depth.

I give you orange robes, but only to remember constantly that you have been initiated into sannyas. Now you have to sit, stand, walk, talk as a sannyasin should. Your actions in the world should not be that of a slave but of a master, which is why I call you swami. Now show that you are a free person, not a captive. I agree that this cannot come about immediately, but you have to make a beginning somewhere. These clothes are like a knot for you. Their usefulness lies in constantly focusing your remembrance on the fact of being a sannyasin from the very beginning.

These words of Nanak are directed towards the holy men of the *Nath-Sampradaya*, an influential sect in those days. Their ashrams were spread throughout the country. Their founder, Gorakhnath, was a potent leader, but after his death the methods fell into the hands of ordinary people and they became shallow and useless. The sadhus of this sect pierce their ears, which is very useful in serving as a knot.

Acupuncture has been a science in China for centuries; now it is gaining recognition in the West. This science believes that there are seven hundred points in the human body from which the life energy flows. The earlobes are very important acupuncture points, very closely connected to remembrance. When the ear is pierced the energy within gets a severe jolt. In fact, piercing the ears was even a well known remedy for certain mental ailments. In China it was the only treatment to cure mental illness.

Because of the profound experience from that energy flow, the sadhus of this sect used to pierce their ears; one group even cut the lobes through and through instead of just piercing them. The energy flows more directly to the brain when an intermediary obstruction is removed. It was a significant device to awaken remembrance.

Try this experiment: when you are feeling sad, worried, downcast or angry, hold your ear lobes and rub them hard; there is no need to pierce the ears. You will find a change in your state of mind. But one thing is certain, merely cutting the lobes or piercing them does not make an enlightened being out of a seeker.

There is an ancient village custom in India that arose during the time of very high infant mortality. Even today you may come upon someone in a rural village whose name is *Kanchchedi-lal,* he whose ears are pierced, or *Natthu-lal,* he whose nose is pierced.

This tradition of piercing the ear or the nose came into vogue, and the children named accordingly, after a great deal of experience; finally it had been realized that it was more likely that the child would not die when the ear or the nose was pierced. The method evolved through the experience of thousands of years, and is the result of a fundamental change in the life energy as a result of the piercing.

In Russia experiments with Kirlian photography have arrived at significant conclusions. The whole play of health, illness, birth and death of a human being involves the flow of electrical energy within. This flow of energy can be diverted at certain points and transformed. It can be made to flow in whatever direction is required, and it can also be stopped from flowing in a particular direction.

The art of acupuncture is based on this. When a person is ill, needles are inserted into particular places on the body. The prick of the needle changes the flow of energy, and alters the disease and effects a cure. China has been using this therapy for thousands of years, and now science has confirmed the existence of these points in the body. Russia has also introduced this form of therapy into their hospitals. They have devised an instrument like an x-ray machine, which can spot trouble-spots in the body by picking up changes in electrical currents in the body-part that has fallen sick. Having discovered the spot, an electric shock at this point reestablishes the energy flow and the illness is improved.

The yogis of Nath-Sampradaya had devised their own significant shock method. Many such techniques have evolved. For example, Jews and the Muslims follow their custom of circumcision, which is also an effective shock technique. The Jews circumcise the male child on the eighth day.

Research has tried to uncover the advantages of this technique. There is no community more intellectual, more brilliant than the Jews. Though small in number they have taken the greatest number of Nobel prizes. They are prominent in whatever field of work they engage in, the leaders of everything they do. People of great influence and power in this century have been Jews: Karl Marx, Sigmund Freud, Albert Einstein, for example. In fact, it is they who have created this age. Among great thinkers or scientist no one can meet their caliber. So now scientists have tried to see whether circumcision in infancy has anything to do with the Jews' genius.

Since Muslims, who also circumcise their children, did not attain to this mark of genius, a suggested cause might be that they perform the circumcision rather late. Jews believe that the first shock the child receives should be directed at the sex organ where the life energy is accumulated. By cutting the foreskin the life energy gets a powerful jolt which sends it straight up to the head. This impact in the head proves very significant for him for all time to come. It changes the course of his life.

Kirlian photography confirms it and acupuncture had known it for ages. The sex organ is the most sensitive part of the human body. To cut the skin is a matter of great shock to the infant, which increases the life energy flow to the head. This method opens many possibilities.

Whenever these things are discovered they are put into use. Then gradually, as time passes, the meaning is lost. Then people go through these practices as a matter of custom, completely unaware of their significance.

Gorakhnath discovered many things. He was a unique researcher. People felt the impact of his genius and millions joined his sect for the results, which were very clear and evident. By the time of Nanak, Gorakhnath's teachings had become vague and foggy; people practiced them as ritual, without meaning. So Nanak tells the yogi to assume the posture of contentment and effacement. He says this because Gorakhnath had evolved many postures, asanas, which were very effective.

You must also have discovered that certain body postures and positions relate to the state of your mind. When you are quiet and tranquil the expression of your face and the position of your limbs are quite different from when you are angry. When you are filled with compassion the body takes on a certain posture; even your hands are filled with compassion, with fearlessness, and a sense of giving.

In compassion the hands cannot do anything but give. When you are filled with kindness, you do not clench your fist as if to fight someone; it would be incongruous. A closed fist is always to destroy someone; it is the sign of a shallow and niggardly heart. The fist opens of its own accord in moments of compassion — you are ready to give everything away.

There is an intrinsic connection between the mind and its moods, and the states of the body. So Gorakhnath devised many postures which when practiced, resulted in a change in the seeker's mind. For instance, if you assume the position of anger — clench your fists and fix your eyes as if ready to attack — you will find the rumblings of anger starting inside you.

There were two significant early psychologists in America, James and Lange, who together developed a theory in which they tried to disprove the idea that a man runs because of his fear; instead they claim that a man experiences fright because he runs away. Many scientists thus give credence to the theory that body position is of critical importance. We say a man runs when he is frightened. James and Lange say, when a man's body makes preparations to run away, then he experiences himself as being frightened. If he were to stop running or preparing to run, he would no longer feel frightened. When the posture is changed, the state within also changes.

With each different state of mind there is a specific posture or position of the body. This means that the mind and the body move in parallel lines. When you are happy your body is in a particular posture; when you are sad your body is in another position. Observe how in moments of joy your body expands and spreads out as if you have become more voluminous. When you are sad or unhappy, you feel yourself contracting, as if your insides are getting narrower and narrower, like a tree that would like to shut itself up in a seed. In studying body postures it was seen clearly that a suffering man appears contracted. By observing body positions alone you can tell the state of the mind. In joy the body is in a state of expansion; in sorrow it is contracted. In anger the lines of the forehead become more pronounced. When you are worried the facial contours change. When you are carefree there are no wrinkles on the forehead.

James and Lange were not the first to make this discovery; it has been known in India since ancient times. From early *hatha* yoga texts to Gorakhnath, millions of yogis have experimented. In fact, no one has experimented in greater detail with the mind and body of the human being, nobody has observed and investigated it in greater detail, than these yogis. They observed that for each state of mind, the body had a corresponding posture. Out of this arose a method: by changing the posture of the body in a particular way, the required change can be brought about in the state of mind. When you feel anger arising, change your body posture to the one you have when you are relaxed and peaceful. You will experience change, a transformation in the state of your energy: the energy that was about to become anger has become tranquility.

Posture is a framework, a template, a die. Energy is neutral. It assumes whatever shape you give it. It is like water. Pour it in a glass tumbler and it assumes the shape of the tumbler; pour it into a pot and it takes the form of the pot. Energy does likewise; give it the form of anger and it becomes anger, give it the form of love and the very same energy becomes love. This is a most profound discovery. When you begin to understand the various postures of the body, you can begin to change the mind within.

But there is a danger: you can get so involved in the study of body postures that you forget that it has anything to do with changing the internal states of the mind. Then you become an adept in the science of body postures, but the mind within remains the same. Remember, this is only an aid; the actual transformation must occur within. Take as much outside help as possible, but concentrate on the internal change.

When a house is being constructed, first the scaffolding is put up. This is a necessary initial step, but if you don't build anything with this structure the house will never be constructed. The structure is not habitable, it was only a prop for an actual house, Once its purpose is served it must be discarded.

Asanas, postures and *mudras* are such aids. From Gorakhnath to Nanak people had begun to consider the scaffolding as the dwelling. The yogi would sit in the posture of compassion, but he has completely forgotten that something needs to be done internally, too. So the posture is of compassion, but he is seething with anger inside. He assumes the mudra of kind-protection, but look inside and there is a dangerous man who might harm you. He stands at your door apparently asking alms, but if you do not give to him he curses you. People were frightened by the *nath*-yogis. Their beggarly appearance was false.

Buddha and Gorakhnath had both directed their disciples to become beggars in order to inculcate humility in them. When the hand is held out to beg, what room is there for haughtiness? When I stand at someone's door with a beggar's bowl outstretched, how can the ego persist? When I am doing something for someone else, the ego is nourished, but to be a beggar is to accept the fact that I am nothing, I am worthless. The begging bowl is my only possession. If you give I shall be happy; it you do not I shall go away silently, for how can a beggar insist? The giver may give or not; it is his choice.

Buddha had told his *bhikkhus* that they should beg, but they must just stand at the door and never ask. Asking also bears weight; perhaps it is coercing the giver, and that would be against the concept of begging, it is too aggressive. So the bhikkhu was directed only to stand before the entrance where he went for alms. If the householder feels like giving, he will; otherwise the bhikkhu leaves quietly. He was to make no effort lest a person give against his will To this end, he was supposed to stand with his eyes closed while he begged. He would stand for a while then move on, thus relieving the householder of any embarrassment in refusing. The bhikkhu had to practice humility. If the giver gives, it is his own will; if he does not, it is his will. In both cases the bhikkhu was to bless him. His blessings had nothing to do with whether the man gave or not.

One of Buddha's bhikkhus, by the name of Puran, gained knowledge and attained buddhahood. Buddha told him, "Go out into the world now and give others what I have given you. Many lamps are unlit, go and light them. You don't need to stay with me any more. You have attained the supreme knowledge."

Puran bowed his head and with folded hands said, "Allow me to go to the village, Sukha, in Bihar."

Buddha said, "It would be well if you do not go there, for the people are crude and heartless. They will abuse you and insult you."

Puran replied, "But master, shouldn't the doctor go where the sick are? Please give me permission to go there. Those people need me."

Buddha said, "Answer three questions before you go. First, if they insult and abuse you what will you feel?"

Puran answered, "I will feel what kind people they are! They only abuse me, they do not beat me. They could have beaten me if they liked."

Buddha said, "And if they were also beat you up? If they welcomed you with stones?"

Puran replied, "I would still feel kindly towards them, for they will only have beaten me, they haven't killed me. They could also have killed me."

"And," said Buddha, "what if they killed you? What would your feelings be at the time of death?"

"I would still feel how kind they were to have relieved me of life where I could have stumbled and erred so many times," Puran replied.

To this Buddha said, "Go forth, Puran. You are truly a perfect bhikkhu. You may go wherever you please."

Only when there is total humility is the person a real bhikkhu. But by the time Nanak appeared on the scene, the Gorakhnath bhiksu had become a terror. He would come before the door of a house and, instead of standing still, walk back and forth, shaking his staff and clanging his tongs. This invariably frightened people into giving. Looking at his straight back and angry eyes, people were afraid that not giving would surely lead to violence.

So people gave alms to the Nath-Sampradaya yogis out of fear. Otherwise their curse was certain. Such was the perverted state of affairs when Nanak came on the scene. The Nath-Sampradaya yogi never blessed anyone. That you gave him alms was of no consequence; rather you should feel grateful that he accepted your alms. He took it as his right.

Gorakh had also exhorted his followers to bless the house they begged from; whether they gave or not was not the criterion, but things had turned topsy-turvy with the passage of time. The postures were maintained but the meaning behind them was lost. There are such yogis in our time too. Certain Nath-yogis have stood for ten years without moving. This posture had significance at one time. If you stand erect while remembering within, the consciousness also stands up; if the body is absolutely still, the consciousness also becomes calm and steadfast; but, unless you remember, the body will become inert while the mind keeps on running until it has crossed a thousand worlds. Thoughts and dreams will continue. Postures will help but they are not an end in themselves.

By Nanak's time the postures had deteriorated and all the sects had become deformed. So Nanak says:

Oh yogi, assume the posture of contentment and modesty.
Pick up the carrying bag of dignity and honor.

Contentment is a significant word that unfortunately has been deformed and mutilated. When a person finds himself helpless he becomes contented. This contentment is only a consolation, not real at all. When he finds himself helpless after all efforts have failed him, and says its all right, this isn't the posture of contentment but a state of helplessness.

A man used to come to Sri Ramakrishna. Every year during the festival of Kali he would sacrifice goats to the goddess, hundreds of them. Suddenly, he gave up this practice. Ramakrishna had tried to dissuade him from doing it many times before, but to no avail. Now he stopped sacrificing the goats. Ramakrishna asked him what made him stop when all the former pleas had failed. He replied, "All this time it wasn't possible to heed your advice. Now I have lost my teeth and cannot eat meat, so I have given up killing goats. I am now quite content to do so."

So people become contented in old age or in poverty but this is pseudo-contentment. Contentment is really a power, not an outcome of weakness. It is a positive energy, not negative. It is not a state of helplessness, but a state of supreme helpfulness, a very high state of being. Contentment implies that you have much more than you require, more than what you need; you have both what you asked for and what you didn't ask for. Contentment includes gratitude: God, your will is wonderful. How much you have given me.

Contentment is not the consolation grasped by a defeated mind in a state of helplessness; it is a victorious journey where there is no question of defeat. It is attained only by glorious victors; it is worthy of heroes. Mahavira says that only Jinas, those who have conquered everything, can attain contentment.

When Nanak says: *Oh Yogi, assume the posture of contentment*, accomplishing physical postures becomes an old story leading to nothing. Nanak means to leave it and practice the inner posture, of which contentment is the highest.

Why? To become contented is to have all anxieties fall away. Anxiety is born out of discontent, out of the feeling that you are lacking something, that you are not getting what you deserve or what you think yourself worthy of. The day you attain contentment, you will sleep like a log — like someone who has sold all his horses, as the saying goes. Then you have no worries, your sleep will be undisturbed by dreams arising out of the day-long anxieties.

Discontentment involves beggarliness whereas contentment leaves you the lord and master. It is the sign of a sannyasin who is happy and contented in every way. You cannot create a condition to make him discontented, for under all circumstances he will see the good. Whatever happens, he spies his hand. In the deepest moments of suffering you cannot take away his rays of joy. He knows that the darkest hour is a forerunner of the coming morn. When he is in utter darkness he laughs and welcomes with song the morning sun that is bound to rise soon. In every dark cloud he sees the silver lining. In the darkest moments of suffering and sorrow, he holds the thread of contentment well in his hand. He accepts all; he has assumed total acceptance.

This is what Nanak means when he says to attain the posture of contentment. By controlling hands and feet and their position, nothing is attained. Control of your consciousness begins with contentment; but do not forget the wrong type of contentment which is born out of helplessness.

Mulla Nasruddin was once traveling with his friend in a bullock cart. Their road led through a jungle where they were suddenly set upon by robbers.

Just ahead of them stood the bandits with guns in hand, shouting, "Halt!"

At that instant Mulla quickly drew five hundred rupees from his pocket and handed them to his friend, saying, "Here is the money I had borrowed from you. Now we are even."

Your contentment is born out of such moments — when you find there is nothing left to be done. When everything is lost, only then you release your hold on it. Actually you don't part with your possessions, they are snatched away from you. So where is the contentment? Only he who lets go of his own accord is contented; he whose things are grabbed from him may shout from the rooftops that everything is all right, but you still hear the note of discontent.

The correct form of contentment requires, first and foremost, a feeling that you have received much more than you need. It requires gratitude, that behind all the apparent sorrow you see the hidden joy. Wherever you see thorns, somewhere there are roses, so why rest your eyes on the thorns.

If you hurl abuse at the contented person he thinks that perhaps it is right; he thanks you for telling him the truth. If it is wrong he thinks, "Poor man, he took all this trouble in vain, to think that he came so far." So there is either a feeling of gratitude or compassion, but never anger. He finds something good and worthwhile in every situation.

There is a story which I like very much of two fakirs: The two fakirs, the old guru and the young disciple, were returning to their hut in Japan for the rainy season. For eight months of the year they traveled from village to village singing the praises of the Lord, but in the rainy season they returned to their hut. When they reached the bank of the lake where the hut stood, they found the roof fallen to the ground by a violent storm that had struck just the night before. It was not only a very small hut, but on top of that, half the roof was on the ground. There were ominous clouds in the sky and darkness all around. Nothing could be done for they were far away from any other habitation.

The younger sannyasin couldn't contain himself. "Look at this. We kill ourselves singing his glories and this is how we are rewarded. What use is all that prayer and worship? What do we get in return? Rich sinners are lying blissfully in their mansions while the gale has carried away the roof of two poor fakirs. The storm is also his."

Having given vent to all his rage, he turned to the guru and what did he see? There knelt the guru with folded hands looking up at the sky, his eyes filled with tears of joy and supreme contentment. He was singing, "Oh Lord, your compassion knows no bounds. The tempest could have blown the whole roof away and you must have stopped it half-way for us. Only you can be so thoughtful."

Then they both entered the hut. Though they seem to enter the same hut, they are different people: one is contented, the other discontented. They both slept. The younger fakir kept tossing and turning, grumbling and worrying about the rain, constantly complaining and filled with anger. But the guru slept very soundly. When he got up at 4 a.m. he wrote a song. He could see the moon above through the half-open roof. He said in his song, "Oh Lord, had we known before, we would not have troubled your tempest to rip off half the roof. We would have done it ourselves. We have been so foolish, but now we can see the wonderful work of the storm; we can watch the moon over the hut! How close is your sky, and we shut it off with a roof! Your moon came and went so many times and we remained behind a roof. We did not know, please forgive us! Had we known we wouldn't have put the storm to so much trouble."

A man who can sing like this under the most direct circumstances is truly a contented person. But he who becomes contented out of helplessness follows the path of impotent and vigorless people; if only they could find contentment before having to lose everything then they wouldn't have to lose anything; for you cannot steal anything from a contented man. You may take away his belongings but not his contentment. His inner equilibrium cannot be disturbed. His true possessions are all within.

When Nanak says to *assume the posture of contentment and modesty,* and *pick up the carrying bag of dignity and honor*, he is hinting at the inner state. In fact, Gorakhnath had said the same thing: all external suggestions were only meant for internal remembrance, but it was forgotten and only the knot in the handkerchief remained. They even forgot what they had come to buy, they even forgot that the knot was meant to remind them about something. Only the knot remained. Now they are left carrying this knot which is only an additional burden.

Oh yogi, assume the posture of contentment and modesty.

Modesty connotes a quality that is totally oriental, unique to the East. The word *lajja* also means shyness and shame. There is no comparable word in any Western language. It is considered the ultimate, supreme state of womanhood. A prostitute is called *nirlajj*, shameless, for she sells her body, which is the temple of God and cannot be for sale. It is meant for worship, the first step to attain the ultimate wealth — not to sell for a few coins.

Shameless implies utilizing the body for anything other than the quest for God. There is no shame in such a person's life. We criticize the whore, but what about others? If you are selling your body to earn wealth or a name in the world, you are no better. The prostitute sells her body to earn wealth, so do you.

The state of shame or modesty insists that the body not be sold for money. Since it is the temple of God, some day he will be a guest there. The body has to be taught to wait for him. This waiting is exactly like the waiting of a beloved for the lover. When the lover approaches she covers her face with a veil, trying to hide so that she does not reveal herself to her lover, for that would be rank shamelessness.

She invites the lover, she waits for him, but when he comes near, she hides herself, covers her face with the veil. To appear before the lover would be egoistic. The desire to reveal oneself is exhibitionism, ego. Would you want to show yourself before God? No, you will hide; you would rather the earth part and bury you. You cover yourself with a thousand veils. To appear before God would be egoistic. You approach him like the love-lost maiden — not like a learned pundit — walking on tip-toe, lest he hear even your foot-steps. You try to

Posture Is a Template 339

hide as best you can, for what have you got to show him? Shyness implies that you have absolutely nothing to show, so you hide your face in shame.

That is why shyness and modesty are considered the highest quality for a woman in India. It explains a certain grace in oriental women which is lacking in the women of the West who were never taught to be shy. For her, shyness is considered a disqualification; she is trained to show, to exhibit, to attract — as if she is a marketable commodity. In the East, when a woman is taught shyness she learns to hide herself and cover herself, thus the custom of the veil. The veil was part of lajja. As the custom began to wane, lajja also began to fade, for the veil is the external expression of lajja. Now, as our women also move about openly and exhibit themselves, they too desire that people should look at them, and so they dress themselves with that in mind. When you desire to be seen like this, you are standing in the marketplace.

Nanak says our modesty before him should be like the maiden's modesty before her lover: she hides, for she is embarrassed by his closeness. She has nothing worthy of his attention — so the shame, so the veil.

To many the more modest a woman is, the more attractive she is; the more she reveals, the less attractive she becomes. To many the woman of the West has lost her charm, for what is readily available in the market loses its drawing power.

We don't go and sell ourselves to God; what have we got to show him? We approach him like a maiden in love — in full modesty. Our feet tremble. Will he or will he not accept me? Am I worthy enough? Such embarrassment, such shyness — we have nothing to offer that is worthy of him.

Modesty is a state of utter humility. Only when a person is so humble is he accepted. The more a devotee hides himself, the more attractive he becomes to God. The more a devotee reveals his devotion by proclaiming his worship, his prayers, his fasts and penance, the further removed he is from God. The union with God is effected only in an egoless consciousness.

*Oh yogi, assume the posture of contentment and modesty.
Pick up the carrying bag of dignity and honor.*

What is the dignity that Nanak talks about? As soon as a person begins to experience the soul and knows that he is not the body, he attains dignity. The feeling of the self is dignity. The body cannot be consecrated, for it is but a temporary resting-place. You tarry there a while, but you cannot make your home here. To be consecrated, to be dignified, means to attain the everlasting, to plant one's roots in that which is forever true.

You cannot be consecrated unless you stand with him. You may sit on a throne but you will attain no dignity and honor. The honor of this world is no honor, for here is merely the play of the waves. Who is going to remember you when you are gone? And who really bothers about you while you are alive — even though you may be sitting on a throne?

Look at those who rule the land. Wherever they go they are received with thrown stones. You look for flowers but you get stones thrown at you. You look for respect and you are insulted. If you gain your place by force, there are always others to pull you down by your leg. Ask the politicians. Their names may appear in the papers and their every action becomes news, but they are equally criticized. In this world if you want to win, you are bound to lose; if you hanker after honor, you are bound to be insulted. Dignity exists only when you are with God.

So Nanak says to pick up the carrying-bag of dignity and honor, throw away the sack of arrogance and ego that you are carrying. Discover egolessness, shyness and contentment, and your roots will have begun to spread towards God.

And apply the sacred ash of meditation.

Merely smearing ash on the body is of no avail. Develop meditation within, Nanak exhorts, let that be your sacred ash; be smeared with meditation.

*Establish death as your bedroll...*so that you are always reminded of him. He who is constantly aware of death cannot forget God. He who forgets death, forgets God. We all have no awareness of death. We live as if we are never going to die, therefore we forget to remember God.

Make a maiden of your body.

The Nath-Sampradaya as well as many *tantric* sects seek a virgin for their *sadhana*. Through a distinctive tantric sexual union meditation is attained. This is true, this is possible, and Tantra has found the method.

But man is dishonest. In the name of Tantra thousands of yogis began to roam about with young maidens. Millions of people used the screen of Tantra to indulge in all kinds of depravity. They had a ready explanation for the girls they kept with them, as also the path they followed. This immorality caused Buddhism to be driven out of the country. Also, a great tantric tradition was lost as a result. Man is very clever; he is adept at finding means to satisfy his lust, and this was a ready-made solution for him. He could move about openly with young girls and masquerade as a tantric seeker.

When Nanak says make your own body the virgin maiden, he is referring to the deepest thread of Tantra. It is your own body that should become your companion; your soul should be the male and your body the female. Intercourse can take place between these two, and that is the supreme union. It is through this intercourse alone that a person attains liberation. The tantric method had the same goal: through the external woman by and by you discover the woman within you.

There is a woman hidden within every man and a man hidden within every woman. When a union of the man or woman within and the woman or man without, takes place, the final state of *samadhi* is reached. Contemporary science has also accepted the fact that man is bisexual. This is natural, for each person is born out of the union of mother and father; so he is a part of his mother as well as a part of his father. Within you there is a man, within you is a woman; and when the two energies combine the result is an eternal intercourse, while physical union is only momentary.

So Nanak is speaking about a very profound theme of Tantra. He says,

> *Oh Yogi, make experience your staff of liberation,*
> *And consider the unity of all as your first principle.*
> *To conquer the mind is to conquer the world.*
> *If you must bow, bow to him.*
> *He is the primal being, pure, without beginning or end. He is the unstruck sound.*
> *He is immutable through all time.*

Bow unto him who is forever the same, the unchanging one. You may break your back bowing in temples and mosques, but if your obeisance is not directed towards him it is of no avail. Always remember, wherever you bow, let it always be at his feet, When you bow before the guru, it is him you are worshipping through the guru and when you bow in the temple, you are bowing to him. All homage is to him. As a reminder the idol in the temple becomes helpful. Otherwise the temple idols pose a danger to you, as does the guru. If your reverence is not directed towards him, whenever you bow you create shackles for yourself; all kinds of obstructions come your way. And if you learn to bow only to him, each stone can become a door for you. Bow anywhere, in temple, mosque, gurudwara, church, but remember one thing, all homage is to him, him who was in the beginning, who is pure and perfect, who is everlasting, who is the primal sound, and who is always the same — forever and forever.

> *Make knowledge your pleasure and compassion your storehouse.*
> *Make a conch shell of the eternal music playing in every being.*
> *He alone is a master in whom all beings are intertwined,*
> *While the search for supernatural powers is a false path.*
> *The law of union and separation governs all things,*
> *And destiny determines our just inheritance.*
> *If you must bow, bow to him.*
> *He is the primal being, pure, without beginning or end; He is the unstruck sound.*
> *He is immutable through all time.*

Make knowledge your pleasure and compassion your storehouse. Knowledge and compassion are the two wings to be mastered in order to fly into the heavens of his abode — knowledge and wisdom for within, sympathy and compassion for without. If there is only knowledge within, but no sympathy and tenderness without, there is the danger of your not attaining perfection. You are incomplete. Who can fly with only one wing? If there is sympathy and tenderness without but no knowledge within, then too you are incomplete. Who can walk with one leg?

Knowledge ultimately refers to oneself; sympathy means to know others. Together the full happening can occur. For wisdom knows its own self; as soon as wisdom dawns, it knows that it resides in everyone. If knowledge is not conscious that it is there in each of us, it is no knowledge.

When the genuine lamp of knowledge is lighted, its light is bound to fall on all. The lamp does not merely illuminate itself, it lights all things around it. This light that falls on others is sympathy, tenderness. Unlimited compassion arises when wisdom is born. You will give freely, even allow yourself to be looted; you will give assistance of every kind to one and all — then do all in your power to help others to reach him, for all are wandering and groping. You will not lose yourself in your knowledge, for that would be selfishness — maybe you are still tied to old attachments or that the ego is not yet conquered.

Some people are lost in their own knowledge, like the Jaina *munis*. They are concerned only about themselves. They are so busy working for their own salvation, they have no interest in things outside. If they are kind it is only to further their own knowledge, therefore their kindness is false.

If a Jaina muni takes a step so carefully that no ant inadvertently dies under his feet, don't think it is out of pity for the ant. Mahavira had done so out of his great compassion, but not so the Jaina muni. He watches his step merely to guard against the sin of killing an ant. Understand his concern: if he commits sin he will have to wander in the cycle of birth and death; so his concern is for himself, not with the ant. If the ant's death were not a sin, he wouldn't bother at all. He even strains the water he drinks — not out of concern for the germs in the water, but for fear of the sin of swallowing the germ. Outwardly his actions are the same as Mahavira's, but he is only involved with his own salvation, trying to save himself from hell.

His kindness is false. It will be genuine only when he is prepared even to go to hell in order to set you on the right path, but his ethics is that of a business man: do only what profits you!

So it is no surprise that Mahavira's followers became the business community. Mahavira himself was from the *kshatriya* caste, the warrior caste, but his followers became shop-keepers. This is strange. All twenty-four Jaina *tirthankaras* were kshatriyas, but those who followed them became traders. What happened? What calamity took place that a whole community became so timid as to restrict itself to working only in the shops? There is a secret in this: Mahavira's kindness was genuine compassion, whereas the kindness of the crafty people who followed him was calculated: they turned it into a business. They shunned all work that entailed sin. They left off farming because plants had to die for the harvest to be collected. They shunned the violence of the battlefield. All that was left was to be a shopkeeper, a tradesman.

It is noteworthy that ninety percent of all wise men of India come from the *kshatriya* caste, including Nanak, Krishna, Rama, Mahavira and Buddha. They have certain qualities which make it easy to attain knowledge — courage and boldness. Not so many Brahmans or other castes have reached the ultimate truth as the kshatriyas. The reason is that the warrior will stake his all; he isn't afraid of danger. It is impossible for a warrior to forget death. It stands at his door at every moment. And he who remembers death begins to be reminded of God also. The kshatriya's trade is the business of death, at any moment death can occur. He who is so aware of death cannot possibly forget God. God has to be remembered as he is the only antidote. When the thought of death grabs hold of you, what else will you do, whom will you remember, whom shall you call, who will save you? It is but natural to recall the nectar.

Make knowledge your pleasure and compassion your storehouse.

Offering of food and feasts for the poor continue in the world, but they are only external expressions. Both the Nath-Sampradayas and the Sikhs have their own kind of feasts, but they are the same, mere outside happenings.

Nanak is saying to make kindness your food offering, your feast for the poor. Let there be kindness in every moment of your life. Think of others. Whatever you do, see that others also profit: let your actions serve their welfare and well-being. Seek knowledge for yourself, but be helpful to others on their quest. Let your feet travel towards liberation, but take others along with you. Remember that as you cultivate both compassion outside and knowledge within, your momentum increases towards the goal. These are the two wings necessary to fly to the destination.

Contrary to the Jainas, the Christians are always busy serving others, opening schools and hospitals everywhere. No one can surpass them for service, they give no thought to knowledge. Like the Jainas they are convinced that what they are doing is enough by itself. The Jainas think it is enough to understand one's own self. The Christians think it enough to serve others, and that service leads to salvation. He is less concerned with the question whether the leper whose feet he washes, or the sick he takes care of, or the orphan he educates, profit by his services or not. He serves in order to attain his salvation. Man's selfishness is wonderfully strange. Even in seeking knowledge he ferrets out his own self-interest, and while serving others he manages to serve his own interests.

There is an old Chinese tale: A fair was taking place in a small village. There were large crowds and many shops selling different wares. A man fell into a small well nearby, and though he began to shout, no one could hear him above the din. Everyone was so involved in his own work — buying things, selling things. It was getting close to evening and people were in a hurry to reach home. Shopkeepers began closing their stalls. Who was to hear him?

Fortunately a sannyasin who was a follower of Confucius came and sat near the well. He heard the man's shouts and he called down, "Hold your peace, brother. I shall go right away to plead your case, for it is against the law to build a well without a wall. You fell because there was no wall. Have faith in me. My colleagues and I will start a movement for you right away, so that not only this well but all the wells in the villages will have walls." And away he went. This was but natural for Confucius was a reformer who believed in society and its laws. He was a revolutionary.

The poor man called out to the sannyasin, "Of what use are future walls? I am drowning right now!"

The sannyasin answered, "It is not just your problem. It is a problem for everyone, for the whole of society, not just one person. If society is saved, the individual is saved." He stood up and began shouting, "Listen, brothers! We must see that each well be surrounded by a wall."

A Buddhist bhikkhu came and sat near the well. He heard the shouting, bent down to look and saw the man in the well. "You are suffering from your actions during your past life," he said to the poor man. "Each of us has to reap the fruit of one's karma. Nothing can be done about it."

"Tell me about it later," said the man in the well. "First get me out of here."

"But I have renounced all actions," said the monk. "Actions lead to attachments, and attachments cause a man to wander in *sansara*. I want to free myself from the cycle of birth and death. I don't want to start another karmic cycle by pulling you out of the well. Who knows what you might do if I saved your life? If you kill someone I shall be a partner in your crime, for had I not saved you you wouldn't have committed the crime. Or if you set fire to someone's house? Why should I trap myself by your misdeeds? Besides, please be quiet, I have come here to meditate. You go through your experiences and I shall go through mine. No one can walk on another's path."

Since the drowning man was making so much noise the bhikkhu got up and left to meditate. Meditation is a great thing. If one is to go around pulling people out of wells, imagine how many wells there are in the village; and there are so many people, so many fairs, you would never get around to meditate. So what can you do? It is better to take care of one's own meditation, then everything else is taken care of.

Soon after a Christian missionary happened along. Hearing the man's cries, he quickly pulled out a rope from his knapsack and threw it down the well. He pulled out the man, who fell at his feet and said, "Thank you. You are really a deeply religious man. A follower of Confucius heard me and went on his way, and a Buddhist monk abandoned me to my fate. They just ignored my cries."

The Christian said, "There is only one thing I ask of you: keep falling into wells so that we Christians can come to help you out. We always carry a rope. If you were not to fall in the well so that we could save you, how can we attain beatitude?"

No one is bothered about any one else. Man's selfishness is so deep-rooted; the one who helps you is only out for his own self-interest. This sort of service is worth nothing. So look at the God within you — that is knowledge; and don't ever forget the God in others — that is compassion.

Make knowledge your pleasure and compassion your storehouse.
Make a conch shell of the eternal music playing in every being.

What is the sense in sounding conch-shells? Blow the conch shell that sounds the unsounded sound within each living being. Pay the music that happens without reason and which plays eternally.

He alone is a master in whom all beings are intertwined,
While the search for supernatural powers is a false path.

You perform a miracle, you produce ashes out of your hand and become a Satya Sai Baba; you produce a talisman from nowhere — to what avail? Supernatural powers are second-rate products for they only nourish your ego. It strengthens your arrogance. You feel you are somebody special. The only power that applies to religion arises out of: "I am nobody, nothing!" He who realizes and knows that he is nothing becomes everything. He who annihilates himself completely on earth, becomes God himself. Do not be satisfied with anything less; if you do then you have opted for the powers of lesser quality.

What will you gain by producing a few amulets? How will your magic help you? You help neither yourself nor others thereby. You may gain a little popularity in the world, but that is all. Is the honor of this world any real honor? What is the value of all this magic before God? Of what worth the ashes that you produce, or the talisman, before him who has created the universe? Your tricks may fool people and satisfy your ego, but it will not lead anywhere towards self-realization. Therefore Nanak has said that attaining supernatural powers are second-rate results.

The law of union and separation governs all things.

Union and separations run the whole show of sansara. So there is only one power worth attaining — to be freed from union and separations. Things that unite must part; things that are formed are bound to disintegrate. He who is born must die. That which is obtained is also lost. That which is a possession today is a calamity tomorrow. Today's happiness is tomorrow's unhappiness. Each thing moves into its opposite. The wheel of sansara turns on uniting and parting. You meet today; you part tomorrow.

He who understands that truth — that the wheel of sansara turns with the help of union and separation, that it works according to the law of opposites, saves himself by going beyond both. He is neither made happy by unions nor unhappy by partings. This is the only *siddhi*, the only real power; master it!

And destiny determines our just inheritance.

Therefore be patient, be tranquil in whatever is given you, for it is a part of your destiny. Things had to happen this way and so they happen. And since only that happens which has to happen, why the discontent? Why the complaints, the weeping and wailing? Accept whatever fate ordains. Try to liberate yourself from unions and separations. This alone is the siddhi, all else is lesser quality stuff.

> *If you must bow, bow to him.*
> *He is the primal being, pure, without beginning or end;*
> *He is the unstruck sound.*
> *He is immutable through all time.*

Posture Is a Template   349

CHAPTER 15

One Becomes Three

By skillful means one Maya has given birth to three disciples:
Brahma, the Creator; Vishnu, the sustainer; and Shiva, the destroyer.
God directs them by his will and his order.
He watches them but they cannot see him;
That is the wonder of wonders.
If you must bow, bow to him.
He is the primal being, pure without beginning or end.
He is the unstruck sound.
He is immutable through all time.
All the worlds are his abode, and all worlds his storehouse.
He has them filled for all time with all worth attaining.
The creator creates, and oversees it all.
Says Nanak, He is the true reality and all his works are true.
If you must bow, bow to him.
He is the primal being, pure without beginning or end.
He is the unstruck sound.
He is immutable through all time.

In the quest for God we have to travel along the same path by which God descended into the world. As God has become the creation, so we, his creation, have to work our way in the reverse direction and become God. The path is the same; only the direction changes.

You have come here from your house; while returning you will cover the same route. The road will be the same, you will be the same, your legs will be the same, the energy to walk is the same; only the direction will be different. When you arrived here, you had your back towards home; while returning you will be facing home.

You have to return to God along the same path as God descended into creation. While coming you had your back towards him; while going you will be facing in his direction. Therefore, indifference is the way to enter into the world and eagerness towards God is the way to approach him. The ladder is the same, the path is the same; only the direction changes.

In this sutra Nanak tells us how God became creation. Whoever has sought him and found him followed just the way that Nanak describes here. Not only religious seekers but also scientific researchers agree on this.

Religion looks at the creator; science looks at creations. Religion seeks from one end, science from another. Science conducts its search where man stands; religion conducts its search where man came from and returns to. Religion seeks your beginning and your end, whereas science probes into the middle.

One of the most valuable discoveries of science is that there is just one force, one energy, that is holding together the whole universe. All the world can be broken down into smaller and smaller bits and pieces, into atoms. The chair, the trees, the stones, the flowers are all made up of the same basic elements; and these atoms have a relationship to one another. Either they come together by attraction, what Nanak called unions, or they push apart, repulse one another; Nanak called it separations. What is pushing apart or pulling together is energy, and all is caused by electric charges, the same electricity that makes the lamp to burn, that makes everything move in our cities. The same energy is the force that holds the world together. Science calls it energy or electricity. Religion refers to it as God.

It is only a difference of words; but the difference in words creates a great deal of difference to us, for how is one to worship electricity? How can you make love to electricity? How will you call out to electricity? How can you build temples to it?

The word *electricity* remains only in the head; it cannot be related to the heart. But God is the name of this same energy. The name makes all the difference. At the very mention of the word *God* it becomes a matter of the heart; it has no longer anything to do with the head. In matters of the heart, relationships can be established. The intellect breaks things down; the heart joins them. It is through the intellect that we break away from people and things, for it is the mind that creates differences. At heart we are one, for the heart has the quality of undivided oneness. Here all boundaries and definitions fade away; they are not created.

As soon as religion declared this energy to be God, we gave it an individuality. Now relationships can be established with it, and everything depends upon this relationship. If you cannot become related you cannot bring about a transformation in your life. Science can make use of energy but it cannot worship it. It is this very energy that religion worships. A scientist can electrify villages, create atomic energy and discover new means of destruction, but will remain untouched by this energy; no flowers will ever bloom in his life. A religious man will not be able to carry electricity to the villages or make atom bombs, but he can illumine each and every heart; and this light is tremendous. He can fill each heart with song and dance, and thus fill life with brightness.

These two, science and religion, agree that it is only one energy working. They agree on another point also: when the one breaks, it splits into three. Science says that each atom breaks up into electrons, neutrons and protons. From these three elements the whole world is formed.

In the Hindu religion the one becomes the *trimurti*, what Christians call the trinity. The Hindus created trimurti, one person having three faces. Each face attaches to the same body. Brahma, Vishnu and Shiva are the names of the three faces. When the one descends into creation, he becomes three.

Another very astonishing fact is that the meaning given to Brahma, Vishnu and Shiva by the Hindus coincides with the meanings the scientists have given to electron, neutron and proton. In the whole process of creation, birth is necessary and also a giver of birth. Then the one who is born must die, so death is necessary and also a giver of death. Then there is bound to be a period of time between birth and death, so there should be a protector or guardian, also. So Brahma is the birth factor, the creator, Vishnu is the protector, and Shiva the destroyer. Electron, neutron and proton have the same qualities: one of them protects, through another there is birth and the third brings about destruction.

The one is divided into three, and then into infinity. Now if we wish to reach God, we shall first have to reduce infinity to three; and the three are then to be infused into one and ultimately become one. This is the reverse journey, like traveling the Ganges to Gangotri — towards the fundamental source.

So from the many we have to concentrate on the three. The three are the intermediary destination. After three the one remains.

The ordinary man wanders in the many. How many desires, how many expectations! Can you count them? And each desire is intertwined with so many other desires, like so many leaves on a tree. They are endless — man's hopes and dreams. There is no way to fulfill them. How many things he possesses! So many arrangements and so much equipment he gathers! And even if you obtain all that you desire, you are not satisfied. The more you attain the more you wander in the multifarious objects of the world and the further you go from the one. And the further you go from the one, the greater becomes your suffering. It is as if, going further and further away from the source of light, darkness increases proportionally till ultimately you find yourself in total darkness.

To go into the many means that there is a great distance between you and the one. We are all in the many. He who has come into the three from the many, we call a seeker. He is in between. And he who has progressed from the three to the one, we say he has attained. He has reached the place where God originally was.

Let us try to understand this further. How will you reduce the many into the three? The method to do this is the method of witnessing. If you observe your desires and do not become the enjoyer of them, you are the witness. If you experience desires as the doer you will lose yourself in the many. By witnessing alone you can reduce the many into the three. Whatever you do, do not be involved in your actions. Observe everything in a detached manner, and one fine day you will suddenly discover that the three have arrived! One is the observer, the other is the multifarious world of objects, which now is like a gigantic screen on which everything moves. The many is no more. And between the two is seeing. So there is that which is seen, the observer or witness, and the seeing. You have reverted from the many to the three.

As soon as the witnessing is cultivated, you have become a seeker. This is the state of the sannyasin. To revert from the many to the three is sannyas. Whatever you do, keep the witness alert; when walking on the road, eating your meals, putting on your clothes. Even in illness or pain, or when you win the lottery — whatever the situation, keep the witness alert inside. Never lose sight of it within.

There are two ways of losing the witnessing state: if you become the enjoyer you lose it, or if you become the doer you lose it. At the moment you say, "I have done this," the witness is lost, and the drug of arrogance begins its work. You are no longer the same person.

One day I asked Mulla Nasruddin, "Mulla, every day I see your servant taking two glasses of wine on a tray to your room. Since you are always alone, for whom is the second glass?"

Nasruddin replied, "Once I take a glass of wine I am no longer the same person. I become a different person altogether. Don't you think it is my duty to offer my hospitality to this other person?"

As soon as you are intoxicated you become a different person; you can never be the same. Being under the influence of intoxicants is the only difference between a sannyasin and a worldly man, for what is the most potent intoxicant but the drug called the ego.

All other intoxicants wear off after a while, but the effect of the ego goes on from birth to birth. You try your best to get rid of it and still you find it standing right in front of you. You try to run away from it, but it follows you like a shadow. You devise a thousand tricks and yet you find it tagging along with you. You practice humility, but there it is stirring inside you.

The ego is the subtlest of all intoxicants. If witnessing is awakening, the ego means you are asleep. As soon as you become the doer, as soon as you become the enjoyer, you fall asleep slumber overtakes you. As soon as you become the witness, awakening occurs and consciousness returns.

As soon as consciousness dawns, the many are lost and only the three remain: that of which you are conscious, the one who is conscious, and the connection between the two. This the Hindus refer to as *triputi*. The one whose triputi is awakened is a sannyasin; he begins to delve into his spiritual practice. As you dwell more and more in the three your wanderings in the many diminish until you reach a stage when the many will no longer form, and there will be only the three; then you are permanently in the witness state. You suddenly find that the three have faded away when the mind becomes still. You discover that the observer, the observed, and their connection are all one and the same.

This is why Krishnamurti says again and again, "The observer is the observed."

But this is the ultimate state. First, through long practice all ways of forming the many are closed, the world is no more and only the three remain. Then gradually you come to realize that the three are one. When you know that, the one who sees is that which is seen. Then the connecting link is also lost, for the relationship between the observer and the observed exists only as long as they are separate. But when only one remains, how can there be any relation? The intermediary connection is thus broken.

This is the journey — the return journey to again become one. You become God. When you became many, you were the world. The trimurti stands in between. This is what Nanak means in these sutras.

> *By skillful means one Maya has given birth to three disciples:*
> *Brahma, the creator; Vishnu, the sustainer; and Shiva, the*
>   *destroyer.*
> *God directs them by his will and his order.*

The descent is from one to three, and from three to many; but however far away you are from the one, you cannot step outside his edicts, his orders. No matter how much you disintegrate, how much divided you are in the many, he is present within you. If he is not, you cannot be. You may wander far, far away. You may go astray, but you cannot go so far that there is no point of return; there is no such point of no return.

Therefore no person is unredeemable. Even if a person has fallen into the lowermost depths of sin, he is not beyond cure. In terms of spiritual knowledge, there is no illness that is incurable, that cannot be remedied. All spiritual diseases can be cured. You cannot go so far that you cannot return.

Wherever you go, he is present. However far you go, it is he who takes you. Even in sin you need his help, because it is he who breathes within the sinner, it is he who beats within the sinner's heart. We can go far, very far. We can forget him, but there is no way of losing him.

So when you ask, "How are we to seek him?" your question is not correct, for you have never lost him. Even if you wish to, you cannot lose him for he is your very nature. Were he apart from you, you could have lost him, forgotten him somewhere, but you cannot do this even by mistake, because he is you.

Then what happens? You merely forget. There is also a way to forget oneself. Man can forget himself, forget his very nature. And yet his nature stands within him.

I have a friend. He is a lawyer, but a more forgetful person is hard to find. He forgets almost everything. On occasions he even forgets whom he was representing in court, who had engaged him to fight the case. But he is a very important lawyer. Once he had to go to another town to fight a case. When he reached there he found to his horror that he had forgotten the client's name. He sent a telegram to his secretary, "What is his name?" The secretary wired back the lawyer's name thinking he had forgotten that this time.

There is every possibility of forgetting one's own self also. The whole world is proof that one's own self can be forgotten. And what is the way to forget? The way to forget is the same as the way to remember.

How can forgetfulness be remedied? By meditation! When you become too much object-oriented, you forget yourself. For through concentration alone one remembers, and through concentration alone one forgets. Wherever you apply your attention, that is what comes to mind.

Whatever you remove your attention from is what you forget. When your attention is directed towards an object, your concentration shifts to the object and illuminates it. You begin to see the world and you forget your own self. You are so enrapt in what you see that you are lost to yourself. The only one way to get out of this and awaken is not be so absorbed in viewing. However beautiful or enchanting the object, shake yourself into remembering yourself.

But you are bound to forget reality. Even when you go to see a movie you forget the simple reality that it is only an empty screen in front of you, that the film is merely a play of light and shadow. People cry in the theater over the tragedy on stage. When you see them after the show you would imagine someone in their family had died. If it is an action film, they sit upright in their chairs, ready to fling themselves into the action, into the fray. And it is not only the simple-minded who forget themselves; even intellectuals get carried away.

There is just such an incident in the life of Ishvarchand, who was a great intellectual in his time. He was given the title of *Vidyasagar*, Ocean of Knowledge. Once he went to see a play in which there was a character who was supposed to be a rogue, a libertine. He harassed people in many different ways, like waylaying a woman and pestering her. Ishvarchand was the honored guest, so he was seated in the front row. He became so angry he jumped onto the stage, took off his shoe and began beating the actor with it.

The actor turned out to be wiser than Ishvarchand. He took the shoe in his hand and holding it to his heart said, "I shall not return this shoe to you, for it is the highest prize I could ever receive for my acting. Never before has anyone been so overpowered by my skill." Vidyasagar later regretted his mistake. He could not understand how he got so involved with the play. He also never got his shoe back.

Whenever something seizes your attention so intensely, you commit this same mistake. In the course of time you forget the seer and the object begins to mean everything to you. When this happens you lose yourself in the mirage, you go astray. If this habit becomes deeply ingrained in you, everything you see becomes real for you.

This is why dreams seem true, just because of this habit. Whatever you see seems true to you. Dreams appear true when you sleep. In the morning you discover they were not. Again when you sleep, dreams look true again...and in the morning you realize they were false. This goes on and on. If someone comes to kill you in the dream you scream and your sleep is broken. You awaken and find your heart beating faster. If someone dies in a dream you cry. You wake up in the morning and find the pillow wet with your tears. How many times have you dreamed? Yet you forget that a dream is a dream in the course of the next twelve hours. How is it possible? It is because you have developed a habit of taking everything you see as true.

There is an old tantric method for this. Unless you know the dream to be false while it is in progress, you will never be able to know that the world is false. This is the reverse of what we know. We still believe *sansara* to be real; therefore even dreams appear real. Tantra says that unless you realize dreams to be false while they are happening you will never understand the ephemeral quality of maya. Tantra has evolved very subtle methods to know a dream to be a dream, and not reality.

You may experiment with this. Decide on something before you fall asleep: for example, decide to raise your left hand with a jerk. Or decide to put your palm over your eye as soon as you begin to dream. You will have to practice this auto-suggestion every night for three months before falling asleep. At the end of that time or sooner, if you do it very regularly, your remembrance will become so intense that it penetrates your unconscious. Then as soon as you begin to dream, your left arm will shoot up with a jerk, or your palm will cover your eyes – whatever you have practiced. As soon as this happens, it will come to you that this is a dream, for these two are connected in your auto-suggestion.

Another tantric method: whatever you see in your dream, concentrate your attention on one object. Let's say you see a marketplace. There are lines of shops loaded with various articles and many people are moving about. Now focus your attention on something, perhaps on one shop. You will be astonished to find that as soon as you fix your attention on this one shop, the shop disappears — because it was never there. Then fix your gaze on other things one by one and you will find them all disappearing in the same manner. If you become adept at watching dreams, dreams will be lost. As soon as dreams are lost, you go into meditation even in sleep; you reach *samadhi*.

Begin with dreams and you find that the whole world is a dream. The world is a dream seen with open eyes because our habits die hard — we get involved in the things we see. This involvement is so intense that we forget ourselves, forget the observer. Our consciousness works in only one direction.

Gurdjieff used to tell his disciples, "When the arrow of your consciousness becomes double-pointed, when your consciousness begins to flower at both ends, you will become an enlightened being." Gurdjieff's efforts in directing his disciples were all to this end. "When you look at someone, look at him, but also keep trying to look at your own self: 'I am looking, I am the observer.' Then you are sharpening the other edge of the arrow of your consciousness. One end is directed towards the object you see; the other points toward you, the seer."

Here you all sit listening to me, and you have lost yourselves in me while listening. You forget the listener entirely — but then you err. The listener should also be remembered while listening. So as I sit here talking to you and you sit there listening, you are also conscious of the fact that "I am listening." When you go beyond the listener, a transcendence occurs. The witness is born.

As soon as the witness is born, the person steps from the many into the three. You have reached the confluence of Brahma, Vishnu and Shiva. Then it is easy to merge into the one from the three, for it is only one more step forward. Similarly, the confluence of great rivers is considered auspicious. Prayag is a unique pilgrimage place because of the confluence of three rivers. Two rivers can be seen, the Ganges and the Yamuna, but the third, Saraswati, lies underground and cannot be seen.

Whenever you focus your attention on something there are two elements: the subject, you, and the object, what you are observing. These are both apparent, but the connection between the two cannot be seen. This is symbolized by the river Saraswati at Prayag. However, all three rivers meet at Prayag, and they naturally become one.

By skillful means one Maya has given birth to three disciples: Brahma, the creator; Vishnu, the sustainer; and Shiva, the destroyer.

There is only one temple dedicated to Brahma in all of India. Brahma is worldly. His only work is to give birth to sansara, the world, so he is not considered worthy of worship.

Shiva's temples are found everywhere. No other deity is worshipped as much as Shiva. In every village, in every lane you will find a Shiva temple. Under trees you will find stones that are revered as Shiva. This is because with Shiva the world comes to an end. He is the deity of death, and hence worthy of worship. Brahma gives birth to the world, Shiva destroys it. India's keenest desire was always how to be rid of sansara, how to attain liberation. Therefore we find Shiva temples abounding.

There are temples dedicated to Vishnu also. Many among us are afraid of annihilation. They worship Vishnu. The shopkeeper worships Vishnu for Vishnu is the treasurer, the keeper of the stores. He is in between Brahma and Shiva, and so he is the Lord of Laxmi, the deity of wealth. So those who lust for wealth worship Vishnu.

This is worth pondering over; if you want to approach a man it is best to go through his wife. Not only in ordinary matters of the world does this method apply, but even in matters of the spirit. The rule is: please the wife and the master is bound to be pleased. Please Laxmi and Vishnu is pleased.

Vishnu looks after the world; therefore, those who want to live in the world worship him. Shiva is the end. He is the supreme death. He is the deity of the sannyasins. Therefore there are so many temples of Shiva. The smallest village is not without its Shiva temple. And because it is the temple of the sannyasin it has to be made as cheaply as possible. You do not need great funds for a Shiva temple. Find a rounded stone and it becomes the Shivalinga, the symbol of Shiva. You do not even need flowers; a few leaves off the woodapple tree, that is all. Temples to Vishnu are elaborate affairs that a millionaire can afford, but who is to erect temples in honor of the lord of death? Certainly not those who cling to life and the world, so Shiva's temples had to be cheap constructions.

These three deities are the three threads of life: birth, life and death. Remember, birth has already taken place, so what need is there to worship Brahma? What has already happened is a closed chapter; there is nothing more to do about it. Life still is; therefore some are absorbed in the worship of Vishnu. But these are not very wise people, for life is ebbing away every moment. Unless the knowledge of death descends into your life, sannyas cannot enter your life; you will remain a worldly man.

What is the difference between a sannyasin and a worldly man? A sannyasin understands that all life ends in death; all being ultimately ends up in nonbeing; that which is formed also decays and disintegrates; that which is decorated becomes desolate one day; the house that is built falls one day. A sannyasin is one who has become aware of death, who has begun to remember death. He is one who knows that this world is a campground where we pitch a tent for a short while. When the knowledge of death dawns a transformation takes place.

Except for man there is no religion, for among the birds and animals there is no knowledge of death. They also die, but they are not aware of that fact because consciousness is needed to see death; this they do not have.

Also, among human beings you are just an animal if you do not have a clear perception of death. As you become aware of the end, what you value in life changes. What was important until yesterday seems worthless today. What was meaningful up to now becomes meaningless as soon as awareness of death occurs. Many dreams were dreamt, many hopes were pinned on the rainbow of desires, but when death knocks at the door these fall like a house of cards.

Death gives the first knock the very day you are born. The day Brahma started his work, Shiva started his also, but we are not aware of it. If you do become conscious of this fact, the very awareness brings about a conversion within you: you turn back towards your source, your direction changes. Then you do not aim towards sansara for you see nothing but death there. Instead you turn towards yourself, and to proceed towards one's own self is to walk in the direction of God. The shock of death reminds you of God. God is forgotten to him who does not remember death. Many times you have died, many times you have been born, but you are still oblivious of death.

Remember death. Make it your focal point in life, for there is nothing more certain than death. Everything else in life is uncertain. Keeping this certainty at your core, set out on the journey of life and you will find that you have begun to proceed from the many to the three.

Nanak says that God directs the three according to his own will and order. Remember, whatever you do, good deeds or bad, sin or virtue, whether you go closer to God or further away, whether you follow the path or go astray, you cannot step outside his boundaries.

If this remembrance is with you then there is a way to step away from sin too. You also step out of the virtuous life for with this remembrance you come to understand that I am not the doer; he is the director. I am only the means, a medium. I do what he directs; nothing is of my doing. Then why the arrogance, and why the ego? It is he who gives birth, it is he who gives life, it is he who takes life. Then why should I strut about? Why should I be conceited and proud?

You must have heard the story of the fly that sat on the wheel of the chariot. The chariot was raising a lot of dust for it was drawn by many horses. The fly looked around and said, "Today I am raising a great deal of dust!" You too are sitting on a chariot wheel and thinking the same thought. There is the gigantic wheel of sansara but the dust raised is not on account of you. The day you understand this you will be filled with great peace. For all restlessness pertains to the ego and the ego has the habit of taking everything upon itself; it even shoulders the burden of things you are not doing, things you have nothing to do with.

The day it dawns on you that you are no better than the fly on the wheel and the dust is raised by the enormous wheel of sansara, you will attain supreme peace. Then you will feel: I am nobody, nothing. Why should I be restless? Who is to be restless? As long as the illusion persists that I am, you will be restless.

People come to me and ask how to become tranquil. "Help me to find peace." I say to them: You cannot be tranquil as long as you are; as long as the you exists, you cannot be given peace. Your not being is peace. Put yourself aside; you are a falsity, a dream. If you understand fully, you will know that you are a dream within the dream.

You do not exist even in dream. You must sometimes have dreamed a dream within a dream. You dream that you are going to bed, you have fallen asleep and you are dreaming a dream.

There is an old Chinese story: A woodcutter was cutting wood in a jungle. He was tired, so he came down from the tree and fell asleep. He dreamed that nearby lay buried a great treasure of diamonds and gold in huge pots that were lightly covered with dirt. In his dream he thought that he would come at night and remove the treasure quietly. If he removed it in the daytime he might be caught. He was a poor man and the treasure was worth millions. When he awoke, he buried a stick to mark the place and returned home.

When it became dark, he went back to the spot. He found the stick in place but the pots had been removed. He went back and told his wife, "I don't understand whether I dreamed about the treasure or actually saw it. The stick is there all right, and there are holes where the pots were, so it is certainly not just a dream. But someone has removed the pots."

His wife replied, "It must be a dream. You must also have dreamed that you went out at night and saw the stick in the ground, and that there was an empty place where the pots were supposed to be. So go back to sleep and sleep in peace."

But it happened that another man also dreamed that he saw these very pots buried in the same place, and that a woodcutter had buried a stick to mark the place. When he got up from his sleep he ran to the place. He found the stick in the ground and also the vessels underneath! He removed the pots and brought them home. He told his wife, "I cannot understand whether I dreamed a dream or I actually saw a vision. Whatever it is, I have brought the pots home. They are proof that it is not just a dream. I must actually have seen the woodcutter burying the stick and therefore I knew where the treasure was."

His wife said, "The pots are here. That much is clear. But if you actually saw the woodcutter marking the spot, it isn't right that we should keep this treasure. Take the pots to the king and let him decide."

He was an honest man, so he took the pots to the king's court where the woodcutter had already lodged a complaint. The king was perplexed. Finally he told them, "It is very difficult to decide whether you were asleep or awake, so I shall divide the treasure equally between you both, for the pots are very much there." So he divided the treasure between them.

That night the king told his wife, "A very strange thing happened today: Two men dreamed the same dream. Now it is difficult to decide whether they dreamed or whether they really saw the treasure. But the pots of treasure were actually there, so I divided them equally between them." The queen said, "Go to sleep, you must be dreaming."

For thousands of years this was discussed in China – *did* they dream it or not? Who actually dreamed? But this is what happens by the time we reach the end of life. All of life seems like a dream. It is difficult to decide whether the stick was really there and whether the pots were really buried; whether the wife and children ever existed, or friends and foes; whether there was poverty or riches; whether there was conflict and competition; whether we really lost or won, were successful or unsuccessful. At the time of death all events pass before a man like a dream. Did we really live, or was it only a dream?

Those who have known say, "This is a dream dreamed with open eyes." It is a dream because it has no relation to that which is. This is an intermediary state of imagination; it is merely a thought. It makes no difference whether you saw it when asleep or when awake. The characteristic of a dream is that it is here one moment and gone the next. At the time of death all is lost.

Within this dream you see another dream that is called the ego. You consider yourself the doer, the author of the dreams. You are filled with conceit, which all the world can see; only you do not see it. Everyone else is in the same state, never seeing their own, but seeing everyone else's ego.

People come to me saying so-and-so is very egoistic. Then that very person tells me the same thing about others.

Mulla Nasruddin used to say, "I can eat ninety-nine cookies at a stretch." Once I told him, "Mulla, why don't you eat one more and complete the hundred?" He was very annoyed with me; "What do you think? Do I have a stomach or a warehouse?"

Through ninety-nine the Mulla has no sense of a warehouse, for that is all his. But if another person adds even one more, the warehouse suddenly appears — stark and clear! We are blind to ourselves. If the other were not there to make it clear we would be oblivious to everything. Therefore the others are a blessing.

And the seeker is very much aware that if the other is not present you cannot be aware of your ego, you will not recognize your ailment. Thus, in the last moments of his life, the seeker thanks all those who reminded him of his ego, all those who fractured his dreams. This is why Kabir says, "Bring the critic and keep him with you. Make a thatched cottage for him in your courtyard, for he can see your ego when you cannot."

As long as the witness is not awakened within you, you are stone-blind. It is a dream within a dream that I am. Sansara is maya. The object world is illusion. And within this illusion you have the feeling of I-ness. The dream also has a dream and that is the difficulty. The day you encounter death, the I is the first casualty.

How will you stand with regard to death? How will you save yourself? If the breath stops what will you do? All your power, your strength, fails before death. This is why we make such efforts not to remember death. If we do remember death our conceit cannot stand up. It falls limp when we confront ourselves helpless before death. Our arrogance cannot accept it. I — a helpless person? I, who am so strong, so powerful; how can I be helpless? So it is best to suppress the fact of death, and then the ego is not hurt! The wise man remembers death.

In the face of death one is always defeated, even the greatest conquerors: not Hitler nor Alexander nor Napoleon has won against death. Therefore we try to hide the fact of death. We hold on to the ego, which is false, and forget death, which is a reality. If you are determined to go towards the one, remember death, for death is a very great truth, and the powerful effect of this truth is that the ego falls away.

Chuang-Tzu was returning home one night. His way led through the royal cemetery. The night was dark and his foot struck against a skull. Chuang-Tzu picked up the skull and said, "Forgive me, I did not mean to insult you. I must ask your forgiveness because this is just a matter of time. Had you been alive today I do not know what I would have done after this affront." He brought the skull home. The disciples pleaded with him and argued that it should be thrown away. Who keeps a skull in the house?

Why don't we keep a skull in the house? We should give it a place of prominence. What better relic can there be? Nothing is more effective than a skull to remind you of death. Keep it on your dressing table so that you can see your face in the mirror and the skull on the table.

Chuang-Tzu kept the skull with him all the time. He might forget everything else, but never the skull. People objected and asked why he kept such a morbid thing with him.

"Why does this skull bother you so much?" Chuang-Tzu would ask. "How does it harm you? I keep it with me to remind me that one day my skull will also be lying somewhere. Perhaps it too will be kicked about by beggars and no one will care even to ask forgiveness, and I shall be unable to do anything about it. The skull is very much there in my head. I keep this skull so that even if you beat me on the head with a shoe, I shall not look at you but at the skull. Then I shall smile, for I know this was to happen one day. This was bound to be. How long shall I save my skull?"

When death becomes an absolute fact the ego is dissolved. Remembrance of death is like poison to the ego. As long as ego persists you cannot awaken. No sooner does death become visible, the ego breaks, because then you understand that all happens according to his will, that you are not the doer.

But God directs them by his will and his order.
He watches them but they cannot see him;
That is the wonder of wonders.

Nanak says God sees Brahma, Vishnu and Shiva, but they are not capable of seeing him. This is a choice statement. The seeker should keep it in mind. You see the whole world with your eyes. The observer within you can also see your eyes, but your eyes cannot see him. You can touch the whole world with your hands; the observer within you can also see your hands, but your hands cannot touch him.

Brahma, Vishnu and Shiva are the three eyes or the three faces of God. These faces can see the object world, but they cannot turn back and see God; for that which is hidden within is beyond their reach. Therefore you can see him only when your external vision is completely closed off. Your physical eyes cannot see him. With this face you cannot see him; only when this face is completely forgotten will you recognize him. If you wish to go within, all external modes of travel have to be discarded. They are useless for the inward journey. Brahma, Vishnu, Shiva are for the object world. The trimurti is on the outside, and that which is hidden with the three is beyond their reach.

There is a delightful Indian story — and there are many such stories — in which, whenever a person attains buddhahood, Brahma himself comes and sits at his feet and begs him to impart knowledge.

Nanak is hinting at this idea, for a buddha is higher than Brahma; he is higher than all the deities. Brahma, Vishnu and Shiva are left far behind for they were merely faces of the three. He who has known the one becomes higher than those who know the three. Even Brahma himself comes and bows at his feet and asks for knowledge.

The fact is Brahma, Vishnu and Shiva are still there, but through them the One cannot be known. Only when the three are dropped can the one be known. In this context, the Hindus have written wonderful stories that are unequaled to this day, but it is very difficult to understand and interpret these stories.

The story I was talking about begins when Brahma created the earth. The earth is thus Brahma's daughter, but as soon as he created her, he was enchanted by her beauty and began to run after her. She took various forms to save herself from him. Whatever form she took, Brahma assumed the corresponding form and ran after her. When she became a cow he became a bull.

When the West first read this story they were uncertain — what kind of a God runs after his own daughter? But these stories are wonderful, for Hindus believe that the deities are also worldly. They are also outward oriented. Thus Brahma can be enchanted by his daughter, meaning by his own creation.

Do we not do the same? Are we not enchanted by our own creations, our own dreams? And don't we run after them? We run after the very desires we create — this is the meaning of the story. The very desire becomes our lifelong involvement. We pursue our desires in many forms. The deities are as involved and as much captives as man. Therefore Brahma also came to Buddha in search of knowledge.

Nanak says that it is a wonder of wonders that God sees the three but he is invisible to them. It is a matter for wonder and yet not so surprising. The wonderment is if the One can see the three, why can't the three see the One? And it is also not so astonishing, since how can the three see the One unless they look back? But as soon as they look back into themselves they become one.

Understand it this way: I always keep telling you that you cannot meet God, for the day you meet him you will no longer be you. You have to annihilate yourself before meeting him. As long as the I in you is present, God cannot be. When you are not, God is. How can the meeting take place?

The same happens to Brahma, Vishnu and Shiva. When they turn inwards within themselves, the one remains, the three are no more. As long as the three remain as three, they cannot turn inwards. Therefore it is a wonder and also not a wonder.

Remember that this is not a discussion of Brahma, Vishnu and Shiva, but concerns you! The three are merely a symbol.

If you must bow, bow to him!

Nanak says: Why bow to Brahma, Vishnu, Shiva? They cannot even see him. He alone can see them, so bow to him if you must bow.

He is the primal being, pure without beginning or end.
He is the unstruck sound.
He is immutable through all time.

Bow to him, the everlasting one. Seek only him who is the primal one; who is the beginning of everything, but who is himself without a beginning; who is the very first, and before whom there is nobody and nothing; and who will be in the end and after whom there is no one! Bow to such a one only. If you bow to a lesser form you will wander.

But we cannot muster the courage to bow to the one, for we bow only to serve ourselves. We have to drop all self-interest in order to bow to the one.

If you want to satisfy your own ends, bow to the deities, for they are like you. You have desires, so have they. Ask them for gifts, they will gratify your wishes. There are comparable values between them and you. They may be more powerful than you but they are not different from you; as you have hopes and expectations so also have they. So sing their praises, worship them and all your worldly wants will be gratified; however, whatever you ask them will pertain only to the world. If this be your end, then you should worship Vishnu.

You can ask for the one only when you are prepared to leave the world. Remember, whatever is attainable is through the one; all else is mere wandering. Whoever has attained has attained through the one; all else is mere wandering. Whoever has attained has attained through the one. You see people toiling so hard to attain worldly gains and they gain nothing, yet your eyes do not open to this fact, yet your understanding is not awakened. There are so many who seek worldly wealth; some achieve it but find they have attained nothing. Those who lose are the losers, but here even the winners are losers.

Two men were sitting at a table in a restaurant. One was young, the other somewhat older. A beautiful woman came in. Seeing her, the young man said, "Whenever I see her my heart misses a beat. I am so mad for this woman that I won't be happy until I have her. Without her I know no peace. I don't know what to do."

The older man said, "When you have succeeded in seducing her, let me know."

"What do you mean?" the lover asked.

The other man replied, "She happens to be my wife. I have lost all peace of mind since I married her and I shall regain my peace only if you manage to entice her away from me!"

Those who do not get, complain, and those who do get also complain. Complaint is the way to being in this world. You find the rich and the poor, the successful and the unsuccessful, the defeated and the victorious, all crying and complaining. In one respect there is a great similarity in all walks of life — all are unhappy.

Only by attaining the one can one attain something. This one has no temple. Brahma has one temple in his honor, Vishnu has many, and Shiva has innumerable. But there is no temple dedicated to the one; there cannot be.

The name Nanak gives to his temple is very beautiful — *gurudwara*. It is not a temple to God, but the entrance of the guru. Through it you can reach the one, but in itself it is only a door through which you have to pass. It is no place to tarry. He who terminates his journey in the gurudwara is a foolish man. We have to pass through the guru's door towards the one who resides beyond the door.

And, says Nanak, if the feeling of obeisance has really and truly arisen within you, then bow your head to the one. He is seated on the throne of the visible and the invisible and therefore there can be no temple to him.

> *All the worlds are his abode, and all worlds his storehouse.*
> *He has them filled for all time with all worth attaining.*
> *The creator creates, and oversees it all.*
> *Says Nanak, He is the true reality and all his works are true.*

All that is relevant to the Lord — whatever it be — is truth.

Whatever is relevant to you is false, for your very being is false. Truth cannot grow from untruth. Whatever you create will be merely a house of cards — a slight wind, and it will fall. Whatever you make cannot be more than a paper boat that will sink as soon as it sets sail. You cannot travel in it. Whatever is created by the ego is false, for the ego itself is false. Whatever belongs to God is true.

The day this truth dawns on you, you will stop wasting your energy in creating untruths; instead you will begin to utilize it to know truth. *Samsari* involves a person who is busy creating untruths. You do not realize the falsity of the world for you are wrapped up in it. Stand a little away and observe your world — how frightening its falsity is!

A man hoards currency notes. He does not realize that these notes are mere bits of paper, only a means of transaction. If the government changes and the new government decides to cancel this currency, they become just paper! So this man is actually gambling on an assumption that cannot be relied on.

There is a hotel in America. During the depression of 1930 when the economy of America crashed, the owner pasted the walls with useless bonds that formerly had been worth tens of millions of dollars. Millions upon millions of dollars turned into useless paper.

On the other hand, there is this man amassing currency notes. He has no other interest but to hoard money. He fills his safe, but he does not know that for each bank note he is selling his own life, for each moment is precious. The energy he could have utilized in attaining God he wastes in gathering the bank notes.

In Mexico pebbles and stones were once used as coins, for it is only a matter of general agreement; you use paper to represent money, but surely stones are more valuable than paper! Gold is gold for we have agreed to its value. If tomorrow the wind changes, iron will be valued in place of gold, and gold will lose all importance. Then jewels and ornaments will be made of iron.

There are tribes in Africa who value bones and not gold. They wear ornaments, necklaces, etc. of bones. Gold has no value for them. They will not exchange it for their bones.

It is all a game of values, and for these values you sacrifice your

One Becomes Three

life. You are willing to sacrifice anything so that people may honor you. What is the meaning of this honor? Who are those people whose recognition you crave? They are the same ones hankering for your honor. What is the value of their respect? What do you gain by being honored by fools? And the crowds of the foolish in this world cannot be counted.

Winston Churchill went to America. He spoke at a meeting before a huge crowd; the hall was filled to capacity. After the meeting a woman came up to him and said, "You must be delighted to see so many people come to hear you. Whenever you speak the hall is packed."

Churchill replied, "Whenever I see a packed hall I say to myself, 'If it was my execution fifty times more people would have come.' How can one trust these people? They hear me and they clap. If I were being hanged, they would still clap. So whenever I see a hall filled with people I remind myself that these very same people would turn out in large numbers and enjoy the sight if I were executed."

The same people will acclaim you when you rise, and applaud even louder when you fall. Where do you want to reach by gathering this crowd and getting their votes? What companionship do you get when they are with you? And how high do you hope to rise by riding on their shoulders? But man wagers his life for these paltry gains — how to win acclaim from people, how to rise in their esteem.

Nanak says that whatever is born out of the ego is false; it cannot but be false. All this is a quest of the ego. The politician comes to your door, folds his hands, bows his head and asks for your vote. You give him the vote; he gets you the position. This is mutual ego gratification.

It happened once: There was a man who used to strike the hour in a clock tower in a town that also had a small telephone exchange. Every morning at nine o'clock the telephone exchange would get a call asking for the time. Now the exchange people would hear the clock tower strike nine and set their clocks by it.

This went on for a long time until one day the operator asked the caller who he was and why he asked the hour at exactly nine every morning.

The caller answered, "I am the man in charge of the clock tower."

You can imagine the state of affairs: this man depends upon the exchange and the exchange depends on him — totally reciprocal!

This mutual interdependence exists in all our dealings. I look at you, you look at me; I respect you, you respect me; you nourish my ego, I nourish yours. Such is this vast network of falsity.

Says Nanak, He is the true reality and all his works are true.

Seek truth first. Do nothing before that. For whatever you do before that is bound to be false. Only one thing is worth doing: recognize truth! Then you may do anything. For once you know truth, it begins to act from within you.

If you must bow, bow to him.
He is the primal being, pure without beginning or end.
He is the unstruck sound.
He is immutable through all time.

Remember this: he is the changeless, always the same form. Whatever changes is maya, illusion; it is sansara, it is falsity, it is a dream. What is eternal, what never changes, is God. If you grasp well the meaning of this sutra, you will one day seek out the changeless one within you.

You may perhaps have observed, or perhaps not, that within you too there is a factor, an element that is changeless. Anger comes but it is not with you all day long. Anger is maya. Sometimes love comes but that too does not remain all the time. Love also is maya. Sometimes you are cheerful, sometimes sad; but all these are passing phases, therefore they are illusions.

Then what is with you all twenty-four hours? It is the witness within — whether you are aware of it or not. Who is it who sees the anger? Who is it who sees the greed? Who sees your love? Who watches your hate? Who knows you are sad? Who knows when you are cheerful? Who is it who tells you: I am ill, I am well? Who is it who knows that you did not sleep well last night, that dreams troubled you?

All day long there is one who knows you inside. He is forever awake, while all else comes and goes. Catch hold of this one, for in this alone can you get a glimpse of him.

> *If you must bow, bow to him.*
> *He is the primal being, pure without beginning or end.*
> *He is the unstruck sound.*
> *He is immutable through all time.*

CHAPTER 16

Your Boat Is Useless on Land

If my single tongue becomes a hundred thousand,
And this hundred thousand becomes twenty times more,
With each tongue would I sing a hundred thousand times
The only name of the master of the world.
These are the steps of the name of the Lord.
By following them does one become twenty-one.
Hearing them speak of heaven's glory,
Even those who are like lowly worms become ambitious to
  emulate them.
Nanak says, He is attained only by his grace.
But the false claimants spread their boastful tales.
The power lies neither in speaking nor in silence;
The power lies neither in asking nor in giving;
The power lies neither in living nor in dying;
The power lies neither in the wealth of kingdoms nor the
  resolves of the mind;
The power lies neither in remembrance nor in knowledge of
  the divine;
The power lies neither in the world nor in the devices to be
  rid of sansara.
The real power lies in his hands — who creates and keeps on
  watching.
Nanak says, No one is high and no one is low before him.

Before proceeding with the sutras, there are a few things we should understand.

Thousands upon thousands of ways have been devised to search for God. But whenever a person has attained, he has found that he could not be attained through any means. Attainment comes always by his grace, as his gift; only through his compassion does a seeker arrive.

But alas, things become very complex, because without effort on the part of the seeker grace does not descend. Understand this a little, for without prior understanding of this complicated puzzle you cannot progress on the path of realization.

For example, you forget someone's name. You try very hard to remember. You feel it is on the tip of your tongue and will come to you at any moment, yet it does not come. You try a thousand ways to remember; you get all worked up inside, for you are so sure the name is so close. Then you give up in exasperation. What can you do if it doesn't come to mind? You go to do something else — read the newspaper, go for a walk or visit a friend's house. You have forgotten all about the name when suddenly, over a cup of tea, the name comes to you like a flash when you least expect it. You are completely relaxed and making no effort.

When we put out a great deal of effort, it becomes a hindrance in itself. Great effort produces great tension in the mind. When we pursue something doggedly and obstinately, the insistence becomes an obstruction. When the mind is concentrated it becomes constricted and we become closed. The mind can become so constricted that not even a single word can find its way out.

Concentration means constriction. The concentrated mind must be closed to all except the object of your concentration. Only a small hole is left open for you to see; all else is closed. For instance, when a person's house is on fire his mind is concentrated on the fire. At that moment if his shoe pinches him, he would be unaware of it. He is oblivious to everything around him. Rushing madly to extinguish it, if his hands burn or his clothes, he is totally unaware. All his energy is directed towards putting out the fire; all else is forgotten. In the same way, when you struggle to remember a certain name, the name doesn't occur to you, because your mind has become so concentrated and constricted.

The complication is that God is so vast that a narrow mind cannot grasp him. If a small word cannot be recalled how can God be remembered? And his name is not on the tongue, it is in the heart. It does not come to mind until suddenly, when you are doing nothing and the mind is relaxed, its gates all open. When the constriction of concentration is gone, you open and God enters.

But the irony is that the second happening can take place only after you have truly tried. Without that initial effort nothing happens, for the happening is the ultimate outcome of the initial effort and struggle. The intense effort ends in apparent failure; but when you give up, this effort slips into the subconscious mind and continues with the same intensity. Then, when you are relaxed, the thought wells up.

So trying is of two kinds: the conscious effort you put in does not lead to God. When you give up and accept defeat all the effort you had put in now penetrates every pore of your body. It spreads with every beat of your heart, in every breath that you take. It becomes a part of your being that you cannot lose. Do what you will, it has gone deep within you as an internal current, a flow in which the advent of God takes place. Scientists would say it has now become an effort of the unconscious.

The conscious mind is a very small segment compared to the unconscious. The ratio is one to nine. It is just like a piece of ice floating on the water; one-tenth is above water and nine-tenths is below.

When you try with your conscious mind you never profit. The imperceptible gain will occur only when your conscious effort reaches its last gasp and you are completely worn out; you will give up but the effort will continue in the unconscious. Though you give up the unconscious never gives up.

This means that the conscious effort gradually becomes the unconscious effort. When this happens the *japa*, repetition, becomes the unpronounced repetition, *ajapa*. Now you needn't repeat the name consciously; it happens inside by itself. Wherever you are — running a shop, marketing, working in the office or even sleeping — the japa continues inside. Once the japa enters your unconscious, it permeates each atom of your being. You may not hear its music but it is sounding within you all right.

The conscious is useful inasmuch as it carries you up to the unconscious. One day the explosion takes place and suddenly you find God before you. Then you will feel that it is only his grace and compassion that have brought you so far. You had long since given up all effort and accepted defeat when suddenly the destination appeared; so it was not your effort. You had stopped traveling and the sacred place came before you. Since at that time you were making no effort, it is natural to feel that it is his grace.

Initially it is necessary to try your utmost through the conscious. Don't think that since your effort yields no result you should not try — that, since it happens only through his compassion, it will happen when it is to happen, so why should we bother? Then it will never happen.

Or if you think your endeavors alone will bring about the result and you keep on struggling consciously, then too it does not happen. Where your effort and his compassion meet, your efforts end, and only his grace remains.

You are restricted only by your conscious self. He is only in your unconscious. You are limited by the boundaries of your conscious mind, your thoughts. Below these, in your very depth, he resides. Although he is already there within you, the door between the conscious and the unconscious has to be broken down by your own effort. The experience of union happens only through his compassion.

Those who wish to seek must first explore thoroughly and entirely; then they have to let go of all searching. Only when they have tried totally should the search be given up, not before that, or else all goes in vain. When the search is complete, when you have staked your all without holding back a single thing, only then does the search slip from the conscious to the unconscious; for there you are not, your ego is no more.

In sleep where is your ego, your arrogance? In sleep there is no one to say I: that "I am a king" or "I am a millionaire". The I is completely lost. In the same manner there is not the faintest inkling of the ego within your unconscious. The I is a product of the conscious mind. With effort his I breaks; when you are exhausted the ego dissolves. As the ego dissolves, the door to the unconscious opens. And the door of the unconscious is the entrance to God. Those who have reached have all passed through this door. But then you are not there, there is no one to say I; therefore in the moment of attainment you will say, "His grace, his compassion."

This gives rise to an illusion, a doubt: you may wonder if his grace is more for some and less for others. If it is his grace alone, a few are attaining but the majority are not. Is this some rank injustice? Remember, through your own efforts alone you become worthy of his compassion. His grace showers on all, all the time, but you are not fit for it. Therefore it is your failure to accept what you are getting, not some discrimination on his part.

Nanak says, No one is high and no one is low before him.

No one is worthy, no one unworthy. He gives, he showers on all alike. But if you are not ready to take, you will keep on missing. You are not ready to take his grace.

If you find a rough diamond by the wayside you will not pick it up, but if a jeweler passes that way, he will because he knows its value. To you it's only a piece of stone. The diamond was equally available to you and to the jeweler; it was there for anyone's taking. The diamond didn't differentiate between you and the jeweler; it hadn't refused you in favor of the jeweler. The fact remains, you did not recognize it; the jeweler did. He had the eyes, the capacity, to spot it.

God, similarly, lies before you, everywhere. Wherever your eyes reach he is there, but you do not have the eyes to see. Your eyes cannot see him, your ears cannot hear him, your hands cannot touch him. You are deaf, dumb, lame! He calls you but you cannot run toward him. He calls from all four sides but, alas, you are deaf. There is no differentiation, no discrimination from him towards anyone. For all come from him and ultimately merge into him. How can there be any discrimination?

Do you differentiate between your right hand and your left hand — that when your right hand hurts it is worse than when your left hand is in pain? Both are yours, left and right, inside you are just one — yourself.

Does he differentiate between the rich and the poor, the learned and the ignorant, the good and the bad? If his gift were conditional, he would give only if you conform to his requirements. It would be a business deal, a bargain. No, God gives unconditionally. If you cannot receive his gift, it is you who are wanting. He knocks at your door, but you think it is the wind. You see his footsteps, but you begin to interpret and offer your comments, which only deepen the darkness in your eyes.

God comes to you from many directions. He does not spare himself at all. He comes to you as much as he came to Buddha, as much as he came to Nanak. For him you are not any different from Nanak. But Nanak recognizes him; he is a jeweler. Buddha holds the hem of his robe while you keep missing him again and again. When you are qualified, when you become an adept in the art of assaying, your blindness will vanish. After all your efforts cause your ego to fall, when through exhaustion you are no more, you find that he was always there before you. He was right at the tip of your nose; wherever your nose turned, there he was. You missed because of your own self.

Keep this well within your heart: if you miss you are the cause, if you attain it is through his grace. This is incomprehensible to those who have not known. Logic would assert: if I miss because of myself, I shall also attain because of myself. While the logic seems tight it is a mistake; you miss because of yourself, you attain because of him, his grace.

What does this mean? It means that as long as you are, you cannot attain him. Then how can you attain through yourself, since your very self is the obstruction? The stronger the I in you, the greater is the obstruction, the stronger is the wall. Once the walls fall, he stands directly before you. Conscious effort will break the wall and the door will open, but the light of God was always outside the door.

When you attain him, many things become clear to you. One: I missed because of myself, I attained because of you. Two: you were near but I sought you in far off places, not where you were. Three: the supports I used in my search were those by which you can never be sought.

In all dimensions of life the mode of travel is different. You can cross an ocean with a boat, but you cannot use it to cross the land. No matter how good a sailor you are, no matter how many seas you may have crossed, or how great your knowledge of the ocean, you cannot sail your boat on the road. Now because of this boat your whole journey comes to a halt. You could even have walked and arrived one day on foot, but now you are stuck with this boat around your neck, so to say. You may try to apply your knowledge and experience of sailing to land, you may have crossed vast oceans, but this small bit of dry land will defeat you for your boat is useless on land, and you don't abandon it.

This is exactly what is happening. The boat of ego is a useful vehicle in the world of *sansara*, the world of objects. You cannot take a step without the ego. Trying to make your way in life without the ego leads to grief; for it is a race of egos. All striving is in the I. The greater the ego, the greater the success. That this success ultimately turns into defeat is a different matter. But in the material world arrogance wins; the psychosis of arrogance is always victorious for this is a world of maniacs.

If however you begin on the path of God with this ego, you shall err. You may have been successful in the material world, your ego may have made a Napoleon, an Alexander of you, but do not make the mistake of carrying the ego along with you on this journey towards God. It becomes a hindrance that you will be caught and bound by. Having boarded the boat, you will simply sit becalmed in it. It won't sail. The journey is impossible.

At the first glimpse of him a person realizes that he missed him all this time entirely because of himself, and that the attainment came by his grace. He realizes that all his efforts that had seemed so intense and exhausting were hardly worth the name compared to the gift of attainment. There is no relation between the two — his effort and his grace.

It is just as if a person travels with the help of a needle to realize the ocean. Really, what connection can a needle have with the ocean? All efforts of man are like the needle — small, very small. Until you meet God you cannot weigh your efforts or know what they mean.

One man says he worships in the temple. What does he do? He sounds the bell, offers flowers to the image. Granted he is performing a worthy act, but has this anything to do with realizing God? Another man sits for an hour every day and repeats his name. He is mad if he thinks that by repeating his name over and over for an hour a day he can attain him! How will his shouts and cries help? What value is his voice; how far will it reach?

When you arrive, you realize at once how childish, how insignificant were all your efforts. They will seem so trivial — all that going to temples, going to Kaaba or Kashi; all your worship, japa and penance; all the topsy-turvy postures, all the shouting and hollering. How much are they all worth? You undertake these puny efforts, these petty, feeble efforts to attain the invaluable, the priceless — that cannot be had at any price in the market of the world? You work for an hour and earn a rupee; you worship for an hour and you expect to attain God? It is understandable and logical that an hour's labor can earn you a rupee, but how can you earn God by one hour's meditation?

That which is realized is infinite. Our labor is insignificant. When you attain you will appreciate the fact that you had set out with a spoon and the ocean poured into it. In that hour you are bound to call out: "Your grace, my Lord, Your compassion!" Saints have exhausted themselves in their endeavors, and in the end declared against their own efforts. Yet they exhorted their disciples to keep on trying, never to stop trying. Their words seem so illogical.

Each time I say that you cannot attain by your effort, that very evening people come and say, "Why go through all the strain of meditation if he can be realized without trying? If as you yourself say, efforts yield no fruit, what is the sense in all of this?"

It happened: Early in this century physicists made a discovery beyond all logic. All their data showed that the ultimate particle of matter, the electron, was operating in a way that was beyond comprehension: it was behaving in two different ways at the same time. It was acting both as a particle of matter and as a wave, a current, a ripple. What conformed totally to the words of the saints was inconsistent in the scientists' laboratories.

If you have studied geometry you will know that a line is a line and a dot is a dot. The line can never look like a dot nor a dot like a line, for the simple reason that a dot is a dot whereas a line is a continuation of many dots. If you have a dot in your book which sometimes becomes a line and sometimes becomes a dot as you are looking, you will be alarmed. You will imagine all kinds of things — that it is black magic or that someone is playing a trick! For a dot is a dot and cannot become a line. One thing cannot be two different things.

In the same way a particle is a particle, and a wave is a wave. But physicists discovered at the beginning of this century that the electron acts as if it is both, it behaves in a dual manner simultaneously. This was a great calamity for science, for all its premises were nullified.

Science is governed by logic, it is not a play of the mysterious. It is not poetry. It is arithmetic where two plus two must equal four. Then what was to be done? The more they explored the atom, the more their troubles increased. Ultimately they had to accept the dual behavior of the electron.

People questioned the physicists: How can this be? Such a discovery nullified Euclid's geometry. It is against all mathematical laws.

The physicists replied: What are we to do if the electrons don't obey the laws of Euclidean geometry? We have verified every aspect of it and have to announce what we saw. If it doesn't conform to logic, let it not. We shall have to change our laws of science; we cannot tell the atoms to behave differently.

So a new geometry was born — non-Euclidean geometry. Geometry had to be changed, for the elements cannot be expected to change their nature and conform to man's theories.

For the first time in the history of science, Euclid was rendered useless and its definitions proclaimed defective. And all the doctrines of logic propounded by Aristotle were invalidated.

Saints face the same difficulty. They have tapped his door long before the scientists and they found that nothing is attained without a full-fledged effort; yet he is not attained through any amount of endeavor. The condition is such that there's nothing to do but try, though he is not to be attained by trying. If you really understand this, you will come to know the profound correlation between the two and you will risk your all in the effort. You will attain him only through his grace, but you have to make yourself worthy of his grace by making an all-out, unsparing effort. This is the quintessence of this sutra.

> *If my single tongue becomes a hundred thousand,*
> *And this hundred thousand becomes twenty times more,*
> *With each tongue would I sing a hundred thousand times*
> *The only name of the master of the world.*

Only then will you be exhausted, not before! How many times have you repeated his name? How many meditations have you done? You have hardly begun! You haven't used your full strength. If your house caught fire you would really run. But you haven't run towards God with half that effort. If your wife were to die, how much you would weep! Have you cried for him in your grief of separation? If your child is lost, you will run here and there like a madman, searching; have you looked for him like this? Your quest is still lukewarm; it hasn't reached the boiling point.

Nanak is speaking of the boiling point when he says in this sutra: If my tongue becomes a hundred thousand, and if this hundred thousand turns into millions, with each tongue shall I repeat endlessly the name of God. Each hair on your body should fill with thirst for him, each pore, every atom, yearning for him. All else but "I must attain him!" should be meaningless in your life. God alone should be your only purpose. When you are ready to renounce all else, when your only goal is his attainment, only then is the concentration enough.

These are the steps of the name of the Lord: that one tongue becomes a million, and then each tongue repeats his name millions of times. When traversed by the seeker, the names of the Lord are the very steps by which he becomes twenty-one — in other words, he attains God-realization.

The word *twenty-one* occurs in the reckoning of the *Sankhya* school of thought. Sankhya discusses the ways a seeker can become enlightened or twenty-one. The calculations of this philosophy are very valuable. The very word *Sankhya* means numbers, numerals. It is the first time man's existence was dealt with numerically; therefore the philosophy came to be known as Sankhya.

Sankhya says the five elements — earth, water, fire, air and ether — are born out of the One. But these elements are gross. There are also five subtle elements that cannot be seen by the eyes. Scientists also agree that the wall we can see with the naked eye is the gross wall; the subtle wall we are never able to see. Scientists have obtained only a bare glimpse of it. The wall that appears so static and immovable to us is not static; it contains a great deal of movement. Each particle moves at incredible speeds, approaching the speed of light; and the light ray travels at 186,000 feet per second. This is so fast, so subtle, that we cannot grasp it.

The microscopic particles that make up the wall revolve at such tremendous speeds. It is so far beyond what the physical eye can observe that the wall appears stationary. The fact is, however, that each thing is vibrating, everything is alive and moving. One day the wall will fall. If it was totally static and devoid of any movement, inside and out, it could not disintegrate; how could it fall? Activity brings about a struggle that results in destruction.

The wall is going through great activity, with tremendous friction between the particles of the wall and the external forces of wind and dust that ultimately causes the wall to break down.

Recent scientific experiments show that the human body can be kept alive for a great length of time if kept below a temperature of zero. It can thus be preserved for an indefinite period. The theory that applies is that the less the activity, the less the disintegration. This is what refrigeration is all about. Keep a fruit in the refrigerator and it can be preserved for a length of time. On a similar basis, we find that people mature sooner in tropical countries and appear to age sooner. The greater the heat, the quicker the movement and the quicker the maturation and eventual disintegration. Because of this increased activity and metabolism we feel restless in the hot season and enjoy the cold season. In winter you often feel healthier.

Sankhya says there are five subtle elements. These subtle elements are related to five gross elements. Together they make ten.

Then there are five organs of perception that are subtle, and five organs of action that are gross. The eye is your organ of action, while the capacity to see is your subtle organ of perception. If you do not have the power of seeing, you are blind in spite of the eye. It sometimes happens that the eye is in perfect condition yet cannot see; this is because the power of vision has shifted away from the eyes. The ears are the gross organs of hearing; but hearing, the power to hear, is the subtle organ of perception.

Therefore when Nanak tells us again and again, "Listen!" he is not referring to your ears. The external organ of hearing, the ear, is always open to sound, unlike the eyes, which can be closed or open. Then why does Nanak say, "Listen"? He is hinting at your subtle ear. He means come nearer to the ear, don't wander here and there because then the ears will hear but you will not listen.

These five gross sense organs and the five subtle organs of perception make ten. Together with the elements they make twenty. Nanak says that he who wagers his all becomes twenty-one, and this is God. If you do not bet your all, you do not seek him, even then you become twenty-one. But this twenty-one is your ego.

So there are two ways of becoming twenty-one. The first twenty are the states of being. Either you attain God or realize your own soul and you become twenty-one, or you visualize a false picture of yourself — that I am this or that, a millionaire, a hero, a renunciate, or a king. There too you will be twenty-one, but this would be the twenty-first lie.

Either you add one lie to the twenty and you have twenty-one lies, or add one truth to the twenty and you have twenty-one truths. In either case you become twenty-one. We are all twenty-one. Nanak is also twenty-one. No one can be more than this, but we have joined one lie to our twenty and we have never sought in the other direction.

You have never tried to know anything about your own self; you are under the illusion that you know yourself and there is no greater lie. You have never tried to know yourself, nor have you even a glimpse of your authentic self. Yet you say, "I am!" You haven't the slightest notion of who you are. You know only as much as the mirror tells you. And how much of you can the mirror show except the external appearance of your body? You can see your body, your clothes — that is all. The mirror cannot reflect the soul within you, your real self. Whatever the mirror shows, you accept as your own self, the I.

And this I you have taken to be the twenty-one. That is the whole trouble; it is hell. If your twenty-first is a falsity, you fall into suffering. The twenty in every case is constant; it is only the twenty-first that is the deciding factor. No sooner is the twenty-first the truth, you experience the bliss of supreme liberation. The twenty are an arrangement of life, they cause no confusion. Only if the twenty-first is inauthentic does it bring untold troubles.

Nothing causes as much pain and suffering as the ego. There is no synonym better suited to express the nature of the ego than suffering. Increase your ego, you increase your suffering. You can contain the whole of hell within your fist.

The more you desire joy, happiness, the less your ego will have to be. The day your ego is no more, the whole of heaven will be in your grasp. It will follow you like your own shadow. Then you cannot be sent to hell. Even if by chance you are sent to hell, you will create heaven there too, for he who has no ego finds heaven everywhere. And he who is filled with ego, will create a hell out of heaven if he happens to go there. Happiness and unhappiness are not connected with situations but with the twenty-one within you — whether it is false or true.

> *These are the steps of the name of the Lord.*
> *By following them does one become twenty-one.*

Nanak says that he who gives his all is taking the steps to the Lord's name. If you keep investing your all, a moment comes when there is nothing left in you. Traveling on that path ultimately makes the seeker twenty-one. In other words, the seeker becomes enlightened.

> *Hearing them speak of heaven's glory,*
> *Even those who are like lowly worms become ambitious to*
>   *emulate them.*
> *Nanak says, He is attained only by his grace.*
> *But the false claimants spread their boastful tales.*

Here Nanak makes a valuable statement about how religion is altered and deformed when his light enters a person, he cannot help talking about him. How can a flower stop spreading its fragrance when it blooms? How can a lamp not spread light once it is illumined? Whenever divinity descends into a person he is bound to talk about it. He will sing his glories, what he has attained will ooze from each pore of his body and will be manifest like fragrance around him, like light. Even if he remains silent, by basking in him his very being radiates news of him.

Nanak says: "Seeing such a person and hearing him talk of divine things, inferior and worthless people, who are no more than worms in human form, feel a sense of competition. These people are filled with envy and jealousy and do their utmost to discount the attainment of such a one."

So the first thing that happens around a person when he attains is that people around him will deny him and his attainment. They will brand him a liar, a hoax. They will set out on a fault-finding mission. This is the *Kali Yuga*, the Age of Darkness, they will say, and who can attain in this era? The days of *Sat Yuga*, the Age of Truth, when so many beings were enlightened, are gone. They will ask for a thousand-and-one proofs and do their utmost to demonstrate that he has not attained.

There is no way to prove one's attainment, neither by one's behavior, one's clothes or one's food. But realization needs no proof; its light manifests all around the person.

Then what do these people do? Those among them whose ego is stronger than the rest proclaim to the world, I have attained! The ego first denies the attainment of a genuine seeker: how could anyone do such a thing before he — the egoist — has realized? When he finds that the man in question cannot be proved wrong, he lets it be known by the beat of a drum that he also has attained!

Nanak speaks of the mean and lowly — for nothing can be meaner or lower than the ego. They are like lowly worms or insects. They are filled with the spirit of competition. Then they give rise to false stories of achievements.

So if there is one *satguru* in the world, for each perfect master there are ninety-nine pseudo-satgurus. This is always the ratio: 1 to 99. And the joke lies in the fact that the pseudo-gurus are more successful in attracting you than the genuine guru, for they speak your language. The pseudo-guru knows you very well and does all that you wish of him deep within yourself. If you want him to produce ashes from his hands, he does go. if you want an amulet to fall from the skies, he gets one for you.

You see the wayside magician performing the same tricks, but you are not impressed. When a holy man or saint turns round and indulges in these same tricks, you go mad after him; you dance with joy that at last you have found the satguru! Then you pour out your desires to him. You want to be rid of your ailment, he blesses you; you desire a son, he blesses you. He tries to satisfy all your desires. Therefore you find crowds of thousands, millions, around a pseudo-satguru, for he is but a reflection of your own life.

It is difficult to recognize a satguru, for it requires a transformation in your life: you must change! A pseudo-guru gives to you and tries to satisfy your desires; an authentic guru snatches away all you have.

And the most interesting part in this whole affair is if you were to light a fire and sit before it blessing whoever comes, it is certain that your blessing will be successful fifty percent of the time! These are significant odds. Whoever comes, bless him! You need do nothing more. If a man wants your blessings to win his law suit, bless him. Fifty percent of lawsuits are bound to be won — with or without your blessings! But now the focus of attention will be shifted to you and your blessing! The other fifty out of the hundred will go to some other pseudo-saint, for you were no good to them.

The fifty who win are now your confirmed followers; they will keep coming to you. Now this crowd of fifty will impress any newcomer with their stories of success; one won a lawsuit, another got back his wife, a third was lucky in love, someone was rid of an ailment, another's child was saved in an accident...and so on. Such is the crowd around the false saints; they are people whose wishes are fulfilled. The disappointed ones continue to move on and one day, when their wish is fulfilled, they will follow the guru they happened to be serving at that moment, presuming it to be the result of his blessings.

If you recognize the guru by your desires, you will err; what has the guru to do with your desires? The true guru is not there to gratify your desires; he is interested in awakening you. To accomplish this it is better for you to be rid of desires — as many as possible. The guru is not interested in your illness, in your court cases or your wife and children; he is interested in you and your God. And his path is not the path of desires, but of desirelessness. Therefore he will not be able to attract you to him.

Thus you usually find crowds around the pseudo-guru. Whenever you see such a crowd, beware! For a crowd is always of deluded people. You will find very few people in the right place, near a satguru. And they are extremely hard to find. You will find only a selected few whose aim is to attain God. A crowd is always made up of desire-ridden people.

Nanak says that the false people then spread false tales. The irony is, the stories of such people often seem to be correct, for life is such that fifty percent of the people will be satisfied and convinced when their desires are fulfilled, and the other half will move further on in search of fresh gurus. When by chance their desire is fulfilled they will take it as the grace of the guru they are currently serving; if not near one Sai Baba, then another. Now each tells the other what he has gained from the guru, and so the crowd multiplies. Then when you see thousands of people have gathered...

You too have come there goaded by your desires. You also have put your faith in someone and many times your good luck is the result of your faith. Psychologists say that most illnesses are mental. If you have full faith that you will get well, you get well.

Many hospitals have experimented with this. Physicians call it the placebo effect. A group of patients with the same illness are divided into two groups. One group is given the regular treatment and the second group is treated with pills made only of plain sugar. The most interesting part is that about three out of five will recover independent of which group they come from, whether they got the regular treatment or the placebo. This is why there are so many "pathies":

allopathy, homeopathy, naturopathy, and what-not. And all these "pathies" work on people and they recover, or else the treatment would have vanished long ago.

It appears that people are cured more by faith than by medicine. If a doctor who has just started his practice, who has just graduated from medical college, prescribes a treatment, it will not work, for you have no faith in him. If he happens to be your son it is bound to fail. What father has ever trusted his son? If a well known doctor prescribes the same treatment it will work. The bigger the doctor and the higher the fees, the more effective the treatment. Half the work is done by your faith in him. A doctor in whom you have no faith can never cure you.

This is why we find a doctor's diplomas and certificates hung on the walls of his consulting room. These are medicines in themselves for his patients. In India if the doctor is "foreign-returned," his cures are certain! Seeing the certificates the patient gets half cured. Have you noticed how many illnesses vanish when the doctor begins to examine you? He may have just taken your pulse, checked your blood pressure, he may just have applied the stethoscope to your chest and you feel the pain half gone.

A crowd gives confidence and faith, and faith yields results, while the phony person at the center of this crowd reaps the profits. You are engrossed in the play of your own mind.

> *Hearing them speak of heaven's glory,*
> *Even those who are like lowly worms become ambitious to emulate them.*
> *Nanak says, He is attained only by his grace.*
> *But the false claimants spread their boastful tales.*

Here worms denote the egoists. The worms are filled with awe and terror. How is this possible? The word *Nanak* means small, wee. This wee man has reached and not we! This man who is way behind us in the world has reached? This illiterate village bum, this penniless farmhand without place, position, or family to boast of? Is anything known of his background; can you name one great man from his ancestors? That this man without heritage, wealth or property has reached while we have not is just impossible!

So Nanak says he can be attained only through his grace, not through your conceit. Who you are does not entitle you to attainment; what you are does not count in his attainment. He is attained only through his munificence. Your conceit and arrogance are only a hindrance in his path.

And yet, false people spread false stories. In the field of religion this is so easily done. Therefore we find the greatest amount of hypocrisy in the name of religion and the greatest amount of untruth.

This is so because the subject is the heavens. The subject is so wide and so far away, so splendid and so mysterious, that anyone can say anything and get away with it. If you set up a shop and begin to sell invisible cloth, how long will your shop last? It will be difficult to get even the first customer. In the marketplace your wares must be not only visible but well displayed and laid out if you want to sell them. How can you cheat now?

I have heard: A store in America began to sell invisible hair pins for women. You may take it as a story of the future. Women would love to have invisible hairpins!

A woman came and asked for a box of them. When she was served she asked the salesman if they were selling well.

He answered, "Madam, we were out of stock these last three days. Thousands have bought them." This was possible, for the primary quality advertised was their non-visibility. Once having advertised them this way, when you open the box and find it empty, whether there are hairpins in it or not is not questioned.

The business of God is just such a business of selling invisible hairpins. Since nothing is visible it is paradise for cheats; that is why we find that the more religions a country has, the greater the hypocrisy prevailing in it.

Our country is proof of this. You will not find more hypocrisy or more humbug anywhere else in the world. Nowhere else in the world has religion been studied as in India. This led to so many satgurus in this country, but each satguru led to ninety-nine pseudo-gurus. You get so tired of all the deceit and fraud, the tyranny and chaos, you come to feel that this whole business of God is one big swindle, a racket. Best to keep away from it all!

Nanak says false people spread false tales and tall stories. And as your faith in them gets stronger, the stories get taller still.

Mulla Nasruddin was telling his little nephew about his experiences. He said, "I was going through the jungle when ten hyenas surrounded me. I killed five at one stroke..."

"But," interrupted the nephew, "Three month ago you said you met five hyenas. Now you say ten."

The Mulla replied coldly, "Then you were smaller. You weren't ready to hear such a frightening and dangerous story. You could not have understood it properly and would have been so shaken with fear."

As your capacity to hear their lies increases, the claims of these hypocrites increases also. They keep watching you to see how much your faith has increased and expand their stories accordingly. Your faith nurtures God knows how many false gurus. When your faith develops you become blind to everything and believe almost anything.

Last night I was reading a discourse of a Christian padre who is well-known in the West. At the very outset he stated an outright lie. I wonder how anyone can believe such nonsense, yet there are people who believe him! He has a following of thousands. He writes in the foreword that very soon the advent of Jesus will take place. He will gather together all the millions of his followers and disappear. He promises that Jesus will not be long in coming now and even mentions the date and day. Tens of millions of Christians will vanish from this earth. Imagine! The rest of the world will look on amazed. And as soon as Jesus collects his devotees and disappears, all kinds of catastrophes will fall on this earth; it will become a veritable hell. He therefore exhorts all people not to waste a single moment, and start believing in Christ — join the flock. In the end he says, "There are only two alternatives before the people who read this book: if he is a sinner he will not believe in what is said in the following pages. If he is a man of good actions and virtue, he should tarry no longer and become his follower at once. He offers you only two alternatives. If you have the slightest sense and if you are basically good, you will follow Jesus. If you don't like the book at all it is because you are a sinner.

There is nothing wrong in going along with Jesus, but this man is exploiting his name. Jesus is a beautiful person, very lovely, but this man — what he says is a brazen lie; yet how can you prove it? I can give you many instances where man's gullibility is exploited.

In 1930 a Christian priest announced that the end of the world would occur on the first of January. Some fifty-thousand of his followers sold all they had and spent the money in merrymaking. There was no sense in keeping the money when the world was coming to an end! They spent as much as they could and gave away the rest. It was a question of believing or not believing. Those who believed were virtuous people. Those who did not were sinners.

The day of resurrection arrived. In darkness they all went up the mountain. When the sun came out, they would be praying on top of the mountain while all the world was destroyed and Jesus would pull all his followers high up into the skies. Morning arrived, the sun came out — nothing happened! All the people of the village headed towards the mountain to question them. They were met halfway — by the followers coming down! When they were asked to explain, they said, "Everything is in order. Our prayers have been heard and accepted. God has postponed the annihilation of creation."

The sect is still very active in spite of this. It is astonishing how blind faith works. And we have no way to prove their falseness. People were prepared to take them to task for playing a hoax on them, but the priests were cleverer. They said it was an even greater proof of their prayers — God had put off the day of judgment because of their intervention!

Mulla Nasruddin sprinkled salt on his doorstep every evening. When someone asked what he was doing so religiously, he said, "It is to keep away wild animals."

"But there are no wild animals around!" people exclaimed.

"That is because I sprinkle the salt every day," Mulla answered.

What can you do to such a man? He leaves you no way out. The proof is before your eyes. Not only do wild animals never come to his doorstep, they do not dare come anywhere near the village!

Man is only too willing to be deceived, for deceit has its own logic. Fraud and deception have their own way of advertisement, their own logic; and they excite your desires. They persuade you in their own insidious way.

Nanak says false people spread empty boastful tales. But he is attained only by him who makes no untoward claims, whose I is completely annihilated. He is attained by him alone to whom he condescends to be gracious.

> *The power lies neither in speaking nor in silence;*
> *The power lies neither in asking nor in giving;*
> *The power lies neither in living nor in dying;*
> *The power lies neither in the wealth of kingdoms nor the resolves of the mind;*
> *The power lies neither in remembrance nor in knowledge of the divine;*
> *The power lies neither in the world nor in the devices to be rid of sansara.*
> *The real power lies in his hands — who creates and keeps on watching.*
> *Nanak says, No one is high and no one is low before him.*

These are revolutionary words. If there is one thing, and one thing alone that Nanak stresses in the whole of Japuji — it is remembrance of his name; yet here in these lines Nanak declares that even remembrance has not the power. This is the last, the ultimate step coming into view. Nanak tries to snatch everything away from you — even remembrance. For if you have the slightest inkling that something has the power, you will protect yourself, your hold on yourself will be strengthened; all strength ultimately proves to be the strength of your ego.

So Nanak says there is no power even in the utterance — that you will take his name and somehow achieve. Then, in order that people not feel that if utterance has not the power perhaps silence does, Nanak says that even silence has no power. He is pulling everything out of your hands, anything he feels you might cling to. You may have thought: "Right! Talking is so much babble; silence is the answer!" So you become silent and go into meditation. But Nanak says that even silence has no power, for there is still the you in you; it is the you that had been talking that has now become silent. The quality of your being does not change. If the one who speaks is a sinner how can he become a saint merely by becoming silent?

Try to understand this business of qualities. If an evil person observes silence, he is still evil. How can his silence bring any change? A good man is a good man whether he speaks or is silent. A bad man is a bad man in both cases. An evil person will contrive some fresh device to harass others even while remaining silent.

Do you think merely by keeping quiet you can bring about a change in yourself or you will gain some power? What difference can there be? You were present in your words; you are present in your silence. You are still there. You will say, "I have become silent. I have entered into meditation." The same arrogance was there before, that you could speak well. Arrogance is blind — whether in silence or in speech.

I have heard: The ministry was being expanded and Mulla became a minister. He prided himself in his oratory and was confident he would impress and influence the public. Instead his speeches proved so long that the audience got bored. Because of the guards' instructions, nobody could leave the hall until the honored minister had finished his speech. He watched people yawning and stretching and squirming right before his eyes.

So he told his press agent to write shorter speeches, because people were getting bored. On the next occasion, Mulla started out hopefully to read the speech prepared for him. Yet the people still became bored; they were squirming in their seats. Mulla again rebuked his press agent: "Didn't I tell you to write shorter speeches? Yet you wrote such a long one that people were thoroughly bored. If this continues I am going to lose all my following."

"But, sir!" said the press agent, "That speech was quite short. No one said you had to read all three copies!"

Intelligence cannot be borrowed. People get speeches prepared, but quality cannot be bought or borrowed. The quality of one's individuality can easily be obtained, for no one else can give it to you.

If you are a Satan at heart and you sit in silence, you are still a Satan. Until yesterday you prided yourself on your words; today you can pride yourself on your silence.

The Zen fakir, Bokoju, went to his guru and said, "Now I have become absolutely silent; the emptiness within is complete. Please speak now."

The guru said "Go out first and throw away this silence, then come in."

"Throw away silence?" asked Bokoju, "All this time you were saying become empty!"

"That was the first step," explained the guru. "Now this is the second: be silent first, then throw away the silence or else your silence will make you stiff with arrogance. Who is it now who says, 'I am empty'? This is the very thing that has to be dropped."

The power lies neither in speaking nor in silence;
The power lies neither in asking nor in giving.

What will you give? What do you have to give? The beggar and the giver stand in the same place. One asks God for wealth, while the other distributes wealth or builds temples or feeds the poor; but both have their eye only on wealth. And it is possible that the beggar is humble, but how can the benefactor be humble? He will say, "I am a benefactor." But there is only one true benefactor. How can you be a benefactor? What have you got to give? You can give only what you have: pebbles and stones, pieces of gold and silver, paper currency. These are all artificially given their value by man.

The power lies neither in asking nor in giving;
The power lies neither in living nor in dying.

You cannot achieve him by living, so people think they should die. You see such people in ashrams everywhere. They don't have the courage to die in one stroke, so they do it gradually. This gradual dying is considered to be sannyas.

First they run away from the world, which cuts out ninety percent of their life. Then they stay in an ashram where they cut down their intake of food by eating only once a day. So one half of the remaining life is lost. Gradually they reduce their food even more; eventually they are walking around almost dead.

Nanak says that neither your living has the energy nor your dying. If you did not attain while alive, how can you attain after death? It is you who will die, is it not? And it is you again who will be born. You only shift positions, places; but you do not change.

What Nanak is saying is very significant.

> *The power lies neither in living nor in dying;*
> *The power lies neither in the wealth of kingdoms nor the resolves of the mind;*

Some people amass wealth, others collect meditation: they sit, they concentrate with great resolve, they do great penance. But Nanak says, even these do not have the power to attain.

And most significant of all, he says:

> *The power lies neither in remembrance nor in knowledge of the divine;*

Thoughts do not have the strength — and many people have said this — for thoughts are on the surface. Knowledge also has no strength, and many people have said it. Reading the scriptures, learning from the world or even from the guru — what power can they have? For it is always you at the center of the vortex.

Now this is interesting. Here all the paradox of the mystery manifests fully. All along Nanak has spoken of *surati*, his remembrance. And here he says: Even his remembrance has not the strength.

The first step is his remembrance, and the second step is what use is mere remembrance? For it is I who will remember. That remembrance will be my very own. It is I who will call out to him, all my qualities will be contained in the remembrance; and what strength can that have?

The second phase is now at hand, when the seeker lets go of everything — but only after doing everything, remember! Don't be in a hurry to stop. If there is the slightest lack, there will be no results. This is only at the very end when nothing is left to be done. The fact is, you do not do it; things fall away by themselves. If you quit consciously, it means something still remains to be done. You strive and you strive and you strive, then the moment comes when you fall down exhausted. This falling is not of your own doing — you suddenly find yourself flat! Nanak refers to this when he says nothing has the strength, the power. For if there is even a little bit of strength left, you are bound to go further.

> *The power lies neither in the world nor in the devices to be rid of sansara.*
> *The real power lies in his hands — who creates and keeps on watching.*

Nanak says that none of the methods and tricks devised to be free of sansara have any strength in them either. The authentic power lies in the hands of him who creates the world and, having created, admires it. It is all in his hands. All strength, all power lies in his hands. Become weak, helpless, you will get his support. If you are strong you need no support. God is the strength of the weak and helpless.

If you become helpless here, God awaits you there; but he belongs to the weak, not to the strong. The strong man does not need him; he believes in helping himself. He denies God from all his endeavors, his arrogance is still strong. He does not feel the need of God's help.

Once it happened this way: there was a Christian saint, Saint Theresa. She was an exceptional woman. One day she went to the village church and announced that she was going to construct a big church. The village was small and the people were poor. They thought it was a worthy idea, but wondered where would they get the funds. Who will give the money? One of them asked her, "How much money do you have to start with?"

Theresa put her hand in her pocket and produced two *paise*. "I have this with me: two paise!" she said exultantly. "We can start with this."

The people laughed, "We already doubted your sanity. Two paise for such a gigantic project! You need tens of millions of rupees, Theresa!"

St. Theresa replied, "You see these two paise? That is all I have, but what about him? He is with me. I have two paise plus God. How much does that make? And these two paise are only for beginning; later it will be he who has to see it through. How much can we poor mortals do? What is our capacity? It is worth not more than two paise; the rest is his. The two paise we have got, we shall go that far. He will see to the rest. Thy will be done! Let us make the beginning."

The church was completed and stands to this day. It is an enormous edifice. It could not have been completed by man's puny effort alone. His effort is worth only two paise. But you can set out to fulfill so grand a dream provided you remember that your own worth is so petty. Realizing your worth and taking shelter in the Lord's grace, you have infinite power and wealth to back you. You can move mountains provided you keep your trust in God and are fully conscious of your own insignificant strength.

No sooner do you become helpless than the fountain of the supreme strength begins to flow for you. As long as you rely on your own strength and give it importance, your power is not worth a penny.

Therefore Nanak keeps repeating again and again: neither this has the power nor that...he is depriving you of all your strength. Therefore, I say, the satguru snatches things away from you; he does not give. He takes away your all, he makes you helpless, he makes you weak. He leaves you in the state of a man in the middle of a desert, dying of thirst and no water anywhere. At the moment of the thirst that arises out of this helplessness — that moment you shall attain. You will call out, "Oh helper of the helpless!" and there he will be! When you are completely helpless you get the supreme help.

And remember: there is no one high, no one low here.

Therefore do not worry about anything else. before him, all are equal, all are the same. So do not fear that the strong will reach, or the virtuous will reach, or the benefactors, or those who meditate, will reach first. There is no one high and no one low here.

If you feel the difference of high and low, it is entirely your own doing; it is not because of him. If you lose yourself entirely, you shall rise high; if you save yourself, you shall be low.

Jesus has said: "He who loses himself will attain, and he who saves himself will lose forever."

Do not save yourself. This is one mistake that man can commit. Then he is left with two paise only; then he is really a pauper. Do not save yourself and you will find the two paise are nowhere – the whole of existence is at your disposal. The full energy of God is at your service. Then you become a king. You can be a beggar of your own making, but a king through his compassion.

CHAPTER 17

The Mines of Meditation

Having made night and day, the seasons, and the dates;
And air, water, fire and the underworlds;
Having made all of this, he established the earth as a
  dharmshala.
In it He created countless creatures of many colors and forms.
Their names are infinite.
Each is considered according to his own deeds.
God is true, and all his court is true.
Only before the Lord is each one tested;
Each is ranked by his glance.
There the raw is sifted from the ripe.
Nanak says, One who is raw will dissolve away.

Some things have to be understood before going into these sutras.

He who takes life to be the goal wanders. Life is only an opportunity and not the goal. It is not the destination but a path; we have to reach somewhere by way of it. Do not assume that the very fact that you are alive means you have arrived. Life is not an accomplishment but only a process. If you pass through it well you arrive; if not, you go astray.

He is an atheist who takes life to be everything. He is a theist whose goal lies beyond life; for him life is a transient camp. Nanak calls the world a *dharmshala*, a traveler's bungalow. It is like an inn or rest place where you have to stop for a while before you proceed onward, but you shouldn't make your home in it. He who makes it his home denies himself the authentic home. You had set out to attain something, but if you took a way station as your abode how would you reach the destination? Who will continue to travel once he has made a home?

Sansara is not a home. Those who make a home of it we call householders. A sannyasin is one for whom samaras is a waiting room, not a house. Both stay in the same world — where else can they go? They stay in the same house, but their attitude towards the house is different. The worldly man thinks his home to be his haven; the sannyasin takes it to be a resting place. He has somewhere else to go, and he never forgets his destination — this is *surati*, remembrance.

One who keeps this remembrance alive, who does not lose the thread of remembrance, will stay in dharmshalas, but will keep moving on. No inn will lure him to stay on. He will stay in the world and out of it. You are what your destination is; where you go, that itself is you. You are not where you physically are, you are where your mind is. This has to be understood.

The majority of people — barring very few — take what they have obtained as the ultimate. Actually, it is not even the beginning, it is not even the door or even the steps leading to the door of your destination. You are still on the path; the steps are yet to come. When the steps begin to appear, know that religion has arrived within you. Those on the path are the worldly people. Those in whose lives the steps have appeared are the seekers; and he who has already entered the mansion of the Lord is an enlightened being. You are still on the path; the steps are far away, for you have not even begun your spiritual practice.

The deep-rooted cause for this illusion is that you are contented with what has been given to you. Remember, a religious man is absolutely contented in one sense; but in another sense it is difficult to find a more discontented person than he. He is contented in that he has no complaints against God. He is discontented in that he is very dissatisfied with himself.

An irreligious person has a thousand complaints against God: You have not given me this, you have not given me that. He has no complaints about himself. He is satisfied with his own self. That is his grave because how can you then develop, how can you progress? How will you open your wings to touch the skies? Instead you will remain a prisoner in your own nest, and will die in your cage.

You should feel contented with God and discontented with yourself, but things are reversed. We are deeply satisfied with ourselves and thoroughly dissatisfied with the world. Only we appear to be right, all the rest of the world is in the wrong. This attitude is the very thing that is wrong with us. Except for man, there is no mistake or miscalculation anywhere in existence. All the world flows in peace and joy except for man. There is no obstruction anywhere; only within you is there something clogged somewhere.

A religious man has a deep sense of dissatisfaction with himself. He feels as if he is not worthy of God, that he is not fit to worship or adore him. He is apprehensive whether God will accept him as he is. One thought keeps hammering in his brain: I must make myself worthy of him, I must be a worthy recipient of his acceptance. I must raise a throne within my heart that befits his majesty. I must be so qualified that he accepts being my guest.

So a religious person is critical of his own self. Gradually a moment comes when he evolves to such a degree, he has cleansed himself sufficiently, that he becomes a throne for the Lord. God is bound to knock at his door — if not today, then tomorrow. Then there will not be a moment's delay. No sooner are you ready than he knocks at your door. The delay lasts only as long as you are not prepared to receive him. Screaming and shouting, weeping and wailing is of no avail. What is needed is your preparation.

And preparation means transformation. You will have to change yourself in many, many ways. If you search within yourself, you will find that not only God but you yourself would not be prepared to step inside you — as you are now. Had you to love a person just like yourself, you would refuse.

Therefore, deep down nobody loves his own self. You are not fit to love your own self, and that is why people are afraid to be alone. If you have to stay alone for an hour or two, you become restless. You look for a friend or go to a club or cinema or market, or play the radio, or watch the TV, or read a paper. How can one sit all by oneself doing nothing you ask. You are bored with yourself. You are not good company to your own self, and yet you desire the company of God? If you yourself are not prepared to stay with yourself, who else could be ready to stay with you?

God is a faraway prospect! To attain God means that the most profound peak of existence enters within you; but then you have to create a space for him within yourself. You are so shallow that a small thing causes a storm within you. A slight movement and you tremble, a slight insult and you burn within, a little suffering and you feel all hell is let loose on you. You are affected by little, little things; there is no depth in you. Someone throws a pebble and a storm rages in you. You are not a deep ocean.

The ocean is so deep that even if the Himalayas fall into it, the waves will be blissfully oblivious of the happening. So many rivers pour into the sea, but the waters of the sea do not rise by even an inch. The ocean stays the same, whatever may happen.

You desire God. Have you ever thought what your state would be if He were suddenly to descend on you? You will be in a dilemma. Where will you seat him? How will you welcome him? You will be so shaken the only thing to do is run away from home.

You have no throne befitting him. Were it to be made of gold and precious stones perhaps you could have had one made, but you have to make a peacock throne of your own heart. You have to fashion a throne of love. You can buy gold in the market, but where can you buy love?

Were a palace required to be made, that would be easy. Then God would already have descended to some king's palace. But you have to build a palace within, a palace of emptiness, a palace of meditation. That is a very difficult task; the journey is long.

If you take as your home the place where you find yourself, you are a worldly mortal. If you take this world as only a dharmshala where you rest for a while and then start again, then you are a sannyasin.

There is a very old Sufi story: A man went to a Sufi fakir asking the secret of attaining God. The fakir proceeded to recount the following tale:

The Mines of Meditation

A woodcutter went every day to the forest to cut wood. Each day he would gather wood, carry it to town and sell it. Whatever he got would be barely enough to give him a meal. Sometimes he managed to buy a little food; at other times he went to sleep hungry.

A fakir who used to stay in the same jungle watched him every day. He was filled with pity for this miserable man who barely managed to keep alive. One day he told him, "Every day for the last so many years I have been watching you. You are such a foolish fellow. Why don't you go still further into the jungle?" The wood-cutter asked, "How will that help?" The fakir replied, "Whoever went deeper within became wealthy. Go in, and you will find mines of copper."

The man went a little further and he found the copper mine. He began to sell copper. Once again he met the fakir who said, "Foolish fellow, go still further. There are mines of silver there." The man went and found the silver mines. He now began to sell silver and became very rich.

One day he met the fakir again who said to him, "Had you any sense you would have taken the hint by now. You have failed to understand. Go still further, you fool, for there are gold mines there!" The man penetrated deeper into the forest and found the gold, but he got totally involved in the gold.

He must have been a man like us, this woodcutter. Wherever we go we get involved. We don't think of getting up from where we sit. The fakir felt sorry for this man. One day he went to him again and said, "You really lack intelligence. So many times I goaded you to go onward to go still further, and you have not understood me. Now you are outwardly very rich, but within you are as miserable a wretch as before. Go still further, there are mines of diamonds." The man went further in.

Then, after some years, the fakir happened to meet him again. He rebuked him as before. Even though he was the owner of huge palaces and all that wealth could buy, the fakir was sorry for him. "You are as poor as ever within," said the fakir. "All this gold and silver and diamonds are on the outside. Go still further.

"Now where?" asked the man. "Why don't you leave me in peace?

Why are you goading me on and on? Now what is left to be attained after getting these diamonds?"

The fakir replied, "Beyond that is my ashram and only I can give you the genuine diamonds. They are diamonds of meditation. Until now you sought the mines outside, now your search for the mines within must begin." And though the man had heard about the jewels within, he was not ready to seek them. Besides, he claimed that this talk was beyond him, so he begged to be allowed to stay where he was.

The fakir said, "As you wish. But remember, these mines within will not remain forever — today I am, tomorrow I may not be. The mines you dig now will remain. They always were, they always will be."

The mines of meditation manifest rarely — sometimes once in a thousand years. Sometimes some person discovers it and becomes an entrance to it. Such a person is the guru, and Nanak refers to his temple as *gurudwara*, guru's door — a beautiful name for a temple. He who comes upon the mine of meditation during his lifetime becomes an opening for others, but he does not live forever.

And you? You are so blind that you go past the door and do not see it! Your eyes are fixed on the visible wealth and not the true wealth that is invisible.

Remember this maxim: Still further. Until you reach God you should hold it always to your heart. If you halt before that, you will wander.

Therefore the thirst, the dissatisfaction of the sannyasin knows no bounds. His thirst is satisfied only when he drinks God. Lesser waters will not do for him. This is exactly why Nanak refers to this world as a dharmshala.

> *Having made night and day, the seasons, and the dates;*
> *And air, water, fire and the underworlds;*
> *Having made all of this, he established the earth as a dharmshala.*
> *In it He created countless creatures of many colors and forms.*
> *Their names are infinite.*

So the first thing is that the world is only a resting place. The deeper you take in this fact, the more useful will it prove that you must not stop where you are, that stagnation is death and that you have to go further and still further...till you reach his door. You may rest if you are tired, but do not make a home out of the inn.

You are bound to get tired, for the journey is long and the destination far away. You will also wander time and again, for it is not a path that is marked out, a highway! Man has to walk himself and carve out his route. Therefore the road to his abode is very long. As birds fly in the air and leave no trace behind, so the enlightened one walks in his path and reaches but leaves no marks behind. The space is as empty as ever.

When you set out, you cannot walk on the footprints of others. There is no loan system in the realm of truth. No one else can give you truth; others can merely suggest, give hints. Love you can get, also the guru's grace, but truth you will have to find yourself. His grace can lend strength to your feet to continue walking but cannot give you the path. His compassion can offer up confidence and encouragement, but not draw a map for you. His compassion can give you the strength to carry on and be persistent in your effort so that you do not waver, you do not give up. But you must walk the path alone.

And the path is such that it is formed only if you begin to walk. It is not a carved-out route marked on a map. There is no ready-made device to take you to God. Each person has to find his own way himself.

This is the difficulty, and this is the dignity of purpose. For if it were a well-beaten track that thousands had trodden before, the joy and fulfillment in reaching and attaining God would not have been so special.

Whenever a person attains God he finds him new, fresh, and original — as if you are the first one he has met! As if this happening has never taken place before. It is not a stale affair, it is not as if others before you have met him — that you find millions of footprints leading to his door. No, it is as if you are the very first person he meets. He is like a virgin waiting for you. God is always a virgin. Had he been married many times before there would be nothing of interest left in him. His virginity is eternal; he is an eternal bachelor. Whoever reaches him finds him fresh, new and chaste, unspoiled as a virgin — just as the morning dew or the first rays of the rising sun.

There is no map that can be handed over to you, for life itself is a constant change. Everything changes every moment. The way I reached will be of no use to you; it was my special way. You will have to find yours.

For Nanak says God has made infinite creatures, infinite souls. He has cast in millions and millions of colors and forms. Each one is unique. If each person is unique, unparalleled, no one person's path can be of use to another. My understanding can be of use to you but not my path. My insight can help you to find your way but your way will be entirely your own personal way. It shall bear your imprint just as your thumbprint can be only yours. There are millions upon millions of people in this world, but never will your thumbprint be repeated. If existence has caused your thumb to be unique, how much more original will your soul be! Imagine it.

New research has involved itself in very deep issues. Science now declares that the internal organs of each individual are peculiar to that person. No two people have kidney, heart or liver exactly the same as another person. Not only the thumbprint but every cell of your body is specially made and designed for you, and you alone. You are incomparable. God creates you, makes each cell, each atom in your body just for you. He never creates another to match you. So your path of attainment will also be unique. This produces a sense of helplessness and many difficulties, but it is also the grandeur and dignity that you have reached by a route that is absolutely new, untrodden; it cannot be stale for you.

If this is understood well, you will know that we are talking of the soul, the *atman*. We can produce machines in tens and thousands. There are millions of Ford cars whose parts fit one another very easily. Sometimes it is impossible to distinguish between two cars, so much alike are they. Not so the soul; no two souls are alike. Each atman is unique.

This means, were we to use the language of poet, saint or devotee, the atman cannot be machine-made. It seems that God makes each and every atman with his very own hands. This is why he is called the creator. If you tell a painter to make another painting to match one he has already done, he will be unable to do so. He cannot make an exact copy of the original. There will be a difference. With the passage of time the painter himself changes; his moods change. He is no longer in the same state of heart and head as when he made the original.

A friend came to visit Picasso when he was making a picture. He was so lost in his work that the friend thought it best not to disturb him. When the painting was put up for sale the friend bought it; it was worth millions of rupees. One day he took the painting along with him when he visited Picasso and asked him to authenticate it. Many fake copies were sold in the market as Picasso's own works, but this one the friend had seen him paint with his own eyes. Picasso replied, "I have made it all right, but it is not genuine." The friend was puzzled, for an authentic painting according to him was one that the painter paints himself. "It is authentic," explained Picasso, "in the sense that I have made it, but it is inauthentic insofar as it is only a reflection of my earlier paintings. I was copying my own style. The creator in me was not present at the time."

"What do you mean by the creator in you?" asked the friend.

"I am the creator when I make a unique painting, when I am totally original."

Therefore poets, painters, sculptors are closest to God when they produce something really original; they are as near God as a saint or devotee. A sculptor carving the images at the caves at Ajanta or Ellora was as close to God when he created these as even Buddha was.

Whenever you create something that is not a copy, not an imitation, there is no prayer that is greater. For you are nearest to God; in fact, in the moment of creation you are like him! You too are a creator. Therefore creativity gives so much joy. How happy and satisfied you feel when you create something, however small, however insignificant.

A small child makes a house of cards and tells everybody, "I have built a house." Another builds a sand castle that he knows will be blown away by the breezes, but how happy he feels! He dances with joy. All moments of bliss in life are moments of creativity. Whenever you make something you get pleasure out of it. And those whose lives pass without any creativity find nothing but sorrow and suffering.

Why is it so? Why do you feel happy when you make something? Because in the act of creativity you get a glimpse of the creator. He is the creator but you too are a creator of sorts in that moment. You plant a seed in your garden. When the plant appears and bears leaves and flowers, how much pleasure it gives you. This joy is the same joy that God feels when He sees the earth bloom. There is only a difference of quantity, not quality.

Nanak says, "He has created lives in many colors and forms; and their names are many, infinite." If you were only able to recognize this creativity, this expanse of creation that spread to eternity! But it is difficult to recognize God. He is forever hidden, but if you can recognize his visible performance then you have made the first acquaintance; the first step is taken. Look at the universe. It is filled with a deep and profound arrangement. The moon rises, so does the sun. The stars revolve, seasons come and go, the morning comes and flowers open, the birds sing. The brooks bubble down the rocks, rivers rush to meet the sea. Clouds gather and pour down the waters that rise by evaporation into the skies. The water goes back again to the stream. It is all a well-organized arrangement. The world is a cosmos, not a chaos...if you understand this significant arrangement of nature.

The more you begin to understand this order of things in the world, and the more you begin to perceive the flow of this order, to the same extent will you begin to remember the hand that directs all things in this world. For no arrangement works without a source of direction, and the hand that directs this vast arrangement must be infinitely vast and powerful. This is why the Hindus say: "He has a thousand hands. He has an infinite number of hands, for this is no small work. The infinite existence can be guided only by infinite hands."

Nanak says, "He made the day, he made the night. He made the seasons, the air, the water, the fire, the earth and the netherworld. He has made all — all! And in the midst of it all he made the earth for you to rest awhile in your journey to the infinite."

This earth is a resting place only. Do not make your house in it. People make all kinds of houses, forgetting it is a resting place. Imagine if a man puts up in a traveler's bungalow for the night, and in the morning he forgets and takes the place as home, takes all its involvements upon himself, all its worries. Weighted down with sorrow and suffering, he goes about asking the way to peace and quiet.

If he is asked, "Why have you made a home of your *dharmshala?*" he replies, "It is difficult to leave so abruptly. I also understand having made a mistake, but it will take me time. I shall leave gradually."

The question is not of leaving gradually. The question is not of leaving at all. It only requires right perception, and that takes time. You can perceive in a moment if you are ready and willing. You can see clearly that where you stand is no more than a waiting room, for you were not always here. Where were you before birth? Where will you be after death? This is a fancy fete that lasts only a few days. In this short span you have clung so tightly to things that are and also to things that are not. A man clings to his wealth or possessions but he also clings to his desires, his dreams of the future.

Mulla Nasruddin built a house for himself. He took me to see it. He had laid out a big garden. As we walked along we came to an artificial pond. "This is the hot water pond for us to bathe in in winter," he informed me. We went a little further and came upon another pond. "And this is the cold water pond for us to bathe in in summer." Then pointing to a third pond which had no water he said, "This is for the days when we do not wish to bathe."

Man makes arrangements for bathing as well as non-bathing. He arranges for what he has and for what he does not have. You are already weighted down by the harassment of your possessions, and also obsessed with the anxiety of things that might have been or might come to be. Look into your mind: you will find it is filled with past anxieties that no longer exist. Some incident that took place twenty years ago is still revolving in your mind. Now this is long past and nothing remains of it. Or you are thinking of something that may happen twenty years from now. You increase your anxieties a thousand-fold this way.

And for whom do you worry? For an inn along the road? You begin to be anxious and worry about those who also happen to stay in this inn while you are there. There is the husband, the wife, the son, the father, the mother, and all of them you just happened to meet in the dharmshala. You have involved yourself completely in them, and taken upon yourself all sorts of anxiety for them, while you have completely forgotten that you have a destination to reach. You have all the concerns except the real one, to reach home!

In it He created countless creatures of many colors and forms.
Their names are infinite.
Each is considered according to his own deeds.

Whatever you do in this world is very significant, for your ultimate destiny is based on your actions. The world is a rest-house where you tarry for a while and then move ahead. But you get involved in so many things. The inn is taken away from you one day but the web of your actions remains with you. You will die, the world will no longer be for you, but what you did in the world will follow you like a shadow. Your actions will hound you for infinite births, and the last judgment will be based on the sum total of all your actions.

Now this is worth pondering over. If the thought remains in your mind that this world is but a resting place where you have pitched a tent for a short while, then many actions will disappear immediately. Will you shout at your wife when you know that this togetherness is but for a short while? What meaning will your anger have? You consider your wife so much your own that you quarrel with her. But when death comes you go alone; she does not go with you. While she is left behind, your anger towards her, the pain you inflicted on her, the words you spoke in displeasure to her, they will go with you. Your dreams likewise will remain behind, but all that you did in your dreams goes with you. In this bargain things turn out to be expensive, for nothing comes to hand save loss and defeat. Man attains nothing from sansara, he only loses everything.

Nanak says that if you keep constantly in your mind that this world is only a resting place, almost all of your actions will stop by themselves. On a railway platform or in a waiting room, what is one's

The Mines of Meditation   413

attitude? If someone steps on your toes you tend to overlook it, for you know that such things are inevitable in a crowd. You do not get angry.

Mulla Nasruddin didn't marry until late in life. When he reached fifty his friends asked him why he was afraid to marry. This is what Mulla said: "Once, while coming out of a cinema house, I happened to step on a woman's foot. She immediately whirled around and pounced on me. Her eyes were raining fire, her face was flushed. I tremble even now as I am narrating this. I was sure she would kill me, squeeze the very life out of me with her bare hands. But the next moment she cooled down. 'Sorry,' she said. 'I thought it was my husband.' That very moment I decided never to marry. A stranger she was ready to forgive. She was ready to concede it was a mistake only because it was a stranger."

We forgive others but fail to forgive our very own. Is it not astonishing? We forgive strangers but not those near and dear to us. What is the difference? A stranger is a stranger. He is a fellow traveler in the dharmshala. The one near you is no longer a stranger. We are under illusions about him; we create a homelike relationship with him.

He who considers the whole world as a temporary inn — for him, everyone is a stranger — and he is! Just because your wife has been with you for the past thirty years, do you think she is not a stranger? You are wrong; this is mere delusion. Long association is no criterion.

Nobody can be your very own in this world. There is no way to make someone your own — except God. God alone can be yours, yet you do not seek him! You have taken strangers to be your own. Because a son is born to you, you take it for granted that he is no stranger to you. Life will prove otherwise. A father can do nothing regarding his son's life. You want him to be one thing; he becomes another. You want one thing; he wants something else. Your expectations are one thing; his desires are something else. What father is ever satisfied and totally accepting with his son? The son is born to you, but he is still very much a stranger to you. No father can predict what turn his son's life will take. There is no way to find out. Husbands fail to reform their wives, and wives fail to change their husbands.

Who can reform whom? We cause more harm, more damage than anything else.

We are all strangers, living according to our own actions, each traveling his own path. No one can reform us or change us. It can be that we meet for a while at the crossroads. We take this meeting so seriously. Can you make a woman your very own merely by walking around the fire seven times, as in the Hindu wedding ceremony? Seven rounds or seven thousand rounds make no difference. Nothing changes. You remain where you were.

In the mundane world no matter how hard you try, you cannot get rid of the other, who must remain the alien. No matter how close you get to a person, there is always a distance. This is the bane of all lovers. The lover wants to come so close to the beloved that there is no distance between them. But the closer he comes, the more he realizes that the differences still persist. When they were far apart there was the hope that closeness would make the separateness disappear, but on coming closer and closer he realizes that the distance can never be eradicated. There is no way to do so. You can sit very close to one another: you bodies will be close, but the distance between you remains the same. You are in your own thoughts, your beloved in hers. You have your own mind; your beloved has hers. How can the two ever meet?

All unions in this world are false meetings. Separation is true. Meeting is but a dream. Your only union can be with God. This is the only possible union; therefore Kabir, Nanak, Dadu kept singing, "I am Rama's bride!" Kabir says, "One thing I have understood, and that is enough — that one can only be the bride of Rama." Only there is the union complete; all distances fall away and there is no without and no within. There alone will your thirst be quenched, where all is one and there are no two. There alone shall we meet him who is our very own, and then the anguish of separation will end. Before that the worry, the unrest will continue.

No matter how many wells you drink from, no matter how many shores you walk on, there is only one river that can actually quench your thirst, and we are not in the least worried about this. All that you do in your state of wandering, gathers around you. The collection of these actions determines your future...every day. If you get up in the morning and you are angry, an impression, an imprint is created. If again you get up the next morning and are angry, this impression becomes more pronounced. If you again are angry on the third day, this impression forms a deep furrow within you. Now there is every likelihood of your losing your temper on the fourth day, for man lives by his impressions till he attains buddhahood. Then habits no longer affect him; he lives in full consciousness. You live by your habits. What happened yesterday is repeated today. What is happening today is sure to happen again tomorrow. So all your actions create your habits.

The doctrine of karma is very scientific. It has nothing to do with philosophy. It is a straight and simple psychological fact that whatever you do and keep on doing, increases your tendency to do the same thing, again and again. Whatever you are not in the habit of doing, increases your tendency to not doing it. Doing becomes a habit. You do things mechanically. Go back into your own past and you shall find that your life is nothing but constant repetition. You do the same things every day.

People come and tell me, "I don't want to be angry, but anger happens." Then I ask them, "Then what do you do after you are angry?" They say, "I feel terrible remorse and I repent. I know I should not have been angry and then I feel so miserable."

I tell them, "Forget about your anger, but stop the worrying. Give up repentance. This at least you can do. I know you cannot control the anger." They are nonplussed. "What kind of advice is this? If despite repenting the anger doesn't leave, how can you say not even to repent? How will I get rid of anger that way?"

I say to them, "Look back at your lives. You've repented a thousand times and yet your anger is unchanged. Just carry out this experiment and see! Do not repent! You must make an effort to break one half of your habit at least. Anger and repentance together make one complete habit. It is not so difficult to do. The need to get angry will be there, which you won't be able to give up, but the repentance is your personal affair. It has nothing to do with anybody else.

Anger always involves the other. If someone calls you names how can you not be angry? If you are not angry what will people think of you? If you let him go the news will spread around town like wildfire, and others may turn around and indulge in the same sport with you. Anger is a collective affair, whereas repentance is simple and doesn't concern anyone else. You repent in privacy. Please just give this up."

The man who had sought advice returned and said to me, "It is as difficult to give up repenting as it is to give up anger."

A lady comes to me whose husband is addicted to alcohol. They were married twenty years ago, and ever since then she has been after him to leave off drinking. He keeps drinking and she keeps reprimanding him. One day she said to me, "For heaven's sake, do something! This man of mine will not stop drinking. I've tried my best. Please make him see sense." I told her, "Stop nagging him! Say nothing to him about it for three months, then come back to me and I shall do whatever is necessary for him. Alcohol affects the chemistry of the system, so it won't be possible for him to give it up so soon. It has permeated his every cell. Anyway, do as I say and then I shall take care of him."

On the third day she returned. "It's impossible. I just can't do it! It's totally habitual to reproach him every time he fills his glass."

I said to her, "Now you can understand how hard it must be for your husband. You can't give up mere speaking, and what kick is there in only talking? For twenty years you have been telling him, now for three months give up saying anything to him about it. If you give me proof that you have broken your habit, I shall take your husband in hand." But she, poor thing, can't complete the three months! And I am adamant. "I won't say anything to your husband until you have completed three months," I tell her.

Now she understands what a difficult task it is. She can't keep quiet for even a day. Her husband drinks twice a day, and she taunts him ten times — that is her drug. All habits are drugs and when repeated they get into your system.

The doctrine of karma says only that when you do a thing, the possibility of your doing it again increases. When you do not do a thing, the possibility of your not doing it increases accordingly. If you put up in a dharmshala and behave as if it is your house, you are forming a wrong habit. The rest-house will one day be no more for you, but what you do in it will stick to you even after death, for that is entirely yours. Nothing but your actions go with you when you leave the world. Remember this and act accordingly.

You picked up a diamond you found along the way. This diamond does not go along with you; it shall remain here, but your act of picking it up and pocketing it goes with you. Your actions are the only possessions you take along with you. If you do wrong, you give a wrong direction to your future; if you act right you give a right direction to your future.

And if you live in full awareness you are preparing for liberation. For the more a person develops his awareness the more his habits break. Then he does not live by habit but by awareness. In every situation he makes decisions in full consciousness and not by sheer past habits.

A man swears at you, you stand up at once, your fists clenched. During a plane flight, the pilot and a passenger got down to hot words. The situation got worse and they began to abuse each other. The other passengers said, "Hey, what are you doing? Can't you see there are ladies in the plane?" The angry passenger replied, "The ladies can leave the plane. I am determined to see this through." In his anger he doesn't even realize what he is saying, suggesting that the ladies can get off the plane in mid-air.

He is not in his right senses. He doesn't know what he is saying, but the fight has to take place because it is beyond his control. How can one who is not conscious be in his senses? And you are all like that. Whatever you do, you go on doing mechanically without ever pondering on what you are doing and why.

Wake up a little. First of all, wake up to the fact that this world is not so valuable that you should be so anxious and worried about it. If a man swears at you, remember, neither he nor his abusive words are so important that you should be so upset about it. Nor is your ego so important that you create an uproar for its sake. This is but a resting place; if someone treads on your feet, do not be upset.

Mulla Nasruddin was coming out of the auditorium during the intermission. He stepped on another man's foot. The man was almost writhing in pain, but considering that it was dark and the lights had just come on, he thought that Mulla just did not see his foot, so he did not say anything. Mulla reentered the hall and went up to the man. "Brother, was it you whose foot I stepped on?" The man thought he had come to apologize. He said, "Yes." Mulla looked back and called out to his wife, "Come this way. This is our row!" He had stamped on the man's foot just so he would be able to identify his own row.

The man who abuses you has his own reasons. There is no need for you to get upset about it. The world is a marketplace filled with crowds and crowds of people, and each is busy searching on his own. You have nothing to do with anyone, nor has anyone anything to do with you. As each one is playing his own game, you are bound to bump into one another at times. It is inevitable with so much traffic on the road.

If you can keep this in mind, your anger will disappear, and so will your hatred, jealousy, envy — and all the actions that spring from them. The day such actions disappear you will feel pity for people, for each man is in a state of unconsciousness. The day before, anger invaded you, and on this day it is replaced by pity and kindness. Each man has gone astray. People live in darkness. It is nobody's fault that they are asleep. If in their sleep they jabber insults and abuses, would you say anything to them? You would note they are asleep and dismiss the incident.

If a drunk hurls abuse at you, you think he is not aware of what he is saying, but, alas, this is the state everybody is in. They have been drugged through infinite births, and are profoundly asleep. If your awareness has developed even to a slight degree, you will feel pity for them — how much they suffer, these people all around you! They have taken the rest-house as their ancestral home and fight in the courts over possession of it.

When you begin to feel pity for others, the shape of your actions will change accordingly. Where your deeds were evil, they will now be good; where you planned and contrived to harm others, you will go all out to help them. You won't even hesitate to help those who revile you, for you will be filled with compassion for them.

What is critical here is the relationship between knowledge and kindness. Knowledge means awakening. Kindness means the qualitative change in your actions due to this awakening. When there is ignorance within, there is violence without; when knowledge is within, compassion is without. They are associated with one another, but knowledge, discernment and intelligence must be based on actions.

This is a funny situation: you think of all the good things in the world and do all the bad. Your thoughts turn to the good, while your actions are bad. But what you think is of no account; only your actions will be your testimony, your measure. Even criminals think great and noble thoughts. Ask a murderer what he thinks and you will find his thoughts soaring into the skies. High thinking is a trick for committing evil deeds.

Understand this subtlety: when a man does evil he is always repentant within. When a man insults someone or is hard on someone, he is filled with remorse. He feels that this should not have happened, so he thinks good thoughts of kindness, of forgiveness, of pity. Next time, he promises himself, he will be kind and understanding. Thus he strikes a balance, enough good thoughts to match the evil deeds, to hide his bad deeds from himself. People who are evil, vile, always think great, noble things.

The reverse is also true. Those who do good deeds have bad thoughts. To the aware person, both these states are wrong. Thieves always think of doing charity; they are very generous. It is they who think of building temples, feeding the poor or clothing them, all because the sting of thieving is with them. They steal a million rupees and give a thousand in charity. In this way they strive to achieve a balance. A sinner bathes in the Ganges, distributes a little here and there to the destitute, and feels he has atoned for his misdeeds. He comes home relieved of his guilt. But what does he do now that he is unburdened of his sins? Exactly what he did before, but now he will do it with an easy mind. This is even more dangerous, this feeling of unconcern.

A woman visited a psychologist. She was in the habit of dropping things, which made her very nervous and restless. She felt herself to be in great trouble.

After six months of treatment the doctor asked her how she felt. "I still drop things, but it no longer makes me feel nervous."

A man does a few good deeds and on the strength of these he is unperturbed about his actions. He feels he has balanced his bad deeds with the good, and now he is ready to indulge in more evil. Now he holds the key to the situation: whenever you do wrong, counteract it with good deeds.

No country is as sinful as India today. It happened when we discovered the device of good deeds. The Ganges flows in this country and it can wash away all sins. Commit a sin, then go and make an offering in the temple; or do evil, and offer a coconut to Hanuman, the Monkey-God. Poor Hanuman! He has nothing to do with your evil; it's not his fault that you sinned. He has no share in your misdeeds, and yet you make him a partner in it. Make your mistake here, atone for it there; and you are ready for fresh misconduct. Whenever you sin you negate it with a good deed so that the sting of misdeeds is eradicated. Thus you repair the harm done to your image of yourself as a good and righteous person.

What you think will hold no water. Your destiny is determined by your actions and not your thoughts. The astonishing fact is that you always put off a good deed, postpone it for tomorrow, but you never say the same when it comes to sin. Then you are eager for it this very moment. If you want to kill someone you kill immediately, for you know that a little delay and you will never be able to do it. When you want to be angry you become angry at once. Have you ever heard anyone say, "All right, I shall come tomorrow and be angry with you. Right now I'm busy." Abuse him and he will drop everything to retaliate, even if he were fetching medicine for his wife on her deathbed. In effect he is saying, "Let her die if she will. She has to die anyhow, but now I have to settle this score." You know very well you won't be able to settle it later.

When his father died Gurdjieff was nine years old. His father's last advice to him was, "Whenever you are incited to anger, let twenty-four hours pass before you retaliate." So whenever anyone abused him, he would say he would reply after twenty-four hours. He had promised his father when he was still a child and understood nothing, but he kept his word.

Because of this promise, Gurdjieff writes, his whole life changed.

Can anyone still be angry a whole day later? In that time the futility of anger becomes obvious, the stupidity of the whole affair! And ninety-nine times out of a hundred, we come to realize that what the man said about us was correct: he didn't abuse me, he described what I am. If that man called you a thief, after a day's reflection you realize he is right – you are a thief! If he called you dishonest you will come to realize that you are dishonest. This is not abuse but an accurate description of what you are, an eye-opener!

Many a time Gurdjieff would go back to the person concerned and thank him, for what he said was absolutely true. As for his anger, he would say that was of no account. He was thankful for his pointing out the fault in him. "What I could not see, you have shown me." He who diagnoses your illness is a doctor; so he is no enemy.

Or, after twenty-four hours his attitude would be: "I have pondered all day over your words but I found they do not apply to me at all. And since they don't apply to me why should I be angry? I have nothing to do with them. Perhaps you were talking about someone else." Or if he found that the epithet applied to him he would thank the person. If it did not apply there would be no need to retaliate.

Whenever you are angry, you are angry because what someone has told you strikes a note of truth. Have you ever thought about this? If you are not a thief this accusation does not bother you.

But the reverse is the case: you are a thief, going about as a holy man. You go to the temple, tell your beads and practice all kinds of camouflage. Now this man has caught on to your authentic character and he calls you a thief. You feel the blow. Remember, truth always hurts, untruth never. For untruths have no strength, no power of their own.

We indulge in bad deeds immediately, and postpone the good ones for later. A Marwari was once sitting behind a vetiver screen, writing his accounts. It was a hot summer's day. A beggar came along and asked for a coin. The Marwari told him to move on; there was no money there.

The beggar said, "Then give me some bread." The Marwari said rudely, "There is no bread."

"Give me some old clothes," the beggar persisted, as beggars usually do. "Get lost!" shouted the Marwari, "There is nothing here."

"Then what are you doing here, sitting behind the screen?" the beggar asked. "Come with me, join me. Whatever we get we shall share between us."

If someone asks you even for two *paise* or a piece of bread you put him off. You postpone doing good, but you gird your loins that very instant when some evil has to be done; for that you are ready and waiting.

Stop the evil and don't defer the good, and your life will change for the better. To evil say, "Tomorrow," the good, do immediately, for who can trust the morrow? If this becomes the thread of your life, you will be incapable of doing evil. Now you act like the Marwari, postponing the good and doing the evil immediately. But then tomorrow never comes for you to do good, whereas evil happens through you every day! The whole chain of your actions becomes a chain of thorns; no flowers ever bloom there.

Each is considered according to his own deeds.
God is true, and all his court is true.

Remember, only if you are true can you gain entry to his court. You may deceive the whole world but can you deceive your own self? You know what you are. The whole world may hold you in awe and reverence, but you know for yourself what you actually are. The existence that is hidden within you is God himself. How can you cheat him? Before him you stand in all your nakedness. Everything is open there, nothing is covered. Therefore, only if you are true can you enter his court.

People ask, "How is God to be attained?" I say they should ask, "How is one to be true?" They shouldn't say, "God cannot be seen," but should ask, "Why can't God be seen?"

False eyes cannot see God. True eyes are needed to see God. A true heart is required to experience truth; for only the like can recognize the like. As you stand now, you are absolutely false. False does not mean only that you do not speak the truth: your very being is false. Your appearance is false, your dealings are false. You say one thing, you think another; while what you do is contrary both to what you say and what you think. Your word, your being cannot be trusted. You yourself have no faith in what you do. Are you doing what you want to do? Are you thinking exactly what you say?

But then the thought is very frightening! For if you begin to be authentic, the house you made within the resting place will begin to crumble. It is but a halt in your journey; that you have made it your permanent abode is the biggest lie. You have set out in a paper boat to sail across the sea of existence. How will you sail? You will have to remain sitting on the shore, for it is too dangerous to lower such a boat into the water. No sooner does it touch water than it will be no more; the paper will dissolve.

People come to me worrying that life will become difficult if they begin to be authentic. Yes, it will! Because you have based your lives on falsity. It will be really difficult in the beginning. If you do not change, then too it is difficult; for what happiness have you attained in your life, what flowers have bloomed in your life, what fragrance have you experienced? What is there in your life, on the strength of which you can say that your life has been worth living? There is nothing. And you know it.

Life as it is is no less difficult, but you have become addicted to it. When you turn towards truth, your old habits will break. Right now when a person you detest visits you say, "Welcome. I am so pleased that you have come." But inside yourself you curse the day for bringing such a person to your door. Now your day is ruined.

If he is even a little intelligent, a little aware, he will see the lie behind your words. No matter what your lips pronounce, your eyes give you away. Your face, your movements will be very different from your words. They will have nothing in common. When a person is truly happy he does not go about declaring his happiness; every pore of his body is filled with joy and cheer. You can make out a person who is really happy. But alas, the other man is also asleep. You think you really mean what you say. This is why flattery pays in the world. The listener can always detect the deception in your words if he listens carefully.

The English poet Yeats was given a Nobel Prize. He was a genuine person, simple and artless. His works were filled with his authenticity. When a meeting was held to congratulate him on winning this much coveted prize, the usual occurred for such a meeting: people began to praise him and his works very profusely. Even those who had criticized him before were now singing his praises. He was very disturbed and perplexed to see the sham, for he knew that all that was being said was never meant. He began to shrivel up in his chair.

When the speeches were over he was sitting in his chair, cowered and shrunken as if all this was beyond his endurance. The chairman shook him and said, "Are you asleep? Did you hear what I have just announced?" A purse of £25,000 was offered him as a gift by his colleagues. Yeats replied, "I am not asleep, but had I known all this would happen I would not have come. To have to listen to such blatant lies for two full hours for the sake of a mere £25,000, I would never, never have come!"

If you have cultivated even the slightest awareness, no one will be able to flatter you, for you shall see the falsity in his expression. But you lack awareness; people all around you pronounce lies and you are not the least aware of it. You yourself are speaking untruths without any awareness of what you are doing. Then you get caught in a thousand difficulties. In your moment of unawareness you tell a woman, "You are so beautiful; I am in love with you." – and land in trouble. Perhaps at that very moment you know that it was a lie but now a whole series of problems begin. You regret it the very next day.

One day Mulla Nasruddin's wife complained to him, "It was you who was running after me and not I. And now look at you, and your ways! If this is how it was to be, why did you run after me?"

Mulla said, "What you say is one hundred percent correct. Have you ever seen a mousetrap run after a mouse? The mouse gets himself trapped. Your statement that I ran after you is absolutely correct."

Women are very clever in this respect. No husband can accuse his wife of running after him. No woman ever makes this mistake, for she knows this problem is bound to arise sooner or later. It is always the man who falls into the trap. The woman watches quietly;

at most she nods her head. All the initiative is taken by the man. Nasruddin is right; men walk into the trap of their own free will.

Mulla Nasruddin was on his death bed.

His son asked, "Tell me something of your experiences in life."

Mulla said, "I have learned three things in life. One: if people are a little patient the fruits ripen by themselves and fall. You need not climb the tree in order to pluck them. Two: if people are patient people die by themselves. There is no need to wage wars in order to kill them. And three: if people are really patient women will run after men on their own accord; there will be no need to run after them."

This is the quintessence of Mulla's life experiences. But who profits by the experience of life? Do you know what you are saying? Do you know what you are doing? If you become aware, ninety-nine percent of your actions that you use to create a house will fall away. Only one percent will remain, which is enough for a dharmshala, and enough for the life of a sannyasin. What is inevitable is what will remain; all that is unnecessary will be cut out. It is the superfluous, the inessential, that causes problems in a householder's life. How many needless things you buy and keep in your house!

I was once a guest in a house so full of things that it was well nigh impossible to move about. They were rich people, but there would be more space to breathe in a poor man's hut. Anything new that came to market was promptly bought; whatever was advertised in the papers had to be in the house. It was so full, it was impossible to live in it. I asked my host, "Is this a house or a museum or some exhibition ground? Most of the things you have collected are useless. Get rid of them. It is space that makes a house. It is impossible to stay here. If this state of affairs continues, soon you will have to sleep outside."

You, too, gather junk in your home. You store useless things, hoping that one day they will be useful. Even things that are broken are stored away for future use.

Eskimos observe a rule that would bring great peace and happiness to the world if it were observed universally. Every New Year's Day they distribute all that they have and start life anew. Everything is got rid of until the house is literally bare. Nowhere are houses as clean as the Eskimo houses. As it is, Eskimos have very little. When they start anew there is a freshness to life. The Eskimo never collects useless stuff for he knows he has to give it away at the end of the year. Imagine, if you had to do likewise, how many non-essentials you would find in your house – things you should never have bought at all.

It is not only household articles that you collect, but also useless thoughts: someone says something and you keep on listening. You read the newspapers mechanically. Have you ever asked yourself whether you want to store all this stuff in your head? Have you ever told someone, "I really have no use for such talk." Someone sits next to you and gossips about other people. Do you ever tell him, "Why are you filling my head with this junk?" It is easy to fill it up, but difficult to empty the head. Ask those who meditate. When they try to remove those thoughts they cannot do so easily; they have firmly struck root. Actions also are gathered like useless articles in the house. Gradually you become a dumping ground of rubbish. There is no difference between the ragman's shop and your life. Become a little more aware!

Nanak says that each action of yours sets the pattern of your life, so think a great deal before each act. Only a genuine person can gain entry to his court. The great, the best, the most authentic — only these can reach, and his compassionate eye will then cause such a person to see his hand in all things. As truth begins to enter your life, you will find proof of his benevolent eye. You will get a hint, a symbol of him in each and every place. Right now you get no hint of him. As yet you do not recognize him. As soon as you begin to become authentic you will feel his commands coming in. Then, in every grain of sand, in every leaf and bud, you will begin to see him.

He wants to lead you on the path. He wants to guide you in what you should do and what you should not, but you do not have the required emptiness within you. Your own tumult and noise is so much that you cannot hear his voice. Every day you find signs of his grace, his compassion. Right now you get no signs. You are living on your own supports, and is your own support worth the name? No sooner does your life begin to become authentic than you begin to live by him. Then life takes on a new momentum, a new dimension.

Nanak says that the test begins only after having reached:

> *Only before the Lord is each one tested;*
> *Each is ranked by his glance.*
> *There the raw is sifted from the ripe.*
> *Nanak says One who is raw will dissolve away.*

Each is examined to determine whether he is ripe or raw. What is meant by ripe and raw? He who disintegrates before God is raw; he who remains integrated before him is ripe. Make this your touchstone: whatever you do, ask yourself, "Will I feel right to produce this act before God, or will I be afraid to show him?" If you are afraid and want to hide, do not do it, for nothing can be hidden from him. He can see you through and through. Nothing is hidden or can be hidden from that mirror.

Before doing any act weigh in your mind whether you can bring it before him, just as a goldsmith tests the gold before he does anything with it. If it passes that test do it with an easy mind. If there is fear or doubt, don't do it!

Then you will ripen. The potter fires his pots. The raw ones dissolve in the rain; the fired ones hold the water. You go to the market and buy a water jug for two paise. You sound it in several places to be sure it is strong. The sound of a well baked, strong pot is very different.

So too, as you ripen, the music of your life begins to change so that you can hear the internal sound. You will get hints and signs of this internal music. Its indications are: you become more peaceful, you are happier, you find yourself filled with joy. A profound contentment envelops you from all sides and you feel grateful, for no apparent reason. Bliss dances softly in you.

Sahajobai was a well known mystic. She said, "There are no clouds and yet it rains." You are happy, cheerful, every hair on your body smiles, every pore overflows with joy — all for no reason. No treasure has been discovered and yet the heart is weighed down with gratitude. These are the signs.

As you begin to ripen more and more, as you get more and more established, the rainwater will fill you. His bliss is pouring, the showers fall every moment, but you are still raw; therefore you melt in it. Because you aren't ready, God's bounty becomes a curse for you. The moment you mature, the moment you are established, the moment you ripen, then what seemed a curse before is clearly seen as a blessing in disguise.

The final test takes place after reaching there. But don't wait until that time, because you are evolving, being constructed every moment. Start this very day and perhaps you will be able to stand before him; perhaps you will be able to reveal yourself to him. You have lost enough time; don't waste another moment. Live always with God in your mind; for he is the destination, he is the abode. The world is but a resting place.

CHAPTER 18

There Is No End to It

The supreme law expresses the Realm of Religion.
Now to understand the conditions of the Realm of Knowledge:
So many winds, waters, and fires; so many Krishnas and Shivas;
So many Brahmas, so many of his creations of so many colors and forms;
So many fields of action and sacred mountains; so many polar stars and so many sermons;
So many Indras, and moons and suns, and galaxies, and continents;
So many enlightened ones, and buddhas, and masters, and goddesses;
So many gods and devils, and munis; so many jewels, so many oceans;
So many species and tongues, so many kings and emperors;
So many remembrances, so many devotees;
Nanak says, There is no end to it, no end.
Knowing is the expression of the Realm of Knowledge.
There is music and mirth and frolic and bliss.
Modesty is the expression of the Realm of Shame.
The experiences that take place are beautiful and incomparable.
He cannot be spoken of in words.
He who tries repents later.
Memory, mind, understanding, and intelligence are all formulated here;
And the consciousness of gods and enlightened ones.

Nanak has divided existence and its quest into four realms. The division is very scientific and worth understanding. He names the realms: Religion, Knowledge, Shame and Grace.

The section of religion deals with the expression of *dharma*, the law, the rule, that governs the whole of existence. The Vedas refer to it as *rut*, which means unchangeable law — what Lao Tzu calls Tao. From rut is derived *rutu*, the seasons. At the time of the Vedas, the seasons were so regular and clear-cut that there was not a moment's difference from one year to the next. Spring would come on the exact day, the rains would start the very day they were supposed to. Man has disturbed nature completely so that the seasons are no longer seasons. The word *rutu* was given specifically to the seasons for they worked exactly according to their timetable, following an unchangeable law. There was a system at work. Because of man's so-called knowledge, everything has gone haywire; even the seasons have gone off the rails, so to speak.

The West is now much more concerned about this state of affairs, giving rise to a movement around a new branch of science: ecology. Ecologists insist that nature be not tampered with. They believe that man should leave nature to God if he wishes to survive. Changes in nature bring about changes in the surroundings, which are being destroyed, and we are approaching a point that is dangerous for mankind.

The art of knowing the most intrinsic discipline of the supreme law of life is called dharma, religion. Buddha used the Pali word, *dhamma*, to mean the rule. When a Buddhist monk says, "Now I surrender myself to the law," he lets go of his self to seek shelter in the supreme law "through which I was born and in which I shall dissolve." To know truth is to know this rule.

To express this fundamental law of life, Nanak says, is the basis for the realm of religion. We live, but we live by our thoughts. We think a thousand times before we take a single step. And the more we think the more our steps fall in the wrong place. Whatever steps we take without the intrusion of thoughts invariably lead us right.

You eat your food but you do not think about digesting it. The rule digests the food. Try this experiment: after meals concentrate on the stomach and the process of digestion — you will end with an upset stomach. As soon as you interfere with the unconscious law you create chaos within. Every night you sleep. One night ponder at length on how you fall asleep, how sleep comes, and what happens — you will pass a sleepless night. It isn't strange that people who think a great deal suffer from insomnia.

Life goes on! The trees never think about when they should let the flowers bloom. The tree knows from its very roots. It does not think, for all its mechanisms are built-in. The rivers flow towards the sea. Do they have any sense of direction? Do they have any maps? An unconscious rule guides their waters towards the ocean.

This gigantic universe works without thoughts; and nowhere do we find a single mistake or mishappening. Everything works according to the rule — except man. Man has gone wrong for he does not obey the rule; instead he is guided by his thoughts. He thinks: "Should I do this or not? Is this right or wrong? What would be the outcome if I...? Will I gain something? What will people say?" In the haze of smoke created by a thousand-and-one such thoughts, the straight line of life gets hidden and lost. He who works in a state of no-thought is an enlightened being.

So religion is not wisdom, nor a decision of your intellect. Religion is a quest by a man who is tired of his intelligence, who is harassed by it, who has tried every direction and finds himself a helpless failure in the end. Such a man lets go of his intelligence and then says, "Your will, not mine, O Lord! Take me where you will." This Nanak refers to as the divine order.

Don't imagine this to mean that there is a huge person sitting somewhere issuing orders, that there is a supreme father, the supreme God! The rule works without the orderer, the rule is God himself. We have to use words that people can understand; so also we have to make use of symbols, signs. Foolish people often cling to symbols; so they think God has hands, mouth, limbs, that he sits on a throne and dispenses justice and gives orders. If we do not obey his orders, we are irreligious; if we do, we are religious. If we don't obey, he will be displeased and angry and then punish us. If we obey he will reward us.

This is all useless nonsense! You are attaching too much importance to mere symbols.

Only the law exists. There is no one sitting there on high who works the rule. When you move in harmony with the rule all wrong actions stop on their own, for the rule knows no wrong. Then when the right actions accumulate through you, the melody of joy begins to play. When your actions are right they will spread a fragrance of happiness and joy all around. This fragrance signals that your actions are correct.

When something wrong happens through you the shadow of sorrow will surround you. The greater the wrong, the greater the anxiety and worry and suffering. Don't look upon suffering as a punishment, but rather as the outcome of wrong action.

If a man leaves the straight road and wanders into a jungle and then thorns prick him, he understands that he has gone off the track. Not being on the road, there are bound to be thorns. The man looks for the right track and gets back to the road; now no thorns prick him because there are none. When you hit against a wall and hurt your head, the wall is not punishing you. What has the wall to do with you? When you find the door you can go out easily without hurting your head.

It is just like this. The day you begin to recognize the law, you will have found the door. As long as you are oblivious of the rule you will keep knocking your head against the wall. How many times have you hurt yourself, how many wounds do you bear on your head? These are wounds you have gathered over millions of births that are oozing, festering, and causing endless pain. And you think someone is punishing you.

No one is punishing you; you are reaping your own harvest. Always bear in mind whenever you are unhappy you have gone against nature; whenever you are ill you are out of harmony with nature. Illness is a warning, a hint to you; as such it is helpful and for your own good. If there were no illness you would never know when you have left nature's path, or when you have gone against the eternal arrangement of life. Then you will keep wandering with no way for you to come back. Suffering and sorrow turns you back to God. This is why you remember him when you are in pain and sorrow. In joy you never think of him.

The saint prays: "Oh Lord, let there always be a little suffering as a reminder, so that we remain constantly in prayer, always calling out to you. If there is no pain or sorrow, we shall have no excuse to call you. In happiness we forget you; we shall be lost!"

Suffering means just one thing: you have wavered in religion somewhere, somehow. Do not blame others, nor your fortune, nor be angry with God. Take it as a hint, a warning, and try to find out where you have slipped. Where have you gone against nature? Then try to fall in line with nature — for that is religion.

Nanak calls the second division the realm of knowledge. Religion exists. The day you recognize this you attain knowledge. Religion is — only you have closed your eyes to it. The sun is shining, only you have closed your eyes to it. The sun is shining, only you have closed your doors and windows; the lamp burns, but you stand with your back to it. It is pouring outside, but you are afraid to get wet, so you hide yourself in some dark cave. Religion is going on all the time but you have kept yourself away — somewhere far away.

To come back, to return and retrace your steps, is called Knowledge. Every man will have to come back. Man is capable of going far. The animals, the plants, the birds have no religion, for they do not have the ability to go outside of nature. Whatever they do is within nature's law. They do not have the sense even to wander. Wandering requires a little intelligence. You need at least a little courage to go wrong; and you need some awareness to step off the path. This much man has, but then to come back to the path you need more awareness.

So the animals are in their right place, for they cannot wander. This is not a very laudable state of being; it is actually a helplessness. The average man has a little intelligence. He can wander; therefore, he has gone astray. Then there are those who attain buddhahood, like Nanak and Kabir. They have the highest awareness at their command; they have come back. What the animals have naturally you have to attain through your *sadhana*, through your spiritual practice. Buddha also returns to the point where the plants always are. The same supreme bliss that the plants enjoy is attained by Buddha but there is a basic difference between the two: Buddha is completely aware of the bliss that rains on him, whereas the plant has no awareness of the bliss that rains on it.

Nature is unconscious, whereas the *Buddha-Purusha* is naturally in full awareness. We are between these two. Nature is not conscious; in nature happiness and joy are natural but the knower, the enjoyer of this happiness is absent. It is just as if you are unconscious while jewels are raining all over you. It makes no difference to you whether it is raining stones or raining jewels. Then if you open your eyes you become aware of the endless bounty that has rained on you.

Buddha has attained only what was so readily available to the stones; he returns to the same place. But this coming back is an absolutely new happening. The place is the same, the rocks are the same; the very tree under which Buddha attained enlightenment is also where Buddha is. And this is bound to be, for God is hidden in every grain, every particle.

But what is the difference between the *Bodhi* tree and Buddha? There is a vast difference. The place is one, but the difference is infinite! The difference is that Buddha is experiencing this bliss in full consciousness; in full wakefulness he feels the infinite glory. The same glory pours on the tree but the tree is oblivious of it. The same glory rains on you also, but you have chosen to stand with your back to it. The trees face towards him but they cannot know him. You can know him but you have turned in the opposite direction! The day you take a full turn, the day your eyes rest on his glory, you shall know. This knowing Nanak refers to as knowledge.

The realm of knowledge is man's attainment. Religion will be even if there is no man left on earth, but knowledge cannot be. Existence has tried to seek knowledge through man; therefore, man is the peak of creation. You do not know how many possibilities of glory are readily available to you. God wishes to become awake through you; he wishes to awaken from within you.

In nature God is dormant. In man he has stirred. He wants to awaken in man. In nature there is the dark, moonless night and deep slumber. In man the moment of dawn has arrived. If you miss, you will remain in the dark night. If you open your eyes and see, you will also be like Buddha, Nanak, Kabir; until then you will suffer. Understand the eternal principle: if you do not become what you could become, you will suffer; if you become what you should have become, your life will be filled with bliss.

Bliss means fulfillment — the attainment of that which you had the power to attain. Until the tree that lies dormant in the seed attains its full growth and bears flowers and fruit, a tension always remains inside.

If you die without singing the song you were born to sing, you will die in sorrow. You shall have to be born again and again in order to sing this song for nature does not accept things in halves. The day you are complete, total, you will be accepted.

Therefore, the Hindus say, "He who is perfect is not born again." He has sung his song and attained his bliss. The stream has met the ocean and there is no reason for him to come back. You return again and again because you fail every time. Nature sends you back again and again, for nature is in no hurry. It has infinite time at its disposal.

I have heard: Two people were traveling in a train. One was from Bombay and the other from rural Bihar. The Bihari gentleman asked, "What is your name, kind sir?"

"Veenu," replied the Bombayite. "And what is yours?"

"Sri Sri Satyadev Narayan-Prasad Sinha."

The Bombayite's eyes almost popped out of their sockets. "Such a long name!" he exclaimed.

"Well, you see," explained the Bihari, "we are not Bombayites. We have enough time at our disposal for such names."

God is not a resident of Bombay. He has plenty of time. Nature is in no hurry. You may fall a thousand times; you may prove worthless endless times, and nature will patiently push you back here. But you will suffer endlessly until you succeed. Unless and until you have sung your song, unless and until you have fulfilled your destiny, you will not be accepted. There is only one sorrow, one anguish, that this existence does not accept you but turns you back again and again. Once you are accepted, you are immersed in it and then there is no return.

Nanak calls the second division the realm of knowledge — to know what is with full awareness.

Third is the realm of shame. When a person knows what is to be known, then only does he realize his own ignorance, hence the shame. The ignorant man swaggers about in arrogance. Without modesty the ignorant are totally unaware of the ignorance that fills them. An ignorant person struts about as a wise man. Only the wise knows how vast is his ignorance. He feels: "What do I know? Hardly anything!"

Socrates said, "When I became enlightened the one thing I knew for certain was that I knew nothing." When knowledge becomes complete this is what you know – that you know nothing, that you are nothing. You become a zero. This zero Nanak calls the realm of shame. Then you are filled with shame: What am I? Nothing worthy of the name, and how I prided myself on my knowledge – swollen like a bubble! How I exaggerated the little I knew.

Mulla Nasruddin had just returned from a journey. He was telling his father, "There was such a storm on the river as was never experienced before. The waves rose fifty feet high."

His father said, "You are exaggerating a bit too much. I have spent fifty years going up and down this river and I have never seen waves like you describe. The river never rises that high."

Mulla said, "Be sensible, father. Everything is increasing. Just look at how the price of grain has gone up."

Man finds ways and means to support his exaggeration. And on this stands his greatest exaggeration — that I am. It is the biggest lie in this world. If the existence of God is the greatest truth, the existence of the I is the greatest lie, for two I's cannot exist at the same time. Existence is one. If all existence is one, it can have only one center. But each man, each individual person constantly proclaims "I am."

The enlightened person is filled with shame at the excesses and exaggerations he formerly engaged in. What proclamations he made over mere nothings! There was only a large bubble that burst at the slightest touch; there were paper boats that disintegrated as soon as they touched the water; there was a house of cards that fell in the

There Is No End to It 437

slightest breeze. But how many exaggerations he indulged himself in for them!

Mulla Nasruddin was arrested and brought before the court for using foul language about a well-known politician. When the magistrate asked him why he called him a big ass, Mulla said, "Your Honor, it was not my fault. I know the high position this gentleman holds. He is our minister. But what could I do when he himself asked me, 'Do you know who I am?' I had to tell him."

Your eyes ask the same question of others: Do you know who I am? If someone's feet trips you, or you are pushed by someone, you turn back as if to say, "Don't you see who I am?" The fact is that you do not know who you are. Who knows himself? Those who really know, their egos are annihilated. As long as you do not know, the I exists. Next time a person asks you, "Do you know who I am?" please ask him in return, "Do you?"

It is all arrogant talk when a man asks, "Do you know how rich I am? Don't you know my status, my position?" He implies that he can get you in trouble, that he is a dangerous man. It is a proclamation of violence. You say that, only when you want to convey your power to destroy the other person.

All your arrogance is violence. Ego is the thread of violence. The one who knows is not even aware of his being; he does not know who he is, he is lost. The ignorant remains arrogant and proclaims, "I am." He who is enlightened stops this language.

So Nanak calls this third part the realm of shame. He says, "When the enlightened one is asked to speak he does not know what to say, and to whom. He has nothing to say, he makes no claims. Even before God he is filled with shame, for in his heart he is aware of the endless false claims he has made before. God in his compassion graced him with enlightenment! If, as he stood before him and conveyed: Here I am! Accept me! it would be total arrogance. If he prayed it was only that he might be accepted by him. If he did a good act, if he built a temple or mosque or *gurudwara*, it was only to show him that he was something."

The wise man becomes overcome with shame; with what face will he stand before him? All your appearances are false, made up to show the world. Just think, if today you were to stand before God which of your faces would you show him? The one you show to your wife, your boss, or your servant? Will you show him the face that you take to your sweetheart or the one you assume before the lowly and poor? Which of these masks will you put on?

Before those who are powerful your tail keeps wagging and you try to please in every little way. Your appearance bears the expression of flattery and wily charm. And how stiff is your posture before a lowly person! From him you expect the same flattery and attention as you give to those who are higher than you. You expect him to wag his tail and appreciate every word that comes out of you. Remember, he who demands flattery has had to flatter someone somewhere, and is actually taking revenge. But the person who has seen himself correctly, never praises anyone nor expects praise from others. There is one God. If he is praised that is enough. From whom is he to ask praise? For everywhere it is he.

Nanak says, one dies of dreadful shame when one stands before truth; for one finds that not a single appearance is worth the name. All are dirty, all are false.

Zen masters tell their disciples: "When you have discovered your original face your search is over." They exhort them to find the face they had before they were born, to look for the face that will be with them after death. All intervening faces are false.

Psychologists say that if a person tries to go back into his past by reawakening his memory he can only go up to the age of five or four, or at the most to three. He cannot go beyond that. The first three years of life cast no imprint on the mind. Why? Because till then you are so artless and simple that you have no mask. To have a memory one has to claim something.

The ego creates memory. All remembrances are the ego, which remembers everything and keeps account of every moment of your life. For the first three years you are so innocent, so guileless, you do not know who you are. You have no claim to anything. A three-year-old comes jumping and prancing and laughing aloud as he tells his mother, "I was last in the class today." He has no idea what it is to be first or to be last. The ego is not yet formed. He has no idea of caste or creed, of his house and home, high caste or low caste. He is blissfully unaware whether he is a *brahmin* or untouchable. He knows nothing yet. His face is without blemish. Only such a face can you present before God.

But the parents begin their vicious training very early in life. They begin to impose the false masks from the very first day. The mother, at the very outset, expects the child to smile when she looks at him. If he does not she feels hurt. The child may not feel like smiling, but soon he learns that he must smile at his mother's glance, whether he likes it or not. The lying has started. The child gets his first mask. Then many, many more masks are added as the child grows up.

It becomes most embarrassing to stand before him with these false faces, says Nanak. Whenever anybody becomes aware of this fact he is filled with shame. Then he looks and looks and cannot discover which one is authentic. The more he seeks, the more he is faced with other appearances, just as when you remove one layer of an onion another one appears; for the false is deposited on the mind in layer upon layer from infinite births. That is all that you have done in your infinite births, but when you remove them layer by layer, you find nothing remains – except emptiness! Nanak says that when the emptiness emerges one is drowned in shame. One feels: What was I? I was nothing and yet I claimed to be this, and that. This is the shame that Nanak refers to as the third realm.

The fourth division is the realm of grace. He says, when you are filled with shame his grace pours on you. When you become zero, emptiness, then perfection descends on you — not before that. Your stiff-backed arrogance is the obstruction between you and his grace. You rely on your own self, you need no help even when you pray. When you ask him for something, it is just one of your many attempts. You are also tapping this source — perhaps something will come of it. And if something does emerge you claim it was your own effort that brought about the achievement.

Mulla Nasruddin climbed up into a cherry tree. The cherries were ripe, but high in the tree so he had to climb way up.

He became frightened and prayed, "Oh, God, if I reach the cherries and get them, I shall offer one *naya paisa* in the mosque."

Now Mulla began to climb with full faith that God would see to him. As he neared the top branch, the thought struck him, "One naya paisa is too much to have committed, and there aren't that many cherries; besides I'm climbing on my own. It wasn't necessary to bring God into this at all."

When his hands reached the cherries he said, "I could buy more than this for one naya paisa in the market and you haven't moved a finger. I'll offer a few cherries in place of the naya paisa."

As he was busy thinking this his foot slipped and he came crashing to the ground. As he lay there he called out to God, "Couldn't you even take a joke? If you had been a little more patient I would have offered the one naya paisa at the mosque as I promised."

When you worship or pray it is all a display of your egotism and arrogance. It is a decoration for your ego. Real prayer is when you are not, when the worshipper is no more, worship starts.

Nanak says, in shame you melt, you are obliterated. On the one hand you are no more, and on the other his grace pours showers of joy on you. Bliss is always pouring down, but you were so filled with your arrogance that there was no place for it inside. So grace only pours constantly when shame empties you inside.

> *These are Nanak's four realms.*
> *Now to understand the conditions of the Realm of Knowledge:*
> *So many winds, waters, and fires; so many Krishnas and Shivas;*
> *So many Brahmas, so many of his creations of so many colors and forms;*
> *So many fields of action and sacred mountains; so many polar stars and so many sermons;*
> *So many Indras, and moons and suns, and galaxies, and continents;*
> *So many enlightened ones, and buddhas, and masters, and goddesses;*
> *So many gods and devils, and munis; so many jewels, so many oceans;*
> *So many species and tongues, so many kings and emperors;*

So many remembrances, so many devotees;
Nanak says, There is no end to it, no end.

No sooner does a man awaken towards existence than he is filled with awe, and great wonder surrounds him. You are not affected by wonder. You go about as if you know everything. A pundit is never astonished; he has an answer for everything. A child is full of wonder. At every step he questions all that he sees and is filled with wonder. Don't think that a child questions because he wants to know; he simply exhibits his wonder and excitement; therefore he doesn't even wait for your answer before he asks another question. He isn't really interested in answers.

He sees the butterfly and asks, "Why does the butterfly have so many colors?" He expects no specific answer. He is merely expressing his wonder. "Why are the trees so green? Why are flowers so colorful? Why are there clouds in the sky? Why does the sun come out every morning?" The child asks because everything fills him with such wonder and mystery, but he is only expressing his astonishment.

A scholar is one who is all answers, but has no questions; he has an answer for everything. A wise man is one who has only questions but no answers. Understand this well. The sage is wonderstruck like a child; he is even more so, for a child sees at most a butterfly or a flower, whereas the sage sees the whole of existence. How far can a child's vision go? The sage can see through and through, and what he sees strikes him dumb with awe.

These words of Nanak convey his wonder and his love, but you want information, you want answers; for then you can be the master. You can't be a master of wonderment. You can be filled with wonder and astonishment, but then they become your masters; they will surround you and drown you. In wonder you cannot survive — you will be lost. You desire an answer, for you can hold an answer in your hand. You can use answers; you can defeat others and cut their questions short. People are not in quest of knowledge, but of answers so they can be known as wise people.

Remember no one becomes a sage by seeking answers. You become wise only by going deeper into the question. The deeper a person delves into questions, the more doors open to wonderment and mystery; enter one door and a thousand others open before you.

This is the wonderment that Nanak is talking about. He is a rustic, an illiterate villager; therefore you shouldn't be concerned about the form of his language. When a villager enters this realm of wonder he too becomes garrulous. In utter amazement he tries to convey the magic of that wonderland! He speaks in his simple dialect:

> *So many winds, waters, and fires; so many Krishnas and Shivas;*

So many Krishnas! When you begin to see, you too will find there are infinite flutes playing; an eternal dance of the *gopis* is going on. Infinite is this existence. It does not end with your earth, but you are filled with much arrogance that you feel that existence ends in you! You might even think the infinite dance of existence is only for your entertainment!

Once a villager was caught by the ticket-taker for traveling without a ticket. The villager begged him to let him go for he hadn't a paisa on him. But the conductor wouldn't give in. He pulled the chain and stopped the train and told the man to get out.

The man pleaded, "Please drop me at the first station, then. It is very dark and there is heavy jungle all around."

But the conductor was adamant and he was forced to leave the train. The motorman suddenly saw the man walking on the tracks, so he sounded the whistle for him to get out of the way. "Let him keep sounding the whistle, I shall not get on the train again," the man said to himself.

You think you might be asked to get back on the train, but the whistle is for you to get out of the way, to leave the path. But each man thinks nature is playing for him alone; each man thinks he is the center, and all of existence revolves around him. This is why ancient people like to believe that the earth is at the center and the sun goes around it.

Bernard Shaw once said jokingly, "I do not believe in the theory that the earth revolves around the sun. I just can't accept that idea. It is wrong." Someone got up from the gathering and said, "Every child of the twentieth century knows that the earth revolves around the sun. What proof do you have to negate the theory?" Bernard Shaw replied, "Who bothers about science and what it proves and does not prove? The proof is only this: as long as Bernard Shaw resides on this earth, it cannot revolve around anything else. The sun has to revolve around the earth."

The joke pokes fun at all of us. It is hard for you too to believe that your earth revolves around the sun.

When Galileo made this discovery there was great commotion. The church objected, the priests rose in opposition, even the popes denied its validity. Galileo was told to ask pardon for making such an outrageous announcement. Galileo was a wonderfully strange person – he asked forgiveness. He was a clever man and a true man. He had no intention of becoming a martyr over such a matter. He was a genuine person who was not afraid of the consequences. He said, "I shall ask pardon. I shall put it in writing that it is the sun that goes around the earth, but how will my words change matters? I have not made up this doctrine. If a thousand Galileos deny the fact, what difference is it going to make?"

Man always thought this way, and that was the only reason. Christianity is far behind Hindu thought. It is a very ancient Hindu concept that there are infinite worlds, that our world is not the only one that has life on it. Science now confirms the fact that there are at least fifty thousand worlds where life is possible. The Hindus have always said there are infinite worlds, infinite species and generations. Things do not finish with this world; it is not the ultimate. In fact it is a mere speck. The sun is sixty thousand times bigger than the earth and this sun is a mere ball compared to other suns! There are suns that are tens of millions times bigger than this sun. With such a mediocre sun, this earth is a mere nothing.

Bertrand Russell has written a story: A priest slept one night and dreamed he had died. He went to the gates of heaven, which were closed. He was rather surprised. He had expected the doors to be wide open and God himself waiting on the steps to welcome him. Hadn't he served the poor and tended the ill? Hadn't he opened schools for poor children? Hadn't he served in the true Christian spirit?

But the door was closed, and it was so enormous that he couldn't see where it started or where it ended. He shouted aloud, but his voice couldn't penetrate the thick door. He banged with his hands. He banged his head against the door, but to no avail. It was just like an ant banging on your door! His ego turned to ashes. He had dreamed of a grand welcome. How much service, how much worship, how much charity he had performed; how many he had converted to Christianity, and here no one seemed to bother about him.

Infinite years passed. He sat crouched near the door of heaven, which still had not opened. He had forgotten everything. Then one day the door opened slightly and a man with a thousand eyes, each eye like the orb of the sun, looked around and spotted him — just as you would spot a tiny object with a magnifying glass.

The priest cringed even more, for he thought it was God. He addressed him: "Oh God, how your eyes frighten me, for each is like a sun. I cannot bear to look into them."

The man laughed and said, "I am not God. I am merely a guard. What are you doing here?"

He lost all courage. This was only a guard! If the guard is like this, what would it be to face God? At last he said, "I have come from earth, where my church is well known. I am a believer in Jesus. I am his devotee..." His courage sank further and further.

The guard said, "Jesus? Earth? Which earth are you talking about? Give the file number. There are infinite worlds. Which earth do you come from and which Jesus are you talking about? Each earth has its own Jesus."

Imagine the state of the poor priest. He said, "I speak of that Jesus who is the only son of God."

The guard said, "You seem to be mad! On each earth such Jesuses are born and their devotees declare them the only son of God. Anyway, we shall find out. First tell me the number."

The poor man said, "We know of no number. We don't think in terms of numbers. We always thought our earth was the only one of its kind."

There Is No End to It 445

"All right," said the guard, "then give me the number of your sun. Which solar system do you come from?"

"We know only one sun and no other," the poor man wailed.

"Then it will be very difficult," said the guard. "But wait here while we make inquiries."

And again infinite years passed. The guard did not return for it was not an ordinary inquiry. It would take ages more, if he ever did manage to identify him. By this time the poor man's ego was turned to ashes; his hopes of a grand reception remained a dream. He had planned everything: there would be bands playing, flowers everywhere and God would make him sit at his right hand. In this state of fear and agitation he awakened. He was covered with perspiration. It was only a dream – thank God! But from that day onward he lost all courage.

And this dream is the truth. Nanak is talking of the truth contained in this dream:

So many winds, waters, and fires; so many Krishnas and Shivas;

If a priest had asked Nanak he would have said: "So many Jesuses! So many Krishnas and Shivas.... There is no end to it, no end."

Nanak is expressing his awe and wonder. This wonder gives birth to shame and all claims fall. What is one to claim?

There is a well known incident in the life of Socrates. A very wealthy man of Athens went to visit Socrates. His arrogance was natural. When people who have nothing are so arrogant, imagine this man who was a multi-millionaire, the very wealthiest man in Athens. When Socrates paid no attention to him, the man could not bear it. He said, "Do you know who I am?"

Socrates said, "Please be seated. We shall try to understand." He had a map of the world brought before them and he asked the visitor, "Where is Athens on this map?"

Naturally Athens was marked by a point on the map. The millionaire pointed, "This is Athens."

"Now please show me where your palace is in Athens," Socrates said.

"How can I show you my palace when the whole of Athens is shown only by a dot?"

"And where are you in this palace?" Socrates insisted. "Remember this is a map of this world only, and there are infinite worlds, infinite suns. Who are you?" As he was about to leave, Socrates gave him the map and said, "Keep this map with you. Whenever arrogance takes hold of you, open the map, locate Athens and ask yourself, 'Where is my palace?' Ask yourself, 'Who am I?'"

We are like nothing, and the obsession of being everything has caught hold of us. This is the bane of all mankind. The day you awaken and look around, what will you be able to say of yourself? What are you? You will begin to lose yourself. As you get lesser and lesser and shrink into nothingness, the vast form of the Lord will manifest. He manifests only when you are completely empty.

Wonder is bound to destroy you. Wonder is suicidal. It kills not only the body but your whole being. It is the death of the whole amness. This is why you seek answers, whereas the wise man gives you questions. And he gives you such questions that have no answers. And this is to kill your arrogance.

Wake up a little, brush the dust from your eyes and see all around you — what answer does a man have? Science has discovered so many answers. Which answer is an authentic answer? No answer is an authentic answer; it merely pushes the question a little further back.

A small child asked D. H. Lawrence while they were strolling in a garden, "Why are the trees green?" It isn't that Lawrence didn't know the answer, for the answer is simple: because of the chlorophyll in the leaves. But then the question would have arisen: Why is there chlorophyll in leaves? And this one question would lead to another and another. Lawrence was definitely a wise man. He would have got along well with Nanak. He said to the child, "The fact is, trees are green because they are green." There was no need for any further explanation.

This is an answer that a poet would give. It is an answer that a master would give. They do not destroy your wonder but enhance it. This is not an answer in the narrow sense of the word. What Lawrence tries to convey to the child is: I too am filled with wonder why trees are green. All I can say is, they are green because they are green — and there is no way of knowing why they are green.

All searching for answers merely pushes the answers further away. Therefore philosophy reaches nowhere. Each question gives rise to ten more. Bertrand Russell has written: "I chose philosophy as my subject in the university so that I might know the answer to every question in life. Now at the end of my life I know only this: that I found not a single answer but my questions have increased a thousandfold."

So there are the philosophers and thinkers who are forever in search of answers. Each answer creates fresh questions. Those who are weak stop halfway and hold on to their answers. Those who are courageous go to the very end. Then they come to realize how useless their labors were. Then religion is born and mystery takes hold of them.

Overpowered with wonder and mystery, Nanak says,

> *Knowing is the expression of the Realm of Knowledge.*
> *There is music and mirth and frolic and bliss.*
> *Modesty is the expression of the Realm of Shame.*
> *The experiences that take place are beautiful and incomparable.*
> *He cannot be spoken of in words.*
> *He who tries repents later.*
> *Memory, mind, understanding, and intelligence are all formulated here;*
> *And the consciousness of gods and enlightened ones.*

In the Realm of Knowledge there is an overbearing power of awakening awareness — an overabundance of consciousness — not of answers or of scriptures or principles, but of awareness. Knowledge means awareness, not scriptural knowledge or information or words.

> *Knowing is the expression of the Realm of Knowledge.*
> *There is music and mirth and frolic and bliss.*

Nanak does not mention scriptures at all, nor does he talk of doctrines or principles. There are no answers, but then what is there? Music...*nada*.

This nada, the sound, the music, is an experience. Before you awaken in the morning the birds may be singing, only you do not hear them. Then your sleep is broken and you begin to awaken; you turn over, your eyes still closed, but you hear the birds outside your window. The fresh morning breeze caresses you tenderly and you begin to hear the sounds all around. As you awaken you begin to experience the music of existence.

There is still another daybreak exactly like this, another awakening. Right now your life is one long slumber: you walk as if asleep; whatever you do is in a trancelike state. You fight, you love, you meet, you part; you do all kinds of things in this unconscious state.

Once it happened: A news editor wrote a scathing article against the town drunkards. The drunkards were very angry. One of them got hold of a stick and went in search of the editor. He entered his room and waving his stick he called out, "Where is that damn editor?"

The poor editor was in a fix! He was a small, weak man, whereas the drunk was a gigantic fellow. Thinking fast, he said, "He has just gone out. Please be seated. I will go and find him." And so he slipped out.

Just as he walked out he met another burly drunk on the steps. "Where is that so-and-so editor of yours?"

He hollered, "Go right in. There he is!" You can just imagine what happened inside.

This is exactly what is happening all around us. Nobody is in his right senses. You are not quite aware of what you are doing, certainly not of why you are doing things. You are completely oblivious of the doer. You live in a crowd of sleepwalkers. If you are unhappy, what else can you expect? And if your relationships turn out to be veritable hells, no wonder!

Nanak says, In the Realm of Knowledge there is profusion of "knowing," of awareness. Right now you are in the field of ignorance, where nonawareness runs rampant. Where being asleep is the ultimate.

The first thing that a man of knowledge experiences is the music,

There Is No End to It 449

the nada. This sound Nanak calls Omkar. He declares: *Ek Omkar Satnam*. It is the sound Nanak talks of. Omkar is only a symbol to convey the message to you. Existence is song — a very deep song — unobstructed music! No one has created it; no instrument plays the melody. It is an unsounded sound, a causeless song that plays without any reason. Music is the very being of existence, therefore you find it so absorbing. And if you find yourself drowning in music, be sure that melody has a shade of the nada.

A great musician is he who can capture the nada in his instrument. He is able to draw down the Omkar to some degree into your otherwise sleeping world. Music is not meant to stimulate your basic desires.

Music is of two types. One is oriental music, which has been deeply explored and studied by the Hindus. Eastern music is based on the nada. When music wafts towards the nada the listener gradually slips into meditation, which means that you become more aware. You are filled with total consciousness, as if a lamp has been lit within you.

You have heard stories of musicians lighting unlit lamps. Do not take these to be external lamps; they have nothing to do with music. It is you who are the snuffed-out lamp, and if the singer is in a state of *samadhi*, then only can he light your internal lamp. He can only integrate Omkar in his music and bring it down to your level if he is in a state of samadhi himself. If he can bring down even a drop of this nectar, a slight glimpse of that divine music, when you awaken you are filled with awareness, as if someone has shaken you from your sleep. Then this music becomes meditation.

Then there is the opposite kind of music: it puts you to sleep, carries you further into drowsiness. This music also excites passion. For this very reason Islam had banned music. The Muslims did not know the music the Hindus had discovered, which was connected with the *sahasrar*, the center of the thousand-petaled lotus located at the top of the head.

There are the two types of music: one is connected with the lowest center, the sex center, and the other is connected with the highest, the sahasrar. The music connected with the latter is the nada. The former only agitates passion, but it was the only music known where

Islam was born; therefore all music was completely banned in the mosque.

And it was just as well, for ninety-nine percent of the music that is prevalent is such that can never lead you to the temple steps. The West has evolved a form of music that is all distorted: The loser loses all sense, as if he is drunk. This music leads you into deeper slumber and deeper passions. Prostitutes make use of this music. Saints have also made use of it, but with the difference that the singer-saint has experienced the nada.

Nanak was a singer. He never spoke. He only sang. He answered in music. His songs are not constructed with due rhythm and meter; they were improvised creations that came straight from his heart. Someone asked a question; Nanak made a sign to Mardana who began to play his *rabab* and Nanak began to sing. Whatever Nanak has said is in song form, for all of existence understands the language of music. And when the singer is himself in a state of samadhi, the nada inadvertently enters into his song.

Nada means the supreme note that forms silently in existence, like the sound of silence on a quiet night. In the same manner, the nada keeps ringing all twenty-four hours of the day. It is the rhythm of existence. When nothing is, it still sounds. But you have to become very, very silent in order to hear it. When all sound within you stops, then only can you hear. Internally you are a thousand-and-one marketplaces, each replete with its noise and tumult; in this tumult you can hear only what is loudest and what satisfies your cravings. Only then are you conscious of it.

Mulla Nasruddin's neighbor has been practicing his music for hours. When it was well past midnight Mulla could not contain himself any longer. He told him, "You should give a performance in Moscow or London or Peking." The man was very moved by this appreciation.

He told Nasruddin, "Mulla, I never knew you took so much interest in music. Did you like my song so much?"

"It's not that," said Mulla. "At least you will be far enough away from here that we can sleep peacefully."

What passes as music is often nothing but noise and chaos. It is better that you not hear it since you are already so filled with dissonance and discord. Why arouse this poison even further? People dance to incite their passions and sing to work up their frenzy.

But the very thing that arouses passion can also calm; poison can be turned into nectar, depending on what use you make of it. Poison can be both a cure or your death, depending on how you use it.

Nanak says the first experience of the Realm of Knowledge is nada. Then the second is mirth, merry-making. This must be examined, for what has mirth to do with a saint? Mirth means that life is no longer grim but pleasant; it means life becomes sweet, light, joyful, and not burdensome. Ordinarily you see our so-called saints with their long grim faces, as if they bear the burden of the whole world.

Nanak says he who has heard the nada can't be sad and despondent, but filled with mirth and laughter. He can laugh. In fact, only he can laugh in the true sense. Your laughter is a sham; your life energy isn't filled with joy, so how can there be a genuine smile on your lips. Only he can truly laugh, who has known. There is no grimness, no gravity in his life; you find him authentic, genuine. His life is filled with joy and cheer; there are no dark circles of suffering under his eyes, only celebration.

The third is frolic, play. Such a person finds wonder in his life. His frolic has come to the fore, filling him with wonder he thrills at everything he sees, at everything he feels and hears — just like a little child. Wherever he looks he finds infinite wonder. He has no answer for anything and others' answers no longer concern him. Wherever an answer is found, the ego gets a foothold; whenever no answer arises the ego dies a natural death.

Mystery means you cannot hold anything in your grip. You can enter into the mystery if you wish, but you cannot capture it in your grasp. You cannot store it in your safe nor make it a captive of your scriptures; it can't be brought under any regulation. Mystery is like the vast space of the skies: you may enter into it as you would enter an ocean.

So Nanak says, first the nada, then mirth, then frolic, then bliss. Mirth is like bliss; bliss is deep mirth. Mirth is the top layer, like the waves in the ocean, while bliss is the ocean depths. Smiles and cheerfulness are the thrills of bliss that come to the lips. You can laugh only if there is bliss within you. So mirth is on the surface; bliss is the depth. When they combine, supreme blessedness descends on you.

But your mirth is diseased and unnatural. You cannot even laugh unless someone cracks a dirty joke; it requires filth and dirt. Most jokes are about sex, which everyone can enjoy because they are dirty and debasing.

A man has to slip on a banana peel in order for you to laugh. Where kindness is needed, you laugh and joke. Your humor is sick, diseased. A man who has fallen needs help. Give him help! How is it an occasion for laughter? Deep within you, you desire to lower and abuse everyone else. The more you want to see a person fall, the greater your mirth. For example, if a beggar falls you won't laugh so much; but if Indira Gandhi falls you'll be unable to control your laughter. What is there to laugh about a beggar falling? He was already fallen. But there is an unconscious desire in you to knock Indira down. That would be hilarious to you. If a servant falls no one laughs so much; if the master falls it is an occasion for mirth.

Your unconscious hostility is contained within your laughter. Your laughter is a poison, your mirth but sarcasm — a sneer. The difference between mirth and sarcasm is the bitterness, the sting to it. It has thorns without flowers.

The saint also laughs. His laughter carries no sting, no thorns, he laughs mainly at himself for he is aware of his own state. When he laughs at you, then he is also laughing at himself, for he sees a glimpse of himself in you. When he sees a man fall, he sees humanity falling — not just a man. He knows that man is helpless and that his arrogance is thus ridiculous.

How well this man was dressed: tie, coat and whatnot, but a little peel of banana and he is flat on the ground — tie and all! A banana peel pulled a joke on him.

The saint sees man's helplessness behind this fall: how weak he is and yet so proud! He had a Himalayan ego, but he is brought down by a lowly banana peel. He struts about with the idea of defeating God, but he is shamefully defeated by a banana peel. So, if a saint laughs when a man falls, he is laughing at his state of helplessness. He laughs at the thought of his own helplessness, and is filled with shame. He never laughs to revile or beat someone else. Within him is the bliss which overflows into mirth and merriment.

Modesty is the expression of the Realm of Shame.

As knowledge deepens, awareness increases and so also modesty. He who has attained buddhahood, the *Buddha-Purusha*, hesitates when he speaks; he doesn't bang the table. Therefore, it is the non-buddhas who gather the followers. They gauge their leader by the force of his words. If a man is hesitant they feel he isn't sure of himself. How can he be our guide? But the Buddha-Purusha is hesitant out of modesty, out of shame, for he knows how difficult it is to tell.

Many people would come to Buddha with new and different questions. Buddha answered very few questions. Some particular questions that have no answer he would not answer at all. Only non-special questions have answers. Whatever troubles man has created for himself have an answer, but the mystery that belongs to existence has no answer.

So Buddha would hold his peace. When he did not answer, many thought he did not know, for they insisted that if he did know he would have answered. This silence of Buddha you will never comprehend; such modesty as was in Buddha very, very few people had. In Buddha's time there were many theoreticians who answered forcefully. People flocked around them. These theoreticians incited their followers to go and ask buddha certain questions: "If he is enlightened he must answer." This is how people generally believe: if knowledge is attained all answers must be available.

All answers are lost when a person becomes enlightened. He has no answer to give; he feels ashamed; what answer could he possibly give to your question? He also is ashamed of the futile question you put forth, and you are so oblivious to it. People walking on the road have sometimes accosted me with such questions as "Does God exist?" I am on the railway platform about to catch a train and someone shakes my shoulder, "Please, one minute — what is meditation?"

What can be said to such people? They do not know what they are asking. They want answers. If I answer them my answer should make two plus two equal four. Would that life were a straight case of mathematics! Everything would have been so easy then.

Life is not an arithmetic problem. Life is a poem and you need the necessary ability to understand it. You need the qualification to hear it in silence. Poetic answers never make two plus two equal four; they arouse wonder, they awaken you from wherever you are. They tear you by your roots and take you on a new journey: from wonder into more wonder, towards greater wonder. Nanak says, it has no end, it has no end.

Buddha remained silent whenever anyone asked does God exist. This gave rise to two misconceptions. Hindus thought this man knows nothing. You can ask the dullest village pundit and he will give you an answer. He says, "God is," and offers proofs. If any ordinary man can give an answer, what about this man?

I have heard: In a land of fools, the worst of the fools among them became a minister. Now this fellow was a very good speaker. He was adept at lecturing, and that is all that is required to become a minister. He used to impress the crowd by his loud talking. People thought: Here is a man who knows something; but he was really an illiterate who could neither read nor write.

The trouble arose when he become Prime Minister, for tradition demands that he read his lecture and not speak extempore. But the man was clever. He thought to himself, "Never mind. I shall find a way out." So he would pick up any old newspapers, hold it before the audience, and speak as if he were reading his speech. As he could not read he sometimes held the paper upside down.

One day it happened that someone brought a friend who had just come from a foreign land to hear the Prime Minister. Now this man was literate and he saw that the Prime Minister held an old newspaper, and even held it upside down. He stood up and announced, "This man is a cheat. He is not reading what is in the paper for he is holding it upside down."

Now the local people were convinced by the stranger that their Prime Minister was illiterate.

The Prime Minister put down the paper and addressed the gathering, "What is up and what is down for a man who knows how to read? You must have heard the saying, He who knows not the dance finds the floor crooked. What difference does the floor make? One should know the dance. One must know how to read! Let the paper be of any kind. I can read this paper from all directions. This man is illiterate."

He is still the leader of the town.

When people asked Buddha, "Does God exist?" Buddha remained silent. The other fallacy, the second misconception that arose was that people thought Buddha's silence meant that there was no God. Because of the silence Hindus thought that Buddha did not know and Buddha's followers thought there was no God. His own disciples took him for an atheist, whereas there was no greater theist to appear on this earth.

You will understand this from Nanak's words when he says, modesty is the expression. When you ask, "Does God exist?" Buddha keeps silent, for how should he speak? With what face can he speak? What is he to say of so great a mystery? Buddha answers through his silence, and you do not understand. However you interpret his silence is wrong.

> *Modesty is the expression of the Realm of Shame.*
> *The experiences that take place are beautiful and incomparable.*
> *He cannot be spoken of in words.*
> *He who tries repents later.*

How does this happen? As soon as the words are spoken the speaker realizes that what he meant to convey remained unsaid, and what he said is not what he intended. Just looking at the listener he knows he has failed to convey the message. Ninety percent falls off as soon as the first words are formed, and the remaining ten percent never reaches the listener's ears. You said one thing; they heard something else.

Buddha would say one thing; the ignorant people would hear something quite different. Then these ignorant people form sects and establish religious traditions. Thus there is no connection whatsoever between the buddhas and these religious organizations. Therefore all of those who have spoken have regretted it. Those who have tried to speak on this mystery have always insisted that the listener should not cling to his words but use them only as guidelines.

Now Nanak must be sorry for having spoken. When he sees the Sikhs today he must be filled with regrets. Likewise Buddha, Mahavira, Mohammed must all be regretting what they started. They must be together in heaven telling one another their sad stories. They are bound to be weeping together.

What the Buddha has to convey cannot be understood by words, for the listener holds on to the words; then he drags them along and forms religions and organizations around these words. Then these organizations go on for thousands of years. Thousands of errors are committed because of these creeds and doctrines, and thousands of deformities arise. It spreads like a wound on the earth, like an illness on man's consciousness. Nanak says, he who tries to speak, repents later. His words then become the code of law, opinions, beliefs, and hence the mind and understanding of man.

Where consciousness awakens in the Realm of Knowledge, in the Realm of Shame all forms of consciousness take shape.

> *Memory, mind, understanding, and intelligence are all formulated here;*
> *And the consciousness of gods and enlightened ones.*

In that consciousness all these forms are seen. Just as a potter makes so many forms with clay, so also the clay of consciousness takes many forms: intellect, mind, wisdom, remembrance, recollection, genius, brilliance.

When you are sufficiently awakened to rise above these, you realize that they are but various forms of the mind. Whatever you know through them is bound to be limited, for you cannot know the formless through form. That which is behind understanding, memory, mind, intellect is awakening — that is realization! that is awareness! that is consciousness!

You must take hold of this formless and let go of the forms

within. As soon as you catch hold of the delicate thread of the formless within you, you begin to recognize the formless in the world outside. Whatever you know through the intellect will be limited by having form. Like seeing the sky through your window, you will see only as much as the window frame permits.

Consciousness takes many forms, just as matter has many forms — somewhere it is a rock, somewhere a cloud, somewhere it is ice, somewhere it is the skies — so consciousness also has infinite forms: intellect, remembrance. Wise men are intelligent, like pundits; holy men have recollection and remembrance, and some have powerful memories. Even if they have no intelligence their remembrance is very strong. It often happens that very intelligent people have hopeless memories; and many whose memories are strong are not intelligent. There are many examples where people with strong memories were found to have dull intelligence. This because the function of memory is different: to store whatever it comes across and recall it. The function of intelligence is different: to make way through the unknown, with which it is unacquainted. Both are oriented differently: remembrance focuses on the past, and intelligence looks toward the future.

Scientists now believe that if memory is very strong, intelligence gets locked up in it thereby preventing intelligence from working freely. At present most educational institutions lay stress on memory, so it is no wonder that the world is so full of dull people. By the time a child finishes his education his brain is so clogged with data and theories that he is lucky if he manages to save anything of his intelligence. Memory is different; intelligence is different; a genius is altogether different. Genius means the natural ability to know life and recognize it. It is the capacity to know and understand in a flash the answer to any question of life. Ask the greatest scientists like Einstein, who would say, "Whatever I have known was not through my intelligence but through my intuition." He has no answer to the how of his achievement. Genius, intuition happens in many, many ways.

Madam Curie was awarded a Nobel Prize for her discovery. For a long time she had sought the answer to the problem but to no avail. One night she got up in her sleep, went to the table and wrote down the key to her work. In the morning she was shocked to see what she had written. Where had it come from? She recalled the previous day's events — how tired she was by the evening, how she had fallen asleep disappointed — another day lost. Things came back to her as in a dream. She saw herself get out of bed and walk towards the table. She saw herself pick up the pen and write the answer. She recognized her own handwriting. What she had vainly sought for days and months had come to her in a flash in the middle of night. This is the experience of all artists and creative people. A poet will tell you that only when he gives up trying does the verse descend on him. This is a part of intuition.

But Nanak says that all this intelligence, understanding, intuition, etc. is a play of the mind. These are different molds, and whatever you know through them will be limited. You have to rise above them. Only one has to be known within; only one has to be known without. And when the one within is known, then only will you know the one without; for when you become an integrated one within, then only shall you recognize the oneness without.

When you know the one within and the one without, it does not mean you know two, rather you find that the one that is within, is the one that is without. You suddenly discover that all these distances and directions of within and without are self-created. The space outside your house is the same space as inside your house; it is you who have created the walls, and made doors and windows. Do you think you have succeeded in splitting space by raising a wall? No! Space is indivisible. Your walls may or may not be but the skies remain forever.

No sooner do you recognize the one within and the one without than both fall and nonduality is born. The ultimate peak is the experience of the indivisible, the experience of the one.

CHAPTER 19

He Exults in His Creation

Power is the expression in the Realm of Grace;
Except this, there is nothing else.
In it are the great warriors and heroes;
There Rama abides in his fullness.
And in its glory also Sita abides,
Whose form is beyond words.
Those in whose heart Rama abides
Never die nor can be cheated.
There live many devotees of many different worlds;
Keeping the true name in their hearts they enjoy bliss.
In the Realm of Truth the formless abides.
He creates the world and exults in it with his vision.
With him are the continents, the suns, the universes;
And they all defy description.
There are worlds upon worlds, and creations upon creations.
All works according to his order.
Seeing all this and thinking of it, He flowers in happiness,
Nanak says, To describe him is like chewing on iron.

Man is helpless — but only as long as he is away from God. Man is weak, miserable, lowly — but only as long as he is away from God. Our distance from him is the cause of our wretchedness; the further we move away from him the more meaningless life becomes.

Many recent thinkers in the Western world feel that life is meaningless, that there is no motive behind our living, nor is there any destiny or order. It is a long story of meaninglessness, uselessness. It is a "tale told by an idiot, full of sound and fury, signifying nothing."

This feeling is bound to exist. Look at your own life — how much noise and fuss over nothing! You engage in great projects. You never walk, you run; but have you ever asked yourself, "Where am I going?" After all the running you find yourself exactly where you started at your birth; you haven't gained even a grain of sand. If you look at your hands, they are empty. The treasure chest may be full, but you must leave it behind; you are empty. All the dreams of fulfillment turned out to be untrue.

No matter how much you acquire of this world, at death it falls away from you. And what falls away is never yours even though it belongs to you. Those who took refuge and solace in worldly goods built their palaces on sand; they are bound to fall. How long can you delude yourself? Someday you will wake up, someday you will ponder and realize: I walked so long and so far and so much, but reached nowhere.

Your condition is like the ox at the oil mill. How much he walks! Round and round he goes all day. There is so much noise around him as oil is being extracted. After a day's work he is at the same place as when he started in the morning, and the next day is exactly the same. And so it goes.

Your life is like that of the ox. You may cleverly try to hide it by painting it in different hues, but you are aware of the quality of your heart — a beggar's bowl that is forever asking and never gets filled. The further from God man is the more beggarly and wretched his inside state. The filling only comes when you are with him.

We are not only distant from him, but, even worse, we are opposed to him. Whatever we do is contrary. Distance is of no concern if we are with him, for then transformation takes place immediately.

If a man swims against the current, trying to go towards its source, he is not far from the river, but against it. And the irony is, the more you fight the river, the more you realize that it is not your enemy. It is not hostile to you. It follows its course, hurrying along to meet the sea, and has nothing to do with you. Whether you sink or swim is none of its concern. It is you who have made an enemy of the river.

It is because of you alone that you find enemies everywhere in this world. When do you find the time to live? All your time is spent trying to save yourself from your supposed enemies.

Life away from God is bound to be meaningless — if not full of misery. It becomes like a nightmare, and you want to awaken but you cannot. You feel somebody sitting on your chest, and your arms are powerless to push him away; or someone is trying to shove you down a mountain and you have no way to save yourself. You try to move your hands but you cannot. You want to open your eyes, but you cannot. You want to shout, but you cannot. This is a nightmare.

Everyone removed from God is in a dream state. Those who are opposed to the flow of existence are in a nightmare. Examine your own life and you will find that such is the condition. The eyes do not open, the hands do not move, the load on the chest does not lessen — and yet you live! Then your life can be nothing but one long tale of woe.

Kierkegaard, Sartre, Marcel, Heidegger, and other great thinkers of the West describe life as anguish and anxiety with no way to be freed from it. They are right to a very great extent. Life as it is generally led is a torment.

But we also know of another kind of life — that of Nanak, Kabir, Buddha, Krishna, Christ. Their lives are just the opposite of ours: where we are weighed down with harassment, their lives are a veritable dance. Where nothing echoes within us except strains of pain and sorrow, their inner self reverberates with music. Whereas we walk as if we have heavy chains around our feet, their step is light; they walk with a spring. While a look at us conveys the fruits of great sin, their appearance glows with the blessings of the divine.

There is another way of living, and the key is to live not away from, but near to God, to live not against his order but in conformity with it. He whose life flows with the law undergoes a change. You may not necessarily struggle against God, but your ego pushes you — it says the more you fight and struggle, the greater you become.

But the joke of the whole thing is, just the opposite happens: the more you win, the less you become. You may find a big heart in a poor man, but not in a rich man; his heart gets smaller with every gain. A poor man may give in charity, the rich man loses his courage to give. A poor man is capable of love, but there is no music of love and cheer within a rich man; and of course, prayer and God are unheard of where he is concerned. He is barely capable of ordinary animal love. The more wealth you amass the narrower your heart gets. It is a contradiction. The internal space gets more and more constricted and you find yourself always anxious and worried about your possessions.

Nanak says, "In the realm of grace power is the expression, yet his compassion is attained only when you genuinely feel absolutely helpless." Not a hint of cunning can remain; the helplessness must be total. By merely saying, "I am helpless," nothing happens. The feeling must enter deep inside, penetrating the core of your heart, pervading every atom of your being. Not mere lip service but a feeling from your heart, it should be evident in your tears. It must permeate your every word, and echo even when there are no words. In your every action should ring the message to him: I am helpless, O Lord! I am helpless!

What can you do? You can neither do anything nor undo anything. Your actions have brought to pass only what should not have happened; you cannot accomplish anything.

There is a saying in English that is similar in many other languages: Man proposes, God disposes! Nothing can be more erroneous. It is just the other way around — God proposes and man disposes! God gives opportunities and proposals, and man refuses them, denies them. God wants to give everything to man.

Existence is waiting to be looted at your hands, but your doors are shut. This existence wants to shower its bounty on you, but alas, your pots are turned upside down. This existence wants to enter you, but out of sheer fright you have not allowed so much as a crack to open to receive it. And you have so filled yourself with junk that even if it enters there is no space for it. You have left no place befitting him within you.

His grace is attained only when you are utterly helpless, rudderless. The total experience of this helplessness is shame. Then you are ashamed even to say I. Then you wonder on what grounds you can claim I am? On what basis can I say that I am capable of doing something?

But our lives tell the opposite story. You have failed in all your ventures. All your efforts ended in vain, turned to nothing. All the fortresses you built fell into ruins and yet still you have not come to your senses, but hold on to doing. As long as this persists shame cannot enter into you, and Nanak says, "Shame is prayer." As long as you say, "I know," you will not bow down. Does a scholar ever bow down? His head never bends. He may bend his body but his head stands stiff in arrogance.

There is a well known event that the Sufis use for teaching. Two friends studied together throughout their school career. When they finished school and went their separate ways, one became a powerful king and the other a fakir. So it was destined! The king lived in the royal palace; the fakir roamed naked from town to town. The king was famous, the fakir no less so.

Once it happened that the fakir came to the king's capital. Since he was a childhood friend the king made suitable arrangements for his welcome; he had the whole town lit with lamps and the streets strewn with flowers.

As the fakir was proceeding towards the town he met some travelers who said, "What an egoist the king is! He has made all these arrangements just to show you his magnificence. He has lamps lit not only in every house but all along the streets. The whole town looks like the Festival of Lights. He has covered the steps you are to climb with sheets of gold inlaid with precious stones. He wants to show you that you are but a naked fakir while he revels in his glory." The fakir said, "We shall see his arrogance."

The day arrived for the fakir to visit his old friend. All the people went to receive him at the gates to the town. The king was also there. He looked at his friend and was dumbstruck. It was not the rainy season but the fakir's legs were smeared with muck right up to his knees! But it would have been embarrassing to ask him about it in front of so many people. When he crossed the glittering steps and entered the palace, the fakir sat on the priceless carpet spread especially in his honor — and dirtied it!

Then the king finally asked him. "Friend, there was no rain anywhere, and it is not the rainy season, then how come your legs are covered with mire?"

The fakir replied, "If you wanted to show off your wealth, I wanted to show off my poverty to you."

The king laughed and said, "Then come, brother, let us embrace, for neither of us has gotten anywhere. We are just where we were when we left school."

Wealth can fill you with arrogance, and so can renunciation. So arrogance is the only obstruction. Once arrogance is obliterated, shame is what remains.

Nanak says, "The he who is filled with shame gets showered with God's grace." Shame and modesty is worthiness. As long as you are arrogant you do not need him, and how can you achieve what you do not need? You have never really called him, wanted him, needed him. If ever you called him it was for other things: when the child was ill, or you had a case in court — but never just for himself!

Until you call him just for himself, all your prayers are false for your prayer has nothing to do with divinity. You want something of the world — perhaps you might get it from God.

A wealthy man was dying. He called his priest and asked him, "If I were to donate one hundred million rupees to your temple, would I get a place in heaven?" This was a natural question from a man who always thought in terms of wealth.

The priest answered, "There is no harm in trying, though I cannot promise anything. I have never heard of anyone booking his seat in heaven this way. Since your wealth is going to be left anyway, why not try?"

If you have acquired anything through wealth, the feeling always remains in your mind somewhere that worship or meditation can also be attained this way. Wealth is gained by ego, by ambition; whereas worship, prayer, meditation are attained through shame. God is attained only when all ambitions fall, when you find yourself utterly useless, when nothing you do turns out correct. At the moment that you are absolutely helpless and incapable of doing anything, his grace showers.

Not only the ego of doing, but the ego of knowing, must also fall. That you know the four Vedas by heart, or the Koran, or that no one is more adept at the Bible — all this knowledge will keep you from his grace. "I know," which is the statement of your knowledge, is a subtle form of doing. Your doing and your knowing are two sides of your ego. Both must fall.

Have you ever asked yourself in full awareness what you know? You do not even know the stone that lies outside your house and yet you claim to know God? You haven't been able to know a flower fully yet.

The English poet, Tennyson, said: If I were to know the smallest flower fully, I would know what God and man is. You will have known everything if you have known the mystery of a flower opening, since it contains all existence. If you have understood and recognized the beauty of one single flower, you have discovered and understood the beauty of all existence. If you penetrate the truth within the flower, what is left? He who has known the drop knows the ocean, for qualitatively they are one. Whatever is in the ocean is contained in the drop. It is a small edition of the ocean. He who knows a single atom knows all.

But what do we know? Whatever information we have is stale, borrowed, belonging to others. It is alien, handed down to you from thousands of hands. If thousands of people have worn the same pair of shoes, you will not be ready to step into them. But this is how your knowledge is. You have not put your feet but your head into such shoes. All your knowledge is borrowed and alien. You read the books, but cannot even be sure if the person is talking from his personal experience or hearsay.

I am told: A certain film actress was very clever. When she removed her jewels each night she left a note next to them, saying: "These are fake jewels. The real ones are in the bank vault."

One morning she got up and found them gone. On the table was a note, "I took the fake jewels, for I am a sham thief. The real one is in jail."

Are you sure that the one whose words you are taking in, whose knowledge you are imbibing, is authentic? You have no way to find out. You have no criterion to judge the true from the false. The only real test is when you have your own experience, but then you have no further need to listen to anyone else.

This is the trouble. When gold is at hand we do not have the touchstone; when we have the touchstone there is no need to test the gold. But as long as you are able to test, you need the touchstone very badly. You cover your knowledge with borrowed knowledge, and this strengthens the spine of your ego. "I know" creates the arrogance and pride that is the hindrance. When there is neither knowledge nor action, you are no more; both your props have fallen, and the castle is razed to the ground. This state where the castle has fallen into ruins is what Nanak calls shame. When shame becomes intense, crystallized, his grace begins to pour. Your shame, his grace: these two are correlated. Shame is like a hollow in the ground and his grace is like the life-giving rains. It also rains on the mountains, but the water slips off into the valleys below that are low, hollow and empty. His grace pours on all and you can either be a valley and receive it or a mountain and allow it to flow off.

Nanak says, for him no one is high, no one is low; no one is worthy, no one is unworthy. He showers his grace on all. There are some like valleys who are filled and blessed, whereas others are like towering mountains, so filled with themselves that there is no place to hold his grace.

Be like the valley, the hollows in the ground, and you shall attain Nanak's shame. Once shame forms and the hollow takes shape, since His grace is always pouring, you will become a lake of knowledge and awareness. Your very way of being will change. You shall no more be as you are now. The hollow contains only God. Then you are no longer helpless; in fact no one is stronger than you.

> *Power is the expression in the Realm of Grace;*
> *Except this, there is nothing else.*
> *In it are the great warriors and heroes;*
> *There Rama abides in his fullness.*

No sooner does a person attain to shame than grace begins to rain on him, and the wretched pauper becomes a king. Saints have said, "Through his grace the lame cross mountains, the blind begin to see, and the deaf begin to hear."

The saints are not talking of the ordinary lame and blind; they are talking about you. As long as you are filled with arrogance your ears remain deaf, your eyes remain blind and your heart will be stone; it will be insensitive and register nothing. Till you are almost as good as dead, the flame of your light will be flickering unsteadily, as if the oil is running out. Your flame will lack the luster. There will be no urgency or intensity or depth of sensitivity in your life to awaken your heart, so that it does not beat with a dull thud as if half dead.

Your life should be like a river in spate; not only are you full yourself but you wish to give to others since you have so much. Within you should be a magnificence, a fragrance. The more of it you spread, the more it grows, and you possess life's infinite source.

This happens with grace. It is paradoxical, which is why the words of the saints appear mysterious. They are simple, artless, but nonetheless mystifying, for they seem to be saying the reverse of things: Die so that you can live; lose yourself in order to be worthy of attaining; or, be no more and the elixir of existence is yours.

You keep saving yourself, therefore you are nothing. The more you hold onto yourself, the more miserable and wretched and meaningless you will be. The more you save yourself, the more shall you wonder. These are paradoxical statements that are not immediately understood, for they are contrary to our logic. It says, "If you want to be, save yourself." The saints say, "If you want to be, lose yourself. Did the savior save even himself?"

Our logic says, "What if we die?" So we cling all the harder to life. But the saint says, "He who clutches harder to life, his death stands at the door long before his time!" Those who accepted death, welcomed it and went to encounter it found the nectar. They found that death was only a mask behind which the nectar was hidden. You run because of fear and deny yourself the nectar. When you embrace death you find the nectar. The characteristic of that aspect of life which is compassion and grace is power.

The fourth book of Carlos Castaneda is called *Tales of Power*. It deals precisely with Nanak's fourth realm. As soon as the rays of his compassion descend on you, you attain infinite power. You become capable of untold power; you touch mud and it becomes gold. Before, it was different: you touched gold and it turned into mud, because then you were. Now wherever you look you see heaven. Before this wherever you turned was hell; wherever your feet fell, the place became inauspicious; whatever you did turned poisonous, even your love turned to hate, your friends turned foes. All this happened because you yourself were wrong. You were going against God so the results were contrary. Because of your own self, the results were unfavorable.

Now you are no more and everything is possible. Now your very shadow holds magic. Wherever your eyes look the gates of heaven will open. Wherever you go, whatever you do, the very air in that place will change. The people who gather around you will be affected by your glory; it will permeate them.

Therefore, Nanak insists on the company of the saints. He says to seek out saints and holy men, for they are the same ones who have attained the source of power. Their company is elevating, glorious. Sitting next to them....

Energy or power is active and infectious. Remember, well-being and health are equally infectious. Not only does evil enter you through others, but also goodness enters you and flows to others. You feel a freshness in the company of a fresh person. Sit a little with stale, sad, half-dead people, and their drawn faces will so affect you that you depart a different person — sad, ready to cry like them. Sit with laughing, gay people and even if you have been sad, their joy will begin to infect you. Man is not different from or separated from man. From within we are all connected and flow into each other.

Nanak stresses a great deal the company of holy men and saints. He says, "How will your efforts help? Instead, stay next to those who have attained his support, and through them his hands will touch you too! Through them the fragrant air will reach your heart." When a person passes through a garden the fragrance of flowers catches onto his clothes. When a person passes a Buddha, knowingly or unwittingly, the fragrance of his buddhahood permeates his clothes. He no longer can remain where he was; somehow he is a changed person.

The company of saints is invaluable. To establish contact with God is difficult for the simple reason that you have no idea whatsoever of him. The saint is his symbol; you can discover his name and address and find him easily, but where will you seek God? Saint means someone in whom God has crystallized — where his rays are so intense, and the heat so terrible! A saint intensifies God within him in much the same way as we concentrate the rays of the sun through a lens. God is in you too but he is more sparse, less concentrated; his rays do not set fire to you. There is only a lukewarmness that somehow gives you life. The saint is full of fire. He is fire! You are bound to feel the heat when you sit next to him. Something within you will also begin to burn and be destroyed.

The day you attain his grace you begin to gain strength. But remember, that strength is not yours. If you become arrogant with it you will lose it, and in all likelihood tumble right to the bottom. For the subtle ego follows you till the end. It is the last thing to fall. It follows you like a shadow; you hear neither its footsteps nor its voice, and because it walks behind you, you cannot see it.

Just as the body has its shadow, the mind's shadow is the ego. That is why there are stories that the person who attains God loses his shadow. By this don't assume that the physical shadow is lost, for this shadow is bound to last as long as the body endures. It is the internal shadow of the mind, the ego, that is lost. Then, he performs all actions required of him in life, but no shadow forms within; his mind has become transparent. It no longer exists.

Remember, don't be under the impression that you will become strong and powerful. His grace and compassion will rain on you — when you are not. That is all the power you will be capable of. You will become a medium, which is an important word. The flute produces notes which do not belong to it, but to the player. The flute is merely a medium. What is special about the flute, its excellence, lies in the fact that it is hollow. The hollowness allows for the notes to flow. The day that God's grace begins to pour on you, you become like the flute.

Kabir said: I am only a bamboo tube. The songs are all his. It is he who sings. I am only the medium, an instrument. And the instrument is such that I am absolutely hollow, like a bamboo. There is nothing within me.

Power is the expression in the Realm of Grace;

The ultimate energy is expressed here. He who attains his grace attains this intense magnetism. You are drawn towards him. You try to stop yourself but cannot, for some magnificent attraction binds you to him in spite of all your efforts.

Power is the expression in the Realm of Grace;
Except this, there is nothing else.
In it are the great warriors and heroes;
There Rama abides in his fullness.

When the moment arrives in a person's life he becomes a Mahavira, a great warrior. When we depend on our own self we are miserable paupers; when we attain his support we become a Mahavira. All energy is his, everything is his. We have only to step aside and give way to this energy.

There Rama abides in his fullness.
And in its glory also Sita abides,

These utterances must be entered into in depth. A person within whom his power descends is bathed in and invested with a double energy: Rama descends into him, and also Sita. These are important symbols. If only Rama descends the person would remain incomplete. He will gain the male energy, but, being incomplete, it is violent. It will lack the glory of the feminine energy, its gentleness, its beauty, its mildness. Rama is only complete together with Sita.

The feminine energy is a different dimension of the same energy, which gives it equilibrium, and maintains the balance. If there is male energy alone, a Hitler will be born who can do nothing but destroy, for he has not the feminine energy for balance. The female energy is a creative energy; it is the mother, the giver of birth. It is joined to the root source of existence; it is mild and gentle. The power of this energy is compassion, affection. This energy is not like the sun but cool like the moon. It is an energy, yet it is cool. And where the sun and the moon become one, where hardness and mildness unite, where violence and humility meet, there both Rama and Sita are.

This is a very deep discovery of Hindu thought that is beyond the understanding of many; Christians, Muslims, Jainas and Buddhists have all been incapable of understanding its depth. The Jainas cannot accept Rama as God because Sita comes in the way. What kind of a God has a female with him? Their contention is that God should be unattached. So for them Mahavira is God, for there is no hint of a woman — even in the far distance.

The Jainas have carried this affair so far as to deny that Mahavira had a wife or that he had children; they changed his whole life history. The fact is that he was married and had a daughter. It is mentioned in the Jaina *shastras* that the girl was married and Mahavira had a son-in-law. But the Jainas erased this portion of his life for it went against their concept of God. How can he have a child? To think of Mahavira going into sex was unbearable to contemplate, so they changed the whole story and made him stand absolutely alone.

We can see the violence in Mahavira but not tenderness. If one side of life is missing, Jaina thought cannot get very far. It did not give rise to any culture or civilization, but remained only an ideology. You cannot find even one town in which only this ideology prevails, for if a town contained only Jainas who would be the cobbler? Who would be a sweeper or cut hair? That is not part of their culture. They are crippled and have to depend on others. They follow a mere ideology.

And the most deep-rooted reason behind their being crippled is denying the feminine element. The Jaina religion does not ever allow for a woman to attain enlightenment. She will have to be born as a man first, then only can she go to heaven. Women must take orders from men. They are granted no equality in Jainism.

And you will be surprised to know the reason: a man attains celibacy, but even if a woman practices abstinence she cannot be truly celibate because her menstrual flow will continue according to the law of nature. For them a person cannot be liberated until celibacy is fully attained.

The Jainas found it difficult to understand Rama and impossible to understand Krishna with all his girl friends. The Buddhist could not understand. And Islam and Christianity were also certainly far removed from it; they couldn't understand either.

The Hindu thought is very deep. It says that energy has two facets; one manifests as male, the other as female. It is not important whether male or female, but the important fact is that the energy balance itself by being both male and female. The male alone has violence, not gentleness. All qualities of gentleness are feminine; even words describing them bear the feminine gender in Hindi, like *compassion, affection, kindness, pity* — as it should be.

When man reaches the supreme state there is a unity within him of the male and female. He is violent and he is also mild, gentle. The sun and the moon combine within him: he is full of fire and cool as moonbeams. When these two facets are integrated, the Supreme Man becomes manifest. This supreme state is beyond both man and woman for it is the union of both their energies. In them is born the One, but only when they are completely and fully drowned in each other.

Therefore, the sutra of Nanak says that Rama alone is not enough:

There Rama abides in his fullness.
And in its glory also Sita abides,
Whose form is beyond words.

Then it is impossible to describe the form. You can discuss the form of a man and you can discuss the form of a woman, but where Rama and Sita merge into one, discussion becomes difficult, for opposite qualities have merged into another. If you say one thing about it now, the opposite is also present.

In Japan there is a statue of the Buddha in which the right half of the face is of Buddha. The hand on this side carries a burning flame whose light falls on the very gentle, beautiful, tender face, which is feminine in all its qualities. The other hand carries a sword whose glare falls on the left half of Buddha's face. Though the face is the same, the expression is not of Buddha but of Arjuna, a warrior.

The samurais, who are the warrior class, worship this image. The image can be said to be half Buddha and half Arjuna. The male and female have been integrated into one.

Nietzsche has criticized Buddha and called him effeminate. There is some truth in it, for in Buddha manifests completely the form of the female. The male energy of Buddha is not characterized, for Budddha had attained to such depths of tranquility: he had become cool as the moon, and the sun was lost.

The Hindu makes a point to stand Sita with Rama, Radha with Krishna. When the name is spoken it is always "Sitaram" and "Radhakrishna." Because the woman is the giver of life, she is the first and the man is placed second. Violence is second; compassion is first. When there is untapped violence hidden behind compassion its beauty is boundless. And when the energy lies hidden behind affection, how is one to express it? If there is cold fire, how is one to describe it? Where the opposites meet, expression becomes impossible.

> *Those in whose heart Rama abides*
> *Never die nor can be cheated.*
> *There live many devotees of many different worlds;*
> *Keeping the true name in their hearts they enjoy bliss.*

There is no death for him in whom Rama abides, in whose heart God dwells and whose heart is overfilled with him. Understand that death is only for you; there is no death for God. Waves are formed and destroyed, but the ocean is forever. As long as you identify with the waves you will die, for the wave considers itself as separate and is sure to die. Therefore, we are frightened of death. Your identity will die. You have made wrong connections. If you join yourself to God, to Rama, then where is death? Therefore the wise man dies before death; he breaks all his connections, separating himself from all identities. He knows he is neither the body nor the mind; both these will die. He knows he is not the ego, which is also sure to die. It is destructible; it is a small form that has appeared like a wave. No matter how beautiful the wave may be, no matter how high it may rise and boast of touching the skies, the very next moment it begins to drop into oblivion. In youth all waves boast of touching the skies. Ask the same people in their old age!

I have heard: A fox set out for food early one morning. The sun was just rising behind the hills and she found her shadow stretched long before her. Seeing her shadow she thought: "Today it seems I shall need a camel for breakfast, for see how big I have become; look at my shadow!"

The poor fox had no other gauge with which to measure herself except the shadow.

She kept looking for a camel. By now it was mid afternoon and the sun was high overhead. She was feeling faint with hunger for there was no camel in sight.

Suddenly she looked down and her shadow was so small as to hardly be there at all. "Now I can do with even an ant!" the poor hungry fox cried.

In youth the wave is at its peak; therefore youth is foolish. The West put its faith in youth and suffered, and that suffering is increasing by leaps and bounds. The Orient never trusted youth or gave it a place of importance, for it would be like giving importance to foolishness. Youth is the peak of the wave, the longest shadow. In the length of the shadow you see all kinds of dreams. What doesn't each of us dream of becoming? The East has venerated old age, for then the shadow contracts to almost nothing, and if old age does not awaken you and make you aware of the ego, then when will you awaken? If you awaken in young age, your life is filled with glory. If you do not awaken even in old age you are the greatest of fools. In youth your not awakening can be forgiven; not so in old age.

As soon as a person begins to observe life with awareness, he discovers that his relationships were of the wrong kind: they were all physical. The cells of the body change completely every seven years yet you continue to exist. One day in the mother's womb you were so small that you could be seen only under the microscope; that too was your body. Then one day, when you die, your relatives will make a small bundle of your remains and throw you in the Ganges; that too is your body! How many ups and downs have you seen in between these two events? If you identify yourself with this body then you will tremble and fear death. Therefore a wise man dies before death — by his own hands.

There is that incident in Nanak's life when his disciples found him at the burning grounds. He said, "I thought it better to come here on my own feet than on the shoulders of others, and if someday I have to come here it is best that I know the place well. There is no better place than this for meditation. Have no fear for me." And he sent his disciples back. He is saying that death is the meditation; there is no other. If you concentrate and meditate on death, by and by death departs. The top layers of death vanish and the hidden nectar comes into view. The wave is lost but the ocean is found.

Buddha would send his monks to the burial grounds. He told them: "Watch people burn. Observe the bones turning into ashes, the smoke rising from the skin, the flowers from the pyre. See the dead man's own people breaking his skull. Those whom he trusted all his life didn't take a moment longer than necessary to prepare him for the last rites. Watch all of this if you wish to reach buddhahood. All those who promised never to part, cry for a few days and then begin again their normal lives. When all are gone and the corpse is left alone, watch it, observe it quietly. This is what is going to happen to you, if not today, then tomorrow or the day after." So Buddha always insisted that his disciples go to the burning *ghat* so they could observe it and begin to die consciously; then only do the practices come easier.

For three months, day and night, the monk had to watch death. There was death and death and death... Death was getting more and more intense. He would begin to see death everywhere, all around him. Everything would seem to be burning; and yet he would sense a point of awareness within him that could not burn. Flames cannot touch consciousness. Flame has nothing to do with it. The monk returns more conscious, more aware; then he breaks his old connections. Only then would Buddha say, "Now it is possible."

There was a fakir by the name of Ebrahim. He was once a king, then he became a Sufi fakir. He used to stay on the outskirts of his own former kingdom. Whenever travelers came to him asking the way to the town, he would say, "Go left." People would walk a mile or two and find themselves at the burning ground. They would turn back very angry with the fakir, and then take the other road to find the town.

When he saw them again Ebrahim would say to them, "I too used to live there. I have now come to understand that it is not a living place but a dying place; every person there is awaiting death. Would you call death's waiting room a living place, a habitation? Would you call it a settlement where people go one by one and never return, where even the very colony one day will be no more? What people call the burning ground is a place where you settle once forever. Now that I would call a real habitation."

Our settlements are death grounds, and our burial grounds are the last of our habitations. A sage dies before death; an ignorant person clings to life, making every effort to survive even with his last breath. A wise man dies but once, but a fool dies several deaths. Until you learn this lesson you will have to die again and again.

Death is an education. It is like a child failing in school who is returned to the same grade. If he fails again and again he remains in the same grade until he learns. In the same way death is a great education. Until you learn to recognize the nectar you will have to come again and again.

A singer was giving a performance. The hall resounded with applause and shouts of, "Encore! Encore!" He sang again. Again they shouted, "Encore!" This went on eight times. His throat became sore, and he could no longer sing.

He told the audience, "I am glad that you enjoyed it with such enthusiasm, but now I can sing no more."

One man got up and shouted, "Who enjoyed your song? You are a rotten singer but until you sing correctly we won't leave you."

The cycle of death and birth is God's request to you to sing properly. It is part of your training and you have to pass through it. He who understands this breaks his identity with death.

Nanak says that those with Rama in their hearts can neither die nor be cheated. And here you are! No matter how clever you are, how efficient, how cunning, you are bound to be cheated; for no one except yourself is cheating you. No one else can rob you; it is impossible, but you have become attached in such a wrong manner that the other can rob you. Your vision is so filled with illusions that all around you see only enemies – everyone seems out to steal from you.

Sri Ramakrishna used to tell this story: There was a kite that found a piece of meat. She held it in her talons and flew away, but it was her bad luck that there were many kites out flying in the skies hunting for food. They saw the piece of red flesh and began to chase her. They swooped down on her, pricking her with their beaks. She tried her best to hold onto the piece of flesh, but there were too many kites and she was badly wounded. They had plucked so many of her wing feathers she could hardly fly. Ultimately she let go of the food in her mouth. No sooner did she do this than all the other kites left her. She flew to the branch of a tree and sat there quietly.

Ramakrishna would say, "From the day I saw this happening I let go of my piece of flesh! Now I have no enemies. Actually I had no enemies before; it was the piece of flesh that was causing all the trouble."

As long as you hold onto wealth, someone is bound to be your enemy; as long as you hold onto your flesh others will not leave you in peace. In truth there are no enemies, only you catch hold of the wrong things. Whenever you grasp hold of something, even your friend will seem an enemy.

Mulla Nasruddin's wife was very angry. She was into a senseless tirade against Mulla. He, poor man, stood quietly with both hands in his pants pockets, as men usually do. After she had said all she wanted to say, and even more, she shouted at him, "And stop this nonsense! I see you clenching your fists at me inside your pockets!" The poor man was just keeping quiet to save his own skin.

If you are angry, fists appear everywhere, gripped and taut. It was only natural that Mulla's wife saw fists in his pockets. In fact your eyes create these illusions for you. If you are holding a piece of meat like the kite, and you have the same understanding as you have now, you are bound to be cheated. The piece of flesh is the body; as long as you hold onto the body you are bound to be cheated. There is no way to save yourself no matter how clever you are.

Kabir says, "Your efficiency has no value — not a tuppence. You hold the lamp of consciousness in your hand, yet you fall into the well."

You are bound to be cheated, for you yourself make the arrangements: you establish wrong contacts and false relationships. And he who relates himself to the wrong, to the false, determinedly arranges to get himself cheated. If you hold onto the piece of flesh the kites are bound to swoop.

Those in whose heart Rama abides
Never die nor can be cheated.
There live many devotees of many different worlds;
Keeping the true name in their hearts they enjoy bliss.

These are the four divisions of the path of the journey. First, in the "Realm of Religion," there is nature. In "Knowledge" there is the awakening to nature — to be aware and conscious of things as they are. In "Shame" it is to be modest, understanding your condition you become humble, helpless, zero. The fourth is to allow his compassion and grace to shower on you without any obstacles.

These four are the divisions of the journey. The fifth is the destination, and that is: truth. In the Realm of Truth abides the formless, God. That is the destination.

He creates the creation and exalts it with his vision. Here the path ends. Now there is no more need to divide it into any divisions. When his grace fills you completely, you are fully bathed; then you have nothing left to call your own. You drown and flow away in the ocean of divinity. You seek: Where am I? Where am I? You have no idea where you have disappeared. You have no knowledge of your own self, of where you are, though you are completely aware. You seek here, you seek there, and find it is he and he alone that is everywhere; you are nowhere, you are zero. When this knowledge becomes crystallized you become a mere medium — no more.

In the Realm of Grace, you will be only a medium, a flute, for the songs are his. Then this too vanishes and even the flute is no more. Only he is there. There is now no one to say even as much as:

"You, you, you! "For as long as this knowledge remains, a little of yourself also remains.

> *In the Realm of Truth the formless abides.*
> *He creates the world and exults in it with his vision.*
> *With him are the continents, the suns, the universes;*
> *And they all defy description.*
> *There are worlds upon worlds, and creations upon creations.*
> *All works according to his order.*
> *Seeing all this and thinking of it, He flowers in happiness,*
> *Nanak says, To describe him is like chewing on iron.*

An important thing to keep in mind, as Nanak stresses time and again, is that God has not stood apart or removed himself from his creation after creating it, nor is he in any way opposed to it, nor has he forgotten it. God's work of creation goes on every minute, eternally. Actually, creation is God's way of being. He creates and creates and creates, and he is always interested in whatever he creates.

This is very significant. We tell the seeker not to be attached to anything in order to attain God, but God himself is not unattached or uninvolved. If he were so, the process of creation would stop; everything would come to a halt. Now what is this? As soon as you become one with God a new kind of involvement arises, a new interest, where there is no difference between attachment and nonattachment, where there is neither desire nor desirelessness, where there is neither enchantment nor otherwise. All differences fall away.

God creates with full interest and desire, yet he is desireless, uninvolved. How will you be able to understand this paradox? Nanak says it is as difficult as *chewing on iron*. God creates, so his interest is natural, his involvement is natural; but it is not a blind involvement as we have with our desires. In his involvement there is no possessiveness, no ownership. He creates you and frees you, and lets you loose. This is why you can wander, commit sin, do evil. He does not bind you in chains to keep you away from evil. He has his relationship with you, all right, but he does not stand in the way of your freedom. It is not that he is against you, yet you are completely independent. This is rather complex.

When a mother is attached to her son, this attachment kills his freedom, for she is always saying: Don't go here, don't go there. Don't do this, don't do that, and a thousand other don'ts. She smothers him with her love, but kills him nevertheless. She doesn't give him enough independence to allow him to stand on his own two feet or gain some experience of life; in this manner she cripples the child. He will never become mature as long as he is under his mother's protection; even when she dies, her hold over her son will continue as before and he will find it difficult, if not impossible, to love another woman. He knows only one love, his mother. Anyone else would be sinful. The mother was interested in the child, but it was blind infatuation.

A relationship with open eyes protects you, and at the same time does not destroy your freedom. It sometimes obstructs with a view to making you worthy of going ahead. It makes you strong. It supports you today and withdraws the support little by little so that you may be able to stand on your own tomorrow. It does not lend the support in order to make a cripple of you.

Then there is another kind of mother: if she is told that her attachment to her child is harmful, she draws back completely and removes all restraint from the child. Now total nonrestraint is not the same as giving freedom to your child. If it is a boy he may go to prostitutes, take drugs, gamble, steal, murder. The mother has given him full freedom to do as he pleases; she has become indifferent to her child. First she cared so much, but her caring was blind; now there is negligence and indifference, which is equally blind. The balance lies between the two.

This balance is the characteristic of God. It is his very nature. His attitude towards his creation is: he protects you so that you may be independent, and gives you independence so that one day you may be able to surrender. These are two apparent contradictions. He gives you the opportunity to go far away, for if you do not go far how will you come close? He gives you license to wander, for if you do not wander how will you gain experience? He gives you a chance to fall, for if you do not fall how will you learn to protect yourself?

And yet he protects you and follows you. His eye watches everywhere; his shadow is everywhere; he envelops you from all sides.

No matter how far from him you go, still he is beside you, so close that whenever you need him you have only to turn and there he is — available to you that very moment.

There is the well known couplet: "In the mirror of my heart is the picture of my beloved. I have only to bend a little to get a glimpse of him."

No matter how far you go, he is always behind you, following you. He causes you no interference, no matter what path you tread. He does not even stop you from going wrong, if that's where you are heading. He allows you to be wrong if you so wish, and in his tender love he does not remove his energy from you, but waits. He awaits your pleasure. He hopes that one day you will return and when you do — ah, what joy, what ecstasy he feels!

Seeing all this and thinking of it, He flowers in happiness, Nanak says, To describe him is like chewing on iron.

This is certainly so, for there all contradictions are laid to rest, and become one.

I have studied the lives of many people and find that we can move towards any extreme and do all kinds of things, but all extremes can be very dangerous.

I know a very possessive husband who follows his wife not just as a shadow, but like a ghost. When he is in the office he is always worried; perhaps his wife is laughing with someone and having a good time. He would leave his work and pay surprise visits home just to check on her. He cannot bear her talking and laughing with others without him. He firmly believes in the descriptions of the wife given by Kalidas, the famous Indian poet. In one of his best known poems he describes a wife so pining away from a fifteen-day absence from her beloved, that she "wilts away and becomes like a skeleton" and then she describes it all in messages sent to him with the clouds.

This constant siege from all sides has filled the wife with boredom and subtle hatred. Theirs had been a marriage of love. They had been very much in love. I could see that, and I knew them for a long time. But when the husbands love became so excessive, his hands no longer formed a garland around her neck, but became a noose. It is not diamonds and gold alone that bind; such love could also be fatal. The wife's love began to diminish and she began dreaming of being freed from her husband. The more independent she tried to become, the more restrictions he created for her.

I explained to the husband that this was madness, that he was killing his wife's love for him with his own hands. Love also wants freedom and a chance to breath. Love needs a little distance, a little aloneness, some time to oneself. I advised him, "Don't be after her so much or you will kill her love for you. Then you will have only yourself to blame."

After a great deal of discussion the husband began to see some sense in it, but then he began to disregard her completely. Now even if he saw her in bed with another man, it would make no difference to him. He says he has given up his possessiveness. He says, "Now I have nothing to do with her. She can do what she pleases. I am in no way connected with her now." The only type of connection he knows is a noose.

This is a natural human trait. If full freedom is given as in the West, it tends to become total indifference, or we set up such a complete subjugation that it can strangle. This is what is happening in the East.

To say anything about God is as good as *chewing on iron*, so difficult is it. He is both: he gives you full freedom, but his love is not an iota less on account of this. He leaves you free, which is the only genuine love. There is no conflict between his love and the freedom he gives you; he does not stop you even if your feet go astray, but waits patiently for you to return. When you retrace your steps and the prodigal comes home – oh the joy, the celebration!

Nanak says: "He worries about you and thinks of you. He rejoices in you. He does not stand apart, unaffected; his nonattachment is filled with a deep essential affection. He is far and yet he is near. He has left you to do as you please, and yet his eye is always on you. He has never, never left you. He always stands besides you. Your sorrow and anguish touch him; your joy and happiness fill him with cheer. You are not a stranger in this universe; it is your house. You are not alone in this world. God is always with you."

This assurance and comfort has deep meaning for the devotee; otherwise there is nothing. If you put aside the thought of God, the world stands untouched, unconcerned beside you; it does not bother what you do or what you do not do, whether you live or whether you die. Let the storm take you; there is no one to care.

But for the devotee there is great assurance and solace in the feeling that "someone is waiting for me." When you return home you will not find it empty; when you return inwards to your own nature you will find God awaiting you. Not only will you find him waiting, but you will be enchanted by all the arrangements for the celebration he has made in your house.

A story that Jesus told time and again is well worth understanding. A rich man had two sons. One boy turned into a vagabond. When he came of age he demanded his half share, which he took and left for the city, for the village offered no means of spending his money: there were no gambling houses, no taverns, no prostitutes. He lost every penny he had in these pursuits and become a roadside beggar. The father was keeping track of him. When he heard of his son's destitution, he was very unhappy. He knew that it was useless to try to bring him back by force, for that might take him farther away. He could only wait, hoping that when his son began to see things in their right perspective he would return on his own.

The elder son remained at home. He worked hard and had doubled the remaining inheritance. He plowed the fields and tended the vineyards, working from morning to night.

Then one day it occurred to the beggar son: "I shall die this way. I still have a home. My father is alive and I can count on his love. He gave me an opportunity to learn for myself what is right and what is wrong, so I am sure his compassion will not fail me now and he will take me back to his heart. I have full confidence in him."

One day he sent word to his father that he was coming home. The father arranged a grand reception. He had lambs butchered and the best of everything prepared, for his son was coming home. He decorated the whole village with flowers and invited everybody in the village.

The elder brother was in the fields. Someone went to him and said, "It is so unjust! You have served your father faithfully your whole life, and have doubled and trebled his assets. You have never gone against his wishes, yet he never arranged such a grand reception in your honor. Now your brother who squandered his inheritance on wine, women and song is returning, and look at what your father is doing for him. It is rank injustice."

The elder brother also felt it was unfair. He returned home saddened and downhearted. He saw the lamps and the flowers set out in his brother's honor and could bear it no longer. He went to his father and said, "I have served you and obeyed you my whole life, but you have never prepared a feast in my honor. Today this prodigal son of yours returns home and look how much you have done to receive him. I can't believe my eyes."

The father replied, "Son, you have always been near me. You never went astray, so there was no need to welcome you. You are always with me and welcome every moment. You are so close to my heart, but this boy who went astray, who wandered and ruined himself, and for whom I spent so many anxious, sleepless nights, he is returning and needs to be welcomed. You gave me no cause for worry; instead I have always been happy and pleased with you, so there is no need to express excessive happiness in your case."

When the prodigal returns a magnificent reception is called for. Jesus would say: Good people, holy men and saints, are like the elder brother; those who have gone stray, sinned, committed crimes, are like the younger brother. Jesus made this a wonderful beginning for his spiritual teachings and because of this, the Jews turned against him. For the Jews believe that he who sins is punished by God; whereas Jesus has said he will welcome him when he returns for he loves him. Do as much wrong as you please, you cannot remove yourself from his heart. You may show your back to him but he will wait. He is the Father of all.

We have a very deep connection with existence, and existence feels pleased — so the Hindus have known from time immemorial. That is why it is said that when a person attains buddhahood flowers bloom out of season. Flowers open when Buddha passes by, whatever the season, for existence is filled with bliss at that moment.

This is what Nanak is saying, that he is so filled with joy and dances in ecstasy whenever the prodigal returns. This is the union of freedom and love. Do what you will, you cannot displease him. His love for you is much deeper than anything you might do. But his attachment is not like yours. He doesn't chain you by the neck. God is not a prison; God is love and freedom. It is difficult to explain, for they appear so contrary, for when you love a person you take away his freedom, and when you give freedom you say good-bye to love.

Where affection and nonaffection both are, where desire and desirelessness both are, where all contradictions unite, there is the great confluence.

Nanak says, To describe him is like chewing on iron.

CHAPTER 20

Patience Is the Goldsmith

Self-restraint is the furnace; patience is the goldsmith;
Intellect is the anvil; knowledge is the hammer;
Fear is the bellows; austerity is the fire;
Feeling is the crucible into which the nectar falls.
The coinage of the Word is cast in the mint of truth.
Only those receiving his grace can succeed in it.
Nanak says, one becomes exalted by his compassionate look.
Epilogue
Wind is the guru; water is the father; the great earth is the mother;
Night and day are midwife and groom; and the whole world is playing with them.
Good and bad deeds are read out in his court by Dharma,
And our own actions determine whether we are near to him or far.
Those who meditate on his name and labor sincerely earn merit;
Their faces are radiant with success,
And many others are liberated by contact with them.
Self-restraint is the furnace; patience is the goldsmith;
Intellect is the anvil; knowledge is the hammer;
Fear is the bellows; austerity is the fire;
Feeling is the crucible into which the nectar falls.
The coinage of the Word is cast in the mint of truth.
Only those receiving his grace can succeed in it.
Nanak says, one becomes exalted by his compassionate look.

Self-restraint means giving direction to life, giving it vision and a goal. A man without restraint runs in all directions, not knowing where to go or what is to be attained; he has no aim, no goal in life. He is like a blind man shooting an arrow. A life of restraint is one in which a person is well aware of his goal; he knows exactly where to let his arrow fly. An arrow that is let fly haphazardly cannot possibly hit the target. No power is attained without restraint and moderation.

So the first quality, self-restraint, involves having a direction, a goal. Once you decide upon a goal then you have to let go of everything that does not further your goal. If you want to achieve one thing you have to let go of a thousand others. He who tries to attain everything ends up with nothing; you have to make a choice.

Now you have come to listen to me here. You had to practice some restraint in choosing to hear me: you left some work half done, or you could have put this much time to some better use, or you could have done some profitable business in the time you spent here. You could have done many things, but once you made the decision to come here, you renounced all the other possibilities for this period of time.

Each moment carries infinite possibilities that can carry you in a thousand directions. A man chooses going to a house of prostitution instead of the temple; another goes to the temple who could also have gone to the prostitute. Both have practiced restraint in not taking the other choice or a thousand and one other possibilities.

You take one step and you leave thousands of steps behind. Only that person requires no restraint who does not walk at all. Whoever walks will have to direct each step of his with the utmost awareness and understanding.

So — direction, path and goal. When these three are in complete harmony you attain self-restraint and balance. Nanak says that is the oven, the furnace where gold is purified and all waste matter burns off. Choose your goal in full awareness, then your life becomes an arrow proceeding in a particular direction, rather than tumbling and fumbling from one corner to another like a blind man; neither are you being jostled about by the crowd, moving helplessly wherever it takes you, nor prodded and kicked from here to there by your own desires.

This is the basic difference between the man of restraint and the desire-ridden man. A man torn by desires runs in a thousand directions simultaneously. It gradually drives him insane trying to do a thousand things at the same time. When he is taking his meals his mind is involved in his shop; when he is in the shop his mind is busy with a hundred other things. Had he a thousand hands, a thousand legs, a thousand eyes, a thousand bodies, you would see the actual state of his mind: his thousand bodies would all go in different directions, with no likelihood of their meeting again.

However, this is your internal state: your mind travels in a thousand directions without any hands and feet, tearing you into fragments. Unless and until you become an integrated whole, you are not fit to be offered at the feet of God.

Many doctrines have been formed since ancient times with regard to the integrity of man. In Islam there is the concept that if a man has any part of his body maimed — whether a finger is cut off or he has undergone an operation — he is unfit to reach the feet of God. Therefore the Muslims are very fearful of operations; if they have to have one they feel guilty and fearful of becoming unfit for God.

In Pakhtoonistan if a limb has to be removed it is severed and preserved until the person dies, and is then buried along with him so that, when he approaches God, he is not incomplete. It is a very significant idea to be a fully integrated whole before approaching God, but here, as elsewhere, a wrong interpretation is being followed.

The Hindus also have this same concept. You must have heard the old stories: when a man had to be burned in a sacrificial fire care was taken that all his parts were intact. If even the slightest defect was present, say a bit of the small finger was chopped off, then he was disqualified.

The finger of a prince got crushed and broken in a door of the palace. Being a devotee who believed and trusted in God, he turned around and said to his attendant, "God be praised! I could have died."

The attendant was surprised. "Your devotion is beyond my understanding. Your finger is broken and you are bleeding badly, yet you thank God. That is carrying devotion too far. You are only fooling yourself by thanking God for this." The attendant was a man of reason.

The prince replied, "Wait awhile, for time will tell." Faith cannot be explained by reason, because faith has no proof.

The prince and the attendant went hunting one day. They lost their way in the jungle and were captured by *avdhoots*, a group of ascetics who were looking for a human being to sacrifice. First they caught hold of the prince, but found that all his parts were not complete — the one finger was missing. He would not do, so they seized the servant and found his body intact. As they were preparing him for sacrifice the prince reminded him, "Didn't I tell you God's grace is on me? I am saved from death." The test, the authenticity of faith, takes time for proof.

Human beings were offered as sacrifice, but this too was a misunderstanding. The sages preached that only he who is total within himself can gain entrance to the Lord's assembly. The lack of a finger does not make you incomplete; even if the head is cut off, a man is not incomplete.

But when consciousness is cut off and his mind falls into fragments, then he becomes incomplete. Your mind is like mercury: let it loose and it breaks immediately into a thousand pieces that cannot be gathered together; touch one small pellet of quicksilver and it will break into ten more. That is how your mind is, broken into thousands of pieces, with each piece going its separate way. If and when you become at all awakened and look within yourself, you will find one part of your mind heading East, one to the West, one to the North, one to the South. One part wants to earn money, another wants to follow the spiritual path, and so on.

Mulla Nasruddin set out to get a beautiful wife. When he married and brought home his wife, his friends were shocked at how ugly she was. They asked Mulla what had happened.

"I was in a terrible fix," he tried to explain. "The girl's father had four daughters and he described the dowry position of each. The youngest was twenty-five years old and very beautiful. For her he had set aside twenty-five thousand rupees as dowry. Feeling the dowry to be rather low I asked about the other daughters. The second youngest is thirty years old and he had provided thirty-thousand rupees for her. The third is thirty-five and he provided thirty-five thousand rupees for her. He was reluctant to mention his eldest daughter but I told him not to worry but just state the facts. She is fifty years old and has a dowry of fifty-thousand rupees. I don't know what came over me then, but here I am stuck with a fifty-year-old hag. I only realized my foolishness on the way home."

The mind is fragmented, so never trust it. One part wants beauty, another wants wealth; you go to fetch one thing and you return with something else; you came on earth to get one thing, but instead you take something very different when you return. Do not trust your mind or you will get nowhere; you will fragment into many pieces like a drop of mercury.

If you do not listen to your mind but instead heed the witness within, you will be able to remember what you have come into this world for, what you have come to buy from the marketplace of *sansara*. That remembrance will become your goal, then you will gain the ability to throw off the fragments that besieged your mind. To practice self-restraint involves the ability to leave the chaff for the wheat, to let go of the useless and worthless in favor of the useful and worthwhile.

The worthless has no value; it serves no purpose in life, brings no peace or joy. It is not designed to reveal the truth, but it has its own attraction, its own temptation and excitement. You can tell yourself: What harm is there in leaving the road to pick some flowers? I can always get back again. But when you take the first steps off the road towards the flowers, you see so many flowers up ahead, and your journey changes course as you shift a little this way or that to savor a little of the fascination of things that are perishable. Lean a little towards them and you are gone!

There are thousand of paths on which to go astray, but only one to reach the right place; therefore you need a very strong memory — uninterrupted remembrance is required. There are many devices and tricks for losing the path, but only one way to reach the destination. There are millions to lead you astray, but only one who can lead you right. If you want to go astray and wander, go ahead. You can err for lives on end. That is what you did, and that is why you are here now, and that is what you still are doing. But there is one path.

Always remember: truth is only one, not many; untruths are infinite, countless. Only the one is worth attaining; the untold others are only worth discarding. It is like a children's maze with many, many paths, but only one exit; the paths all look as if they lead somewhere, but ultimately they arrive at a dead end.

Life is such a puzzle. Whereas children's puzzles are small and contained on a single piece of paper, life's puzzle is endless. It has no beginning and no end; therefore the need for a guru. If you try to solve life's mystery and persist in walking on your own, you will wander for millions of lives.

There is the danger that you might feel that there is no way to get out of the rut of the mundane world; you have tried so many times that you may be disheartened. You might become so despondent you will give up all hope. There is another danger, that you get habituated to wandering. When we do something so many times we become quite efficient at it. Then it doesn't matter what the work is; you've become such an expert wanderer that even if you come across the right path you will shun it.

Guru only means a person who has found the door and can stop you from wandering. He will warn you from treading a path that may seem very attractive and very promising but is only a pseudo-path. You may attain wealth — untold wealth, but what will you gain in the end? Where will you reach? You will find yourself smack against a wall. What will you attain through position? Ultimately you will find the path is lost. Protect your reputation as you will, but what does it yield in the end? Those who respect you have nothing themselves, so what will they give you? What value is the opinion of worthless people? From whom do you seek honor and respect — from those without eyes to see? Even if they pay homage to you, what is it worth? It is like a bubble; no sooner do you get it, it bursts into thin air.

Self-restraint is the furnace;

He has used the word *furnace* after long deliberation. For restraint is not a bed of roses; it is fire. The mind would crave a bed of flowers, and find all logical excuses for non-restraint. The mind refers to non-restraint as enjoyment and it calls self-restraint suffering; whereas the reality is just the opposite.

Enjoyment is suffering because the more you enjoy the more you rot. Every sense-enjoyment leads you ultimately to gloom and dejection. After each enjoyment you find yourself a little more broken in body and in spirit, a little uglier and more deformed. You had hardly anything to call your own, but whatever little you possessed is lost, and you are left a beggar, wanting more. And still the mind urges you on for more and more pleasures telling you that time is running out. Who knows whether this opportunity will come your way again?

The mind never says: "Practice restraint! Who knows whether this moment will come again in this lifetime, or not?" It never urges you forward on the path for fear of time running out, because the mind always hankers after pleasure.

Try to recognize how the mind always yearns for happiness, but instead always gets unhappiness. It seems as if on the door to happiness is written: Sorrow and Suffering, and on every door of unhappiness is written: Happiness. Seeing the sign the mind enters, but it is deluged by suffering and sorrow.

Kahlil Gibran has written a very nice story. He says when God created the world He created a Goddess of Beauty and a Goddess of Ugliness. He sent them both to earth. Since the road from heaven to earth is very long, they were both tired before they reached halfway. They looked at their clothes so covered with dust that they could hardly make one another out. So they halted beside a lake and decided to take a bath and wash their clothes. There was no one around so they removed their clothes and stepped into the water without fear. The Goddess of Beauty loved the feeling of the cold, soothing waters. She swam far out. The Goddess of Ugliness grabbed the opportunity and quickly came ashore, put on her companion's clothes and disappeared.

After some time the Goddess of Beauty, having had her fill and realizing it was getting late, decided to come ashore. To her surprise her companion was missing and so were her clothes. What was she to do? The people from the village were arriving. She was obliged to put on the ugly one's clothes. Gibran says, "Ever since then ugliness masquerades on earth in the clothes of the Goddess of Beauty, while the latter moves about in her clothes."

This is exactly what has happened. Suffering goes about in the garb of happiness; untruth masquerades as truth, and the mind is deceived by it. It fails to see what is behind the mantle.

Self-restraint requires first that you begin to see the suffering. You will experience great difficult initially. How difficult it is to get up at five o'clock in the morning. The whole body revolts, the mind refuses and offers excuses: "It is too cold to get up today, and you need the sleep. You can get up early tomorrow." You gain nothing by sleeping that much longer, but the mind coaxes you into thinking how lovely it would be.

You have no idea of the happiness outside: the sun is rising, birds are singing, flowers are opening, dew is on the leaves — all the beauty hidden in the early morning! There is no more beautiful time of the day, no moment so refreshing. Missing the morning, you can never regain that freshness during the day, but the mind whispers otherwise: "Stay and rest a little longer in that world of oblivion." Waking seems so difficult, but only by awakening does one reach happiness; asleep, a man only loses.

Therefore Nanak says that self-restraint is a furnace where the gold is purified. But you must be prepared to pass through the fire. Only by going through the difficulties and troubles does a person attain the supreme happiness. You also pass through suffering and sorrow, but you resent it; then it is not restraint. When you pass through suffering in full awareness, when you accept the anguish and pain it brings, and when you look upon it as the path, the inevitable furnace of life through which you must pass in order to be purified, then the whole alchemy of suffering changes.

Everyone passes through pain and sorrow, be he in the world or a sannyasin. The worldly man weeps and wails and misses. He who passes through suffering with full awareness, with the attitude of acceptance, makes his suffering a stepping stone and goes beyond suffering. To practice restraint is to accept the suffering as the spiritual path. One should not be vanquished by it, but on the contrary, make it a stepping stone and rise above it. Therefore, it is like a furnace.

...patience is the goldsmith;

When gold is thrown into the furnace, one has to exercise great patience. He who is impatient fails; he who is patient is successful. If you hurry, become impatient, it means you have not accepted suffering and are eager to be done with it. In that case you have not understood the glory of suffering. You do not know that as you suffer you are being cleansed and purified and absolved from all that is worthless and useless. You have not recognized suffering as a friend yet. It is only at that point that you attain to self-restraint. He who recognizes suffering as a friend is in no hurry. He can maintain his patience, and God is attained only through patience — infinite patience. To attain God is not a paltry thing to be instantly attained.

You plant a seed. Seeds of seasonal plants take two to three weeks to sprout. By the sixth week they begin to flower, and at the end of twelve weeks their life cycle is over. When you plant a cedar tree it lives for one hundred years, or perhaps two, three, or even four hundred years. There are trees in America thousands of years old. They take such a long time to grow that the seed remains under the soil for years before it sprouts.

The baser pleasures of this life are quickly attainable, but they vanish as quickly. Remember the equation: the quicker attained, the earlier lost. If you want to attain God you will have to practice infinite patience.

And remember another fact: the more patiently you observe, the earlier you attain. The more you rush the later you attain. You are the cause of the delay. Why does this happen? Because the more patient you are, the deeper inside you go. Impatience is characteristic of a shallow person; it is a sign of childishness. When little children plant a mango seed, after an hour they take it out to see whether it has sprouted yet. Then they put it back in the soil. Again they remove it to see whether it has sprouted, and again they return it to the soil. That seed will never sprout.

You must have noticed the patience and tranquility of the villager. The city shopkeeper has little patience. The further into the countryside you go, the more peaceful and tranquil they are, because they have learned to be very patient with nature. You plant the seeds today, but you can't gather the harvest tomorrow. Long association with nature and observing the law of patience, and they become tranquil. But he who wishes to reap the harvest of the infinite must sow and toil in the field of God.

Nanak's father was always after him to do something and not be idle. "At least plow the fields," he would tell him.

"That I do, father," Nanak would reply.

"What field did you ever plow? What harvest have you ever gathered? What money have you ever earned? I always see you sitting home doing nothing."

Nanak answered, "You are right, father. You see me always sitting at home. The field I plow is of a different sort, and whatever I earned is all within me. May he pour his compassion on you so that you may have the eyes to see what I have attained. I have earned a great deal and harvested much, but it is so subtle that the ordinary eye cannot see it."

He who has walked on the path of religion has desired to reap the harvest of the infinite, for which unlimited patience is required. It only means having no expectations. You must not ask when it will happen. Leave it to him; when it happens is his will. Whenever it happens, be ready to accept. Let eons pass but never complain: I have been waiting so many years.

There is a very ancient Hindu story: Narada, the heavenly messenger, was once going to Heaven to see the god Vishnu. On the way he met an old sannyasin and asked him, "I'm going to meet God. Is there any message you would like me to give?"

The old sannyasin replied, "When you meet him please ask him how much longer I shall have to wait? I have been a sannyasin the last three births."

Narada said he would surely give the message. He went a little further and found another sannyasin sitting under a tree. He was young and lost to this world as he sat playing his one-stringed instrument. Narada asked him jokingly, "Well, brother, have you any message for him? I'm on my way to Vishnu's abode." The young man kept singing, his eyes closed. Narada shook him by the shoulder and asked again.

He answered, "No, brother, I have nothing to ask. His grace is boundless; whatever my wants he has already provided. Don't trouble him on my account. You needn't even mention my name because I have everything I could wish for and more. If possible just convey my gratitude to him."

When Narada returned and met the old sannyasin, he told him, "Forgive me, brother, but Vishnu said, 'As many leaves as there are on this tree, so many births will this man have before attaining.'"

The old sannyasin was filled with rage. He tore the book he was reading, threw away the *mala*, and shouted in anger, "What injustice! For three births I have done penances, tortured myself, and still so many births to go! It cannot be!"

Narada then approached the young man under the second tree. "You didn't request it, but I asked God on your behalf how long it will be before you attain, and he said, 'As many leaves as there are on the tree where he sits, so many births must he take before attaining.'"

The young man jumped up with his instrument and began dancing with glee. "So soon? How high has he rated my worth! Look at the ground! There are so many leaves. Look at the other trees covered by leaves, but he has counted only the leaves of this tree for me. Only so many births? How wonderful! I am not worthy of it. How will I bear his grace? And how will I express my gratitude to him?"

He was mad with joy and danced round and round the tree, and danced around Narada. He could not contain his joy. The story goes that thus dancing, he attained samadhi. His body fell away. What was to have happened after infinite years happened immediately. For him who has such patience, attainment does not take a moment longer to come.

...*patience is the goldsmith;*
Intellect is the anvil; knowledge is the hammer;

We can use our intellect in two ways. We have already made use of it as a knapsack, but not as an anvil. We fill it with information, just as a ragman fills his bag. We hear scriptures and listen to *satgurus*. Whatever we get, no matter what its source, we dump into this bag, this beggar's sack. It contains everything: scriptures, masters' teachings, newspapers, Vedas, radio advertisements, movie songs. If someone abuses you, you tuck away the abuse in the sack. If someone gives you a mantra to recite, you store it there. Your mind is a sack in which the mantra mingles with foul words. Vedas are lost in everyday news. And such a bag we constantly drag behind us.

This we call memory. It is not knowledge, just rubbish. Genuine knowledge is that which is attained from our own experience. The intellect is filled with borrowed knowledge; everything is stale. Nanak says, however, that intellect is the anvil and knowledge is the hammer.

Nanak says knowledge is the blow of the hammer. Whenever you attain knowledge, howsoever infinitesimal, every hair of your body trembles with its impact. This is why we avoid knowledge, because we don't want to bear the shock of it. Instead we merely gather information, because this gives no shock. You read in the *shastras*, "God is the ultimate truth." What shock is there in that? You read, "Meditation is the way." You have learned it by heart; you even tell it to others. What impact does it have?

A little girl was playing in her courtyard when her mother called her from the top of the stairs for her bath. The little girl didn't want to leave her game. Her grandmother, who was herself sunning in the courtyard, told her daughter many times, "Let her play. You can give her a bath later on." But the mother was adamant.

At last the child left her playing and began to climb the stairs. When she saw her mother she said to her, "How strange that you always tell me to 'listen to your mother' but you don't listen to your mother at all."

Do you ever heed the advice you give others? No, it's just stale stuff that you pass on to others. Once you give it away you are free of it. There's no more to it. It never did anything for you; nor will it for others.

Advice is given so freely, and taken so rarely. People feel so free to distribute knowledge, but who takes it? On the contrary, you avoid such people because they bore you. They fill your sack of intellect with all the trash that lies in their sack. The joke is they have never put it to any other use.

Real knowledge carries an impact; it is born out of life's experience, the friction of life. When you take a jump into existence, knowledge is born — not through scriptures and words. Experience is a blow, so we try to avoid it to save ourselves.

Gurdjieff used to compare our knowledge with the buffers of a train or the springs of a car. Both are shock absorbers. When there is an impact they absorb the shock, whereas authentic knowledge is a shock in itself.

When someone close to you dies, you say, "The soul is eternal." This knowledge has never shaken you in your life. You use it merely as a shock absorber. The sages who have declared this truth of the immortality of the soul, have practiced self-restraint. They have passed through many furnaces and fires. This knowledge has been like a hammer of the anvil for them. This knowledge has completely crushed them; it has broken their skulls open, so to speak. Their ego has been reduced to dust. It has severed all their connection with the body. This knowledge has caused their whole world to reel and fall to pieces. This is the knowledge that initiated them into sannyas. This knowledge has made them as good as nobodies in the mundane world. It has uprooted them completely from sansara. It came as a hurricane and swept them away completely.

What has your knowledge done for you? It is like a lullaby. When you do not fall asleep you hum your knowledge, and so fall asleep. When someone dies, you use it to absorb the shock, because you are afraid of death. It could also have been possible for a death in your family to become a full-fledged experience for you, by which you attained knowledge. In that case, the event of death becomes the hammer and you are the anvil; and when the hammer fell on you, the blow would have awakened you.

No one ever awakens in this world without a blow; you have placed shock absorbers all around you so you are safe inside. Nothing can affect you.

Someone dies, and you say, "The soul is immortal." You see a beggar on the road and say, "Poor man. He is paying for his past actions." You are loathe to give him a paltry two *paise*! You really have to believe he is suffering from past actions or you would consider yourself partly responsible, which would be a blow to you, so you create a shock absorber. You say, "Poor man, he suffers because of his own actions." And you go on your way. His plight creates no anxiety in you, no worry, no food for thought.

You are very efficient. Your cunningness knows no bounds. The sages attain knowledge by the impact of events, and you use that very impact as a shock absorber. Whatever happens you save yourself. You take great care to protect your ego, the very thing that needs to break.

Intellect is the anvil; knowledge is the hammer;

But where is the hammer to descend — on whose head? Only if you place your own self between the anvil and the hammer can knowledge be created in you. Only when you break into fragments — only then! But you save yourself in a thousand ways.

One day, early in the morning, I called on Nasruddin. The poor man had a bad cough. His tongue hardly remained in his mouth; he was panting for breath. Doctors had told him time and again to give up smoking but he just would not. "Why don't you give up smoking, Mulla? You see how ill it makes you."

He told me, "Since you asked, and since you are my good friend, I must tell you what actually is my reason for not giving it up." He drew closer to me and whispered, "Last time I gave up smoking the second World War started that very day. Do you really think I wouldn't otherwise give it up?"

Look at the ego of this man! He has the power to start world wars. You devise methods for your ego. You think the whole world is at your beck and call; you are the ruler, and if you die the world will die with you. How can the world go on without you? Wars are started or stopped by your smoking habits! Look around and you'll discover many similar stories about yourself.

Nanak says that knowledge is the hammer. Don't use your intellect as a sack or else the sack will grow and grow, while you get smaller and smaller, until one day you'll get lost in your own sack. You will die beneath its weight; that's how pundits and scholars die, crushed under their own knowledge.

Make your intellect into an anvil and its shine will improve with every experience of life. Each blow will cleanse and polish it. If you ask a goldsmith or blacksmith they will tell you that hammers often break as they strike, but the anvil remains intact. The anvil even begins to shine more and more as the hammers break.

Lao Tzu asked why the anvil does not break. He answered that it is because it bears the blow, and the hammer breaks because it attacks. Aggression always breaks by itself. You need not worry about it, just develop the ability to endure; then every situation that is aggressive, that shakes you up, will make you all the stronger. Ask the goldsmith and he will tell you how many hammers he has broken on his anvil, while the anvil remains intact. Though you would think that the anvil should break after so many blows, what hits breaks itself, while what bears the impact is saved. The secret lies hidden in the anvil.

Nanak says the intellect is the anvil, so the intellect will not break. Don't be afraid, but make it vulnerable to the blows of experience. Let the blows fall — as many as life lets fall on your consciousness, so shall you be purified. Make life an adventure. Don't run away from where you think the blows will fall. He who flees is defeated already; he has not accepted the challenge. His anvil will get rusted even if he sits in the Himalayas. Don't be a coward or a deserter but stand up to the challenges of life!

Therefore, I don't call him a sannyasin who has run away from life. He has run away from the hammer, his anvil is sure to get rusted. Look at our sannyasins sitting in the Himalayas and you will not find the shine of intelligence; they look rusted. If you have eyes to see you will find that their understanding and intelligence are almost nonexistent; they are as if dead. The lamp of life does not shine in them as it should; everything is dull, despondent inside them. Struggle and friction is necessary for the flower of life to burn, because that is its food.

Intellect is the anvil; knowledge is the hammer;

Whenever the hammer falls on the intellect, the impact produces a moment of knowledge, just as on a dark night the lightning flashes. Don't miss it although you are afraid and trembling. The flash will light things around you for a great distance and all the roads will appear clear for a moment.

Each blow of knowledge is a flash of lightning. When there is friction in the clouds, lightning is formed. Similarly, when there is friction in life the flash of knowledge appears; so don't run away from any situation in life. Stop; go through it. That gives you maturity and wisdom, and only that gives rise to understanding.

Nanak never told his disciples to run away from sansara, because that would be running away from the hammers, where all knowledge is born. If you run away from your wife you remain childish; there is growth and maturity in the friction with her. Run away from your children and you will fail to develop the art of extending your strength, your firmness.

Have you ever realized how a woman changes once she becomes a mother? Not only is the child born, but the mother is born along with it. Before she was an ordinary woman; now she has a special quality that a childless woman can never know. When a child is born, a young man, who had been a mere boy until then, becomes a father; there is a maturity, a firmness in being a father. The thought of being a father, the state of fatherhood, is the beginning of an altogether new experience. Don't run away from it. Make use of all the doors that life has opened for you.

This is why Nanak never advised his disciples to run away to the jungle, but exhorted them to remain in the mundane world to allow all the blows of the hammer to fall on their anvil. They were not to fight shy of it.

Fear is the bellows; austerity is the fire;

You can make use of fear in two ways. The one you use now is to run away when there is fear. You believe in the logic of the ostrich and bury your head in the sand. How will you progress if you run from fear? Fear is an opportunity. The basic fear is that you might not exist! And if you are not prepared to annihilate yourself, how can God happen within you?

There is no fear except death: Perhaps I might die and be no more! He who is unprepared to die cannot go into God or enter into prayer.

The other possibility with fear is to surrender. Accept the existence of death; do not turn your eyes away from it. The day you encounter death with open eyes, you will see death disappear into oblivion. You had never come face to face with death, and therefore it existed for you. All fears of life flee in this manner if you face them in full awareness.

Nanak says that fear is the bellows. Don't be afraid of it, because the more you flee from danger the more you fear it; your life's austerity and fire will dwindle to that extent. Wherever there is fear, accept the challenge and enter into it. This is how a warrior is born. He enters wherever there is danger. Where death stands lurking, he accepts the invitation. Where there is danger he walks right into the heart of it. The further you penetrate the fear, the more fearless you become; the more you run away from it, the more fearful you will become.

He who learns the art of using fear, for him fear becomes like a bellows. And every moment of fear ignites the flame of austerity yet more. There is fear in the devotee, but he has transformed his fear into devotion. Now he fears only God, so that through the fear he can maintain restraint and balance in his life. With the help of this fear, he can regulate his life so that it is kept from going on the wrong path. This is not an ordinary fear. Ordinarily, when you fear someone you make an enemy of him; but the fear of God is wonderful, unique. The more you fear him, the more you fall in love with him.

You are anxious not to miss him for a fraction of a moment. Only your fear shows the possibility of your going astray. "Do not let me go astray, O Lord! May your remembrance never leave me. Only your grace can keep my remembrance constant. I search for you, dear Lord, but without your help, how can I?" This fear reflects his helplessness, his state of poverty. The devotee converts fear into prayer. He does not run away from it. Every fear, every danger he turns into prayer. Whenever fear takes hold of him, he utilizes it as an occasion for prayer.

Nanak says austerity is the fire. Whenever you complete a work you have started in all earnest and resolve, a wonderful heat is created within you. Then it doesn't matter how small or unimportant the work. This is the meaning of austerity.

Suppose you have decided to fast today. It is not that you want to do it to go to heaven; if this were possible, going to heaven would be an easy matter. You are not fasting because you want to perform a good deed. Your fasting involves a process of austerity and resolve. You have resolved not to eat today. The body will make its daily demands when the mealtimes come. You will hear its hunger cries without letting them pass unheeded. You will not deny the hunger, but say to the body: I agree that you are hungry; it is time for your food, but I have decided to remain hungry today. Sorry, but you'll have to go without food.

You will not abandon your resolve for the sake of the body. This requires a good deal of awareness. The body's demand is not wrong, but today you are going to live by your resolve. What does this mean? It means you are placing yourself above the body. You are becoming bigger than your body; you are making the body obey you. The mind will think of food, but you say: That's all right. You may think what you please, but I shall only witness it, and not join in. I abide by my decision; that is my resolve. Then you will experience a heat, a kind of fire, an energy being born within you, an energy you have never known before. This power comes by the mastery of resolve. You are now your own master.

Then you will get up the next morning in quite a different way. You will find you can rise above your body. A new experience — you can rise above the mind. You will get a new experience that you are apart from both body and mind. You will get a faint glimpse of this experience.

This is austerity. It is neither for gaining salvation nor going to heaven. Austerity is meant for knowing that one's life and consciousness is beyond the body and the mind. But he who thus raises himself above the mind and body invariably finds the door to beatitude opened wide for him.

What Nanak means when he says that austerity is the fire and fear the bellows, is that one should not run away from anything; rather find some use for it. Each thing has its proper use. There is nothing in life that cannot be put to use: sex energy turns into celibacy, anger turns into compassion, fear becomes prayer, suffering becomes penance. What is required is an artist with the necessary skill. This life which can be a king's domain for you becomes a prison otherwise. Everything depends on you.

Everything is already present within you. All you need is the proper art of putting them together well. This putting together is what is known as self-restraint. You have everything within you, but you have never put them together with the proper system, proper tuning and music. They all lie inert within you, but you don't know what to do with them. A stone lies in front of your house and you think it a nuisance. Another man uses it to cross to the other side; for him it becomes a stepping stone. Everything is within you. God has given everything complete to man, but the freedom to gather himself together to make use of the gifts God has given him lies entirely with man.

If you observe well you will find exactly the same qualities in a criminal or thief or a sinner as you find in a virtuous, good man. The only difference is the arrangement and use to which it is put.

A thief enters somebody's house at night. It is not an easy job. He also has to transform his fear. He enters a house where he is a complete stranger as if he couldn't care less! He makes a hole in the wall and breaks in. He does it so efficiently and quietly that there isn't the slightest sound. Then he enters, in full awareness. It is someone else's house, where he is not welcome, so he has to move in the dark and be so alert and concentrated lest something fall and the people awaken.

Zen fakirs say: "If you want to go to the house of God, you must learn the burglar's art." You need as much alertness as the thief uses. You also must transform your fear and enter like the thief, as if it is your own house.

There is a Zen story: There was a very well known thief who was considered number one in the hierarchy of thieves.

He was so adept at his art that he had never been caught, yet everyone knew he was a thief. The news even reached the ears of the king who called him, and honored him for his wonderful efficiency and skill.

As he became older his son said to him, "Father, it is time for you to teach me your art, because who knows when death may come?"

The thief replied, "If you wish to learn I shall teach you. Come with me tomorrow night."

The next night both father and son set out. The father broke through the wall as the son stood watching. His absorption in breaking in would have put any artist to shame. He was lost in his work as if he were lost in prayer. The son was awed by his father's proficiency. He was a master thief, the guru of so many thieves.

The son was trembling from head to foot, though it was a warm night. Fear arose again and again, chilling his spine. His eyes darted everywhere, watching all directions, but his father was lost in his work and didn't lift his eyes even once. When they entered through the hole the son was trembling like a leaf; never had he felt so afraid in all his life, but the father moved about as though the place belonged to him. He took the son in, broke the locks, opened the lock of a huge wardrobe filled with clothes and jewels, and told the son to get inside.

No sooner did the son enter but the father closed the cupboard, locked it, and taking the key with him, left the house shouting, "Thief, thief!" and returned home. By then everyone had awakened. The son was caught in the worst dilemma of his life. What was he to do? He was worried about the footprints and the hole in the wall. At that moment the servant come right up to the wardrobe. The poor boy was at his wits end, his mind completely blank. At such a time the mind does not work, because it is full of stale knowledge and doesn't know how to deal with fresh situations. He had never heard of such a thing arising in the whole history of thieving. His intellect became useless.

At the moment the intellect became useless, the consciousness within was awakened. Suddenly, as this energy caught him, he began making a noise as if a rat was gnawing at the clothes inside the cupboard. He was shocked at himself; he had never done such a thing before. The woman servant brought a bunch of keys and opened it. He immediately puffed out the lamp she was holding and, giving her a push, ran out of the house through the hole in the wall. Some ten or twenty people gave chase. There was a great deal of noise, because the whole village was awake. The thief ran for his life — ran as he had never run before. He had no idea it was he who was running. Suddenly, as he reached a well, he picked up a big stone and threw it in the well — all this without the slightest idea of what he was doing. It seemed to him it was not he but someone else directing him. At the sound of the stone falling in the water the crowd gathered around the well, thinking the thief had fallen in.

He stood behind the tree to rest a bit, then continued home muttering to himself. When he went in he found his father fast asleep with the blanket over his head. The son pulled off the cover and said, "What are you doing?" The father continued snoring away. He shook him hard. "What did you do to me? Did you want to see me killed?"

The father opened his eyes for a minute and said, "So you have returned? Good. I'll hear the rest in the morning," and appeared to fall back asleep.

The son pleaded with him, "Say something, father. Ask me what I went through or I shall not be able to sleep."

The father said, "Now you are an expert; you don't need to be taught. Anyway, say it if you must." After the son recounted all that had happened the father answered, "Enough! Now you know even the art that cannot be taught. After all you are my son! My blood flows in your veins. You know the secret. If a robber uses his intelligence he gets caught. You have to leave your intelligence behind, because each time it is a totally new experience, a new moment; each time you are entering a different person's house and every house is new. The old experience never comes of use. Use your intelligence and you land yourself in trouble. Rely on your intuition and you succeed."

Zen masters always mention this story. They say the art of meditation is like house-breaking — you need as much awareness. Intelligence should be put aside and awareness should come into play. Where there is fear there is bound to be awareness. Where there is danger you become absolutely alert and all thoughts stop.

Nanak says fear is like the bellows, so make use of fear. If there is fear, awake! Don't protect yourself from it. But what do we do? We take precautions whenever we sense danger: we take a sword or a gun along to the trouble spot, or we take a few servants along to protect us, or we build high walls so that no one can come in. We protect ourselves form fear.

This depletes our consciousness even more. As it is, we are well nigh unfeeling, insentient, and this will make us more so; therefore, the more protected a people the less intelligent they are. It is rather difficult to find an intelligent person among the rich. The rich man has all the arrangements for protection, therefore he doesn't have to use his brains. Others serve him; what his intelligence should be doing is instead done by others.

Thus you often find the children of rich families tend to be dullards. At best they will be mediocre. You will not see the luster of consciousness in them or the sharpness of understanding, and never the brilliance of genius. Their servants need to be brilliant, but what need is there for the master to be clever?

Nanak says to make fear the bellows. Wake up in fear; it is a wonderful state. Your whole body trembles; each hair of your body stands on end. At that time, when the whole body trembles, your consciousness should be stable and unmoving like a steady flame. Then fear becomes the bellows.

Austerity is the fire. Wherever there is suffering in life, take it as an exercise in austerity. Accept your suffering fully and openly, and be resolute. When you fall ill accept the illness. Do not fight against it. Then you will find that not only does the body get well but also the mind attains a new kind of health. When you fall ill, don't fight the illness; rather look it straight in the face and accept it: You have come? Welcome! Don't quarrel with it; don't avoid it. Don't involve your mind in other things, or you will miss the opportunity. Each condition in life that we encounter can become a path that leads to him. Remember this: each event is a step towards his gate. If you know this you will make use of it.

Feeling is the crucible into which the nectar falls.

Nanak specifies not thoughts but feeling. Feeling is the consciousness beyond your thoughts. Thoughts flow in your mind; emotion is the force of the heart. Feeling is not logic; it is love, and so it is within the heart. It does not fit any calculations. It is a state of intensity, ecstasy, exhilaration. When you are emotional you are united with the depths of the universe. Thoughts are your most superficial layer, like the outer fencing of your house. It is not even part of the house, only an outer limit to keep away outsiders. This is not you. You are your emotions.

But we become frightened of our emotions. Gradually we have clogged our emotions, if not cut them off completely. We don't listen to our hearts at all. We heed only the intellect, and act according to our reasoning. And where does your intellect take you? It is the shallowest thing within you, so it guides you only towards superficial things. That is why you are out to amass wealth — you gather all the trash — and why you are so concerned about your honor and position.

Stand a little away from your thoughts and drown your feelings. It is difficult. How do you drown in emotion? In olden days the Hindus would get up in the morning and bow to the rising sun. They would accept the grace and kindness of the sun in all humility. They would pray to him in thankfulness that he had come yet once again and given them one more day of light; and with it the flowers will open, the birds will sing and the story of life will go on. They would bow with both hands and thank him for his kindness to them. As they stood with hands folded they drank in the light of the sun, and a feeling of gratitude would thrill their hearts.

When they went to the river they would bow to it before stepping into the waters; thus they would establish an emotional relationship with the river. Truly the river washes the body, but something else gets cleansed inside as well. The river is pure and it belongs to him — this feeling gets intensified internally.

When they sat down for meals they would remember him first, set his plate apart, and eat only after first offering to him. The Hindus have called grain Brahma because it gives you life. They have turned everything into the remembrance of God. From everywhere and every place, they have taken care to see that the impact of his remembrance falls on us. Therefore when they sit, when they sleep, when they stand or walk or work, or do anything — his remembrance!

We have turned around and denied all of this. We say: What is this bathing in the river? It is only water, mere H20. Where is God in it? You bow to the sun! What is the sun but a ball of fire? To whom are you bowing? If the river is only water and the sun is only fire, then where will you find God? Then what is your wife, your son — only a collection of flesh and bones. Then how will you awaken your emotions?

To awaken the emotions is to know that the world is full of consciousness. Whatever is seen does not end there; there is much more within, deep within. Emotions means the universe has an individuality, a soul. Granted that the child is a collection of flesh and bones, but within the child something has incarnated. Within him, God has descended. He is a guest in this house.

The tree is a tree — that is true — but there is something within the tree that is growing and developing. Within the tree there is also someone, something, that feels joy, that feels sorrow. The tree also has different moods, different emotions and experiences. Within the tree there is even sleeping and waking. The latest discovery of science is that trees feel, much as human beings do, and their experience is deep and their knowledge too. They are also sensitive like human beings, as are also rocks and stones.

Everywhere there is sensitivity. Man alone has lost his sensitivity and his emotions; therefore the world is so sad and gloomy. Without gaiety or mirth it seems a useless place. As soon as your emotions awaken, the world becomes transformed. In fact, the earth is the same, the people are the same, everything is the same — nothing changes, except you.

Feeling is the only vessel into which the nectar is poured. If you have no feelings you will remain bereft of God. The only obstruction to awakening feeling is that emotion is absolutely the reverse of intellect — totally different from it. In sansara intellect is of great use, and not emotion. If you want to amass wealth you cannot afford to be emotional or you will be ruined. If you want to succeed in politics, you cannot use your emotions, because you need the utmost heartlessness and hardness to be in politics. You need excessive, aggressive thoughts; peace and silence will be of no value. You have to forget completely that there is something called a heart within you.

I have heard: It is said that in the very near future all parts of the human body will be readily available, just as we now get spare parts for our cars. Already there are blood banks and eye banks and kidney banks.

So it once happened, in this story of the future, that a man's heart was not working very well, and he wanted to change it. He went to a heart bank and asked to be shown some hearts. There were many kinds of hearts: one belonged to a laborer, another to a farmer, yet another to a mathematician, and there was one of a politician. The last one was the most expensive. "Why?" asked the customer. The shopkeeper replied, "It is brand new. It has never been used."

Thinking his customer could not afford much, the shopkeeper took out yet another heart and said, "This is the cheapest I have. You see it is secondhand and quite worn. It belongs to a poet who has used it to the maximum."

The politician has no use for such a dangerous organ.

Begin to use your heart gradually — and it can only be done gradually. Remember only one thing: put aside thoughts for a while and bring in feelings. Sit near a tree, look at a flower without thinking it a rose or gladiolus. What does it matter, the name? Don't think of its bigness or smallness. What has that to do with you? There is an invisible beauty around every flower. Drink that beauty in but don't think about it. Just sit silently beside the flower and be a witness to it.

Soon you will discover that the process that has now started within your heart has stopped the process of thoughts within your mind. This is because energy can work in only one direction. The thrill you feel in your heart only you shall know; no one else can ever know it or be told about it. It is like a mute eating a candy; how can he tell the taste to others? The heart has no language for communication.

Sit next to the flower and hear the song of the birds. Rest your back against the trunk of a tree and feel its roughness. Lie down on the soil and feel its cool touch. Sit under a waterfall and let the water flow all over you. Let its lovely feeling go deep within you. Stand facing the sun, close your eyes and let its rays touch you everywhere.

You have only to feel. You need not think about what is happening. Whatever is happening, let it happen; allow your heart to thrill with ecstasy. You will soon discover a movement starting within your heart as if a new mechanism that had been lying dormant has begun to function. A new melody now begins to play in your life. Your life center changes, and it is on this new center that nectar pours.

The coinage of the Word is cast in the mint of truth.

What Nanak means by the word is Omkar. As truthfulness fills your life, Omkar will begin to be molded within you, and you will be immersed in it. You harm others with lies, but the greater harm is that untruth prevents you from being the mint of truth where Omkar is molded, where the highest experience of life will form.

Only those receiving his grace can succeed in it.

Nanak reminds us after every couplet to remember, when the event takes place, when grace descends, it will not be because of you. Don't be filled with pride that "I am a great devotee," or "My heart is so sensitive," or "My austerity is great!" No, this does not help. Only he who is fortunate to receive his grace can do this work.

> *Nanak says, one becomes exalted by his compassionate look.*
> *Wind is the guru; water is the father; the great earth is the mother;*
> *Night and day are midwife and groom; and the whole world is playing with them.*
> *Good and bad deeds are read out in his court by Dharma,*

*And our own actions determine whether we are near to him
or far.
Those who meditate on his name and labor sincerely earn merit;
Their faces are radiant with success,
And many others are liberated by contact with them.*

Nanak's symbols are invaluable. They have been chosen with great feeling. He says the guru is like the wind. He cannot be seen, only experienced. Those who try to see him will miss, because who can see the wind? You can only experience it and feel its touch, but you cannot bind it in your fist.

The guru cannot be held captive; the guru who is willing to be enclosed in the disciple's grasp is no guru. Most gurus are like that, directed by their disciples telling them what should be done, what shouldn't be done. There are assemblies of disciples who run the holy men. They decide which holy man is worthy and which is not. The association decides which should be worshipped and which should be kicked out. How topsy-turvy this world of ours! We direct our gurus: how they should sit, how they should walk, what they should say. Remember, such gurus are not real.

You will not find true gurus in our ashrams and monasteries; you will find fakes masquerading as gurus. A true guru cannot be held captive. You cannot direct a Mahavira, a Buddha, a Nanak. They obey only their own will. The wind blows where it will. Where it does not blow, there is nothing you can do. If you try to gasp it in your fist, whatever little was there, that too will go out. Those who liberate others cannot be taken captive. How can you bind the very person from whom you seek liberation or beatitude?

*Wind is the guru; water is the father; the great earth is the
mother;*

Your body cannot exist without the earth; the mother is absolutely necessary. No birth can take place without the earth, but the earth is the grossest of matter. Birds and animals have mothers but no fathers. Fatherhood requires a higher level of culture and conditioning. The mind is the father, the body is the mother; wherever there is a body, there is mother. The father begins where the mind is born, so the institution of fatherhood is a very new happening.

Only man has fathers, and they too are not very ancient if you measure human history. Before that there was no father, because the woman was a possession of society; she was wife to many men so it was difficult to name the father. The state of man was just like the animals. You will be surprised to know that the word *uncle* appeared earlier than father. This was because those who were big and capable of being fathers were all uncles; it was impossible to trace the individual father of any child.

Father came much later because father is the mind, the impressions of previous lives, the culture. Therefore father is a social achievement, not a natural phenomenon. In nature there is no way to recognize the father. When the society develops to a great extent the father steps in.

Therefore Nanak says the mother is like the earth. No one can be without her. It is the grossest form of matter. Father is more fluid; his relationship is not as fixed, as material, as the mother's. To show the fluidity of the father relationship, Nanak compares it to water.

These are the three steps: mother is symbolized by the earth, which is very gross, material; therefore woman is called *prakriti* or nature. Over this, one stage higher, is the relationship of father, representing culture, society and past impressions. The third stage is still higher, where the relationship with the guru begins; it involves religion, yoga and tantra.

If you stagnate at the level of the mother you remain virtually an animal. If you stagnate at the level of the father, you remain a mere man. As long as you do not reach the guru level, your spiritual state does not form. These are the three steps in life. All animals reach up to the level of the mother. All men reach up to the level of the father. There are very few who reach up to the guru. And as long as you do not reach the guru, you will not attain your full stature, because the mother is the body relationship, the father is the mind relationship, whereas the connection with the guru is the relationship of the soul.

This latter relationship is the greatest of all; there is no connection deeper or higher. Those who are without a guru are as if incomplete. With a guru your journey of this world ends and a new journey starts. The guru is the end of this world and the beginning of the next. He is the gate; therefore, Nanak called his temple, *gurudwara. Dwara* means gate. This side of it is the world, that side is the other world. The guru is in between.

> *Night and day are midwife and groom; and the whole world is playing with them.*

The whole universe is a game involving time. There are two kinds of players: one has turned the servants into masters, and the other has understood the servant to be a servant.

Time is not your master but your slave. Make use of it, but do not let it use you. The state of affairs as we see it is just the opposite: time uses us.

People come to me and say they want to meditate but have no time. You have no time for meditation? Is time your servant or are you time's slave? People complain they don't know how to pass the time, but when it comes to meditation, where has the time gone? And it is the same people! They have a lot of time — watching television, going to movies and clubs — and yet there is no time to spare. The question arises how to spend it.

On holidays people do not know what to do. They get very tired doing nothing. On Sundays they don't know what to do, so they go for a long drive or go to the beach or climb a mountain. One day in the week they get to rest and relax and this is how they spend it; ultimately they get so tired that they look forward to going back to work. On Mondays they are happy again as they head towards the office. It is said in America that people get more tired on holidays than on working days.

Time is using you. If you are the master you have all the time at your disposal. If you are a slave, you have no time at all. What can a slave possess? His time is not even his own.

Nanak says all the world plays with them. There are two types of play going on: in one, he who is the master utilizes his time to find the path to the one beyond time, which is meditation; the other is to be consumed by time.

I have heard: A beggar went to a grain shop and told the grocer, "I have no money today. You will have to give me grain on credit."

The grocer was a kind man. He gave him some grain, but at the same time he said, "Look, brother, I have given you grain on credit, but I hope you will not sell it to buy a ticket for the circus that is in town!"

The beggar laughed and said, "You needn't worry. I have already bought my ticket."

For the useless you have already saved enough time. For the meaningful it is difficult to find time. Be the master of time. Then alone will you be able to go beyond time.

> *Good and bad deeds are read out in his court by Dharma,*
> *And our own actions determine whether we are near to him*
> *or far.*

God is near everybody. For him you are neither near nor far. He is equally near to everybody. It is you who are either near or far from him. Your actions take you either closer to him or further away.

If your actions are such that they make you insensitive and unfeeling, then you are standing with your back towards him. The sun is the same whether you face towards it or away from it. If your actions are such that it has filled you with consciousness, awareness, wakefulness, then you are facing the sun. You are the same; the sun is the sun. The difference is wrought by the direction you choose.

"God is consistently near you," Nanak says. No one is high, no one is low in his eyes; no one is worthy, no one unworthy. If you are unworthy you are the cause of your unworthiness. Bring about a little change within yourself and you shall become worthy. For there is only one difference between you and the worthy; the worthy person stands facing towards God, while the unworthy stands with their backs to him.

> *Those who meditate on his name and labor sincerely earn merit;*
> *Their faces are radiant with success,*
> *And many others are liberated by contact with them.*

Nanak says whenever a person becomes liberated many others are liberated by contact with them. Liberation is such a great and superb occurrence and it is such a beatific occasion — even a single person's liberation — that whoever comes near him is filled with his fragrance, and his life journey changes. Whoever comes near him is filled with the resonance of Omkar; infected by the flavor of liberation, they get a taste of it, which, though very little, can bring a complete change into a life that has until now been mundane and worldly.

A light shines within them. Look with love at such a person and you will see it. If you see with a worshipful eye, you will soon recognize it. A light shines within them and its rays spread out from within them to everyone around. This is why the faces of the saints and incarnates have been depicted with halos around their heads. This aura cannot be seen by all; it can be seen only by those who have faith. And those who can see this aura light their own darkened lamp with the lamp of such a one; whenever a single person attains salvation, thousands who stand within his shadow are also liberated. Liberation never takes place for one single person, because when this supreme moment arrives he becomes a gate for many others.

Keep awakening your faith and your feelings so that you can recognize the guru when he comes. He who has recognized the guru, has discovered the hand of God; he has recognized that which is beyond the universe. He has found the gate, and once the gate is found, everything is attained. You have never lost anything, everything is intact within you, and when you pass through the gate you recognize your own being. You reawaken to the light, the brilliance that is yours. What treasures you always held within you are now unfolded. The guru acquaints you with the self that you always were, and which was not for a single moment lost.

The story is very sweet: Kabir said, "The guru and God are both standing before me. Whose feet should I touch?" Kabir is in a fix. If he bows to the guru, God will be insulted. If he bows to God, the guru will be insulted. What a dilemma! Whose feet should be touched first?

When the guru saw Kabir's dilemma, he told him, "Touch his feet, because I only existed till here." The story is so very endearing. The guru signals to Kabir to touch his feet. "I no longer exist for you. The Lord is before you waiting for your greeting."

But Kabir falls first at the feet of the guru: "It is your glory, my guru, that you brought God down to meet me."

If there is faith in you, you will recognize it. All that is required is faith, feeling; thoughts and the intellect have never helped anyone to reach. Don't expend that useless effort, wasting you time, trying the impossible. You cannot be an exception.

The guru is always present. Among the infinite people in the world at any given time, it has never happened that none has attained him. Some people at all times and in all climes have always attained him, so the earth is never without gurus. This misfortune never takes place; but a different type of misfortune does occur, that sometimes a guru is not recognized by the people around him.

518   *2*   *The True Name*

Information about the Original Audio Series

Books by Osho are transcriptions from discourses given before a live audience. All Osho discourses have been published in full as books and are also available as original audio recordings. Information about the audio recordings and the complete text archive can be found at the OSHO Library at www.osho.com.

About Osho

Osho defies categorization, reflecting everything from the individual quest for meaning to the most urgent social and political issues facing society today. His books are not written but are transcribed from recordings of extemporaneous talks given over a period of thirty-five years. Osho has been described by The Sunday Times in London as one of the "1000 Makers of the 20th Century" and by Sunday Mid-Day in India as one of the ten people – along with Gandhi, Nehru and Buddha – who have changed the destiny of India.

Osho has a stated aim of helping to create the conditions for the birth of a new kind of human being, characterized as "Zorba the Buddha" – one whose feet are firmly on the ground, yet whose hands can touch the stars. Running like a thread through all aspects of Osho's talks and meditations is a vision that encompasses both the timeless wisdom of the East and the highest potential of Western science and technology.

He is synonymous with a revolutionary contribution to the science of inner transformation and an approach to meditation which specifically addresses the accelerated pace of contemporary life. The unique OSHO® Active Meditations™ are designed to allow the release of accumulated stress in the body and mind so that it is easier to be still and experience the thought-free state of meditation.

OSHO® International Meditation Resort™

Every year the OSHO® International Meditation Resort welcomes thousands of people from over 100 countries who come to enjoy and participate in its unique atmosphere of meditation and celebration. The 28-acre meditation resort is located about 100 miles southeast of Mumbai (Bombay), in Pune, India, in a tree-lined residential area, set against a backdrop of bamboo groves and wild jasmine, peacocks and waterfalls. The basic approach of the meditation resort is that of Zorba the Buddha: living in awareness, with a capacity to celebrate everything in life. Many visitors come to just be, to allow themselves the luxury of doing nothing. Others choose to participate in a wide variety of courses and sessions that support moving toward a more joyous and less stressful life, by combining methods of self-understanding with awareness techniques. These courses are offered through OSHO® Multiversity™ and take place in a pyramid complex next to the famous OSHO® Teerth Park.

People can choose to practice various meditation methods, both active and passive, from a daily schedule that begins at six o'clock in the morning. Early each evening there is a meditation event that moves from dance to silent sitting, using Osho's recorded talks as an opportunity to experience inner silence without effort.

Facilities include tennis courts, a gym, sauna, Jacuzzi, a nature-shaped Olympic-sized swimming pool, classes in Zen archery, Tai chi, Chi gong, Yoga and a multitude of bodywork sessions.

The kitchen serves international gourmet vegetarian meals, made with organically grown produce. The nightlife is alive with friends dining under the stars, and with music and dancing.

Online bookings for accommodation at the OSHO˙ Guesthouse which is inside the meditation resort can be made through the website below or by sending an email to guesthouse@osho.com

Online tours of the meditation resort, how to get there, and program information can be found at: www.osho.com/resort

For More Information
www.OSHO.com
a comprehensive multi-language website including OSHO books, talks (audio and video), a magazine, the OSHO Library text archive in English and Hindi with a searchable facility, and extensive information about OSHO Meditation techniques.

You will also find the program schedule of the OSHO Multiversity and information about the OSHO International Meditation Resort.

To contact **OSHO International Foundation** go to www.osho.com/oshointernational

OSHO International Meditation Resort
17 Koregaon Park
Pune 411001, MS, India
resortinfo@osho.net

Books by Osho in English Language

Early Discourses and Writings
A Cup of Tea
Dimensions Beyond The Known
From Sex to Super-consciousness
The Great Challenge
Hidden Mysteries
I Am The Gate
The Inner Journey
Psychology of the Esoteric
Seeds of Wisdom

Meditation
The Voice of Silence
And Now and Here (Vol 1 & 2)
In Search of the Miraculous (Vol 1 &.2)
Meditation: The Art of Ecstasy
Meditation: The First and Last Freedom
The Path of Meditation
The Perfect Way
Yaa-Hoo! The Mystic Rose

Buddha and Buddhist Masters
The Book of Wisdom
The Dhammapada: The Way of the Buddha (Vol 1-12)
The Diamond Sutra
The Discipline of Transcendence (Vol 1-4)
The Heart Sutra

Indian Mystics
Enlightenment: The Only Revolution (Ashtavakra)
Showering Without Clouds (Sahajo)
The Last Morning Star (Daya)
The Song of Ecstasy (Adi Shankara)

Baul Mystics
The Beloved (Vol 1 & 2)

Kabir
The Divine Melody
Ecstasy: The Forgotten Language
The Fish in the Sea is Not Thirsty
The Great Secret
The Guest
The Path of Love
The Revolution

Jesus and Christian Mystics
Come Follow to You (Vol 1-4)
I Say Unto You (Vol 1 & 2)
The Mustard Seed
Theologia Mystica

Jewish Mystics
The Art of Dying
The True Sage

Western Mystics
Guida Spirituale (Desiderata)
The Hidden Harmony (Heraclitus)
The Messiah (Vol 1 & 2) (Commentaries on Khalil Gibran's The Prophet)
The New Alchemy: To Turn You On (Commentaries on Mabel Collins' Light on the Path)
Philosophia Perennis (Vol 1 & 2) (The Golden Verses of Pythagoras)
Zarathustra: A God That Can Dance
Zarathustra: The Laughing Prophet (Commentaries on Nietzsche's Thus Spake Zarathustra)

Zarathustra: The Laughing Prophet (Commentaries on Nietzsche's Thus Spake Zarathustra)

Sufism
Just Like That
Journey to the Heart
The Perfect Master (Vol 1 & 2)
The Secret
Sufis: The People of the Path (Vol 1 & 2)
Unio Mystica (Vol 1 & 2)
The Wisdom of the Sands (Vol 1 & 2)

Tantra
Tantra: The Supreme Understanding
The Tantra Experience
The Royal Song of Saraha (same as Tantra Vision, Vol 1)
The Tantric Transformation
The Royal Song of Saraha (same as Tantra Vision, Vol 2)
The Book of Secrets: Vigyan Bhairav Tantra

The Upanishads
Behind a Thousand Names (Nirvana Upanishad)
Heartbeat of the Absolute (Ishavasya Upanishad)
I Am That (Isa Upanishad)
The Message Beyond Words (Kathopanishad)
Philosophia Ultima (Mandukya Upanishad)
The Supreme Doctrine (Kenopanishad)
Finger Pointing to the Moon (Adhyatma Upanishad)

That Art Thou (Sarvasar Upanishad, Kaivalya Upanishad, Adhyatma Upanishad)
The Ultimate Alchemy, Vol 1&2 (Atma Pooja Upanishad Vol 1 &2)
Vedanta: Seven Steps to Samadhi (Akshaya Upanishad)
Flight of the Alone to the Alone (Kaivalya Upanishad)

Tao
The Empty Boat
The Secret of Secrets
Tao: The Golden Gate (Vol 1&2)
Tao: The Pathless Path (Vol 1&2)
Tao: The Three Treasures (Vol 1-4)
When the Shoe Fits

Yoga
The Path of Yoga (previously Yoga: The Alpha and the Omega (Vol 1)
Yoga: The Alpha and the Omega (Vol 2-10)

Zen and Zen Masters
Ah, This!
Ancient Music in the Pines
And the Flowers Showered
A Bird on the Wing
Bodhidharma: The Greatest Zen Master
Communism and Zen Fire, Zen Wind
Dang Dang Doko Dang
The First Principle
God is Dead: Now Zen is the Only Living Truth
The Grass Grows By Itself
The Great Zen Master Ta Hui

Hsin Hsin Ming: The Book of Nothing
I Celebrate Myself: God is No Where, Life is Now Here
Kyozan: A True Man of Zen
Nirvana: The Last Nightmare
No Mind: The Flowers of Eternity
No Water, No Moon
One Seed Makes the Whole Earth Green
Returning to the Source
The Search: Talks on the 10 Bulls of Zen
A Sudden Clash of Thunder
The Sun Rises in the Evening
Take it Easy (Vol 1 & 2)
This Very Body the Buddha
Walking in Zen, Sitting in Zen
The White Lotus
Yakusan: Straight to the Point of Enlightenment
Zen Manifesto : Freedom From Oneself
Zen: The Mystery and the Poetry of the Beyond
Zen: The Path of Paradox (Vol 1, 2 & 3)
Zen: The Special Transmission
Zen Boxed Sets
The World of Zen (5 vol.)
Live Zen
This. This. A Thousand Times This
Zen: The Diamond Thunderbolt
Zen: The Quantum Leap from Mind to No-Mind
Zen: The Solitary Bird, Cuckoo of the Forest
Zen: All The Colors Of The Rainbow (5 vol.)
The Buddha: The Emptiness of the Heart

The Language of Existence
The Miracle
The Original Man
Turning In

Osho: On the Ancient Masters of Zen (7 volumes)*
Dogen: The Zen Master
Hyakujo: The Everest of Zen– With Basho's haikus
Isan: No Footprints in the Blue Sky
Joshu: The Lion's Roar
Ma Tzu: The Empty Mirror
Nansen: The Point Of Departure
Rinzai: Master of the Irrational

*Each volume is also available individually.

Responses to Questions
Be Still and Know
Come, Come, Yet Again Come
The Goose is Out
The Great Pilgrimage: From Here to Here
The Invitation
My Way: The Way of the White Clouds
Nowhere to Go But In
The Razor's Edge
Walk Without Feet, Fly Without Wings and Think Without Mind
The Wild Geese and the Water
Zen: Zest, Zip, Zap and Zing

Talks in America
From Bondage To Freedom
From Darkness to Light
From Death To Deathlessness
From the False to the Truth
From Unconsciousness to Consciousness

The Rajneesh Bible (Vol 2-4)

The World Tour
Beyond Enlightenment (Talks in Bombay)
Beyond Psychology (Talks in Uruguay)
Light on the Path (Talks in the Himalayas)
The Path of the Mystic (Talks in Uruguay)
Sermons in Stones (Talks in Bombay)
Socrates Poisoned Again After 25 Centuries (Talks in Greece)
The Sword and the Lotus (Talks in the Himalayas)
The Transmission of the Lamp (Talks in Uruguay)

Osho's Vision for the World
The Golden Future
The Hidden Splendor
The New Dawn
The Rebel
The Rebellious Spirit

The Mantra Series
Hari Om Tat Sat
Om Mani Padme Hum
Om Shantih Shantih Shantih
Sat-Chit-Anand
Satyam-Shivam-Sundram

Personal Glimpses
Books I Have Loved
Glimpses of a Golden Childhood
Notes of a Madman

Interviews with the World Press
The Man of Truth: A Majority of One

For any information about Osho Books & Audio/Video Tapes please contact:
OSHO Multimedia & Resorts Pvt. Ltd.
17 Koregaon Park, Pune—411001, MS, India
Phone: +91-20-66019999 Fax: +91- 20-66019990
E-mail: distrib@osho.net Website: www.osho.com